HANDBOOK

THE
MACMILLAN

THE MACMILLAN HANDBOOK OF ENGLISH

FIFTH EDITION

John M. Kierzek
Walker Gibson

THE MACMILLAN COMPANY · NEW YORK
COLLIER–MACMILLAN LIMITED · LONDON

Library of Congress catalog card number: 65–16933

THE MACMILLAN COMPANY, New York
COLLIER–MACMILLAN CANADA, LTD., Toronto, Ontario

PRINTED IN THE UNITED STATES OF AMERICA

ACKNOWLEDGMENTS

The authors acknowledge with thanks the permission of the proprietors to quote from the following copyrighted works, listed in the order of their first appearance:

The Parable of the Seed, from the Revised Standard Version of the Holy Bible. By permission of the National Council of Churches of Christ in the United States and Thomas Nelson & Sons. Copyright 1952 by the National Council of Churches of Christ in the United States.

John S. Kenyon, "Cultural Levels and Functional Varieties of English," *College English*, X (October 1948), 31–36. By permission of The National Council of Teachers of English, copyright owners.

Winston Churchill, speech to the House of Commons. From *Blood, Sweat, and Tears*. Copyright 1941 by Winston S. Churchill. Courtesy of G. P. Putnam's Sons, Cassell & Company, Ltd., and McClelland and Stewart, Limited.

Learned Hand, *The Spirit of Liberty*. Copyright 1960 by Alfred A. Knopf, Inc.

Oscar Handlin, *The Americans*. Copyright © 1963 by Oscar Handlin. From *The Americans* by Oscar Handlin, by permission of Little, Brown and Co.–Atlantic Monthly Press and The Hutchinson Publishing Group.

J. Robert Oppenheimer, *Science and the Common Understanding*. Copyright 1953, 1954 by J. Robert Oppenheimer. Reprinted by permission of Simon and Schuster, Inc., Dr. Oppenheimer, and the Oxford University Press, London.

Alexander Eliot and the Editors of *Life*, *Greece*. From *Greece*, by Alexander Eliot and the Editors of *Life*. © Time Incorporated, 1963.

Marchette Chute, *Ben Jonson of Westmin-*

ster. From the book *Ben Jonson of Westminster* by Marchette Chute. Copyright, 1953, by Marchette Chute. Reprinted by permission of E. P. Dutton & Co., Inc., and Martin Secker & Warburg, Limited.

Edwin Way Teale, *The Strange Lives of Familiar Insects*. Reprinted by permission of Dodd, Mead & Company from *The Strange Lives of Familiar Insects* by Edwin Way Teale. Copyright © 1962 by Edwin Way Teale.

Joseph Wood Krutch, *The Desert Year*. From *The Desert Year* by Joseph Wood Krutch, copyright 1951, 1952 by Joseph Wood Krutch, by permission of William Sloane Associates.

E. B. White, "Calculating Machine." "Calculating Machine" from *The Second Tree from the Corner* by E. B. White. Copyright 1951 by E. B. White. Originally appeared in *The New Yorker*, and reprinted with the permission of Harper & Row, Publishers, Incorporated, and Hamish Hamilton, Ltd.

Robert Penn Warren, *All the King's Men*. Copyright 1946 by Harcourt, Brace & Co. Reprinted by permission of Harcourt, Brace & Co., and of Eyre & Spottiswoode, Ltd., London.

E. B. White, "Once More to the Lake." Pp. 252–3 "Once More to the Lake" (August 1941) from *One Man's Meat* by E. B. White (Harper & Brothers, 1944).

Alan B. Shepard, Jr., and Walter M. Schirra, Jr., from *We Seven* by the Astronauts Themselves. Reprinted by permission

PREFACE

THE fifth edition of *The Macmillan Handbook of English*, like its predecessors, is a rhetoric and handbook combined. It may be used as either or as both. Material that can be most profitably used in classroom instruction has been placed in the rhetoric. Material most useful in the marking and revision of papers has been placed in the handbook. Of course, one part supplements the other and enables the teacher to repeat instruction, when necessary, with new materials and a fresh approach.

The first part of the book attempts to give the beginner the sort of helpful, common-sense advice about writing that he most needs. The student is introduced to the concept of English as a living and growing language. He is then taken through discussions of grammar as a tool of effective writing, of building good sentences and good paragraphs, to the process of planning, writing, and revising various kinds of compositions. The first section includes a discussion of a long paper based on the investigation of published material, the most elaborate and ambitious project the student will undertake.

The first seven chapters of the book—the parts constituting the rhetoric—have been substantially rewritten. In several of these chapters there is a more detailed analysis of structure and language than in former editions, a more detailed commentary on the illustrations used, and a firmer linking of rhetorical discussions with the specific problems of writing facing the student. The section dealing with rhetorical patterns of sentences has been strengthened and enlarged. It is now a separate chapter. The chapter dealing with the paragraph has been enriched by the addition of new examples with a running commentary on each selection. In the chapter on planning and writing, a new arrangement of the parts will make this complex material clearer and more usable. Here we now have three areas of attention: problems of subject and focus (deciding, in effect, what to write about and how to limit it), problems of outlining, and problems of writing and revising. The section on revising has been enlarged materially. Throughout these chapters we have followed the general principle that must be familiar to users of past editions—that many short passages of good writing quoted can do what is so difficult to do with a large anthology. These carefully selected passages can isolate specific devices of rhetoric and structure to illustrate theoretical discussion at the moment when the illustration is most needed and most pertinent.

The chapter on the library paper has a new sample research paper. The methods and principles discussed in this chapter apply both to the paper based on research in a library and to the one based on casebooks or controlled sources. The system of documentation in footnotes and bibliography has been adapted to suit the needs of undergraduates from the revised *Style Sheet* of the Modern Language Association.

The material of the second part of the book—the handbook itself —is organized under forty-four divisions. A comprehensive index and a theme-correction chart help both the student and the teacher to find any section easily and quickly.

Most of the illustrative material in both parts of the book is new. All of the exercises have been rewritten.

For valuable criticism of the fourth edition, or of the manuscript of this revision, or of both, we are indebted to Professor Harris W. Wilson, of the University of Illinois, and members of his Freshman Rhetoric staff; to Professor Robert C. Rathburn, of the University of Minnesota; and to Professor Lynn Altenbernd, of the University of Illinois. We are grateful to Professor Ben R. Schneider, Jr., of Lawrence University, for his help in obtaining a new model library paper, and to many others for numerous helpful suggestions.

John M. Kierzek
Walker Gibson

CONTENTS

[ix]

6 WRITING THE LIBRARY PAPER 149

7 LETTER WRITING 202

PART TWO
A Handbook of Writing and Revision

GRAMMAR AND USAGE ✓ 217

MECHANICS 268

PUNCTUATION 290

SPELLING ✓   337

WORDS AND PHRASES   350

EFFECTIVE SENTENCES   388

THE PARAGRAPH 433

PART
ONE

THE
EXPRESSION
AND
COMMUNICATION
OF
THOUGHT

1 THE ENGLISH LANGUAGE

"þyslīc mē is gesewen, þū cyning, þis andwearde līf manna on eorðan tō wiðmetenesse þǣre tīde þe ūs uncuð is, swylc swā þu æt swǣsendum sitte mid þīnum ealdormannum ǫnd þegnum on wintertīde, ǫnd sīe fȳr onǣled ǫnd þīn heall gewyrmed, ǫnd hit rīne, ǫnd snīwe, ǫnd styrme ūte; cume ān spearwa ǫnd hraedlīce þæt hūs þurhflēo, cume þurh ōþre duru in þurh ōþre ūt gewīte. Hwæt hē on þā tīd þe hē inne bið, ne bið hrinen mid þȳ storme þæs wintres; ac þæt bið ān ēagan bryhtm ǫnd þæt lǣsste fæc, ac hē sōna of wintra on þone winter eft cymeð. Swā þonne þis mǫnna līf tō medmiclum fæce ætȳweð; hwæt þǣr foregange, oððe hwæt þǣr æfterfylige, wē ne cunnan. For ðon gif þēos lār ōwiht cūðlīcre ǫnd gerisenlīcre brǫnge, þæs weorþe is þæt wē þǣre fylgen."

—From the Anglo-Saxon version of Bede's *Ecclesiastical History*

If you could take yourself back more than thirteen centuries to a place near York, England, you would hear a man speaking in a language that would sound very strange to you, and yet he was speaking in English—Old English or Anglo-Saxon, we call it now. The exact year was A.D. 627. King Edwin, the ruler of Northumbria and a good part of northern and central England, had called a solemn council of his wise men, his thanes and elders, to consider a momentous decision. One of his trusted thanes arose and spoke his counsel in phrases that to this day, even in translation, have a simple dignity, a directness, a nobility that we find in some of the best of modern formal English:

"It seems to me, O King, that this present life of man, in comparison with that which is unknown to us, is as if you sat at the banquet table in the wintertime, with your chiefs and your men about you, and a fire burned, and the hall was warm, while outside it rained and snowed and stormed. There came a sparrow and swiftly flew through the hall. It came in through one door, and it flew out through the other. Now, so long as he is inside he is not cuffed by the winter's storm, but that is for only a moment, the twinkling of an eye, and at once again he goes from winter back into winter. So this life of man appears but for a moment. What went before it or what comes after it, we do not know. Therefore if this new teaching brings anything more certain or fitting, it deserves to be followed."

If you examine some of his words as they are set down here, you will see that the language is indeed not so strange and different. In the first two lines you easily recognize a number of familiar words: *cyning—king, līf—life, manna—man, eorðan—earth, tīde—tide* or *time, uncuð—unknown*. This is our language. This, more than any other tongue, in spite of all the intermarriages and all the additions of new blood, is the one important great-ancestor of the English language that you and I speak and write.

We know what language and what dialects the Anglo-Saxons spoke. We may go a little farther back and say with some assurance that we know what languages their ancestors on the continent of Europe spoke. Beyond that, if we go far enough, most of our assumed facts are theoretical or conjectural, and beyond theory and conjecture there is only a great mystery. Nobody knows how language originated. Probably no one will ever know. Scholars amuse themselves with ingenious guesses, but they do not pretend that their guesses are hypotheses.

THE DEVELOPMENT OF ENGLISH

English in the Family of Languages

The English language that you and I use has developed through many stages and many centuries. The earliest parent language of the family of which English is a member has been identified by scholars as the Indo-European. The position of English in the scheme or family tree of languages is shown by the table on page 5. English is one of a number of West Germanic languages. The Germanic group is one of a number of groups of languages, all descended from a hypothetical parent language, the Indo-European. The statement that English is one

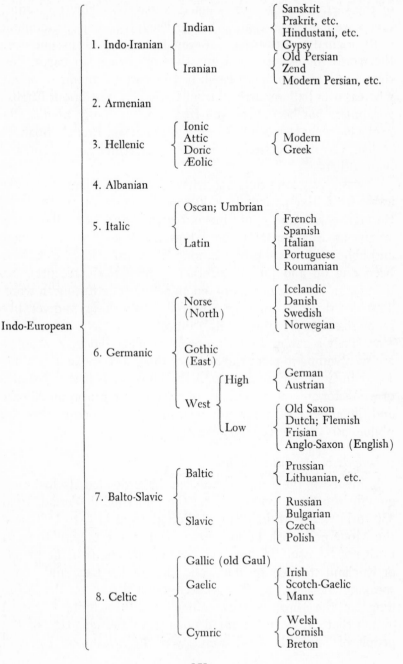

Indo-European

1. Indo-Iranian
  - Indian
    - Sanskrit
    - Prakrit, etc.
    - Hindustani, etc.
    - Gypsy
  - Iranian
    - Old Persian
    - Zend
    - Modern Persian, etc.

2. Armenian

3. Hellenic
  - Ionic
  - Attic
  - Doric
  - Æolic
    - Modern Greek

4. Albanian

5. Italic
  - Oscan; Umbrian
  - Latin
    - French
    - Spanish
    - Italian
    - Portuguese
    - Roumanian

6. Germanic
  - Norse (North)
    - Icelandic
    - Danish
    - Swedish
    - Norwegian
  - Gothic (East)
  - West
    - High
      - German
      - Austrian
    - Low
      - Old Saxon
      - Dutch; Flemish
      - Frisian
      - Anglo-Saxon (English)

7. Balto-Slavic
  - Baltic
    - Prussian
    - Lithuanian, etc.
  - Slavic
    - Russian
    - Bulgarian
    - Czech
    - Polish

8. Celtic
  - Gallic (old Gaul)
  - Gaelic
    - Irish
    - Scotch-Gaelic
    - Manx
  - Cymric
    - Welsh
    - Cornish
    - Breton

of the Germanic group of languages may be highly misleading unless we remember that, although English is mainly Germanic in its original history and in the way it relates words in sentences, the words themselves come mostly from other languages. Less than a quarter of modern English words are Germanic in origin, whereas over half are derived from Latin. The rest of our English vocabulary has been borrowed from a whole range of miscellaneous languages: ancient Greek, Scandinavian, French, Spanish, Italian, German, Russian, Arabic, Persian, American Indian, and many others.

It was a very long time ago when families or tribes first broke away from the parent Indo-European group of people and, through separation, made inevitable the formation of separate languages. But the facts about how this must have happened, and about the relationships among the various languages, have been dug up and pieced together comparatively recently. No living man has ever heard or seen an actual Indo-European word. The idea that this language existed is a hypothesis, and yet, like many scientific hypotheses, it is almost as good as a proved fact. Very likely a parent Indo-European language did exist; scholars are even willing to place the home of those who spoke it as somewhere in Central East Europe. A few clues, such as the existence of words for animals and plants of a temperate European climate and the absence of any words relating to sea or ocean, gave the philologists their interesting lead.

Periods of Linguistic Change

Students of the English language have divided its historical growth into three main periods: the Old English Period, from 450 to 1100; the Middle English Period, from 1100 to 1500; and the Modern English Period, from 1500 to the present time. It must not be assumed, however, that in any one year the people of England stopped speaking one kind of language and began speaking another. The changes were gradual, and yet the beginnings of the three periods coincided with definite historical events that caused more rapid changes in the language of the people of England. These events were the invasion of England by the Angles, Saxons, and Jutes in 449, the Norman Conquest in 1066, and the coming of the English Renaissance about 1500.

There were, of course, people in England before 450. The earliest known inhabitants of England were the Britons, a Celtic branch of the Indo-European family, with whom Caesar's Roman armies came into contact in the summer of 55 b.c. Almost a century later the armies of the Roman Emperor Claudius returned to England and proceeded in earnest to conquer and enslave the native Britons. Four centuries of Roman rule left the natives so thoroughly Romanized and dependent upon their masters that when trouble at home forced the Romans to pull in their armies from their distant colonies, the Britons were helpless against the attacks of their northern neighbors.

One of the native princes, Vortigern, made the fatal mistake of calling in some Saxon tribes from the mainland of Europe to fight the northern invaders. Unfortunately for the Britons, these "liberators" quickly took the entire country into protective custody, and proved that spears and axes can be instruments of genocide as devastating as an atom bomb. What Britons survived the wars and massacres retreated westward and northward; a few must have remained, existing as best they could in unhappy servitude. First Britons and then Britons and Romans occupied the English land for five hundred years of known history, but they left practically no trace upon our English language. The real history of our language begins with the Angles, the Saxons, and the Jutes.

The Old English Period. From 449, the date of the coming of the Angles and Saxons to England, to 1066, when William the Bastard defeated and killed the Saxon King Harold at the Battle of Hastings, is a period of 616 years—a time span almost four times as long as the present life span of the United States. Many things can happen in 616 years, and many things did happen. England became civilized, prosperous, and largely Christianized. Under the influence of Christian missionaries and the organized church, schools and monasteries were set up. Politically, the English land was divided up among four important kingdoms

—Northumbria, Mercia, Wessex, and Kent—which at various times rose to temporal importance and then declined, as kingdoms do in the space of six hundred years. These kingdoms, too, were visited by trouble of the kind that they had brought upon the Britons. Another Germanic people, the Danes, descended upon the island in raids of growing magnitude over two centuries of time. The Danes and the Anglo-Saxons were, in a way, kinsfolk, and although kinship did not mellow the savagery of feud or war, it may have been one reason why the two peoples could arrange to live together at first in a sort of cold war and later in an armed friendship. Gradually the Danes were absorbed by the more stubborn and also more civilized breed, and although the Danes, like most invaders, wantonly pillaged libraries and burned books, enough of the written language of the Anglo-Saxons survived so that we know pretty well what sort of speech our ancestors used. The language remained predominantly Anglo-Saxon. From the Danish, however, we do have such everyday words as the verbs *give, hit, raise, take, want;* the nouns *law, sister, skirt, sky, window;* the pronoun forms *they, their, them;* the adjectives *odd, low, ugly, wrong.* These Danish borrowings are important in that they are mainly short, simple words relating to family life and daily work—words in constant use.

The Middle English Period. About a century and a half before the end of the Old English Period, another Scandinavian people, the Normans (Norsemen), landed on the Normandy beaches of France, took over the country, settled down, and adopted the language and culture of the French. It was done gradually, of course, with many intrigues and the usual political deals and battles. In 1066, William, Duke of Normandy, after a tempestuous and unsavory career in his own country, laid claim to the English throne. The Norman Conquest followed his decisive victory in the Battle of Hastings. What eventually happened to the language of England can be better understood if we remember that the Norman Conquest was not a mass migration of one people intent upon displacing another, but rather the personal adventure of a dictator grasping for more power and distinction.

William the Conqueror, like other ambitious lords of his day, was interested primarily in defeating possible rivals to his throne and eliminating them by imprisonment, torture, and death. Their positions of power he filled with his own henchmen. To pay for his campaigns it was necessary for him to take what property was worth taking. Meanwhile, life went on; the work was done, crops were grown, trade revived, and the common people continued to speak the native Anglo-Saxon speech. The language of the court and the upper classes was Norman French. The language of the church was Latin, the universal language of that day.

For a time England continued to be trilingual. In the course of years a number of things happened that tended to separate the English people from their neighbors across the Channel. For the rulers it became increasingly important to be kings of England rather than to remain dukes of a small French province. Wars with France and Scotland, the Crusades, a break with the Church of Rome, a rise in the middle classes, all encouraged a sense of national unity and importance. By the middle of the fourteenth century, English, not French and Latin, became the accepted language of the ruling classes, the law courts, and the church. More than that, one dialect of the three that had persisted since the earliest Anglo-Saxon times, the East Midland dialect of London and its governmental agencies, emerged as the leading language of England, a position it has held to this day. The fact that Chaucer, a Londoner, wrote his popular stories in this dialect may have helped to establish it.

Naturally, the English that emerged was greatly enriched by additions of Norman French words. As one might expect, most of these words came out of the social, political, and economic life in which the Normans dominated. From the language of government we get such words as *parliament, crown, duke, sovereign;* from the law courts *judge, jury, justice, jail, plaintiff;* from feudal life and the life of the higher social classes *castle, count, baron, vassal, liege, war, prison, barber, grocer, tailor, mantle, labor, chamber.* A Norman word did not necessarily displace an Anglo-Saxon word. Quite often two sets of words survived; thus for the native Saxon words *work*, *stool*, *swine*, *sheep*, *cow*, *calf*, and *deer* we have parallel Norman French words *labor*, *chair*, *pork*, *mutton*, *beef*, *veal*, and *venison*.

By the end of the fourteenth century the language had taken on a distinctly modern look. If you examine closely the following samples, the first in Anglo-Saxon, the second from the time of Chaucer, the third from the time of Shakespeare and King James I of Great Britain, and the last from the present, the whole evolution may become clearer. You recognize a few of the Anglo-Saxon words on a first reading. Gradually the strange-looking Anglo-Saxon words become less strange and puzzling.

Notice how the modern translator, in the fourth passage, is limited by the change in the structure of the language and by the prestige of his predecessors. The essential difference in structure is that Anglo-Saxon functioned largely through coordinate clauses, whereas modern English has developed and perfected the subordinate clause as a means of indicating relations and shades of meaning. Note the repetition of "and . . . and . . . and" in the translation. Furthermore, the translator's problem was to write a version of the Bible that would be easily understood by modern readers, yet would also carry the flavor of the older familiar translations. Hence his style differs somewhat from that of modern idiomatic prose.

And eft hē ongan hī æt þǣre sǣ lǣran. And him wæs mycel menegu tō gegaderod, swā þæt hē on scip ēode, and on bǣre sǣ wæs; and eall sēo menegu ymbe þā sǣ wæs on lande. And hē hī fela on bigspellum lǣrde, and him tō cwæð on his lāre, Gehȳrað: Ūt ēode sē sǣdere his sǣd tō sāwenne. And þā hē sēow, sum fēoll wið þone weg, and fugelas cōmon and hit frǣton. Sum fēoll ofer stānscyligean, þār hit næfde mycele eorðan, and sōna ūp ēode; and for þām hit næfde eorðan þiccnesse, þā hīt ūp ēode, sēo sunne hit forswǣlde, and hit forscranc, for þām hit wyrtruman næfde. And sum fēoll on þornas; þā stigon ðā þornas and forðrysmodon þæt, and hit wæstm ne bær. And sum fēoll on gōd land, and hit sealde ūppstīgendne and wexendne wæstm; and ān brōhte þrītigfealdne, sum syxtigfealdne, sum hundfealdne.

—*The Anglo-Saxon Gospels,* about 1000 A.D.

And eft Jhesus bigan to teche at the see; and myche puple was gaderid to hym, so that he wente in to a boot, and sat in the see, and al the puple was aboute the see on the loond. And he taughte hem in parablis many thingis. And he seide to hem in his techyng, Here ye. Lo, a man sowynge goith out to sowe. And the while he sowith, summe seed felde aboute the weie, and briddis of heuene camen, and eeten it. Othere felde doun on stony places, where it had not myche erthe; and anoon it spronge vp, for it had not depnesse of erthe. And whanne the sunne roos vp, it welewide for heete, and it driede vp, for it hadde no roote. And othere felde doun in to thornes, and thornes sprongen vp, and strangliden it, and it yaf not fruyt. And other felde doun in to good loond, and yaf fruyt, springynge vp, and wexynge; and oon broughte thretti foold, and oon sixti fold, and oon an hundrid fold.

—John Wycliffe, about 1380, revised by John Purvey, about 1388

And he began again to teach by the sea side: and there was gathered unto him a great multitude, so that he entered into a ship, and sat in the sea: and the whole multitude was by the sea on the land. And he taught them many things by parables, and said unto them in his doctrine, Hearken; Behold, there went out a sower to sow: And it came to pass, as he sowed, some fell by the way side, and the fowls of the air came and devoured it. And some fell on stony ground, where it had not much earth; and immediately it sprang up, because it had no depth of earth: But when the sun was up, it was scorched; and because it had no root it withered away. And some fell among thorns, and the thorns grew up, and choked it, and it yielded no fruit. And other fell on good ground, and did yield fruit that sprang up and increased, and brought forth, some thirty, and some sixty, and some a hundred.

—The King James Version, 1611

Again he began to teach beside the sea. And a very large crowd gathered about him, so that he got into a boat and sat in it on the sea; and the whole crowd was beside the sea on the land. And he taught them many things in parables, and in his teaching he said to them: "Listen! A sower went out to sow. And as he sowed, some seed fell along the path, and the birds came and devoured it. Other seed fell on rocky ground, where it had not much soil, and immediately it sprang up, since it had no depth of soil; and when the sun rose it was scorched, and since it had no root it withered away. Other seed fell among thorns and the thorns grew up and choked it, and it yielded no grain. And other seeds fell into good soil and brought forth grain, growing up and increasing and yielding thirtyfold and sixtyfold and a hundredfold."

—The Revised Standard Version, 1952

Modern English. The year 1500 has been arbitrarily set as the beginning of the Modern English Period because near that time two events of superlative importance took place: William Caxton set up his printing press in England in 1476, and England began to feel the first impulses from the continental European Renaissance. The history of the English language since 1500 is one of gradual growth and enrichment, not of violent change, mainly because no foreign invader has again succeeded in setting foot on the tight little island. There have been, it is true, literary fashions or movements, like the swinging of a pendulum, which hurried or retarded the changes. The Elizabethan Age enriched the language in both flexibility of structure and added vocabulary. The Classical Period, which followed, stressed correctness, conciseness, and simplicity. In the Romantic Period the pendulum swung to the other extreme. In addition to this rhythmic swing from the liberal attitude to the conservative and back to the liberal, there were other influences at work. The simple dignity of the King James Bible of 1611 acted as a brake upon the exuberancy of both Romanticists and Latinists. From time to time some writer or group of writers rediscovered the virtues of the speech of the common people. England became first a world empire and then the mother country of a world commonwealth of nations, and the speech of a people who inhabited one half of a little island became a world language.

Several other profound influences upon the course that the English language has taken must be mentioned here. One is the standardizing influence of the dictionaries, the grammars, and the printing houses, which beginning in the eighteenth century set up standards of correctness first in spelling, then in pronunciation and meaning, and more recently in good usage. Another is the influence of almost universal education. A third, and now probably the most powerful influence, is that of television, radio, the theater, and motion pictures. The speech of the radio and television announcer and newscaster has emerged as the standard speech of our nation today—and tomorrow, it seems probable, of the whole English-speaking world. This standardizing influence is extremely powerful; regional differences in America, although they may always remain, tend to grow less prominent and less important. Two world wars have done their bit to scramble dialects in this country, and, on the international scene, to mix Australians, Americans, and British; hence it need not be a rash prophecy to assume that national differences in pronunciation and usage will in time become less noticeable.

Our Changing Language. When one looks back upon the fifteen hundred years that are the life span of the English language, he should be able to discern a number of significant truths. The history of our language has always been a history of constant change—at times a slow, almost an imperceptible change, at other times a violent collision between two languages. Our language has always been a living, growing organism; it has never been static. Another significant truth that emerges from such a study is that language at all times has been the possession not of one class or group but of many. At one extreme it has been the property of the common, ignorant folk, who have used it in the daily business of their living, much as they have used their animals or their kitchen pots and pans. At the other extreme it has been the ward of those who have respected it as an instrument and a sign of civilization, and who have striven by writing it down to give it some permanence, order, dignity, and, if possible, a little beauty.

As we consider our changing language, we should note here two developments that are of special and immediate importance to us. One is that since the time of the Anglo-Saxons there has been an almost complete reversal of the different devices for showing the relationship of words in a sentence. Anglo-Saxon was a language of many inflections. Modern English has few inflections. We must now depend largely on word order and on function words to convey the meanings that the older language did by means of changes in the forms of words. Function words, you should understand, are words such as prepositions, conjunctions, and a few others that are used primarily to show relationships among other words. A few inflections, however, have survived. And when some word inflections come into conflict with word order, there may be trouble for the users of the language, as we shall see later when we turn our attention to such matters as *who* or *whom* and *me* or *I*. The second fact we must consider is that as language itself changes, our attitudes toward language forms change also. The eighteenth century, for example, produced from various sources a tendency to fix the language into patterns not always in accord with the way people actually used it. Gradually a reaction against this authoritarian attitude set in and grew, until at the present time there is a strong tendency to restudy and re-evaluate language practices in terms of the ways in which people speak and write.

LEVELS OF USAGE

A generation or so ago students in schools and colleges were taught that good English was a set, standardized way of writing, roughly similar to what we now call formal written English, and that any deviation from the standard was bad English. Many educated people objected to this inflexible attitude toward correctness, inasmuch as they themselves wrote and spoke in a formal manner when the occasion called for formality, and in a looser, informal manner in an informal situation. Some scholars propounded the theory of "levels of usage" to explain how language actually functions. Although the original form of this theory has been modified, it should be explained here and set in a historical perspective. It is part of the history of attitudes toward language. By *levels* was meant social or cultural levels. Persons living at different levels spoke differently. At the top level was formal English; at the bottom was the spoken language of the uneducated—call it the "vulgate" or the vernacular. Between the two extremes was the level of informal writing and everyday speech. This classification, however, like most attempts to classify and formalize the complexities of human behavior, is too neat, too precise. The language habits of people refuse to conform to these classifications, as they refused to conform to the rules of eighteenth-century grammarians. The college professor, the governor of your state, and the editor of your paper usually speak and write a little more elegantly than an ordinary laborer, but the fact remains that educated people make a practice of suiting their language to the occasion. That is, they do not always speak in one way, but choose their words, in speech and writing, in recognition of the *functions* those words are to perform in a given situation.

Functional Varieties of English

You must understand that serious students of our language, like scientists in other fields, are constantly propounding new ideas, new hypotheses and generalizations. The "levels of usage" formula has been modified, with distinctions based not on levels of culture but on differences in function—that is, differences due to place, situation, occasion, or purpose.

The clearest statement of this new formula was set forth by John S. Kenyon, phonetician and lexicographer, in an article entitled "Cultural Levels and Functional Varieties of English." [1] His views have found general acceptance.

The word *level,* when used to indicate different styles of language, is a metaphor, suggesting higher or lower position and, like the terms *higher* and *lower,* figuratively implies "better" or "worse," "more desirable" or "less desirable," and similar comparative degrees of excellence or inferiority in language.

The application of the term *level* to those different styles of language that are not properly distinguished as better or worse, desirable or undesirable, creates a false impression. I confess myself guilty of this error along with some other writers. What are frequently grouped together in one class as different levels of language are often in reality false combinations of two distinct and incommensurable categories, namely, *cultural levels* and *functional varieties.*

Among *cultural levels* may be included, on the lower levels, illiterate speech, narrowly local dialect, ungrammatical speech and writing, excessive and unskilful slang, slovenly and careless vocabulary and construction, exceptional pronunciation, and, on the higher levels, language used generally by the cultivated, clear, grammatical writing, and pronunciation used by the cultivated over wide areas. The different cultural levels may be summarized in the two general classes *substandard* and *standard.*

Among *functional varieties* not depending on cultural levels may be mentioned colloquial language, itself existing in different degrees of fa-

[1] *College English,* X (October 1948), 31–36. By permission of The National Council of Teachers of English, copyright owners.

miliarity or formality, as, for example, familiar conversation, private correspondence, formal conversation, familiar public address; formal platform or pulpit speech, public reading, public worship; legal, scientific, and other expository writing; prose and poetic belles-lettres. The different functional varieties may roughly be grouped together in the two classes *familiar* and *formal* writing or speaking.

The term *level*, then, does not properly belong at all to functional varieties of speech—colloquial, familiar, formal, scientific, literary language. They are equally "good" for their respective functions, and as classifications do not depend on the cultural status of the users.

The two groupings *cultural levels* and *functional varieties* are not mutually exclusive categories. They are based on entirely separate principles of classification: *culture* and *function*. Although we are here principally concerned with the functional varieties of standard English (the highest cultural level), yet substandard English likewise has its functional varieties for its different occasions and purposes. Thus the functional variety of colloquial English may occur on a substandard cultural level, but the term *colloquial* does not in itself indicate a cultural level. So the functional variety of formal writing or speaking may occur on a lower or on a higher cultural level according to the social status of writer or speaker, and sometimes of reader or audience. It follows, for instance, that the colloquial language of cultivated people is on a higher cultural level than the formal speech of the semiliterate or than some inept literary writing.

What then is the student's interest in levels and varieties? In our society, the student's task is not simply to master the techniques of one set way of composition, appropriate to his class or profession. On the contrary, he must be aware of the various kinds of communication available to him, and he must choose, from hour to hour, almost from moment to moment, that organization of words which will be most appropriate to achieve his purpose. A major goal of this book is to introduce the student to some of these varieties, and to help him choose intelligently. As may be expected, the emphasis in this book will be on the formal kinds of speech and writing. One reason for such an emphasis is that formal expository prose is a difficult medium to learn, simply because for most people it is relatively unfamiliar. A second reason is an overwhelming one: as we shall be pointing out again later, most of the significant work of the community is handled in fairly formal prose exposition.

[16]

Let us see now what the differences in the varieties of standa
English are and how they affect our choice of appropriate la
guage to use in various situations. These varieties we shall classi
as "the more formal," "the more informal," and "the verna
ular," trying to indicate by the label that there is no clear-c
division between formal and informal, but rather a gradual mer
ing of one type into the other.

Standard English: The More Formal Varieties. The difference
between varieties of English have often been explained by liker
ing language to clothes. For formal occasions we put on ou
formal clothes; for a tennis match we dress in sports clothes; fo
driving a truck or roofing a house or digging a tunnel we put o
overalls or dungarees. Similarly, we suit our language to the occa
sion, to the subject, and to our readers or listeners. So far th
comparison is good. When we pause to analyze the analogy
however, we are trapped by the word "formal," which to mos
people means "white tie and tails," a costume that millions o
Americans have never worn, or perhaps have never seen worn
except by actors on a motion-picture or television screen. And ye
every American home that can afford a radio or television set and
a newspaper has been exposed daily to both spoken and written
formal English. We must amend our analogy by extending the
range of "formal" clothes to include the well-pressed business
suit.

The language that we call formal—for want of a term with less
unfortunate connotations—is far from being cold, reserved, or
stodgy. It has warmth, strength, beauty, and an infinite range
and variety. It is not confined to a few scientific and scholarly
treatises. The great body of our literature, from Shakespeare and
Bacon down to the latest book on the international crisis, is written in formal English. It is the language of most books of history,
sociology, political science, botany, chemistry—every textbook
that you use in college. It is the language of the professions, such
as law, medicine, teaching. It is the language of all serious essays,
of a good part of all novels and poems, and of radio and television
newscasts and commentaries. Most business letters are written in

formal English. So are the news and editorial sections of many newspapers. As a matter of fact, a good share of the nation's private and public daily work is done with the help of formal English.

Let us now examine a few examples of the formal style and try to learn from this study what are the distinguishing marks of standard English in its more serious and dignified uses. The first three examples are from public utterances by men whose primary interest was not in professional writing. The occasions were as solemn and formal as any in the history of mankind.

I expect that the Battle of Britain is about to begin. Upon this battle depends the survival of Christian civilization. Upon it depends all our British life, and the long continuity of our institutions and our Empire. The whole fury and might of the enemy must very soon be turned on us. Hitler knows that he will have to break us in this Island or lose the war. If we can stand up to him, all Europe may be free and the life of the world may move forward into broad, sunlit uplands. But if we fail, then the whole world, including the United States, including all that we have known and cared for, will sink into the abyss of a new Dark Age made more sinister, and perhaps more protracted, by the lights of perverted science. Let us therefore brace ourselves to our duties, and so bear ourselves that, if the British Empire and its Commonwealth last for a thousand years, men will say, "This was their finest hour."

—WINSTON CHURCHILL, speech to the House of Commons, June 18, 1940

I see a book kissed which I suppose to be the Bible, or at least the New Testament, which teaches me that all things whatsoever I would that men should do unto me, I should do even so to them. It teaches me further to remember them that are in bonds as bound with them. I endeavored to act up to that instruction. I say I am yet too young to understand that God is any respector of persons. I believe that to have interfered as I have done, as I have always freely admitted I have done in behalf of His despised poor, I did no wrong, but right. Now, if it is deemed necessary that I should forfeit my life for the furtherance of the ends of justice and mingle my blood further with the blood of my children and with the blood of millions in this slave country whose rights are disregarded by wicked, cruel, and unjust enactments, I say, let it be done.

—JOHN BROWN, last speech

With malice toward none, with charity for all, with firmness in the right as God gives us to see the right, let us finish the work we are in,

to bind up the nation's wounds, to care for him who shall have borne the battle, and for his widow and his orphans, to do all which may achieve and cherish a just and lasting peace among ourselves and with all nations.

—ABRAHAM LINCOLN, Second Inaugural Address

Let us pause to examine these selections. Obviously they are not brief portions of run-of-the-mill prose. There would be no point in using ordinary, pedestrian prose in a book that has as its purpose helping you to write better than average composition. In these three samples, note how the speaker's sincerity and intense earnestness come through to us by way of words that are, for the most part, simple, homely, everyday words. As you read, you may be conscious of the heavy use of monosyllables, as for instance the fourteen words out of the sixteen in this sentence: "Hitler knows that he will have to break us in this Island or lose the war." Note in all three the rhythms of spoken prose, the balance of phrase against phrase, and the dramatic climax in the Churchill selection. The sentence quoted from Lincoln's address is in itself a fine example of climax. The style of the speech by John Brown, you will notice at once, is strongly influenced by his knowledge of the King James Bible. All three should be read aloud.

Now let us study two other examples of serious prose, this time the work of two of our most distinguished jurists, Oliver Wendell Holmes and Learned Hand. Both are discussing an aspect of law; in a way they are saying the same thing—that the knowledge of law, the interpretation of law, and the making of law depend on our knowledge of the past. Yet how different are their styles of writing. Their vocabularies are a mixture of everyday words and scholarly words. Both depend for their style on balanced elements—phrases, clauses, words—Judge Holmes more so than Judge Hand. Judge Holmes makes use of antithesis—which is a form of balance—as you may notice in almost every sentence of the paragraph, notably in this one: "The life of the law has not been logic; it has been experience." In the paragraph by Judge Hand we have interesting examples of complex sentences, of clause piled upon clause, each succeeding clause helping to clarify and illustrate and strengthen the author's central idea.

The object of this book is to present a general view of the Common Law. To accomplish the task, other tools are needed besides logic. It is something to show that the consistency of a system requires a particular result, but it is not all. The life of the law has not been logic: it has been experience. The felt necessities of the time, the prevalent moral and political theories, intuitions of public policy, avowed or unconscious, even the prejudices which judges share with their fellow-men, have had a good deal more to do than the syllogism in determining the rules by which men should be governed. The law embodies the story of a nation's development through many centuries, and it cannot be dealt with as if it contained only the axioms and corollaries of a book of mathematics. In order to know what it is, we must know what it has been, and what it tends to become. We must alternately consult history and existing theories of legislation. But the most difficult labor will be to understand the combination of the two into new products at every stage. The substance of the law at any given time pretty nearly corresponds, so far as it goes, with what is then understood to be convenient; but its form and machinery, and the degree to which it is able to work out desired results, depend very much upon its past.

—OLIVER WENDELL HOLMES, JR., *The Common Law*

A constitution, a statute, a regulation, a rule—in short, a "law" of any kind—is at once a prophecy and a choice. It is a prophecy because it attempts to forecast what will be its effects: whom it will benefit and in what ways; on whom its impact will prove a burden; how much friction and discontent will arise from the adjustments that conformity to it will require; how completely it can be enforced; what enforcement will cost; how far it will interfere with other projects or existing activities; and in general, the whole manifold of its indirect consequences. A thoroughgoing and dependable knowledge of these is obviously impossible. For example, although we can anticipate with some degree of assurance who will pay a steeply graded income tax and in what amounts, there is no way to tell what its indirect effects will be: what activities of the taxpayers in the higher brackets it will depress; if they do not work so hard, in what way will they occupy their newly acquired leisure; how any new activities they may substitute will affect others; whether this will be offset by a loss of the mellowed maturity and the wisdom of those who withdraw. Such prophecies infest law of every sort, the more deeply as it is far-reaching; and it is an illusion to suppose that there are formulas or statistics that will help in making them. They can rest upon no more than enlightened guesses; but these are likely to be successful as they are made by those whose horizons have been widened, and whose outlook has been clarified, by knowledge of what men have striven to do, and how far their hopes and fears have been realized. There is no substitute for an open mind enriched by reading and the arts.

—LEARNED HAND, *The Spirit of Liberty*

And here is formal standard English as a historian uses it. His vocabulary, as in the preceding selections, is a mixture of the homely words and the scholarly words. His sentences show the effects of care, a regard for structure, for an easy rhythmical flow of sounds—all these the obvious qualities of a pleasing style in good formal writing.

For the mass of men in 1600, the ocean still held the terrors of the past. That a succession of adventurers had reached the outer shores of these uncharted wastes did not in the least allay the fears of the earthbound. Nothing in the chronicles or in the tales that passed by word of mouth gave a friendlier aspect to the waters of the Atlantic.

Yet soon, in their scores, in their hundreds and thousands, and later in their millions, the earthbound men and women of Europe passed across the unfriendly sea. In their coming they created a nation.

Tiny vessels, sixty to two hundred tons in the main, bore the voyagers westward. Riding at anchor in the sheltered bays of the homeland, the ships seemed substantial enough. Their sturdy timber and looming masts, their cabins that rose like castles several stories high in the stern, were impressive in comparison with the harbor craft that flitted about them. At sea, it would be another matter. All became precarious as the isolated specks, buffeted by the elements, beat their way into the unknown immensity before them; and the men below huddled fearfully in the cramped space that set their condition of life.

—OSCAR HANDLIN, *The Americans*

A scientist, when he is not thinking and communicating in terms of mathematical and chemical symbols, when he is discussing a subject that the common man can understand, may write like J. Robert Oppenheimer, the nuclear physicist.

Each of us knows from his own life how much even a casual and limited association of men goes beyond him in knowledge, in understanding, in humanity, and in power. Each of us, from a friend or a book or by concerting of the little we know with what others know, has broken the iron circle of his frustration. Each of us has asked help and been given it, and within our measure each of us has offered it. Each of us knows the great new freedom sensed almost as a miracle, that men banded together for some finite purpose experience from the power of their common effort. We are likely to remember the times of the last war, where the common danger brought forth in soldier, in worker, in scientist, and engineer a host of new experiences of the power and the comfort in even bleak undertakings, of common, concerted, co-operative life. Each of us knows how much he has been transcended by the group of which he has been or is a part; each of us has felt the solace of other men's knowledge to stay his own ignorance, of other men's wisdom to stay his folly, of other men's courage to answer his doubts or his weakness.

—J. Robert Oppenheimer, *Science and the Common Understanding*

Finally, as an example of formal, serious writing that is aimed at a very wide reading public, let us quote from one of a series of "interpretations in depth" of modern nations—this one of Greece.

An immortal tale tells of a "Clear Land" where colors are purer and the forms of things are finer than on earth. At first the Clear Land seems only a radiant reflection of earthbound countries. The trees, houses and mountains known to everyday experience are all outlined there with dazzling clarity upon the shining air. "Then comes the strange part. When you are perfectly at home there you see again that it is very like our lower world!" Such conditions seem to come true in Greece. Even the Greek battle cry has unlooked-for resonance. *Aera!* the fighting men sing out, meaning "Air!" Greece is a Clear Land, where the sun caresses the mountains and where life itself has a clearer shape. It does not seem surprising that Greece was the setting, some 2,500 years ago, for one of man's best efforts to define the nature and purposes of life on earth.

Awakening in this Clear Land is often an especially keen delight. The roosters which are everywhere about help you to it at an early hour. With luck you may see the first pale rosy rays spiking out from behind a dark mountain. This is the hand of "rosy fingered Dawn," the same that Homer, the first and greatest of the poets of western civilization, knew so many dewy mornings ago. And once again the god Apollo's golden chariot comes winging up over the steep countryside, making the bare peaks shine like crystal above the cold violet valleys and the still dark sea.

The roosters crow the louder; in this country nothing quiets them. But the nightingales fall silent now, or rather their rich silver improvisations vanish like light into light. The thrilling shriek of Athena's silent-winged owl too is stilled. The owl huddles deep in a plane tree by a bubbling spring; it fears the ravens whose black-suited flocks are flapping heavily to their larcenous work in the sun-swept fields. Sarcastically the black robbers light on a breeze-teased scarecrow, a tattered coat upon a stick, while cawing up the sudden warmth of day.

The village innkeeper puts out a single table and chair, tentatively, like a tortoise thrusting out a foot. Sparrows peck and chitter on the cobblestones of the village's steep and winding street. Now they fly up like brown leaves in a gust as a peasant girl appears. She is all in black, but her smile and her glancing eyes gleam white as the morning. The innkeeper's mangy hound stretches out his forepaws and growls approval as the girl goes by. Her thick black hair is coiled in a single braid to signify maidenhood. She passes, straight and graceful, with a tall brown jug upon her head. The girl is on her way to the spring beneath the plane tree, where the owl dozes already and a serpent sleeps too beneath the roots.[1]

. . . .

Amongst these old mountains Pan and the nymphs are dancing still, and sometimes voiceless invisible hunger also dances. Greece as a whole resembles an improbable rock garden, fragrant with herbs and wild flowers, sea-bathed on every hand, beautifully sculptured and yet harsh in its own way. Like marble it is gleaming and lovely in the distance, hard-edged close by and chill beneath the fingers. This rocky southeast corner of Europe has given more to the world perhaps than any other place. But its fruits are of the spirit.

—Alexander Eliot and the Editors of Life, *Greece*

When we examine the last two selections, we see that in one respect they differ vastly and in another respect they are alike. Mr. Oppenheimer has used balance and repetition to give his writing continuity and unity. By repeating the opening phrase of each sentence—"each of us knows . . . each of us has broken . . . each of us knows the great new freedom . . ."—he leads up to the climax of the last sentence—"the solace of other men's knowledge . . . of other men's wisdom . . . of other men's courage to answer his doubts or his weakness." Mr. Eliot, on the other hand, writes in shorter and simpler sentences, and depends for his effects on color, on clarity, and on a subtle use of words, especially adjectives, that echo the epic style of Homer. Such descriptive epithets as "shining air," "pale rosy rays," "dewy mornings," "still dark sea," "silent-winged owl," are here not by

---

[1] Two paragraphs of the text have been omitted here. Note that omissions of any significant extent are indicated by a single typed line of spaced periods. Refer to this for illustration when you study the use of quoted matter in your research paper, Chapter 6.

accident but by most careful design. That is the way Homer wrote.

There is one thing, above all others, that we can learn from this brief analysis of formal English. It is that the writers feel a care for structure. Their sentences are *built*; they are not thrown together. The various devices that writers have at their disposal are discussed more fully in Chapter 3. It will be profitable for you to return to these illustrations when you study the various devices of structure and style discussed there.

Characteristics of the Formal Style. Let us now summarize what we have carefully pointed at in the preceding pages. What are the marks of standard English in its more serious and dignified uses? First, restrictions upon vocabulary, although important, consist almost entirely of excluding words and expressions labeled "colloquial" or "substandard" in your desk dictionaries. Slang and vulgarity are, of course, inappropriate. It is untrue that formal English demands only big words, bookish words, the cold impersonal words of pure science, though such words are probably more common here than in the very informal writing. But the simple, homely, everyday words are as much a part of the vocabulary of formal English as the multisyllabic words.

In the second place, standard English on the more formal levels is characterized by orderly structure. The expression and communication of ideas are a planned process, not a spontaneous outpouring. Ideas are grouped and arranged in some logical sequence. There is a serious attempt to show the interrelationship between ideas. As a consequence, paragraphs tend to be more fully developed than in the informal varieties of English; sentences acquire increased complexity as the thoughts they express become more mature.

Third, those who use the language in formal situations, in the serious discussion of serious ideas, tend, as a rule, to be relatively conservative in their attitude toward matters of grammar and usage. It matters little whether the writer is a statesman like Churchill, a scientist like Oppenheimer, a historian, a sociologist, a college professor, or just an ordinary layman who faces the problem of giving a talk before the Rotary Club or the Chamber of Commerce. The deference to what is known as correct usage is strong in his mind. He wishes to learn what the correct forms are and to act accordingly.

And finally, standard English in the more formal situations is characterized by an impersonal or objective attitude toward the subject matter communicated and by a relatively distant, rather than intimate relation with the reader. One must not assume that the exclusion of the writer's or speaker's self is a requisite of the formal style. Indeed, some of the finest formal writing is intensely personal in nature. In most cases this writing is personal because it is the personal element that is the vital substance of what is being said. Subjects in which the personal element is not vital, however, are usually treated objectively. More specifically, the sort of papers, reports, term essays, and discussions that college students write for their various courses are usually best treated impersonally and objectively.

Standard English: The More Informal Varieties. Before we begin to examine the characteristics of informal English, we must reaffirm the statement that the essential unity of standard English is much more important than the differences among its varieties. One does not stop writing formal English and begin writing informal English as if he were stepping through a door from one room to another.

A great deal of good writing lies in an area somewhere between the intensely serious varieties we have quoted and the chatty, familiar essays, often flavored with wit and humor, that anyone would accept as informal. This intermediate kind of writing has a serious intent, but it is written for the common reader, who is expected to enjoy his reading in a relaxed mood. Here are two examples:

> Every grammar school in England taught each little Elizabethan schoolboy the same thing. It taught him Latin. Sometimes an exceptional school like Westminster went a step further and taught one other subject, and in that case the subject was Greek. The explanations in the Greek grammar were of course in Latin, for the boys of Westminster School

were expected to use nothing but Latin in their school hours. If anyone forgot and spoke in English it counted against him as much as three mistakes in spelling.

It might be said in general of the Tudor school system that its aim was to turn out little Roman-Christian gentlemen who could write exactly like Cicero. To this end the boys struggled through the Stoic precepts of the *Disticha* in the first form, learned elegant Latin colloquialisms from Terence in the second, and emerged on the great plateau of Cicero—"the very foundation of all"—in the third. Throughout, there was a stern emphasis on the two great principles of Tudor education: the gentlemanly Christian virtues on the one hand and a sound Latin style on the other.

The emphasis on character development was not new, and Ben Jonson started school with the same moral maxims that had been inculcated in young Geoffrey Chaucer. The teaching of Latin, however, had changed. Chaucer was taught a Latin over which the dust of centuries had been drifting; no one knew exactly what "correct" Latin was supposed to be and no one cared. But by the time Ben Jonson went to school it had been decided that "correct" Latin meant the Latin that Cicero wrote. The blurred medieval theories on vocabulary and syntax were replaced by a single standard, and the great Roman orator became the emperor of all the English schoolrooms of Queen Elizabeth's day.

Education is a curious thing. All over England the wriggling young Elizabethans sat in their classrooms and studied the classic ideal of gravity and control. They learned elegance and restraint from Horace; they learned a balanced and antithetical prose from Cicero; they learned the tight rules of dramatic construction from Terence. And then they went forth and produced the tangled, loose, barbaric magnificence of the Elizabethan drama.

—MARCHETTE CHUTE, *Ben Jonson of Westminster*

Is this formal or informal writing? Although it really does not matter, it is worthwhile to point out some characteristics of Marchette Chute's style. Her sentences are built with care, but they are more relaxed than the stately rhetorical structures that Judge Learned Hand builds. Since informality depends partly on situation, partly on the reader addressed, and partly on the attitude of the writer to his reader and to his material, note here above all the hint of good-natured irony that lies under what she says and comes out in the last paragraph.

A naturalist writing for other scientists writes in the formal style, using a scientific vocabulary and perhaps a complex sentence structure; writing for the common reader, with the intention to give enjoyment as well as information, he changes his style materially, as you see in the following:

An insect walks in a manner that is unique among animals. If you possessed six legs and had to use them in walking, how would you move them? That is the problem which instinct has solved for the infinitely varied hosts of the adult insects.

The six legs are usually moved as a series of tripods, three legs at a time. The front and rear legs on one side, and the middle leg on the other, move in unison. Thus, the insect is always securely planted on the ground. It does not have to use a large number of muscles, as we do, just to maintain an erect posture. In walking, the average adult person employs a motor mechanism that weighs about eighty pounds—sixty pounds of muscle and twenty pounds of bones. Each step we take puts about 300 muscles in action. One hundred and forty-four are employed just to balance our spine and keep it upright.

Many insects use their legs in specialized ways. The common water-strider employs its forelegs to capture its prey, its oarlike middle legs to propel itself over the water, and its rear legs to guide it in the manner of a rudder. The legs of a dragonfly are held together to form a basket for scooping victims from the air. They are set so far forward on the insect's body that they are almost useless for walking. A dragonfly clings and climbs but hardly ever tries to walk. The monarch is sometimes called "the four-legged butterfly" because of a peculiarity in its use of its legs. This insect holds its forelegs against its body as a general rule and uses its middle and rear pairs of legs for walking. Male monarchs have short atrophied legs that are virtually useless.

For a cow or horse, cat or dog, legs are used almost exclusively as a means of transportation. Among the insects, however, legs have innumerable other uses. Often they are whole tool kits. The rear legs of the bumblebee and the honeybee contain spine-ringed depressions—baskets for carrying pollen home from the fields. The forelegs of the mole cricket and the seventeen-year cicada nymph are enlarged into digging shovels. The swimming legs of the diving beetle are fringed with hairs to increase their effectiveness as oars.

Some insects use the claws on their feet to hang themselves up for a night's sleep. The praying mantis employs its spined forelegs as a trap for catching prey. The water-strider has legs with "snowshoes" formed of hairs that help keep it from breaking through the surface film. When not in use, these hairs fold up into a slot in the insect's leg. A few moths have similar masses of hairs that open out into "powder-puffs" just below the knees on the forelegs as a means of attracting their mates. The legs of no other living creatures have as great variety in form and uses as the legs of the insects.

—EDWIN WAY TEALE, *The Strange Lives of Familiar Insects*

Note in the above selection the relatively simple sentence structure, the economy and directness of diction, and, incidentally, the scientific neatness with which the author wraps up this segment of exposition by the first and the last sentences. As a carry-over from his formal style, one might note in passing that he always uses *employs* instead of employing the simpler and more familiar *uses*.

In some writing traditionally labeled informal, the total extent of informality consists of the attitude of the writer toward his material and toward his reader. You may find in them the same discriminating taste in choice of words, the same respect for present-day standards in grammatical correctness and in usage, the same mature structure as in the best formal writing. The only difference is that the writer frankly and freely interprets his subject through his own personality or through his own likes and prejudices.

In the following selection from *The Desert Year* by Joseph Wood Krutch, American critic, essayist, and naturalist, note the flashes of wit that accentuate his easy informality, his familiar relation with his readers.[2]

Perhaps because life presumably began in hot places, such creatures as the scorpions, lizards, and spiders, who represent ancient ways of life, either survive only in regions still conspicuously warm or at least continue only there to flourish in large, bold forms. Farther north, our spiders are small and inconspicuous, as though they had been able to meet competition in a new world only by fitting themselves into the crevices which a more up-to-date population had overlooked. The wolf spider and the gaudy garden spider are the most imposing we can produce. Nothing comparable to the tarantula, nothing which looks so ancient and so typical of the bad old days, stalks boldly about. One need not be learned in evolution to guess that he was more at home before braininess became so common.

But at least we do have spiders everywhere and a tarantula is obviously a spider. For a real glimpse into an almost vanished world, one should

[2] From *The Desert Year* by Joseph Wood Krutch, copyright 1951, 1952 by Joseph Wood Krutch, by permission of William Sloane Associates.

look instead at a scorpion who so obviously has no business lingering into the twentieth century. He is not shaped like a spider and he has too many legs to be an insect. Plainly, he is a discontinued model—still running but very difficult, one imagines, to get spare parts for. His translucent flesh —if scorpions can be said to have flesh—makes him look as though he were made of wax rather than clothed in armor like an insect or in skin like a vertebrate. High over his back he holds the conspicuous thornlike sting which he is ready to throw forward over his head, with surprising speed, into the finger of a human being unwise enough to molest him.

I have seen none of the small, deadly kind, only two inches long. I have, however, seen several of the more dangerous looking but actually less dangerous sort, five inches from tail to claw, who threaten with their harmless pincers while the sting poises quietly to strike. I wonder if they court in the same quaint way as the one Fabre describes found in the hottest and driest parts of southern France. There, after much preliminary waving of claws, the male takes the female by the hand and quietly backs into his burrow, leading her after him. I hope that as he does so he sings the antediluvian equivalent of Don Giovanni's "Lá ci darem la mano," which Zerlina found irresistible.

—JOSEPH WOOD KRUTCH, *The Desert Year*

The following passage, written by an acknowledged master of the informal style, is serious enough in its content; yet the tone is obviously personal and the diction is varied enough, ranging from the solemn to the disrespectful.

A publisher in Chicago has sent us a pocket calculating machine by which we may test our writing to see whether it is intelligible. The calculator was developed by General Motors, who, not satisfied with giving the world a Cadillac, now dream of bringing perfect understanding to men. The machine (it is simply a celluloid card with a dial) is called the Reading-Ease Calculator and shows four grades of "reading ease"—Very Easy, Easy, Hard, and Very Hard. You count your words and syllables, set the dial, and an indicator lets you know whether anybody is going to understand what you have written. An instruction book came with it, and after mastering the simple rules we lost no time in running a test on the instruction book itself, to see how *that* writer was doing. The poor fellow! His leading essay, the one on the front cover, tested Very Hard.

Our next step was to study the first phrase on the face of the calculator: "How to test Reading-Ease of written matter." There is, of course, no such thing as reading ease of written matter. There is the ease with which matter can be read, but that is a condition of the reader, not of the matter. Thus the inventors and distributors of this calculator get off to a poor start, with a Very Hard instruction book and a slovenly phrase. Already they have one foot caught in the brier patch of English usage.

Not only did the author of the instruction book score badly on the front cover, but inside the book he used the word "personalize" in an essay on how to improve one's writing. A man who likes the word "personalize" is entitled to his choice, but we wonder whether he should be in the business of giving advice to writers. "Whenever possible," he wrote, "personalize your writing by directing it to the reader." As for us, we would as lief Simonize our grandmother as personalize our writing.

In the same envelope with the calculator, we received another training aid for writers—a booklet called "How to Write Better," by Rudolph Flesch. This, too, we studied, and it quickly demonstrated the broncolike ability of the English language to throw whoever leaps cocksurely into the saddle. The language not only can toss a writer but knows a thousand tricks for tossing him, each more gay than the last. Dr. Flesch stayed in the saddle only a moment or two. Under the heading "Think Before You Write," he wrote, "The main thing to consider is your purpose in writing. Why are you sitting down to write?" And echo answered: Because, sir, it is more comfortable than standing up.

Communication by the written word is a subtler (and more beautiful) thing than Dr. Flesch and General Motors imagine. They contend that the "average reader" is capable of reading only what tests Easy, and that the writer should write at or below this level. This is a presumptuous and degrading idea. There is no average reader, and to reach down toward this mythical character is to deny that each of us is on the way up, is ascending. ("Ascending," by the way, is a word Dr. Flesch advises writers to stay away from. Too unusual.)

It is our belief that no writer can improve his work until he discards the dulcet notion that the reader is feeble-minded, for writing is an act of faith, not a trick of grammar. Ascent is at the heart of the matter. A country whose writers are following a calculating machine downstairs is not ascending—if you will pardon the expression—and a writer who questions the capacity of the person at the other end of the line is not a writer at all, merely a schemer. The movies long ago decided that a wider communication could be achieved by a deliberate descent to a lower level, and they walked proudly down until they reached the cellar. Now they are groping for the light switch, hoping to find the way out.

We have studied Dr. Flesch's instructions diligently, but we return for guidance in these matters to an earlier American, who wrote with more patience, more confidence. "I fear chiefly," he wrote, "lest my expression may not be *extra-vagant* enough, may not wander far enough beyond the narrow limits of my daily experience, so as to be adequate to the truth of which I have been convinced. . . . Why level downward to our dullest perception always, and praise that as common sense? The commonest sense is the sense of men asleep, which they express by snoring."

Run that through your calculator! It may come out Hard, it may come out Easy. But it will come out whole, and it will last forever.

—E. B. WHITE, "Calculating Machine"

More extreme varieties of informal writing are to be found everywhere in our society, where the friendly touch is often the way to riches, as in advertising. Sportswriting too has been notoriously informal for half a century and has influenced other branches of journalism. Here is an example by a professional golfer, whose prose may strike you as affected in its efforts to be pals with the reader:

Show me a really morose, down-at-the-mouth, give-up-the-game, leave-me-alone-at-the-clubhouse-bar golfer and I will show you a golfer who is having trouble with one of two clubs, the putter or the driver. We all have a way of surviving those weeks when our long irons aren't long or our sand blasts move lots of sand instead of the ball. But when our putting is sour or our driving is awful, then we are in honest, interminable, miserable trouble. Consequently, the putter and the driver are two clubs that merit some special attention, and that is what we are going to give them now. Then we will add a quick word about club selection for when you don't happen to be using the putter or the driver.

—ARNOLD PALMER, in *Sports Illustrated*

The intimacy of tone and the calculated effect of slapdash characteristic of the farther reaches of informal writing are much in evidence in some modern fiction, particularly in America. The modern novelist strives for informality with all the discrimination that was required to write the more formal nineteenth-century novel. In the following famous opening paragraph observe the consistency of the tone in vocabulary and structure, and see how the reader is constantly appealed to, so that he is forced into assuming a close contact with the narrator:

To get there you follow Highway 58, going northeast out of the city, and it is a good highway and new. Or was new, that day we went up it. You look up the highway, and it is straight for miles, coming at you, with the black line down the center coming at and at you, black and silky and tarry-shining against the white of the slab, and the heat dazzles up from the slab so that only the black line is clear, coming at you with the whine of the tires, and if you don't quit staring at that line and don't take a few deep breaths and slap yourself hard on the back of the neck you'll hypnotize yourself and you'll come to just at the moment when the right front wheel hooks over into the black dirt shoulder off the slab, and you'll try to jerk her back on but you can't because the slab is high like a curb, and maybe you'll try to reach to turn off the ignition just as she starts the dive. But you won't make it, of course.

—ROBERT PENN WARREN, *All the King's Men*

The Vernacular. There is a language below the level of standard English—more accurately, there is an endless variety of languages—in which the college student has only an academic interest. Teaching a college student how to use those languages is not the province of this book. Most of these varieties—call them vernacular or vulgate, if you wish—are not the natural speech of so-called cultural levels, but made-to-order dialects, such as the language of jive, of subdebs, of racing, of airmen and marines, of the various occupations. As an illustration of what a fine writer can do with the vernacular, note the famous description of a storm in Mark Twain's *The Adventures of Huckleberry Finn:*

This place was a tolerable long, steep hill or ridge about forty foot high. We had a rough time getting to the top, the sides was so steep and the bushes so thick. We tramped and clumb around all over it, and by and by found a good big cavern in the rock, most up to the top on the side toward Illinois. The cavern was as big as two or three rooms bunched together, and Jim could stand up straight in there. . . .

We spread the blankets inside for a carpet, and eat our dinner there. We put all the other things handy at the back of the cavern. Pretty soon it darkened up, and begun to thunder and lighten; so the birds was right about it. Directly it begun to rain, and it rained like all fury, too, and I never see the wind blow so. It was one of those regular summer storms. It would get so dark that it looked all blue-black outside, and lovely; and the rain would thrash along by so thick that the trees off a little ways looked dim and spiderwebby; and here would come a blast of wind that would bend the trees down and turn up the pale underside of the leaves; and then a perfect ripper of a gust would follow along and set the branches to tossing their arms as if they was just wild; and next, when it was just about the bluest and blackest—*fst!* it was as bright as glory, and you'd have a little glimpse of treetops a-plunging about away off yonder in the storm, hundreds of yards further than you could see before; dark as sin again in a second, and now you'd hear the thunder let go with an awful crash, and then go rumbling, grumbling, tumbling, down the sky towards the underside of the world, like rolling empty barrels downstairs —where it's long stairs and they bounce a good deal, you know.

—MARK TWAIN, *The Adventures of Huckleberry Finn*

Now set against this another description of a storm, this one written also as a personal experience, but by a sophisticated city-bred man, who interprets the scene in terms of drama and orchestral music.

One afternoon while we were there at that lake a thunderstorm came up. It was like the revival of an old melodrama that I had seen long ago with childish awe. The second-act climax of the drama of the electrical disturbance over a lake in America had not changed in any important respect. This was the big scene, still the big scene. The whole thing was so familiar, the first feeling of oppression and heat and a general air around camp of not wanting to go very far away. In midafternoon (it was all the same) a curious darkening of the sky, and a lull in everything that had made life tick; and then the way the boats suddenly swung the other way at their moorings with the coming of a breeze out of the new quarter, and the premonitory rumble. Then the kettle drum, then the snare, then the bass drum and cymbals, then crackling light against the dark, and the gods grinning and licking their chops in the hills. Afterward the calm, the rain steadily rustling in the calm lake, the return of light and hope and spirits, and the campers running out in joy and relief to go swimming in the rain, their bright cries perpetuating the deathless joke about how they were getting simply drenched, and the children screaming with delight at the new sensation of bathing in the rain, and the joke about getting drenched linking the generations in a strong indestructible chain. And the comedian who waded in carrying an umbrella.

—E. B. WHITE, "Once More to the Lake"

Varieties of Spoken English. In a course devoted primarily to written composition, a few words about spoken English are nevertheless proper and important.

Spoken language differs from written language in a variety of ways. Perhaps the primary distinction between the two is that speech depends on sound, whereas writing depends on sight and on those strange processes of the mind that translate written symbols into sound and meaning. There are other differences, important to the linguist, of course. But the odd quirk in this main distinction is that speech also has the help of certain "visual aids" that writing does not have. In speech we add to and qualify our meaning by our physical gestures, by movement of the hands, by shrugs, by our facial expressions, such as smiles, frowns, or even the lifted eyebrow. Our resources of sound are many—intonation, the rise and fall of the voice, the changes in pitch. We can vary the intensity or the volume of sound; we can, on occasion, whisper, shout, mumble, or even snarl. All these add to meaning. These are a strength that written language does not have.

On the other hand, spoken language has obvious weaknesses. That collection of fleeting, ephemeral noises that we call human speech is gone a moment after it is uttered. Oftentimes it is gone even before it has been heard accurately. Perhaps it lingers for a while in someone's memory. After a minute or so it cannot be called back to life. A little of it, here and there, may be caught and preserved on tape or on a phonograph record, it is true, but most of what has been thus saved was probably first worked over and shaped and set down in writing before it was read off as speech. It is only partly spoken English. Written English has a longer life, a greater permanence. It is a more accurate form of communication because it can be reread, examined, and studied. For these reasons it demands greater care in its composition. Because the writer has time to think ahead and plan, he assumes a responsibility to build his sentences, to select and arrange his words, and to use the rhetorical and stylistic devices that past writers have created and developed.

Functional varieties exist in spoken English as they do in written English. In general, we can distinguish two main varieties, cultivated speech and common or general speech. We use cultivated speech where a degree of formality and dignity is essential or appropriate. We use common or general speech for our everyday communication and exchange of ideas. In speech as in writing we select, consciously or subconsciously, the forms and patterns that seem to fit the subject matter, the occasion, and our attitude toward our listeners.

The Student's Choice. A college student should know something of the history of the English language, its forms and varieties, its resources and limitations, so that his attitude toward self-improvement will be realistic. The history of the language has been a history of innumerable changes. It is still a changing language. What, then, *is* the realistic attitude in the face of changes in usage? The commonsense procedure is to ask, "What *is* being done at the present time by people of education, of taste, of social importance, people whose opinions I value?" The standards of the educated must be your standards for the simple reason that you as a college student and graduate will live among and communicate with those who have these standards.

What these standards are you could probably discover for yourself by wide reading and by long and careful observation of the practices of educated men and women. That is the way the authors of handbooks, grammars, and dictionaries find out what current usage is. Of course you have neither the time nor the opportunity for this sort of individual research; you have to defer to the judgment of others. It is realistic to do so, but do not give up entirely your research and observation, for such study may be rewarding. Observe current usage in the books that you read; listen to prominent men and women whom you may hear on television, and always, when you are in doubt or in a hurry, remember that a good dictionary will provide you with a pretty good reflection of general usage.

In most of the papers that you will write in college you will make a conscious choice of style, language, attitude, and point of view. Many times, it is true, your choices will be determined for you by the situation. If your instructor asks you to write a discussion of the causes of the First World War, you will naturally decide to give him, not a slangy, breezy sketch, but a serious, well-planned, and well-constructed essay in standard English. It is hard to see that any other decision is appropriate in such a situation. Similarly, a professional writer writing for *The New*

Yorker uses the *New Yorker* style; a writer hoping to sell his essay to *Harper's* uses the *Harper's* style. Writing for *Time,* he uses the *Time* style. For a newspaper he uses a journalistic style.

Frequently you will have to decide between a formal and an informal treatment of a subject. A subject such as "Women Drivers" may be handled with deep seriousness or with a light, perhaps with a humorous, touch. It depends on the particular phase of the subject that you decide to use, on the situation, and on the readers for whom you are writing. Your choice, whatever it is, should always consider writing as communication. You are not merely writing—you are writing for someone to read.

Bibliography. The following books dealing with some of the matters mentioned in this chapter—the history of language, its levels and varieties, the sources of its vocabulary, and so forth —will be found in almost every college library:

Adams, J. Donald. *The Magic and Mystery of Words.* New York: Holt, Rinehart & Winston, 1963.

Allen, Harold B. *Readings in Applied English Linguistics.* New York: Appleton-Century-Crofts, 1958.

Bloomfield, Leonard. *Language.* Henry Holt & Co., 1933.

Bloomfield, Morton W., and Leonard Newmark. *A Linguistic Introduction to the History of English.* New York: Alfred A. Knopf, 1963.

Bryant, Margaret M. *Modern English and Its Heritage, 2nd ed.* New York: The Macmillan Company, 1962.

Carroll, John B. *The Study of Language.* Cambridge: Harvard University Press, 1958.

Dean, Leonard F., and Kenneth G. Wilson. *Essays on Language and Usage.* New York: Oxford University Press, 1962.

Evans, Bergen, and Cornelia Evans. *A Dictionary of Contemporary American Usage.* New York: Random House, 1957.

Fowler, H. W. *A Dictionary of Modern English Usage.* Oxford: Clarendon Press, 1926.

Fries, C. C. *American English Grammar.* New York: D. Appleton-Century Co., 1940.

Greenough, James B., and George Lyman Kittredge. *Words and Their Ways in English Speech.* New York: The Macmillan Company, 1901, 1923.

Jespersen, Otto. *Growth and Structure of the English Language, 9th ed.* New York: Doubleday & Co., 1955.

Krapp, George Philip. *The Knowledge of English.* New York: Henry Holt & Co., 1927.

McKnight, George H. *English Words and Their Background.* New York: D. Appleton & Co., 1923.

Nicholson, Margaret. *A Dictionary of American-English Usage.* New York: Oxford University Press, 1957. [Based on Fowler's *Modern English Usage*]

Pei, Mario. *The Story of English.* Philadelphia: J. B. Lippincott Co., 1952.

Pyles, Thomas. *Words and Ways of American English.* New York: Random House, 1952.

Robertson, Stuart. *The Development of Modern English.* New York: Prentice-Hall, Inc., 1934.

Sapir, Edward. *Language.* New York: Harcourt, Brace & World, Inc., 1921.

Smith, Logan Pearsall. *Words and Idioms.* Boston: Houghton Mifflin Co., 1925.

2 THE SENTENCE: GRAMMATICAL PATTERNS

WHAT IS GRAMMAR?

Grammar, as we use the term here, is a description and analysis of the facts of language as it is used today. Other definitions of the term "grammar" are possible. A linguist such as Professor Charles F. Hockett, who speaks of the phonemes and morphemes of a language, not necessarily English, says that grammar is "the morphemes used in the language, and the arrangements in which these morphemes occur relative to each other in utterances." [1] Another linguist, Professor Margaret M. Bryant, dealing primarily with English, uses a much simpler definition: "Grammar is the analysis of communication in words." [2] And the editors of *Webster's Third New International Dictionary*, who try to phrase their definitions for the layman as well as for the scientist, define grammar as "a branch of linguistic study that deals with the classes of words, their inflections or other means of indicating relation to each other, and their functions and relations in the sentence as employed according to established usage and that is sometimes extended to include related matter such as phonology, prosody, language history, orthography, orthoepy, etymology, or semantics." [3] Our primary interest in this book, however, is descriptive grammar, a label that explains not only itself but also the methods of the scientific grammarian. A scientist first observes and gathers the facts; then he tries to organize and analyze his facts, and finally to formulate certain generalizations that he calls laws. In grammar, similarly, the facts of

[1] *A Course in Modern Linguistics*, p. 129.
[2] *Modern English and Its Heritage*, p. 190.
[3] *Webster's Third New International Dictionary*, p. 986.

usage always come first; the generalizations are based on usage.

Unfortunately, if we use the definition of the scientific grammarian or linguist, we are up against a real problem. If we study our definitions carefully, it becomes obvious that there can be no such thing as good grammar or bad grammar. In the judgment of a linguist, everyone, from the college professor to the illiterate, speaks grammatically, for the way each uses words for communication is *his* grammar. The complication arises from the fact that most educated people still do not believe this; to them grammar still means *good* grammar, and to them a person who speaks grammatically is a person who uses language according to certain generally accepted standards and conventions. Their conviction on this matter is a fact of language that we cannot brush away by a definition.

Distinction Between Grammar and Usage

To avoid confusion we must define our terms. The scientific grammarian or linguist makes a distinction between grammar and usage; the ordinary person does not. The fact that certain speech patterns are inappropriate or unacceptable on formal or dignified occasions among educated persons, to a grammarian, is a question of usage. It is a matter of choice, of preference, a matter of what is socially acceptable among the educated and what is not. When we say that something is a matter of usage in speech or writing, we mean that it is a matter of the way people talk or write. And in a college textbook that has as its objective the improvement of a student's use of his language, we must make judgments, make comparisons, point out that certain language patterns are more appropriate or more effective than others. A scientific grammarian or linguist merely says that this is the way things are; he makes no judgments.

Is a Knowledge of Grammar Helpful?

Many students, at some time or other, question the value of a knowledge of grammar as an aid to better writing. What part of grammar is useful? What part is useless? The answer must be different for every different person. Many people write well and speak well without knowing much about grammar, but for those who by reading this book admit their capacity for self-improvement, grammar is both a convenient chest of tools and a practical code of communication. It is like a chest of tools in that it enables the student to build effective sentences and to repair faulty ones. It is a code or a technical vocabulary, understood by both teacher and learner, necessary in learning and teaching. How, for instance, can a student correct a sentence such as, "This is strictly between he and I," if he does not know something about pronouns, about prepositions, and about the uses of the objective case? How can a teacher explain the punctuation of phrases and clauses in a series if the student does not know what phrases and clauses are? When a person says, "I done pretty good in the test today," he expresses his thought with absolute clearness—but clearness is not enough. How can this person learn what is acceptable among educated people, and how can a teacher help him learn it, if he does not have some understanding of verb forms in current usage? Or the accepted use of adjectives and adverbs? The least we can say in defense of a knowledge of grammatical terms is that it is usually well for teacher and student to speak the same language—here, the technical language of the subject that is being studied.

THE PARTS OF SPEECH OR WORD CLASSES

Words are classified according to their *function* or *use in the sentence* into what are called parts of speech. Notice that in this system of classification it is the *use in the sentence* that always determines the part of speech of a word in a given situation. Many words, especially those that have been in the language for a long time, have acquired several uses, just as they have acquired many meanings. In your desk dictionary, look up a few simple, everyday words that occur to you as you glance about the room: *glass, floor, wall.* You immediately think of such uses as *the glass in the window, you live in a glass house, we glassed in our porch,* and you see the word *glass* used as a noun, as an adjective, and as a verb. Now make the same test for *floor* and *wall.*

[40]

The parts of speech are *nouns, pronouns, verbs, adverbs, adjectives, prepositions, conjunctions,* and *interjections.* If you wish to group these parts of speech according to their functions, you may think of them as follows: nouns and pronouns are *naming* words; verbs are *asserting* words; adjectives and adverbs are *modifying* words; prepositions and conjunctions are *joining* words; interjections are *independents.* Another possible classification, useful in certain areas of the study of English, is to call prepositions and conjunctions *function* words or *empty* words. Words that can convey ideas or images, such as nouns, pronouns, adjectives, adverbs, verbs, are then called *full* words.

The Noun

A noun is a word that names something. It may name a person, a thing, a place, an animal, a plant, an idea, a quality, a substance, a state, an action. Use each of the following properly in sentences and try to determine under which classification each noun falls: *man, lion, city, oak, book, liquids, beauty, affection, flight, stupor, relativity.* When a noun names a person, a place, an object, it is called a *concrete noun;* when it names a quality, an idea, a mental concept, it is called an *abstract noun.* Concrete nouns name physical, visible, tangible objects; abstract nouns name things that do not have a physical substance. For the practical value of this information, see Sections 22, 25, 27. A proper noun is the official name of some individual person, place, or object; a common noun names any one of a class or kind. In English, proper nouns are capitalized; common nouns are not. See Section 8.

NOUNS

When the *inverter* was fixed, the *gantry* moved away, the *cherrypicker* maneuvered its *cab* back outside the *capsule,* and the *count* went along smoothly for 21 *minutes* before it suddenly stopped again. This time the *technicians* wanted to double-check a *computer* which would help predict the *trajectory* of the *capsule* and its impact *point* in the *recovery area.*

—Alan B. Shepard, Jr., *We Seven*

The *knowledge* he has acquired with *age* is not the *knowledge* of *formulas,* or *forms* of *words,* but of *people, places, actions*—a *knowledge* not

[41]

gained by *words* but by *touch, sight, sound, victories, failures, sleepless-ness, devotion, love*—the human *experiences* and *emotions* of this *earth* and of oneself and other *men;* and perhaps, too, a little *faith,* and a little *reverence* for the *things* you cannot see.

—ADLAI STEVENSON, speech at Princeton

The Verb

A verb is a word (or group of words) that expresses action, occurrence, being, or mode of being. See Sections 3 and 6.

VERBS

We *were* late. The day *had been spent* in play. The girls *did* not *meet* us there. *Have* you *heard* the latest story?

The Pronoun

A pronoun is usually defined as a word that takes the place of a noun. This brief definition, useful enough as a practical short-cut, must be modified by pointing out that certain pronouns, such as *none, nobody, anything,* and the impersonal *it,* do not take the place of any noun but are words more or less arbitrarily classified by grammarians and lexicographers as pronouns. Pro-nouns are further classified as personal, demonstrative, relative, interrogative, and indefinite. See Section 4. The following table indicates how certain words usually function in these classes. It must be understood, however, that some of these words may also be used as other parts of speech.

PERSONAL
I, you, he, she, it, they, we, them, thee, thou

DEMONSTRATIVE
this, that, these, those

RELATIVE
who, which, what, that, whoever, whatever, whichever

INTERROGATIVE
who, which, what

INDEFINITE
one, none, some, any, anyone, anybody, someone, each, somebody, no-body, everyone, everybody, either, neither, both

The Adjective

An adjective is a word that modifies (describes or limits) a noun or pronoun. It may denote quality, quantity, number, or extent. It is most useful here to consider the articles *a, an, the,* and the possessive forms of nouns and pronouns, when used to modify nouns, as in the classification of adjectives. Pronouns have two forms of the possessive: the first form (*my, our, your, her, his, its, their*) when placed before a noun functions as an adjective; the second form (*mine, ours, yours, his, hers, theirs*) functions as a pronoun.

ADJECTIVES

It was *an eloquent, sharp, ugly, earthly* countenance. *His* hands were *small* and *prehensile,* with fingers knotted like *a* cord; and they were continually flickering in front of him in *violent* and *expressive* pantomime.

—R. L. STEVENSON

The place through which he made *his* way at leisure was one of *those* receptacles for *old* and *curious* things which seem to crouch in *odd* corners of *this* town, and to hide *their musty* treasures from *the public* eye in jealousy and distress.

—CHARLES DICKENS

One of *our* men saw *your* horse throw you and break through *the* fence. They left *their* work, at *my* suggestion, and ran to see if you needed help.

PRONOUNS

That horse of *mine* is a problem. May I borrow one of *yours* to get me back to the ranch?

The Adverb

An adverb is a word that modifies a verb, an adjective, or another adverb. Less commonly an adverb modifies a preposition, a phrase, a clause, or a whole sentence. Adverbs express the following relations in a sentence: time, place, manner, degree, frequency, affirmation or negation. See also Section 5.

TIME

It will rain *tomorrow.* The guests will *soon* be here. They are *now* arriving.

[43]

PLACE

Come *in*. Leave your umbrellas *outside*. Place them *here*, please.

MANNER

She expresses herself *crudely*. Her sister sings *beautifully*. She learns *quickly*.

DEGREE

You are *very* kind. This is *too* good. It is *entirely too* expensive.

FREQUENCY

She is *always* pleasant. She called *twice*. It rains *often*. It *never* snows.

AFFIRMATION OR NEGATION

Do *not* go there. *Certainly*, he will return. *Yes*, he was there. *No*, you must *not* see him. *Perhaps* he will call you. *Undoubtedly* he is busy.

The Preposition

A preposition is a word used to show the relation between a substantive (noun or pronoun), called the object of the preposition, and some other word in the sentence. A preposition thus forms a group of words called a phrase, which may be used as an adjective, an adverb, or, less frequently, as a noun. Many prepositions are single, short words:

at the game, *by* the house, *in* the room, *for* payment, *from* home, *off* duty, *on* land, *above* the clouds, *after* the ball, *around* her neck, *before* dawn, *behind* his back, *between* dances, *below* the covering, *over* the top, *through* the skin, *until* daybreak

There are also a number of so-called "group prepositions," the use of which you can readily see:

by means of, in front of, on account of, in place of, with respect to, and others.

The Conjunction

A conjunction is a word that connects words, phrases, or clauses. Conjunctions are either coordinating or subordinating. Adverbs used as connectives, either coordinating or subordinating, are called *conjunctive adverbs*.

The words commonly used as coordinating conjunctions are

*and, but, for, or, nor, yet, both—and, not only—but also, either
—or, neither—nor.* At the present time, *so* is used as a coordinating conjunction in loose, informal writing and in speech, but its use should be avoided in most serious writing except in direct quotations.

Some of the words used as subordinating conjunctions are *if, although, though, that, because, since, so that, in order that, as, unless, before, than, where, when.*

Correlative conjunctions (conjunctions used in pairs) are *both—and, not only—but also, either—or, neither—nor.*

Some words commonly functioning as adverbs may be used as conjunctions: *how, why, where, before, after.* Such connectives as *however, therefore, nevertheless, hence,* and *accordingly* are often classified as conjunctive adverbs. In modern prose they are commonly used as transitional expressions. There is no profit in quibbling over the question of whether they are transitions or conjunctive adverbs; the only important fact here is that in modern writing these expressions, with the exception of *hence, thus,* and *still,* are *not* placed at the beginnings of clauses in compound sentences. They function more accurately when they are tucked away within the clauses. See Section 14 for a discussion of the punctuation that should be used with these transitional expressions.

The Interjection

An interjection is a word or group of words used as an exclamation expressing sudden or strong feeling. Note that an exclamation point is not the inevitable punctuation of an interjection. For most interjections, especially the mild ones, a comma or a period is sufficient.

THE VERBALS

The verbals—gerunds, participles, and infinitives—are hybrid forms. They are derived from verbs and have some of the forms and functions of verbs, but they serve primarily as other parts of speech. Verbals may have tense forms, they may take complements, and they may be modified by adverbs. In these ways they are like verbs. Their primary function, however, is as nouns, adjectives, and adverbs.

The Gerund

A gerund is a verbal used as a noun.

The man began *shouting* incoherently. [Note that *shouting* is the object of the verb *began*. It is modified by the adverb *incoherently*.]

Writing a poem is not easy. [*Writing* is the subject of the verb *is*, and has *poem* as its object.]

His eligibility for office was established by his *having been* so successful as governor. [Note the form of the gerund. Note also that it takes the adjective *successful* as its complement.]

The Participle

A participle is a verbal used as an adjective. It is, of course, also used as a part of a verb phrase, as in "He *was reading* a book." It may appear in a few uses with an adverbial sense, as in "They came *bringing* gifts" or "The boys ran off, *shouting* protests." Our main concern, however, is with the adjective use of the participle. Note also such sentences as "He *was asking* you a question" and "Teasing him was *asking* for trouble," in which *asking* is a part of the verb phrase in the first combination and a gerund in the second.

The *tired* men again faced the *howling* wind. *Gripping* the rope, they slowly pulled the *mired* truck past the *waiting* soldiers. They noted a staff car *turning* in their direction. *Having saved* the truck, they relaxed for a moment. [Note here the tense forms and the positions of the participles.]

The Infinitive

An infinitive is a verbal that may be used as a noun, an adjective, or an adverb. The infinitive may be recognized by its sign *to*. Occasionally the sign is omitted.

Mary did not want *to drive* her car. [Used as a noun object of the verb *did want*. Note that it takes an object.]

Mary hoped *to be taken* home. [Note the passive form.]

[46]

We did not dare *refuse* her request. [Note the omission of the sign *to.*]
She had no car *to drive.* [Used as an adjective to modify *car*]
She was happy *to come* with us. [In adverbial sense, modifies *happy*]
To watch her happiness was a pleasure. [In noun sense, as subject of verb *was*]

E X E R C I S E S

EXERCISE 1, PARTS OF SPEECH AND VERBALS. *Identify the parts of speech and the verbals in the following selections:*

I have but one lamp by which my feet are guided, and that is the lamp of experience. I know of no way of judging of the future but by the past. And judging by the past, I wish to know what there has been in the conduct of the British ministry for the last ten years to justify those hopes with which gentlemen have been pleased to solace themselves and the house.

—PATRICK HENRY

We hold these truths to be self-evident, that all men are created equal, that they are endowed by their Creator with certain unalienable rights, that among these are life, liberty, and the pursuit of happiness. That, to secure these rights, governments are instituted among men, deriving their just powers from the consent of the governed.

—*The Declaration of Independence*

EXERCISE 2, VERBALS. *Identify the verbals in the following sentences. The verbals are gerunds, participles, and infinitives.*

1. Attending a church wedding is fun; I usually like to go.
2. Being a devoted clubwoman, Mother has social obligations to consider.
3. Father, a tired and harried executive, tries to avoid being involved in her affairs.
4. Coming home, still absorbed in his office problems, he tries to be courteous to a roomful of chattering women without revealing that he is unable to recall a single name.
5. Having finished his social chores, Father retreats to his study.
6. One day Mother took my protesting father to church to watch two strangers being married.
7. The day being hot and muggy, Father sat there sweltering in his tight formal suit.

[47]

8. Wishing to avoid an argument, Father pretended to be enjoying himself.
9. Sitting in the next pew were two old and respected friends of the family.
10. Having bowed politely, he began to study the expressions on the faces of the assembled guests.

THE ELEMENTS OF THE SIMPLE SENTENCE

Defined in terms of form or pattern, a sentence is a basic unit of language, a communication in words, having as its core at least one independent finite verb with its subject. The sentence gives the reader or hearer a feeling that it is a relatively complete unit, capable of standing independently or alone. Now this may seem a bit complicated, but it will gradually clear itself up as you study the explanations and examples below.

For a discussion of the various verbless, subjectless, or fragmentary units that are acceptable in writing and in speech, turn to Section 1.

On the basis of the types of clauses, coordinate and subordinate, that enter into their structure, sentences are classified as simple, complex, and compound.

Subject and Verb: The Independent Clause

The *simple sentence* is one that contains a single independent clause, with or without modifiers. In a simple sentence either the subject or the verb or both may be compounded.

S V
Men are working.

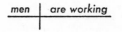

S S V
Boys and girls play.

  S   S   V   V
Boys and girls laugh and shout.

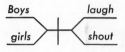

Complements

You can see that some verbs express a general action, and that the sentences they help to form have a sense of completeness. Other verbs, however, require a third element—in addition to subject and verb—to form a complete expression. That element is called a *complement*. There are three main types of complements: *direct objects*, *indirect objects*, and *subjective complements*. Less common are the *objective complement* and the *retained object*.

The Direct Object. The direct object of a verb denotes that which is immediately acted upon.

  S   V   O
Mary bought a hat.

| Mary | bought | hat |

  V   O
Read this book.

| (You) | read | book |

  V S   V   O
Did you hear him?

The Indirect Object. The indirect object names, without use of a preposition, the one to whom or for whom the act is done.

Mother told *me* a story.

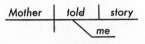

[49]

He taught *us* a lesson.
I gave the *dog* a bath.

Note that when *to* or *for* is expressed, the substantive following becomes the object of a preposition, as in "Mother told a story to me," "Dr. Jones taught mathematics to us," "She gave a dollar to the man."

The Subjective Complement. The subjective complement refers to the subject and describes or limits it. It is often called a *predicate substantive* if it is a noun or pronoun, and a *predicate adjective* if it is an adjective. See also Section 5.

Tom is a *major* now. [Predicate substantive]

| Tom | is \ major |

It looks *good* to me. [Predicate adjective]

| It | looks \ good |

He became very *rich*.
The music sounds *loud*.

The Objective Complement. The objective complement, used with verbs such as *elect, choose, make, call, appoint,* and the like, refers to the direct object.

They made him their *chairman*.

| They | made / chairman | him |

They called him *crazy*.

The Retained Object. The retained object is used with a verb in the passive voice.

They were given *food*.

| They | were given | food |

He was taught a good *lesson*.

[50]

A simple sentence may have adjectives, adverbs, and phrases as modifiers.

The little boy gave his mother a red rose.

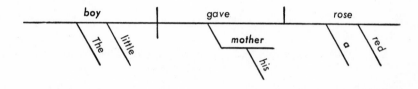

Phrases

In its general, loose sense, a phrase is any group of words. Thus we say that a man "phrases his thoughts" when he puts them into words, or that he expresses his ideas in "well-balanced phrases" when his sentences are well-built and rhythmical. The word *phrase* in its general sense has its legitimate place in the language. In the study of grammar, however, the word refers to one of three kinds: the verb phrase, the prepositional phrase, or the verbal phrase.

The verb phrase, which is not discussed in this chapter, is actually a verb consisting of more than one word, such as *have been persuaded, has loved, will be honored.*

The Prepositional Phrase. A prepositional phrase consists of a preposition, its object, and modifiers of the phrase or any of its parts.

A prepositional phrase may be used as an adjective.

A graduate *with a knowledge of mathematics* and a desire *for advancement* should find a job *in one of the new industries.* [Note that the first phrase modifies *graduate*, the second modifies *knowledge*, the third modifies *desire*, the fourth modifies *job*, and the fifth *one*. Note also that the second phrase is a part of the first and the fifth is a part of the fourth.]

He must have studied several subjects *of no particular value.* [The phrase, a modifier of *subjects*, has within it two modifiers. Note also the verb phrase *must have studied.*]

The father *of the child* [adjective] watched *from the window* [adverb].

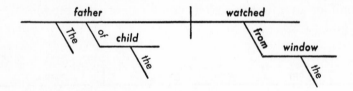

A prepositional phrase may be used as an adverb.

Slowly he walked *toward the door.* [The phrase functions as an adverb of place or direction, modifying the verb *walked.*]
She sat *on a stool* and selected a cherry *from the basket.*
If you are angry *at your best friend,* you must be careful *with your speech.* [Here the phrases function as adverbs modifying adjectives.]
Under the bridge two tramps had built a fire.

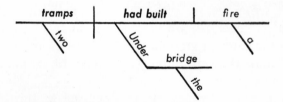

A prepositional phrase may be used as a noun. This use is quite rare.

The best time for study is *in the morning. On the mantel* would be a good place for it. [The first phrase is used as a noun subjective complement; the second is used as the subject of the verb *would be.*] *For me to criticize his work* would be presumptuous. [With *for*]
The best time *for study* is *in the morning.* [As adjective and as noun]

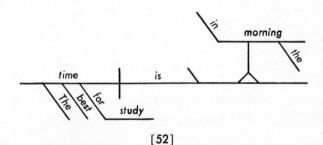

[52]

The Verbal Phrase.   A verbal phrase consists of a participle, a gerund, or an infinitive and its complements and modifiers.

The Participial Phrase.   A participial phrase consists of a participle, its complement, if it has one, and any modifiers of the phrase or any of its parts. It is generally used as an adjective. A thorough understanding of the uses of participial phrases is of practical value to any writer because their misuse results in a stylistic fault known as the *dangling modifier*. For a discussion of dangling modifiers, see Section 32.

The car *now turning the corner* belongs to my father. [The phrase modifies *car*. The participle is modified by the adverb *now*, and it has for its object the noun *corner*.]

The letter, *stamped and sealed*, lay on the table. *Distracted by the sudden noise*, the speaker hesitated and then stopped in his oration. [Note the possible positions of the participle in relation to the word it modifies.]

Having given him the required amount, I left the store. [Notice that within the participial phrase there is another participle, *required*, modifying *amount*.]

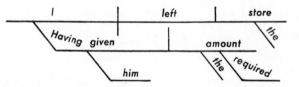

The Absolute Phrase.   The absolute phrase is made up of a noun or pronoun (a substantive) followed by a participle. The substantive has no grammatical relation to any word in the sentence outside the phrase; it stands as an independent element. An absolute phrase cannot become a dangler. Note the following examples carefully.

Our assignment having been finished, we asked for our pay. [*Having been finished* modifies *assignment*.]

The class having been dismissed, the teacher wearily picked up his books.

We hunted toward the north, *each taking one side of the ridge*. [The substantive is *each*.]

The Gerund Phrase.   A gerund phrase consists of a gerund, its complement, if it has one, and any modifiers of the phrase or any of its parts. A gerund phrase is always used as a noun; it may therefore function as the subject of a verb, as a complement, or as the object of a preposition.

Arguing with him does little good. *Piloting a speed boat* requires great skill. [In both sentences the gerund phrase is used as a subject. By this time you should be able to identify the modifiers and the complements.]

Willard enjoyed *watching television*. [Direct object]

You can get the address by *stopping at our house*. [Object of preposition]

I should call that *violating the spirit of our agreement*. [The phrase is used as an objective complement referring to *that*.]

Hearing that song brings back sad memories to me. [Subject of verb]

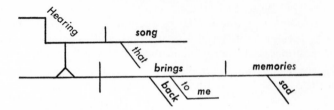

Mary objected to *my telling the story*. [Object of preposition]

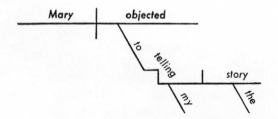

The Infinitive Phrase. An infinitive phrase, like other verbal phrases, may have a complement and modifiers. In addition it may have what is called the *assumed subject* of the infinitive. The assumed subject of an infinitive is in the objective case. An infinitive phrase may be used as an adverb, an adjective, or a noun.

We stood up *to see better*. [Modifies the verb]

We are happy *to have you back with us*. [Modifies an adjective]

Whether to believe him or to call mother was a real problem for me. [A noun, used as the subject of the sentence]

We knew him *to be the worst troublemaker in school.* [Notice that the infinitive *to be* has *him* as its assumed subject.]

My orders were *to deliver the guns.* [Noun used as subjective complement]

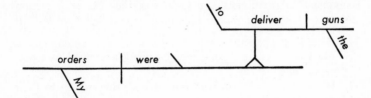

I am happy *to see you again.*

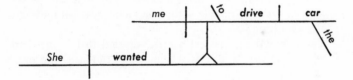

She wanted me *to drive the car.*

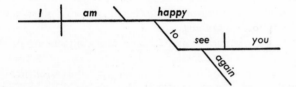

EXERCISES

EXERCISE 1, PARTICIPLES. *Pick out the participles in the following sentences and tell what word each participle modifies.*

1. The astronauts' spacecraft is a complicated machine.
2. Compressed to a minimum, it is the size of a telephone booth.
3. In spite of its reduced area, it contains thousands of instruments.
4. In it are over seven miles of wire winding back and forth.
5. Only a genius could design this amazing machine.
6. The engineers were faced with several puzzling limitations.
7. Every bit of needed equipment had to be miniaturized.
8. Having succeeded in solving one problem, they faced another.

9. The completed system had to have duplicates for safety.
10. In addition, this seemingly snarled and confused mechanism had to be made to function automatically.

EXERCISE 2, PARTICIPLES AND GERUNDS. *Pick out each gerund and participle in the following sentences and tell how each is used.*

1. Most boys entering college enjoy being welcomed to a new experience.
2. Having been duly warned and advised, they return to their normal routines.
3. Some boys, impressed and perhaps disturbed by the advice, resolve to become devoted scholars.
4. Urged on by curiosity, some begin exploring their new and exciting surroundings.
5. Finding old friends and making new contacts are in themselves rewarding experiences.
6. There are always a few lost, unhappy souls who, unable to make new friends, amuse themselves sadly by browsing in the library.
7. Some even think of writing home to surprised and pleased parents, thereby revealing their homesickness without actually admitting it.
8. The happiest are the extroverts, adjusted to life anywhere, taking life day by day as it comes and not worrying much about it.
9. Classes soon start, and then loneliness is forgotten in the excitement of meeting new professors, buying books, and getting a routine of studying established.
10. College life becomes a challenging adventure, demanding much from each boy and giving much in return.

EXERCISE 3, PHRASES. *In the following sentences pick out each phrase and tell whether it is prepositional, participial, gerund, or infinitive.*

1. My brother urged me not to miss the concert.
2. I telephoned to Margie early in the afternoon.
3. Thanking me sweetly, Margie agreed to accompany me.
4. Getting two tickets was the problem of the moment.
5. Knowing the condition of my purse, I decided to get help from my friends.
6. A friend in need seems to be the only kind of friend that I have.

7. I found everyone in great need of financial help.
8. In despair I decided to test my brother's fraternal loyalty.
9. He had a long sermon to give me, but in the end he agreed to help me.
10. Looking very pretty, Margie added charm to an evening of pleasant music.

THE ELEMENTS OF THE COMPOUND SENTENCE

A compound sentence, as the name indicates, is made by compounding or joining two or more simple sentences. Such joining may involve the use of conjunctions and proper punctuation. See Sections 13 and 14. The examples used here are shorter than the typical compound sentence.

She should not take risks; she has three small children.
I warned her, but she was persistent.

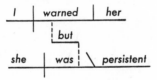

The walk was slippery, and she fell and hurt herself badly.

THE ELEMENTS OF THE COMPLEX SENTENCE

We have seen that simple sentences are units structurally and grammatically complete, and that compound sentences can be broken up into such complete and independent units. A thought expressed in a simple sentence is thereby given primary rank or importance. Ideas expressed in the coordinate units of a compound sentence are given equal billing, as it were. It is of course quite possible for communication to exist on that one level; the Anglo-Saxons came pretty close to writing and speaking in that manner. Turn to page 3 and then to page 10 and note in the excerpts from Old English writing how true that statement is. Modern English, however, has developed a system whereby many differences in the relationship of one idea to another, or of one fact to another, can be expressed by differences in grammatical structure. It has developed and perfected the dependent clause and the complex sentence.

Clauses

In the many possible variations of the useful complex sentence, the notion that main clauses are for big ideas and subordinate clauses are for lesser ideas is often completely lost. Perhaps it is better to think of a complex sentence only in grammatical terms—main or coordinate clauses are at the top level structurally; dependent clauses are dependent structurally. In the following examples pick out what you think is the important idea in each sentence and then decide whether it is in the grammatically independent clause.

He had a feeling that his number was up, that he would die on the beach.
It seems that the entire invasion fleet was heading for the wrong beach.
It should be added that a sudden and unexpected last-minute order from Hitler kept the Germans from moving up their panzer divisions.

These sentences are quite common, normal sentences. For an example of an awkward inversion, called the "upside-down subordination," see Section 29.

A complex sentence, let us repeat, has at least one main clause, grammatically independent and able to stand alone, and one or more dependent clauses. A dependent clause is joined to the main clause by a relative pronoun, *who, which, that,* or by one of the numerous subordinating conjunctions, such as *after, although, as, because, before, if, since, unless, when, where, why.* Dependent clauses are used as nouns, as adjectives, or as adverbs. You can ordinarily recognize a dependent clause by the sign of its dependence or subordination, but occasionally the sign is missing, as in the following examples:

The progress [*that*] *they made in college* depended on the friends [*whom*] *they had found.*
I realized [*that*] *he had not understood the error* [*that*] *I had pointed out to him.*

[58]

The boy [*whom*] *he referred to* was the one who had begged, "Say [*that*] *it isn't so, Mister!*"

The Noun Clause. A dependent clause may be used as a noun.

AS SUBJECT OF A VERB
What he says means little to me.

AS OBJECT OF A VERB
She thought *that she would go to Paris.*

AS SUBJECTIVE COMPLEMENT
Her explanation was *that she was bored with life.*

AS OBJECT OF A VERBAL
Be sure to accept *whatever she offers you.*

AS OBJECT OF A PREPOSITION
It depends upon *how many can play Saturday.*

AS AN APPOSITIVE
His first argument, *that women are inferior to men,* was easily proved untrue.

EXAMPLES
What he told the officers was never revealed. [Noun clause used as subject]

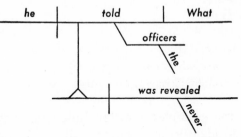

The teacher said *that the answer was correct.* [Noun clause used as object]

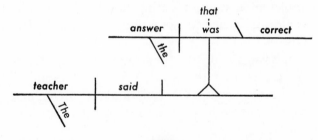

Give it to *whoever calls for it*. [Noun clause used as object of a preposition]

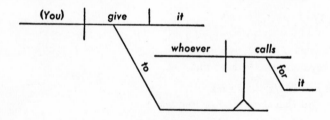

The Adjective Clause. A dependent clause may be used as an adjective. Adjective clauses are either restrictive or nonrestrictive. An important thing to remember in this connection is that restrictive clauses are *not* set off by commas. See Section 13.

RESTRICTIVE

We needed a car *that was rugged and light*.

Do you know anyone *who has two tickets to sell?*

A teacher *who speaks poor English* is badly handicapped.

Try to remember the exact time *when you saw the accident*.

Isn't this the shop *where you found your bargains?*

NONRESTRICTIVE

I have been reading W*e Seven, which was written by seven astronauts*.

We camped that night near Maupin, *where we found some moss agates*.

My father, *who is a lapidary*, was delighted with the find.

I am rooming with John Cooper, *who is now a sophomore*.

Notice in the examples you have just read that a restrictive clause helps to identify the word it modifies. It points it out. It says, "That particular person or thing and no other." In the second group of sentences, no identification is needed. The person or thing is already identified, sometimes by name, sometimes by other means.

Note also, if you are looking for structural signals as a means of identifying clauses, that the words *where, when*, and *why* may introduce adjective clauses. If you think of them in terms of "place where," "time when," and "reason why," you will not be confused. These three words, however, have other uses too. See the examples given below.

ADJECTIVE CLAUSES

We found no reason *why he should be held.*

He was seen near the place *where the crime had been committed.*

It was the hour *when graves and tired students yawn.*

This is the boy *who brought the papers.* [Adjective clause modifying *boy*]

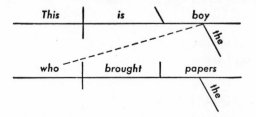

ADVERBIAL CLAUSES

You will begin writing *when I give the signal.* [Modifies the verb]

Put it back *where you found it.* [Modifies the verb]

NOUN CLAUSES

We never did know *where he found it.* [Object of *did know*]

Why he went home is a mystery to me. [Subject of verb *is*]

The Adverbial Clause. A dependent clause may be used as an adverb to show time, place, cause, condition, concession, comparison, manner, purpose, or result.

TIME

You must sit still *while the orchestra plays.*

Parents may come in *before the main doors are opened.*

He played professional football *until he was drafted.*

After you finish your test, hand in your papers to me.

PLACE

I will go *where they send me.*

He hid *where no one thought to look.*

CAUSE

He grows roses *because he loves flowers.*

Since no one volunteered, James finished the work himself.

I can't go with you, *as that would be breaking my promise.*

CONDITION

If I were he I should invest in tax-exempt bonds.

Children will not be admitted *unless they are accompanied by their parents.*

In case you have no parents, any adult will do.

CONCESSION

I agreed to go with him *although I was very tired.*

No matter what he says, I shall not be angry.

COMPARISON

He is as honest *as the day is long.*

Jack is older *than I am.*

MANNER

Marion looks *as if she were ready for bed.*

He speaks *as a tactful man should speak.*

PURPOSE

They came to America *in order that they might find religious freedom.*

RESULT

The night was so stormy *that we could not see the highway.*

EXAMPLES

Carol is prettier *than I am.* [An adverbial clause of comparison]

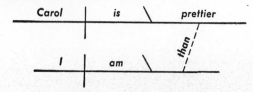

The whistle blew *before the ball was fumbled.* [An adverbial clause of time, modifying the verb *blew*]

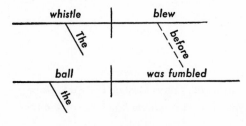

EXERCISES

EXERCISE 1, NOUN CLAUSES. *In the following sentences pick out each noun clause and tell whether it is used as the subject of a verb, as the complement of a verb or verbal, or as the object of a preposition.*

1. At ten they told me that I was chosen to go up in the capsule.
2. Why they were in such a hurry puzzled me at the time.
3. I forgot to tell them what my blood pressure was.
4. We joked about what we had planned to do that night.
5. Then we remembered that our wives must be informed.
6. The engineer wanted to show me what I should do with the oxygen valve.
7. Of course I realized that he was joking.
8. I had expected severe vibration after the final count and the start.
9. That there was little vibration came as a pleasant surprise.
10. I reported that everything was going according to plan.

EXERCISE 2, ADJECTIVE CLAUSES. *Pick out the adjective clauses in the following sentences and tell what word each clause modifies. Be able to tell which clauses are restrictive and which are nonrestrictive.*

1. I have been reading books that tell about human rights.
2. One writer asserts there is no such thing as a natural right.
3. His contention, which I agree with, is that all rights are made by man.
4. I asked him where we got the rights that are mentioned in the Declaration of Independence.
5. The author I speak of is a man whom my father knew at Harvard.
6. He rubbed his chin with a gesture that indicated he was thinking deeply.
7. I understood the reason why he was careful about his choice of words.
8. "The rights you mention," he said, "are rights that men had to fight for."
9. We talked about the reasons why Jefferson called them unalienable.
10. It is a pleasure to know men with whom you can discuss ideas.

EXERCISE 3, ADVERBIAL CLAUSES. *Pick out the adverbial clauses in the following sentences.*

1. The rain that had been threatening us all day came before we had finished our work.
2. We were working where the rocks had to be blasted out.
3. Because the traffic was heavy, we kept one lane of the road open.
4. Before each blast was set off, two men waved the traffic to a halt.
5. Ashley, who was more experienced than I, told me what to do.
6. Although we had never had an accident, we worked under constant tension.
7. When the highway was clear, I pressed the handle down, and a long strip of roadway shuddered as if it were writhing in agony.
8. While the traffic waited, the bulldozers quickly shoved loose rocks off the open lane so that the cars and trucks could proceed again.
9. I think that some of the drivers were as relieved as we were.
10. While we were clearing off the rocks, the downpour came; soon the cut was so muddy that we had to stop work for the day.

3 THE SENTENCE: RHETORICAL PATTERNS

THE PROBLEM OF EFFECTIVENESS

Although we discuss the grammatical and the rhetorical patterns of a sentence in separate chapters, you must not assume that your consciousness and your use of these patterns has developed separately or at different periods of your life. No one can say when your language habits began to form. If you are like most American college students, you picked up the beginnings of your language skill at home, in the form of speech, but usually, in degrees varying with each different home, the written language begins to exert its influence very early. As a child you probably discovered the world of books. Picking up one of your children's books, you pleaded, "Daddy, read. Mamma, read me a story," and as likely as not you had picked out a story that interested and excited you through the way it was written. It was lively or spirited or rhythmical or whimsical or imaginative—whatever quality you can name that lifted it above the humdrum. In other words, you were becoming conscious of style; without having the slightest notion that such a thing as "effectiveness" existed, you were already being strongly influenced by it.

In all of your school studies, correctness of language has been stressed above effectiveness—and rightly so. By correctness we mean the language practices of people of some education, among whom you expect to live and with whom you will have to work. Correctness is indeed important, for a misspelled word in a business letter or a misused verb in an interview can brand an otherwise able teacher or professional man as careless and perhaps unreliable in his own field. Bad spelling and bad grammar show; educated people notice them immediately. Crudity in vocabulary or usage makes many persons squirm. In your college courses, many an otherwise excellent answer, test paper, or report will get a lower grade because of slips in spelling or grammar. Outside of college, in industry, in business, in the professions, these mistakes can be even more important. It is no mystery, then, why we stress correctness in our language studies.

To be realistic about effectiveness, as distinguished from correctness, let us admit freely, before we go into this matter of improving something that is adequate, that for most routine occasions routine writing is good enough. We are here concerned with the student who is not satisfied with routine writing, the student who is disturbed by the fact that although he writes correctly and honestly, he is yet ineffective. Some of the qualities of effective communication are stressed elsewhere in this book. It is well to review them here briefly before we continue discussing sentence patterns. Diction is important. The words a writer uses should be exact, fresh, alive. Picture-making words are better than vague, general words. A fresh point of view can flavor a style. Humor can lighten and liven it. Even such devices as spacing on the page and using opaque paper are important. And as for speech, everyone knows how much depends on voice, tone, inflection, gestures, pauses, facial expression, and a pleasing personality.

In this chapter we are dealing primarily with the grouping or arrangement of words in sentences—not entirely, of course, inasmuch as no skillful juggling of poorly chosen words can make effective sentences.

USES OF SUBORDINATION

A child normally expresses his thoughts and impressions in simple sentences. He will say, for instance, "My trike was lost. I found my trike. It was back of the garage. I lost it last night. It was wet. It rained on it." The child's baby-sitter, several years older than he, probably would report the situation like this: "Bobby found his tricycle behind the garage. He left it there last night when it began to rain." An older person might have said,

15924

"Bobby found his tricycle behind the garage, where he had left it last night when it began to rain." As a child's mind matures and he begins to perceive that not all details and thoughts are of the same importance, he learns to give certain details of his communication a primary or a lesser position in a sentence. In other words, he learns to use subordination. He learns to place minor or contributing facts and ideas in dependent constructions in his sentences. The use of the complex sentence, it has often been said, is a sign of maturity in a person. The same thing can be said for the use of verbal phrases, prepositional phrases, appositives, and various types of single-word modifiers, which are also forms of subordination.

Let us first look at parallel versions of the same paragraph, the first written largely on the same plane, a little like the Anglo-Saxon writing you have sampled, the second as a modern author wrote it. Compare the two carefully.

VERSION A

The Canadian North has a harsh terrain. Yet it has always exercised a mysterious and compelling attraction for men and women. These people come from all walks of life. It is like the great desert. The desert promises death to the unwary. But once you visit it, it invites your return. You may stand among the isolated buildings of an arctic settlement. You watch a plane circle and disappear in the skies. Aside from radio, it is your only link with the outside world. You experience the twin feelings of elation and fear. The Arctic inspires these feelings in you. A strange sense of peace inhabits the wilderness. Your elation comes from this. But day after day you will wait for the plane's life-giving return. This fact inspires fear. Man is an interloper here. Here death is constant—dead earth, dead snows and a cold that kills.

VERSION B

And yet, for all its harsh terrain, the Canadian North has always exercised a mysterious and compelling attraction for men and women from all walks of life. Like the great desert, which similarly promises death for the unwary, it is a place which, once visited, invites return. Few who have stood among the isolated buildings of an arctic settlement, watching the plane—their only link aside from radio with the outside world—circle and disappear in the skies, have escaped the twin feelings of elation and fear which the Arctic inspires. The elation comes from that strange sense of peace which inhabits the wilderness. The fear is that, day after day, one will wait in vain for the plane's life-giving return. Man is an interloper in this place where death is constant—dead earth, dead snows and a cold that kills.

—BRIAN MOORE AND THE EDITORS OF LIFE, *Canada*

Accuracy and Variety: The Dependent Clause

Now that you have compared these two styles of writing, and inevitably felt the greater accuracy, ease, maturity, and economy of the second, let us analyze a few isolated sentences to see what we can do with them. By this time you must be familiar with the various types of dependent clauses and with the structural signals that show their dependence. In the following examples, does the revision improve the accuracy of expression, give unity to sentences, or relieve the monotony of too many clauses on the same level?

A. I well remember a strange conversation I had with a man once. This man was a friend of mine. He and I had served together in the Marines.
B. I well remember a strange conversation I once had with a friend of mine, with whom I had served in the Marines.

A. Do not be in too much of a hurry to join an organization. Study its membership before you join.
B. Before you join an organization, investigate its membership.

A. Space suits are personalized garments. You must make many alterations on one of them. Otherwise it will not fit properly. In this respect it is like a bridal gown.
B. Because space suits are personalized garments, you need to make more alterations on one of them to make it fit properly than you do on a bridal gown.

—WALTER M. SCHIRRA, JR., *We Seven*

The Useful Participial Phrase

The substance of a coordinate clause may often be better expressed in a participial phrase. You should remember, however, that the participial phrase, useful as it is, contains several built-in dangers against which you must guard. In the first place, as used by inexperienced writers, it may easily become a dangler (see §32). If used too often, it produces a stiff, awkward style.

And finally, it can distort rather than clarify the writer's thought if he has subordinated the wrong detail. With these cautions in mind, study and analyze the following examples:

A. A law school or a medical school can be an essential part of a great university. Each school must be properly staffed and directed.
B. A law school or a medical school, if properly staffed and directed, can be an essential part of a great university. [Past participles]

A. I could not overcome my difficulty. I could not understand it.
B. Being unable to understand my difficulty, I could not overcome it.

A. My decision to enter college came suddenly, and I encountered several obstacles.
B. Having made a sudden decision to enter college, I encountered several difficulties.

A. There was one problem not solved by the Commission. This was how to widen the highway without moving the old historic church.
B. The problem left unsolved by the Commission was how to widen the highway without moving the old historic church.

Gerund and Infinitive Phrases

Gerund and infinitive phrases may be used on occasion to gain economy and compactness in writing.

A. For three days he punished me. He refused to eat my desserts.
B. For three days he punished me by refusing to eat my desserts.

A. Their working hours were shortened. This resulted in more spare time for recreation and enjoyment.
B. Shortening their hours of work resulted in more time available for recreation and enjoyment. [Note how the vague *this* has been avoided.]

A. The wife has children whom she must clothe. She must take care of them and worry about them. The business woman has nobody except herself to whom she is obliged to pay any attention.
B. The wife has children to clothe, to care for, to worry about; the business woman has no one to think of but herself.

Conciseness: The Prepositional Phrase

A prepositional phrase may be used to express a detail more accurately and more concisely than a clause or a sentence.

[69]

A. We wrote our papers at separate tables. There was a proctor in front of us. Another one stood behind us.

B. We wrote our papers at separate tables, with one proctor in front of us and another behind us.

A. The professor repeated his instructions. It was to help those who came late.

B. For the benefit of the latecomers, the professor repeated his instructions.

A. The examination was over. Then the students got together and compared their answers.

B. After the examination the students flocked together to compare answers.

A. I turned in my paper. I did not stop to go over my answers.

B. I turned in my paper without a second glance at my answers.

Compactness and Economy: The Single Word

A minor detail worth only a single word instead of a whole sentence or a clause is better expressed in a single word.

A. There were two new girls, and they both wore green rayon dresses that had short sleeves.

B. The two new girls both wore short-sleeved dresses of green rayon.

A. The house was old. The lawn around it was enclosed by yew hedges. These hedges were neatly clipped.

B. The lawn around the old house was shut in by neatly clipped yew hedges.

Uses of the Appositive

Like clauses, phrases, and verbals, the appositive may be used to express details the writer wishes to subordinate. Consider this piece of autobiographical writing:

A. I was born in Middleville, Ohio. It's a real small town. Most of the people in it are farmers. They raise cows for milk and a lot of apples. Still, it's the county seat of Whiteside County.

Obviously this is a wordy passage, marred by many faults in addition to a lack of subordination. However, let us see what the use of appositives will do:

B. I was born in Middleville, Ohio, a small dairy and apple-farming community and the seat of Whiteside County.

The following groups of sentences will further illustrate the resources of the appositive:

A. Lutetium was discovered in 1905. It is a chemical element. It is one of the rare-earth elements. The name comes from *Lutetia.* In ancient days Paris was called that.
B. Lutetium, a chemical element, member of the rare-earth group, was discovered in 1905; its name was derived from *Lutetia*, the ancient name of Paris.

A. The custom of kissing under the mistletoe was once an old Druid religious ceremony. It is now a pleasant part of our Christmas.
B. The custom of kissing under the mistletoe, once an old Druid religious ceremony, is now a pleasant part of our Christmas.

A. Father is a congenial sort of person, and he hasn't made an enemy in his life.
B. Father, a congenial sort of person, has not made an enemy in his life.

Before we leave the subject of subordination, let us examine two parallel versions of another paragraph, and note again, in a piece of connected writing, the principles of subordination we have pointed out in isolated sentences. In the second version, sentences are reduced to dependent clauses or to phrases, and thereby given a more exact meaning and emphasis. As you read the two versions, you feel at once that the second is a more mature, more sophisticated kind of writing, more accurate in conveying the different shades of meaning, and more pleasing in style.

VERSION A

A great deal of traditional cultural education was foolish. That must be admitted. Boys spent many years acquiring Latin or Greek. At the end they could not read a Greek or Latin author. Neither did they want to. Of course this was not true in a small percentage of cases. Modern languages and history are preferable to Latin and Greek. This is in every way true. They are more useful, and they give much more culture, and it all takes less time. An Italian of the fifteenth century had to learn Latin and Greek. Everything worth reading was in those languages or in his own. These languages were indispensable keys to culture. Since that time great literatures have grown up in various modern languages. Development of civilization has been very rapid. A knowledge of antiquity has become less useful. A knowledge of modern nations and their comparatively recent history has become more useful in understanding our problems. The traditional schoolmaster's point of view was admirable at the time of the Revival of Learning. Now it is unduly narrow. It ignores what has been done since the fifteenth century. History and modern languages are not the only things contributing to culture. Science contributes too. But science must be properly taught. Education should have other aims than direct utility. It is possible to maintain this viewpoint. It is not necessary to defend the traditional curriculum. Utility and culture are not incompatible. They only seem to be. But they must be understood broadly.

VERSION B

It must be admitted that a great deal of the traditional education was foolish. Boys spent many years acquiring Latin and Greek grammar, without being, at the end, either capable or desirous (except in a small percentage of cases) of reading a Greek or Latin author. Modern languages and history are preferable, from every point of view, to Latin and Greek. They are not only more useful, but they give much more culture in much less time. For an Italian of the fifteenth century, since practically everything worth reading, if not in his own language, was in Greek or Latin, these languages were the indispensable keys to culture. But since that time great literatures have grown up in various modern languages, and the development of civilization has been so rapid that the knowledge of antiquity has become much less useful in understanding our problems than knowledge of modern nations and their comparatively recent history. The traditional schoolmaster's point of view, which was admirable at the time of the Revival of Learning, became gradually unduly narrow, since it ignored what the world has done since the fifteenth century. And not only history and modern languages, but science also, when properly taught, contributes to culture. It is therefore possible to maintain that education should have other aims than direct utility, without defending the traditional curriculum. Utility and culture, when both are conceived broadly, are found to be less incompatible than they appear to the fanatical advocates of either.

—BERTRAND RUSSELL, *In Praise of Idleness and Other Essays*

LONG AND SHORT SENTENCES

Has the length of sentences anything to do with effectiveness, as it certainly does have a great deal to do with style? Turn back to the last two selections, which you have just studied for subordination. Version A contains twenty-eight short sentences; version B has only ten sentences, most of them fairly long. Both selections say essentially the same thing—but the first seems aimless, immature, and at times highly inaccurate in its emphasis.

Before we arrive at any hasty decision that a paragraph of long complex sentences is more effective than a paragraph of short, simple ones, let us compare the ways in which two men, both good writers, chose to report similar situations. The first man wrote his piece in very short sentences.

Across the open mouth of the tent Nick fixed cheese cloth to keep out mosquitoes. He crawled inside under the mosquito bar with various things from the pack to put at the head of the bed under the slant of the canvas. Inside the tent the light came through the brown canvas. It smelled pleasantly of canvas. Already there was something mysterious and homelike. Nick was happy as he crawled inside the tent. He had not been unhappy all day. This was different though. Now things were done. There had been this to do. Now it was done. It had been a hard trip. He was very tired. That was done. He had made his camp. He was settled. Nothing could touch him. It was a good place to camp. He was there, in the good place. He was in his home where he had made it. Now he was hungry.

He came out, crawling under the cheese cloth. It was quite dark outside. It was lighter in the tent.

Nick went over to the pack and found, with his fingers, a long nail in a paper sack of nails, in the bottom of the pack. He drove it into the pine tree, holding it close and hitting it gently with the flat of the ax. He hung the pack up on the nail. All his supplies were in the pack. They were off the ground and sheltered now.

Nick was hungry. He did not believe he had ever been hungrier. He opened and emptied a can of pork and beans and a can of spaghetti into the frying pan.

"I've got a right to eat this kind of stuff, if I'm willing to carry it," Nick said. His voice sounded strange in the darkening woods. He did not speak again.

—ERNEST HEMINGWAY, *In Our Time*

And now observe how differently another man says almost the same thing, "This is the place I have searched for, where for the moment I am happy and at peace."

There is a valley in South Fngland remote from ambition and from fear, where the passage of strangers is rare and unperceived, and where the scent of the grass in summer is breathed only by those who are native to that unvisited land. The roads to the Channel do not traverse it; they choose upon either side easier passes over the range. One track alone leads up through it to the hills, and this is changeable: now green where men have little occasion to go, now a good road where it nears the homesteads and barns. The woods grow steep above the slopes; they reach sometimes the very summit of the heights, or, when they cannot attain them, fill in and clothe the combs. And, in between, along the floor of the valley, deep pastures and their silence are bordered by lawns of chalky grass and the small yew trees of the Downs.

The clouds that visit its sky reveal themselves beyond the one great rise, and sail, white and enormous, to the other, and sink beyond that other. But the plains above which they have travelled and the Weald to which they go, the people of the valley cannot see and hardly recall. The wind, when it reaches such fields, is no longer a gale from the salt, but fruitful and soft, an inland breeze, and those whose blood was nourished here feel in that wind the fruitfulness of our orchards and all the life that all things draw from the air.

In this place, when I was a boy, I pushed through a fringe of beeches that made a complete screen between me and the world, and I came to a glade called No Man's Land. I climbed beyond it, and I was surprised and glad, because from the ridge of the glade I saw the sea. To this place very lately I returned.

The many things that I recovered as I came up to the countryside were not less charming than when a distant memory had enshrined them, but much more. Whatever veil is thrown by a longing recollection had not intensified nor even made more mysterious the beauty of that happy ground; not in my very dreams of morning had I, in exile, seen it more beloved or more rare. Much else that I had forgotten now returned to me as I approached—a group of elms, a little turn of the parson's wall, a small paddock beyond the graveyard close, cherished by one man, with a low wall of very old stone guarding it all around. And all those things fulfilled and amplified my delight, till even the good vision of the place, which I had kept so many years, left me and was replaced by its better reality. "Here," I said to myself, "is a symbol of what some say is reserved for the soul: a pleasure of a kind which cannot be imagined save in the moment when at last it is attained."

—HILAIRE BELLOC, *Hills and the Sea*

We may notice that out of the thirty-seven sentences in the Hemingway selection, twenty-seven are less than ten words long.

Hemingway was obviously striving to give the effect of random thoughts and impressions going through the mind of his character, who at the end of a long day of tramping was relaxed and happy and not disposed toward much thinking. In the Belloc selection, all except two sentences are over twenty words long. There is an air of reserve here; one feels that this is an occasion worthy of a bit of reverence. And yet both men wrote about the same kind of thing and for the same kind of reader.

VARIATIONS IN ORDER

In writing and speaking our primary concern must always be that our sentences fit the thoughts they are communicating, or, as in the Hemingway selection we have just analyzed, the mood they are creating. Most of our sentences, without any conscious effort on our part, will fall into an established pattern—that of subject–verb–complement. There is nothing *much* that we can do about this normal order or pattern, or should wish to do about it, but occasionally we can be a little more exact, a little more attractive, in our writing by inverting the basic elements or shifting the modifiers about. In the following pairs of sentences, consider how the change in emphasis affects the meaning of the sentence:

A. They elected him their president. [Now change the basic S–V–C order.]
B. Him they elected their president. [What word is emphasized here?]

A. All six hundred rode into the valley of death. [Normal order]
B. All in the valley of death rode the six hundred. [Note the change of emphasis because of the inversion.]

—ALFRED, LORD TENNYSON

It is much easier to throw your modifiers about or to shift from the active to the passive than to invert the order of the basic elements, but here also you are restrained by the need to link sentences together. The following parallel versions may indicate a few possibilities—and a few difficulties—in shifting sentence parts for the sake of variety.

VERSION A

If you want to see and hear what happens and to be so close to the bull that you will have the bullfighter's point of view, the best seat is the barrera. The action is so near and so detailed from the barrera that a bull-fight that would be soporific from the boxes or the balcony is always interesting. You see danger and learn to appreciate it from the barrera. An uninterrupted view of the ring is also available from it. The sobre-puertas are the only other seats, besides the first row in the gallery and the first row in the boxes, where you do not see people between you and the ring. You see these seats as you enter the various sections of the ring as they are built over the doorways through which you enter. You get a good view of the ring and a good perspective from them, as they are about half-way up the sides of the bowl, yet you are not as distant as in the boxes or gallery. They are good seats, yet they cost about half as much as the barreras or the first row of gallery or boxes.

VERSION B

The barrera is the best seat if you want to see and hear what happens and to be so close to the bull that you will have the bullfighter's point of view. From the barrera the action is so near and so detailed that a bull-fight that would be soporific from the boxes or the balcony is always interesting. It is from the barrera that you see danger and learn to appre-ciate it. There too you have an uninterrupted view of the ring. The only other seats, besides the first row in the gallery and the first row in the boxes, where you do not see people between you and the ring, are the sobrepuertas. These are the seats that are built over the doorways through which you enter the various sections of the ring. They are about half-way up to the sides of the bowl and from them you get a good view of the ring and a good perspective, yet you are not as distant as in the boxes or gallery. They cost about half as much as the barreras or the first row of gallery or boxes and they are very good seats.

—Ernest Hemingway, *Death in the Afternoon*

LOOSE AND PERIODIC SENTENCES

A periodic sentence is a complex sentence in which the main clause comes at the end, as "Just as the technicians were locking the hatch in place, one of the bolts broke." A loose sentence is a complex sentence in which the main clause comes first, followed by dependent clauses and other modifying elements, as "I real-ized that I had discussed the wrong topic only after I had handed in my paper." Short sentences are often periodic; long sentences tend to be loose. Since the mind grasps the thought of a short sentence, or even of a moderately long one, so quickly, it is only in long sentences that periodic structure has any noticeable psychological effect.

The periodic sentence builds suspense. It tends to hold up the meaning until the end, to force the reader to consider first the various details upon which the main thought is based. It makes him wait. Overuse of periodic structure is a little like an Ancient Mariner holding your lapel and breathing into your face while he tells his urgent story.

Notice in the following paragraph how a skillful writer can combine the two types of complex sentences. In the writing of beginners, which at times tends to flabbiness, the occasional conscious change from a loose to a periodic sentence is like tightening the bolts and screws on a car—it helps to stop the squeaks and rattles.

For the kind of courage which does not consist in repression, a number of factors must be combined. [Periodic] To begin with the humblest: health and vitality are very helpful, though not indispensable. [Loose] Practice and skill in dangerous situations are very desirable. [Simple: periodic effect] But when we come to consider, not courage in this and that respect, but universal courage, something more fundamental is wanted. [Periodic] What is wanted is a combination of self-respect with an impersonal outlook on life. [Periodic] To begin with self-respect, some men live from within, while others are mere mirrors of what is felt and said by their neighbors. [Loose] The latter can never have true courage; they must have admiration and are haunted by the fear of losing it. [Loose] The teaching of "humility" which used to be thought desirable was the means of producing a perverted form of this same vice. [Periodic] "Humility" suppressed self-respect but not the desire for the respect of others; it merely made nominal self-abasement the means of acquiring credit. [Loose] Thus it produced hypocrisy and falsification of instinct. [Simple: periodic effect] Children were taught unreasoning submission and proceeded to exact it when they grew up; it was said that only those who have learned how to obey know how to command. [Loose] What I suggest is that no one should learn to obey and no one should attempt to command. [Loose] I do not mean, of course, that there should be no leaders in cooperative enterprises; but their authority should be like that of a captain of a football team, which is suffered voluntarily in order to achieve a common purpose. [Loose] Our purposes should be our own, not the result of external authority; and our purposes should never be forcibly imposed upon others. [Loose] This is what I mean when I say no one should command and no one should obey. [Loose]

—BERTRAND RUSSELL, *Education and the Good Life*

PARALLEL STRUCTURE AND BALANCE

One of the rhetorical devices that skillful writers resort to is known as the balanced or parallel construction. Let us examine this at two levels. First, we may see it as a pedestrian and thoroughly practical means of improving awkward sentences, by making a noun parallel with another noun, a gerund with another gerund, a phrase with another phrase, a clause with another clause. Notice how rephrasing the following sentences improves their effectiveness:

A W K W A R D
Choose a house that is spacious, with a good exposure to the sun and that people like to look at. [An adjective, a phrase, a clause]

P A R A L L E L
Choose a house that is spacious, sunny, and attractive. [Three adjectives]

A W K W A R D
I was glad to be there for the lecture and to see how the models work. [A noun and a clause]

P A R A L L E L
I was glad to be there for the lecture and the demonstration of models. [Two nouns]

A W K W A R D
I have only one suggestion to make: cultivate friends who you think are loyal, have a cheerful disposition, and who are ambitious. [An adjective, a verb, and an adjective]

P A R A L L E L
I have only one suggestion to make: cultivate friends who you think are loyal, cheerful, and ambitious. [Three adjectives]

For a discussion of the "false parallel," see Section 35.

When used beyond this workaday tightening up of flabby sentences, parallel structure becomes a conscious art. It could become a quaint mannerism, it is true, if it were carried too far. If it is used naturally, to fit the thought and the occasion, it will seldom be overused. Even Francis Bacon, writing in an age when rhetorical mannerisms were fashionable, did not often find it possible to balance phrases as he did in his essay about studies:

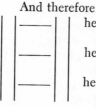

Reading maketh a full man;
conference a ready man;
writing an exact man.

and
And therefore

if a man write little

if he confer little

if he read little

_____

_____

_____

he had need to have great memory;
he had need to have a present wit; and
he had need to have much cunning,

to seem to know what he doth not.

You can find examples of skillful parallelism in the work of present-day writers, as in many of the selections quoted in Chapter 1: Winston Churchill, page 18, Judge Oliver Wendell Holmes, page 20, and J. R. Oppenheimer, page 21.

In the following selection,[1] notice the pleasing rhythm throughout, the frequent use of balance, and here and there the effective use of climax: "... the sudden sobriety of unexultant victory and unregretful defeat, the firm acceptance of the goodness and wisdom and finality of the night's doings, without remorse, without headache.... You are the rulers and the ruled, the lawgivers and the law-abiding, the beginning and the end. ... I say these things to you not only because I believe them to be true, but also because, as you love your country, I love my country, and I would see it endure and grow in light and become a living testament to all mankind of goodness and of mercy and of wisdom."

In theory, there is no duck so dead as a defeated candidate on the morning after election. To test this theory—and perhaps for other reasons, vaguely sentimental in nature—we picked up a book of Stevenson's

---

[1] From "Notes and Comments," *The New Yorker*, November 15, 1952, Reprinted by permission. Copr. © 1952 The New Yorker Magazine, Inc.

speeches on the morning of November 5th, when we were punchy after the night's vigil with Univac and the pasty-faced characters on the television screen. Methodically we read a page or two, expecting to taste stale wine at the bottom of the glass. Greatly to our surprise, we found ourselves reading on and on, responding to familiar words that seemed not to have wasted or faded.

"You are the rulers and the ruled, the lawgivers and the law-abiding, the beginning and the end." (Surely we had had enough of speechmaking; surely there was a saturation point beyond which no further word could add its weight to the almost intolerable burden of the conscientious mind.) "I say these things to you not only because I believe them to be true, but also because, as you love your country, I love my country, and I would see it endure and grow in light and become a living testament to all mankind of goodness and of mercy and of wisdom."

The words still had the power to lift, to strengthen, and to reassure. They even furnished the text for the day: "Who leads us," we read, "is less important than what leads us." And "A wise man does not try to hurry history."

The nourishment, the durability of this collection of campaign utterances struck us as something of a political miracle, in a time of wonders. And it seemed to us, too, that the new President-elect, if he should be in search of a small, inexpensive guidebook covering the main exhibits of the Fair, could hardly ask for a more compact and useful volume to steady him in hours of perplexity and trouble. With minor allowances for differences in party philosophy, there is not much in the published speeches of Adlai Stevenson that General Eisenhower couldn't, or doesn't, subscribe to with all his heart, and it is the country's good fortune that this is so.

We like America on the morning after election. It goes to work with a unique hangover—the sudden sobriety of unexultant victory and unregretful defeat, the firm acceptance of the goodness and wisdom and finality of the night's doings, without remorse, without headache. ("Your public servants serve you right.") There is little reason to believe, looking at the figures, that Governor Stevenson ever stood the remotest chance of getting elected in this year and under these circumstances. But because he was articulate beyond the usual powers of candidates, and because he chose to speak to the voters in exact, rather than in round, phrases, he performed a special service—not only for Americans but for people all over the earth. It is almost as though he served a three-month term of office that will be long remembered.

Governor Stevenson (who has been in politics only four years) had a way of pronouncing the word "political" that invested it with honor even in the middle of a slugging match, and that made politics seem the

[80]

noblest of all works. He pronounced every syllable of the word "political," and he pronounced the first syllable "po," not "puh." He always seemed to utter the word with a mixture of affection, awe, and delight—as a mother bathes a brand-new infant. By so speaking, and so believing, he unconsciously elevated the theater of politics for millions of astonished and attentive listeners, and made the play exciting and at times great. For the millions who found the play, as he read it, exciting and rewarding, and who share his unflinching belief that politics is the noblest as well as the most dangerous of arts, we thank him for the infinite pains he took, for the courage he breathed, and for raising, for everyone, not only the standard of the Democratic Party but the standard of a democratic people.

—*The New Yorker*, "Notes and Comments"

REPETITION, SOUND, AND RHYTHM

Balance and parallel structure are, in a sense, forms of repetition—repetitions primarily of phrasing or structure rather than of words, although within balanced phrases words may be repeated. Note this repetition in the quotation from Bacon on page 79:

a full man	write little	he had need to have great memory
a ready man	confer little	he had need to have a present wit
an exact man	read little	he had need to have much cunning

Then in the selection just quoted note the repetition of structure:

unexultant victory	unregretful defeat
without remorse	without headache
the rulers and the ruled	the lawgivers and the law-abiding

Single words may be repeated for emphasis or for a smoother rhythmic flow of sounds, quite apart from a balance of structural units, as you will notice in the following:

as you *love* your *country*, I *love* my *country*. . . .

—ADLAI STEVENSON

Before *parents* can be *parents* they must have lived a good part of their lives.

—CARL VAN DOREN

[81]

we shall fight in France, *we shall fight* on the seas and oceans, *we shall fight* with *growing* confidence and *growing* strength in the air . . . *we shall fight* on the landing grounds. . . .

—WINSTON CHURCHILL

Good prose should be easy to read aloud. The pleasing sound effects of prose read aloud depend partly on an avoidance of harsh sounds or combinations of letters difficult to pronounce and partly on combinations of sounds, stresses, and variations in pitch that appeal somehow to our sense of hearing. *Cacophony* is the name we give to jarring and harsh sounds. Familiar examples of cacophony are some of the tongue twisters:

She sells sea shells. . . .
Peter Piper picked a peck of pickling peppers. . . .

Euphony is the word that describes pleasing sounds. Some of the pleasure we get from good prose comes from various patterns of stresses that we call *rhythm*. Occasionally—and largely by accident—prose rhythms approach the regular metric forms of regular verse. You may even feel the patterns of poetic feet, the iambus or the trochee, but any conscious effort to arrange prose accents in poetic forms is usually felt to be out of place. Iambic or trochaic feet in prose had better be avoided. The rhythms of prose are irregular—and yet one feels that in rhythmic prose there is a music that is appropriate. Read the following bit aloud, always remembering that the syllables stressed here may be stressed in many different degrees:

Thus from the grim gray of their skies they had alchemied gold, and from their hunger, glorious food, and from the raw bleakness of their lives and weathers they had drawn magic. And what was good among them had been won sternly, sparely, bitterly, from all that was ugly, dull, and painful in their lives, and, when it came, was more rare and beautiful than anything on earth.

—THOMAS WOLFE, *Of Time and the River*

The final selection in this chapter was written many, many years ago—when giants walked the earth—but it has lost none of its freshness and power. The prose rhythms in it cannot be felt through silent reading. It should be read aloud.

A man may read a sermon, the best and most passionate that ever man preached, if he shall but enter into the sepulchres of kings. In the same Escorial where the Spanish princes live in greatness and power, and decree war or peace, they have wisely placed a cemetery, where their ashes and their glory shall sleep till time shall be no more; and where our kings have been crowned, their ancestors lie interred, and they must walk over their grandsire's head to take his crown. There is an acre sown with royal seed, the copy of the greatest change, from rich to naked, from ceiled roofs to arched coffins, from living like gods to die like men. There is enough to cool the flames of lust, to abate the heights of pride, to appease the itch of covetous desires, to sully and dash out the dissembling colors of a lustful, artificial, and imaginary beauty. There the warlike and the peaceful, the fortunate and the miserable, the beloved and the despised princes mingle their dust, and pay down their symbol of mortality, and tell all the world that when we die our ashes shall be equal to kings', and our accounts easier, and our pains and our crowns shall be less.

—JEREMY TAYLOR (1613–1667)

4 THE PARAGRAPH

WHAT IS A PARAGRAPH?

The word *paragraph* comes from two Greek words, *para,* "beside," and *graphein,* "to write." It was at one time a mark, usually ¶, written in the margin of a manuscript beside the place where a unit or subdivision of the text was to begin. The conventional signal now used to indicate a new paragraph is of course indention—that is, beginning a line a little to the right of the margin. (In some situations paragraphing is indicated instead by a skipped line and a new sentence beginning at the left-hand margin.) However it is marked, paragraphing can be considered as a form of punctuation. It suggests that the reader is to make a major pause in his progress—as much as several seconds if he is reading aloud—and that he is to prepare himself for a new unit of discourse following, in some reasonable order, the one he has just finished.

The function of this punctuated, or paragraphed, unit, however, varies considerably with different kinds of prose. In dialogue, the paragraph often marks off a single speech of a character. In description it may divide the details of a scene or object being presented. Paragraphs may be organized in a simple sequence of time, as when one writes instructions on the operation of a machine or the performing of a technique. They may mark off units into which a subject has been divided, a familiar textbook formula (three causes of a war, four classes of a society). In discussions of facts and ideas—usually spoken of as exposition—a common paragraph unit contains a step in a logical argument. Since it is the writing of exposition that mostly concerns students, we shall be giving our major attention here to such paragraphs. If we speak of a paragraph of exposition, for the moment at least, as a related group of sentences calculated to advance an argument, with or without a summarizing or topic sentence, we probably come as close as we can to describing the actual practice of writers.

Almost anyone who begins a sentence with a dependent clause —for instance, "When I saw him on the street yesterday..." —has a pretty good idea as he does so what his main clause is going to say. "When I saw him on the street yesterday, he looked perfectly well." Similarly an experienced writer, composing an introductory sentence in a paragraph, has a pretty good idea how that sentence is going to relate to the major point of his paragraph—a point he may be preparing to state in a so-called topic sentence later on. And then—to speak of even larger structures —a really skillful writer is aware what a particular paragraph he is working on is going to contribute to the whole point of his article or even his book. A writer must be constantly ready to change these schemes, for he learns as he composes, but enormous quantities of waste motion are saved if there is maximum awareness, in the back of the writer's mind, of the various relationships between a particular unit being written down and all the other units of which this one is to become a working part.

For the beginning writer, these things come hard. And it might be advisable, in the study of paragraphs, to try planning them almost as one has to plan whole papers. A scratch outline of a difficult paragraph is often a wise procedure. A draft of a possible topic sentence is sometimes helpful, even when the writer knows that it may not be his opening sentence, and that it may have to be rewritten. Obviously there is no formula for composing the perfect paragraph, but this we can say: any procedure that helps the student to bear in mind a number of possible relations between sentences is useful.

It is relation that matters. The most familiar complaint about the paragraphs composed by students is that they lack organization. By this one usually means simply that there are insufficient relations between the parts of the paragraph—namely, between the sentences. A major concern in this chapter will be the in-

[85]

ternal organization of paragraphs: how sentences can be arranged to lead a reader reasonably and gracefully through the steps of an exposition. How can sentences be connected, or linked, to produce paragraphs that any reader would have to call organized?

As we have already hinted, however, it is, strictly speaking, improper to consider paragraphs in isolation from the larger units of which they are a part. Perhaps the fairest way to approach the paragraph as a single piece is to concentrate on introductions, the first paragraphs in expository essays. At least, one can study an introductory paragraph without the sense that one has missed what went before it, for there is nothing before it except the title. What we shall do here, therefore, in the next few sections of this chapter, is to consider in some detail several introductory paragraphs of the sort found in essay collections intended for freshmen. In each case, the writer is *introducing* his reader to the exposition that is to follow; we can learn much by examining how he does it. This work on the paragraph can then be related to the section "Beginnings and Endings" in Chapter 5, where larger problems of organization are considered.

KINDS OF INTRODUCTORY PARAGRAPHS

We have said that the writer in his first paragraph is introducing his reader to his exposition, but introducing can be done in so many different ways that the statement is not very helpful as it stands. Let us consider here three common and useful ways in which a first paragraph can introduce a piece of expository prose.

First, the paragraph can contain a statement of a thesis to be argued. This is an obvious and sensible mode of beginning, as if to say, "Here is what I am going to show you." Often such a paragraph will include a reference to general opinion on the subject and how the writer's treatment will differ.

Second, the paragraph may tell a story, or begin to tell one, even though it will be clear that the whole essay is not fiction at all. The story will then be used as an example or piece of evidence to support a thesis being argued.

Third, the paragraph may concentrate on a single key term to be defined, as a way of approaching the demonstration to come.

In addition to the logic of such beginnings, there is something else being introduced in an opening paragraph that is of immense importance: the writer himself. Or rather, we should say, that particular self that he wishes to put forward for these particular circumstances and purposes. As we examine the paragraphs to follow, then, we will be asking not only how the sentences have been interrelated to introduce an argument in one way or another, but also how the language expresses a kind of personality talking to us, with a particular relation (or *tone*) toward us. Thus, while the writers here are exposing *arguments* for us, they are simultaneously dramatizing through language a kind of *person* addressing us, formally, informally, intimately or from a distance, as the case may be. The composition of a well-organized paragraph requires attention to this matter of tone just as much as it does to the logical arrangement of ideas being presented —and in fact, for the good writer, the argument being made and the voice doing the arguing become fused, or, as we say, composed.

The Paragraph as a Statement of a Thesis to Be Argued

In expository writing it is of course common practice to state at the outset the thesis or argument that the writer proposes to advance in his essay. For one thing, this is simple politeness to the reader. Often the statement is preceded or immediately followed by a reference to general prevailing opinion on the subject, or to past treatments of it by other writers. We are to assume that such opinion and such past treatments are due to be qualified, or perhaps demolished utterly, by the new treatment the author is putting forward. This approach can, however, come dangerously close to a formula: Contrary to the view generally held on the subject, which naively assumes thus-and-so, I shall soon convince you that this-and-that is really the case. The student using this approach, therefore, should take note of the various ways in which professional writers modify the formula.

Let us begin with an uncomplicated piece of prose from a leading American magazine, *The Atlantic Monthly,* and watch the formula at work.

[1] Anyone who has casually turned on his television set since the beginning of the 1963–64 season might gain the impression that television is in the same old rut, only deeper. [2] A closer examination of the landscape, however, discloses that the world of television is in quite an upheaval. [3] Strange new forms of television are starting to emerge, some of them never anticipated, even by most insiders. [4] New hybrids and seemingly implausible alliances are taking shape. [5] As a consequence, decisive changes appear to be in prospect, with a wider diversity of programming from which to choose and, hopefully, an improvement in what is available to the discerning viewer.

—VANCE PACKARD, "New Kinds of Television"

[1] The first sentence expresses the general opinion from which the writer will differ; he is going to do more than "casually" turn on a television set. Note his informal air with his reader, as in that final colloquial phrase, *same old rut.*
[2] Here is the topic sentence, linked with the preceding one by the transitional adverb *however* and by the repetition of *television.*
[3] This sentence spells out the "upheaval" by presenting evidence, or at least by restating the theme of change in other terms.
[4] These phrases are variations on *strange new forms;* note the biological metaphor.
[5] The opening phrase here is another clear transitional expression, apparently referring not only to the preceding sentence but to the entire paragraph, as the author gives us another restatement of *upheaval.* He ends with language in dramatic opposition to his beginning, where television was assumed to be "in a rut."

As you see, the writer has taken pains to connect his sentences to one another by the use of transitional phrases and by seeing to it that succeeding sentences enlarge upon or define references in previous sentences. A clear case is the fourth sentence, as it plays variations on *strange new forms.* Throughout, his tone, as we have suggested in our analysis of his first sentence, is informal and easy with the reader, and perhaps his slight jokes based on clichés from botany, geology, and evolution (*strange new forms, world in upheaval, new hybrids, implausible alliances*) help to maintain this pose of comfortable knowledge held in common with the reader. But we cannot believe that the writer is thoroughly serious in suggesting an analogy between the great theory of evolution, on the one hand, and the current situation in television, on the other.

Some readers would call this tone unpleasantly chummy, and some would point to a word like *hopefully* in the last sentence to justify a charge of mere journalism. However you may respond to the writer's tone, his thesis, following the formula we have suggested, is easy enough to state: Contrary to general opinion that television is in the same old rut, it is in fact in a state of rapid change that may produce better programs for discriminating viewers. In our next passage, from the same magazine, you will see an opening paragraph that employs the same formula, but with a very different tone. Read it through rapidly before studying it, to see whether you can feel the difference in the sort of person you can imagine addressing you.

[1] The conflict of the generations is neither a new nor a particularly American story, but it is perhaps exacerbated by the self-consciousness and the partial segregation of teen-age culture, to such an extent that both old and young are exceptionally vulnerable to their mutual criticisms. [2] I do not care to add to the complacency of my agemates who, from their clubs, pulpits, and other rostrums, attack the alleged "softness" of the young, whom they have themselves brought up, while failing to see the difficulties young people face today precisely because the manifest hardships with which earlier Americans coped have been, for millions, attenuated. [3] These hardships cannot be artificially restored, at least for people over twelve; however, I believe that college students are now beginning to find new ways to become active politically, and hence responsible humanly.

—David Riesman, "Where Is the College Generation Headed?"

[1] The first sentence connects what is to follow with an ageless problem —the conflict of the generations— and suggests a modern climate of opinion in which the assumptions the author is about to attack can flourish.

[2] Here the author, aware of the climate of opinion he described in his first sentence, explicitly separates himself from those holding the prevailing view of teen-age "softness." He does so because he recognized (first sentence) how vulnerable the young are to such attacks. Note the subtle but clear relation between the two sentences.

[3] *These hardships* repeats an important word from the preceding sentence. Then the key clause of the whole article follows, introduced by the connective *however*. In spite of their loss of traditional hardships, young people are learning to act responsibly.

The difference in tone between the two paragraphs, which should be obvious on a first quick reading, may be explained by a number of differences in the rhetoric, at least some of which we can mention here. For one thing, note the length of the sentences: whereas Vance Packard, in a paragraph of just over one hundred words, writes five sentences, David Riesman, in a considerably longer paragraph, writes only three. Riesman's vocabulary is also strenuous; some of his words (*exacerbated, attenuated*) may have sent you to the dictionary. Riesman expects a good deal of his reader. He addresses him formally, he does not avoid complex ways of talking, and he does not make things any easier by introducing colloquial language or an intimate tone, as Packard did. The relations between Riesman's sentences are not immediately obvious. There are no little jokes, about evolution or anything else, and indeed we may feel some bitterness in this speaker's crack about his agemates in their pulpits and rostrums. How to account for such difference in rhetoric and tone? We cannot assume that the two writers are addressing different audiences, for both these articles appeared in different issues of the same magazine. Nor is the difference primarily that they are dealing with different subjects, though this no doubt has something to do with it. Rather, the answer is to be found in the individual decision of each writer to put forward to his reader a different speaking personality. His precise motives for making such a decision are mysterious, and would probably be as difficult to ascertain accurately as the motives for most other human behavior.

Let us now examine one more introductory paragraph built on the same formula, contrary-to-general-opinion-I-shall-demonstrate-thus-and-so. This one is from a famous article about language itself.

[1] Most people who bother about the matter at all would admit that the English language is in a bad way, but it is generally considered that we cannot by conscious action do anything about it. [2] Our civilization is deca-

[1] Informal, abrupt, colloquial (*in a bad way*). Realistic, almost tough, in the admission that not many do bother about language. *It is generally considered* introduces the prevailing view which the writer will oppose.

dent, and our language—so the argument runs—must inevitably share in the general collapse. [3] It follows that any struggle against the abuse of language is a sentimental archaism, like preferring candles to electric light or hansom cabs to aeroplanes. [4] Underneath this lies the half-conscious belief that language is a natural growth and not an instrument which we shape for our own purposes.

—GEORGE ORWELL, *Shooting an Elephant and Other Essays*

[2] The words between the dashes relate to *it is generally considered* and make it clear the writer does not agree.

[3] *It follows that* relates to the *argument* preceding and is ironic insofar as the writer is opposed to the logic he is reproducing.

[4] *Underneath this* provides the transition, continuing the bogus argument. Language is not a natural growth at all, it is an instrument which we shape.

In this clear expression of a point of view about language, note the signals by which the writer keeps reminding us that we are not to agree with general opinion. What we *are* to do is to "struggle against the abuse of language"—and note the favorably loaded implications of a word like *struggle*. This is a vigorous, serious voice addressing us, even though it speaks to us at some points informally and even colloquially.

We have now seen three examples of expository paragraphs, all employing variations of a familiar formula: Contrary to a generally held view, I propose the following thesis. Each paragraph is constructed out of sentences knit together with transitional devices, some more obvious than others, but all at least competently handled. The tone of the three writers, however, is quite different, from Packard's easy informality, to Riesman's academic distance, to Orwell's mixture of tough-colloquial intimacy with a very serious purpose. Note that the writer's choice about his tone is not necessarily a function of his subject: Orwell's subject is at least as important as Riesman's, yet his tone is considerably lighter.

The Paragraph of Anecdote as Evidence for a Thesis

We begin this section with an article which, written about the same time as Orwell's and on the same subject, takes a similar stand on the abuses of language. But see how differently the argument is begun by Jacques Barzun.

[1] Like five million other people I spend part of each day in a New York bus, and some of that time my eyes rest on the sign:

PLEASE REFRAIN FROM
CONVERSATION WITH OPERATOR
WHILE BUS IS IN MOTION

[2] After some years of dumb staring, it has come over me that this foreign-language text means, "Please do not talk to the driver between stops." [3] But this knowledge does not make me sure that I shall ever understand that other sign, found in every shop, which reads: "Illumination is required to be extinguished before these premises are closed to business." [4] Before it, I find I have only one thought: "WHOM is speaking?"

—JACQUES BARZUN, "How to Suffocate the English Language"

[1] A disarming opener: note how the author specifically makes himself no better than anyone else.

We are to sense the humor of this pretentious sign even before he labels it with *this foreign-language text.*

[2] Three linked phrases: *part of each day, some of that time, after some years.*

[3] *This knowledge* refers to *it has come over me.*

That other sign, yet similar, of course, in its stuffiness.

[4] *Before it:* note the transitional phrase, with its reference to the *other sign.*
The author's joke on grammar at the end implies that his reader shares his immediate recognition of absurdly ungrammatical forms.

The next sentence of this article, beginning its second paragraph, opens with the phrase "These public displays of literary ineptitude..." The anecdote of seeing the sign on the bus, it is clear, is to be taken as one piece of evidence for a larger fact. The sign about illumination is another piece of evidence. This technique is a form of what is called the inductive approach, starting with a specific occasion or instance and leaping upward to a generalization. One advantage to using a personal anecdote as evidence is that the reader may momentarily enjoy the comfortable feeling of being told a story. It provides a pleasant avenue into what may turn out to be a tough neighborhood before the trip is over. And the speaker's relation to his reader, of course, is easy and good-humored; he is having fun with his subject.

We return to teenagers now, to see how another author leads us into a serious and even solemn discussion of educational values by the same device of amusing us at the beginning with an entertaining anecdote. In this case—note that we are dealing with dialogue and a narrative method—we will need to quote two paragraphs.

During a sunny day one autumn a colleague of mine was counseling a freshman girl at the University of Georgia. He explained that a certain course could not be taken without prerequisites amounting to about two years' work. "But I won't be here that long," the lass protested. "At the end of this school year I'm getting married."

Just to be nice my friend asked who the lucky man was. "Oh, I've just got here," said the miss, "and haven't met him yet." Out of curiosity, the professor kept tabs. The wedding took place in a burst of orange blossoms just after the close of the next semester, as planned.

—JEROME ELLISON, "Are We Making a Playground out of College?"

Note the brisk style of this little story, which uses ordinary, informal language of the sort anyone uses in telling an anecdote to a group of acquaintances.

The short sentences are linked in a chronological sequence appropriate to simple narration, where obvious transitional phrases such as *after that* would seem unnecessary.

Note the disparaging attitude implied in *the lass* and *the miss*.

An easy kind of unity is maintained by repeating the professor's motives: *just to be nice, out of curiosity*.

The third paragraph, immediately following those quoted, begins "This sort of thing . . . ," thereby making the anecdote stand for or represent something-or-other not yet defined. But by now the article is more than just entertainment. We read on: "This sort of thing is so common in the large, tax-supported coeducational plants . . . that most people assume it's probably all right." Note the reference to general opinion, so familiar in our earlier examples, an opinion from which the writer will explicitly diverge. He goes on this way: "I, for one, am not at all sure it's all right. It's part of a growing national inclination to push education aside whenever it interferes with love or comfort, money or fun." *Now* we know that we are expected to take the anecdote as a piece of evidence for a much larger concept, namely, a "national inclination to push education aside." But the writer does not entirely lose his good-natured story-telling manner, as his colloquialisms (*not at all sure it's right*) continue to remind us.

The use of stylistic techniques borrowed from fiction has been increasing in expository writing, especially in some journalism. The two samples of exemplary anecdote we have been looking at both originated, presumably, from the writers' own experience, something they saw or directly heard about. When a reporter, for example, takes the larger step of assuming he is a kind of novelist, describing scenes he has never seen and thoughts of people he could not have known about, then the dangers are obvious. Newswriting that attempts to be especially lively, such as you will find in *Time*, runs this risk of dishonesty. But the novelist's manner is tempting to more aspiring writers too, especially to historians who wish to paint the actions of the past with color and vividness. Here is a serious professional historian beginning a piece of writing on early America.

[1] Out to the limitless distance ran the ocean. [2] From its near edge, the generations of Europeans had watched the turbulent waters recede into the unknown space, within which imagination crowded all the fantastic beings of fable. [3] Here began the end of the world; the mariners hugged the margins of the continent, fearful as in Odysseus' day of losing sight of the familiar universe of rising cliffs and jutting promontories that was their home.

—OSCAR HANDLIN, "Shaped in the Wilderness: The Americas"

[1] Note the suspense created here: "What ocean?" we ask.

[2] *Its:* a simple, clear transition by means of a pronoun.
See how the historian takes the liberty of assuming how their imaginations worked.

[3] *Here:* transition.

More subtle links provided by *limitless distance, turbulent waters, unknown space, fantastic beings, fearful of losing sight of . . . home.*

We may have to read on a bit, beyond this theatrical opening, before we know what Handlin is talking about (the European coastline, it turns out, about 1600). The mystery and suspense created here, as we have said, are traditionally characteristic of the novelist, not the writer of exposition. The student expositor, needless to say, should imitate this kind of paragraph with caution.

The Paragraph as a Definition of a Term

Very often we read or write pieces of exposition whose whole point depends on the significance attached to one or two particular words. These are usually words that have been so bandied about by others for so many years that they can mean anything. *Liberal, idea, tolerance* are three examples. Anyone writing an essay making important use of such terms must anticipate his reader's very proper question: What do you mean by that? In the following three opening paragraphs, definition of one of these terms is the central problem the paragraph must solve, or at least face. Within this identity of common function, however, the paragraphs again differ markedly in tone, as you will see.

[1] Any education that matters is *liberal.* [2] All the saving truths and healing graces that distinguish a good education from a bad one or a full education from a half-empty one are contained in that word. [3] Whatever ups and downs the term "liberal" suffers in the political vocabulary, it soars above all controversy in the educational world. [4] In the blackest pit of pedagogy the squirming victim has only to ask, "What's liberal about this?" to shame his persecutors. [5] In times past a liberal education set off a free man from a slave or a gentleman from laborers and artisans. [6] It now distinguishes whatever nourishes the mind and spirit from the training which is merely practical or professional or from the trivialities which are no training at all. [7] Such an education involves a combination of knowledge, skills, and standards.

—ALAN SIMPSON, "The Marks of an Educated Man"

[1] Strong, terse statement, italicizing the crucial term.
[2] Links: repetition of *education* and the final phrase, *that word*, which refers to the italicized term.

[4] *Pedagogy* is a linking echo of *education.*
Note again the repetitions of *liberal*, the key word.
[5] The phrase *liberal education* combines the two.
[5, 6] Sentences 5 and 6 are linked and balanced by the references to time in each: *in times past* and *now.*
[6] This is the crucial sentence of the definition.

[7] *Such an education*—i.e., a liberal one—again reinforces the links between the sentences.

[95]

The writer is now ready to proceed with his discussion of "knowledge, skills, and standards." He has set up a working definition of *liberal,* however general it may be, and he has set it off from its political connotations. The tone is serious, and the reader, although he is expected to share the values of education here referred to, is certainly not left with the impression that the speaker knows him intimately. This is formal discourse.

We now look at another problem with a word, the word *idea.* Here is a distinguished composer beginning an essay on the creative process in the writing of music.

[1] The word "idea" is a very vague term for what we really mean when we talk of the composer's creative imagination. [2] The German word *Einfall* is the perfect expression needed in our situation. [3] *Einfall,* from the verb *einfallen,* to drop in, describes beautifully the strange spontaneity that we associate with artistic ideas in general and with musical creation in particular. [4] Something—you know not what—drops into your mind—you know not whence—and there it grows —you know not how—into some form —you know not why. [5] This seems to be the general opinion, and we cannot blame the layman if he is unable to find rational explanations for so strange an occurrence.

—PAUL HINDEMITH, "How Music Happens"

[1] The speaker concedes immediately that he has a problem of definition.

[2] *Word* is repeated; *in our situation* refers also, more generally, to the first sentence.

[3] *Einfall* repeated; *describes beautifully* refers to *is the perfect expression* in the sentence preceding.

[4] This unorthodox punctuation is Hindemith's attempt to express in words *the strange spontaneity* he mentioned in the previous sentence.

[5] *This* refers, perhaps a little vaguely, to the thought processes just described.

Hindemith's tone is a good deal lighter and friendlier than that in our previous passage, partly because of his bizarre mimicking of popular responses to the word *idea* in musical creation. (All those dashes!) Notice that the writer expresses some charity for those who know less than he does—"we cannot blame the layman." He is a little more human, a little less formidable, than the preceding writer.

You will observe the reference to "general opinion" in the

final sentence, an opinion with which Hindemith is about to disagree in the rest of his article, at least to the extent of describing a composer's process of creating music in something like rational terms. The paragraph of definition, in this case, not only deals with a term, but in doing so also uses the first technique we outlined in this chapter, the argument in contrast to prevailing opinion. Methods, it is important to make clear, are often successfully used in combination, and that is the situation here. Our process of critical analysis, after all, comes long after the writing process is all over, and in practice the writer does not ask, "Now which of three, or six, or fifteen techniques should I use in this paragraph?" Rather he asks a much harder question: "How can I so organize this paragraph that the reader will respond just as I want him to?" The student writer, who sometimes has to be more self-conscious and deliberate about his choices, can often be helped by categories of critical analysis. But he must not expect such analysis to solve all his problems of paragraphing, just as he is certain to find, in his reading, plenty of fine introductory paragraphs that seem to fit none of our categories here.

Of the three words to be considered in this section—*liberal, idea, tolerance*—which would you say most requires a formal, solemn treatment? Whatever your answer, you would probably agree that *tolerance* is a very serious topic, and that one's appropriate tone in defining it should be impersonal or even strictly formal. But such is not the case at all. We must not press too hard our notions of appropriateness, for the fact is, as we have already noted, subject matter and tone are not the same thing. It does not follow that because a topic is supposed to be serious, we must necessarily speak of it serious*ly*. The matter of tone is the writer's own decision, and in the case of some great writers, as the following passage should show, the decision can be surprising.

[1] Can you define tolerance? [2] I can't, any more than I could define love or faith, or fate, or any other abstraction. [3] My mind slips about, tries a definition, finds it won't quite

[1] Definition problem immediately stated, and the reader directly involved (*you*).
[2] The speaker, with his informal contractions (*can't*), cheerfully admits his own limitations.

work, drops it, tries another, and so on. [4] And people whose minds are better than my own seem to be in the same plight here. [5] They propound definitions, they defend them stoutly and philosophically, but sooner or later the definition crumbles under the onslaught of some other philosopher, and the world is left where it was. [6] Well, not quite where it was. [7] Despite the failure, two valuable things have occurred. [8] Firstly, the human mind has been exercising itself, and, my goodness, how desirable that is! [9] It has been trying to discover something, and it has become stronger and more agile in consequence, even though nothing has been discovered. [10] And, secondly, the abstract subjects on which it has exercised itself have gained in prestige. [11] Tolerance is important, no one can deny that, and if it is talked about so that people dispute what it is, or isn't, its importance should be maintained or increased.

—E. M. FORSTER, "Toward a Definition of Tolerance"

Links: *define*, sentence 1; *define*, 2; *definition*, 3; *definitions*, 5.
[4] *And* connects the writer's mind with everyone else's.
[5] This sentence echoes, in more elegant language, the way in which the speaker described his own train of thought in sentence 3.

[6] *Well*: highly informal. *Where it was*: another linkage by repetition.
[7] *The failure* summarizes what has been described so far.
[8, 9, 10] Familiar logical organization: *firstly, secondly.*
The speaker is jocular, of course, about minds exercising themselves, implying it does not happen very often!

[10] *Gained in prestige* links with *important* and *importance* in the final sentence.

[11] *Tolerance* returns us neatly to the first sentence.

On the basis of what we have seen of these introductions, suppose we conclude that success in creating such paragraphs in exposition is a matter of at least two interrelated processes. First, it is necessary to have logical internal *organization:* to provide links between sentences so that the reader has a sense of rational sequence as he moves through the paragraph. Second, it is necessary to maintain a consistent personality, or *tone* (speaking voice), throughout the paragraph.

We are now ready to go ahead into the body of expository writing, to observe how other kinds of paragraphs can be organized, and to learn something of how paragraphs themselves can be linked together by transitional elements to produce a coherent discourse.

PROBLEMS OF INTERNAL ORGANIZATION

What we have already noted about internal structure in opening paragraphs applies to a considerable extent to paragraphs within the body of an essay. Most paragraphs, wherever they may appear, are built around a central theme or idea, which is often expressed in a single topic sentence. And most paragraphs are made up of sentences connected by transitional devices that can be identified. We will now take a look at some additional techniques for organizing, or unifying, or holding together expository paragraphs.

In the following paragraph, notice how all the details have been chosen to relate to the initial topic sentence and its key phrase, *horse-and-carriage life*. This is a simple approach—seeing to it that all the items of a list belong in that list—but it is not so easy as it looks.

The sights and sounds and sensations of horse-and-carriage life were part of the universal American experience: the clop-clop of horses' hoofs; the stiff jolting of an iron-tired carriage on a stony road; the grinding noise of the brake being applied to ease the horse on a downhill stretch; the necessity of holding one's breath when the horse sneezed; the sight of sand, carried up on the tires and wooden spokes of a carriage wheel, spilling off in little cascades as the wheel revolved; the look of a country road overgrown by grass, with three tracks in it instead of two, the middle one made by horses' hoofs; the special male ordeal of getting out of the carriage and walking up the steeper hills to lighten the load; and the more severe ordeal, for the unpracticed, of harnessing a horse which could recognize inexperience at one scornful glance. During a Northern winter the jingle of sleigh bells was everywhere. On summer evenings, along tree-lined streets of innumerable American towns, families sitting on their front porches would watch the fine carriages of the town as they drove past for a proud evening's jaunt, and the cognoscenti would wait eagerly for a glimpse of the banker's trotting pair or the sporting lawyer's 2:40 pacer. And one of the magnificent sights of urban life was that of a fire engine, pulled by three galloping horses, careening down a city street with its bell clanging.

—FREDERICK LEWIS ALLEN, *The Big Change*

Still another technique of unifying a paragraph is to build all or most of the sentences around a comparison or a contrast.

Comparison is telling what a thing is like. Usually the more familiar thing or idea is used to explain the less familiar one. If you were to explain the game of badminton, for instance, you could show how it was similar to tennis, the more familiar game. In what ways is piloting a plane like driving a car? How are Canadians like their friends in the United States? Contrast, on the other hand, is telling what a thing is not like. How does college life as you see it now differ from college life as you thought it would be? How does the American way of living differ from the Oriental way? How does democracy differ from communism? How does propaganda differ from news? These are typical subjects that invite treatment by contrast, not in paragraphs alone but also in entire essays or articles.

A *white-collar employee of an American corporation visiting a Soviet institution of comparable rank will be in for some surprises.* [Topic sentence] For one thing the offices of the establishment will be secondary to the plant, instead of vice versa which is usually the case in the United States. Also the visitor will note that a considerable number of executive officers in a Russian industrial organization, even engineers, are women. On a superficial level other points can be mentioned. First, there is little of the personal byplay and banter that accompany much American business endeavor and office routine; no coffee break, for example. Bosses are aloof. Second, lunch takes place in a cafeteria on the premises, maintained by the establishment; no corner drugstore, bar, or hotdog stand. Third, nobody has to catch the 5:25; commuting, if any, is by bus. Another point is that jobs are different in function. No Soviet plant has a public relations department or advertising department, office for employer-employee relationships, or even a sales manager and staff. Salesmanship, the first of all occupations in America, does not exist in our sense at all.

—JOHN GUNTHER, *Inside Russia Today*

The following, with its sparks of grim humor that so few people associate with the author, may inspire you to compare and contrast your chosen occupation with others:

The great liability of the engineer compared to men of other professions is that his works are out in the open where all can see them. [Topic sentence] His acts, step by step, are in hard substance. He cannot bury his mistakes in a grave like the doctors. He cannot argue them into thin air or blame the judge like the lawyers. He cannot, like the architects, cover his failures with trees and vines. He cannot, like the politicians, screen his shortcomings by blaming his opponents and hope that the people will forget. The engineer simply cannot deny that he did it. If his works do not work, he is damned. That is the phantasmagoria that haunts his nights and dogs his days. He comes from the job at the end of the day resolved to calculate it again. He wakes in the night in a cold sweat and puts something on paper that looks silly in the morning. All day he shivers at the thought of the bugs which will inevitably appear to jolt its smooth consummation.

On the other hand, unlike the doctor his is not a life among the weak. Unlike the soldier, destruction is not his purpose. Unlike the lawyer, quarrels are not his daily bread. To the engineer falls the job of clothing the bare bones of science with life, comfort, and hope. No doubt as years go by people forget which engineer did it, even if they ever knew. Or some politician puts his name on it. Or they credit it to some promoter who used other people's money with which to finance it. But the engineer himself looks back at the unending stream of goodness which flows from his successes with satisfactions that few professions may know. And the verdict of his fellow professionals is all the accolade he wants.

—HERBERT HOOVER, *The Memoirs of Herbert Hoover: Years of Adventure*

As we have analyzed paragraphs, we have noted dozens of specific transitional words and phrases by which sentences have been related to one another. We have been using such terms as *echo, refer,* and *link* to signify these relations. We can now summarize these connecting expressions as follows:

1. *Conjunctions and transitional adverbs,* which include words and phrases such as *and, but, yet, however, therefore, consequently, moreover, accordingly, at the same time, as a result, for example, on the other hand, finally.*
2. *Pronouns,* such as *this, that, these, those, his, her,* and *its,* which refer to an antecedent in a previous sentence. It is extremely important that the young writer make sure references of pronouns are clear. See Section 30 in the Handbook.
3. *Repetition of key words,* of which examples, particularly clear in paragraphs of definition, appear in earlier pages of this chapter.
4. *Parallel structure,* through which the reader is led back to sentences phrased in similar forms.

For a close study of connectives, transitions, and internal organization, follow the themes and variations, almost like musical motifs, in the following passage:

[1] The first sentences of this book were written nearly two years ago. [2] *Outside my window* on *that* spring *morning*, as on *this*, a *bird sang*. [3] *Outside a million windows*, a million *birds* had *sung* as *morning* swept around the globe. [4] Few men and few women were so glad that a new day had dawned as *these birds* seem to be.

[2] Introduces key words. Pronouns *that* and *this*.

[3] Repeats *Outside . . . window, bird*, and *morning; sung* echoes *sang*.

[4] Pronoun *these*. Repeats *birds*.

[5] Because my *window* looks out on a southern landscape, my *bird* is a cardinal, with feathers as bright as his half-whistled song. [6] Farther *north* in the United States he would be a *robin*, more likely than not—less colorful and somewhat less melodious but seemingly no less pleased with the world and his place in it. [7] Like *us, robins* have *their* problems but *they* seem better able to take *them* in *their* stride. [8] *We* are likely to awake with an "Oh, dear!" on our lips; *they* with "What fun!" in their beaks. [9] Mr. Sandburg's peddler was remarkable because he seemed so *terribly glad* to be selling fish. [10] Most robins seem *terribly glad* to be eating worms.

[5] Again repeats *window*. Repeats *bird*.

[6] Contrasts *north* with *southern* in sentence 5. Introduces key word.

[7] Repeats *robin*. *Their* contrasts with *us*. Pronouns.

[8] *We* ties in with *us*.

[9, 10] Repeated phrase, *terribly glad*.

[11] For some time I have been thinking that I wanted to write a book about the *characteristics* and *activities* of living things. [12] During the week or two just before, I had been wondering with what activity or characteristic I should begin. [13] Reproduction, growing up, and getting a living are all, so I said to *myself*, fundamental *activities*. [14] Combativeness in the face of rivals, solicitude for the

[11] Introduces two key words— *activities* and *characteristics*.

[12] Repeats key words.

[13] Pronoun refers to *I*. Repeats key word.

[14] Repeats key word.

young, courage when danger must be
met, patience when hardships must be
endured, are all typical *characteristics.*
[15] But *my cardinal* proposed a different solution. [16] Is any *characteristic* more striking than the joy of life
instead?

[15] *My cardinal* refers to *cardinal*
in sentence 5.
[16] Repeats key word.

—JOSEPH WOOD KRUTCH, *The Great Chain
of Life*

ORGANIZING PARAGRAPHS IN SEQUENCES

To understand how paragraphs are related to one another is to
begin to see how a whole essay is organized. We begin with an
obvious kind of illustration: paragraphs that reflect a list of items
to be considered. But note that in the following piece of historical writing, the authors have subtly given their third "factor" an
added importance by granting it a paragraph to itself.

As late as 1808, when the slave trade was abolished, numerous South-
erners thought that slavery would prove but a temporary evil. [Summary
of preceding paragraph]
  *But during the next generation the South was converted into a section
which for the most part was grimly united behind slavery.* [Topic sentence
of the paragraph] How did this come about? Why did the abolitionist
spirit in the South almost disappear? [Questions to be answered by what
follows] For one reason, the spirit of philosophical liberalism which
flamed high in Revolutionary days gradually became weaker. [One possible answer] For another reason, a general antagonism between puritan-
ical New England and the slaveholding South became evident; they differed on the War of 1812, the tariff, and other great issues; and the South
felt less and less liking for the so-called Northern idea of emancipation.
[A second possible answer] But above all, certain new economic factors
made slavery more profitable than it had been before 1790. [This third
possible answer provides a topic sentence for the whole section to follow,
comprising the following two paragraphs.]
  *One element in the economic change is familiar—the rise of a great
cotton-growing industry in the South.* [First example of an "economic factor"; topic sentence of the first half of the paragraph] This was based in
part on the introduction of improved types of cotton, with better fibers
[one explanation of the rise of the cotton industry], but in much larger

[103]

part on Eli Whitney's epochal invention in 1793 of the "gin" for clean-ing cotton [second explanation]. Cotton culture rapidly moved westward from the Carolinas and Georgia, spreading over much of the lower South to the Mississippi River and, eventually, on into Texas. *Another factor which placed slavery on a new basis was sugar growing.* [This second "eco-nomic factor" provides a topic sentence for the second half of the para-graph.] The rich, hot delta lands of southeastern Louisiana are ideal for sugar cane; and in 1794–1795 an enterprising New Orleans Creole, Étienne Boré, proved that the crop could be highly profitable. He set up machinery and vats, and the crowds which had come from New Orleans to watch the boiling-off broke into cheers when the first sugar crystals showed in the cooling liquid. The cry, "It granulates!" opened a new era in Louisiana. A great boom resulted, so that by 1830 the state was supply-ing the nation with about half its whole sugar supply. This required slaves, who were brought in, in thousands, from the Eastern seaboard.

Finally, tobacco culture also spread westward and took slavery with it. [Third "economic factor" and topic sentence of this paragraph] Constant cropping had worn out the soil of lowland Virginia, once the greatest tobacco region of the world, and the growers were glad to move into Ken-tucky and Tennessee, taking their Negroes with them. Thereafter the fast-multiplying slaves of the upper South were largely drained off to the lower South and West. This diffusion of slavery relieved many observers, because it lessened the risk of such a slave insurrection as Nat Turner's Rebellion, a revolt of sixty or seventy Virginia slaves in 1831—which, incidentally, did much to increase Southern fear of emancipationist doc-trines.

—ALLAN NEVINS AND HENRY STEELE COMMAGER,
The Pocket History of the United States

Here is a similar technique of dividing one's subject into parts and permitting the paragraph divisions to punctuate these parts.

The Soviet Union's cosmic rocket added a new member, if a miniscule one, to the system of planets revolving around the sun since eons past. Its success is a dramatic step toward sending rockets to seek out secrets of the solar system—and perhaps to explore some of the measureless space be-yond. And it has stimulated men further to look up at the "stars that sweep, and turn, and fly," and ponder the nature of the universe. [This statement introduces the next idea, which is the heart of the piece.] *Space, from earthman's point of view, has three main divisions.* [Main topic sentence] *The first and smallest is the solar system.* [Topic sentence of first subdivision] The sun, with a diameter of 864,000 miles and its mighty force of gravitation, holds the nine known planets in their elliptical orbits. In addition, the solar system includes thirty-one satellites of the planets (not counting the earth's artificial satellites); thousands of asteroids, which are rather like tiny planets; comets and meteors. As astronomical distances go, the size of the solar system is not astronomical: it is only about 7,350,000,000 miles across. [Particulars and details to clarify the topic sentence]

The next division of space is "our" galaxy: an aggregation of about 100 billion stars. [Topic sentence of second subdivision] Our sun is an average star in this "Milky Way." The nearest star to us after our sun is so distant that it takes light four and one-half years to travel to us. The galaxy itself is so vast that it takes light 100,000 years to travel from one edge of it to the other. Yet ours is a medium-sized galaxy. [Particulars and details]

Beyond our "Milky Way" is the third division of space—all the rest of the universe. [Topic sentence of third subdivision] In the unimaginable reaches of this really outer space are countless numbers of aggregations of suns. All these galaxies rotate and move in space. The most powerful telescopes can find no end to them. [Again, particulars and details]

—*The New York Times Magazine,* "To the Planets and Beyond"

Here is an example of autobiographical writing whose major device for linking paragraphs is the repetition of the word *embroiled, embroilment.* See what other ways of making transitions you can observe.

I often think of that dinner party in Richard's rooms as the midmost point of my life. I have spent my years almost equally between two centuries, and that was the last year of the first of them. People are apt to see this twentieth century in which humanity now weeps and mourns as a time of cataclysm. We are living in a loft over the stable; the floor is desperately thin; and we can hear the beasts stirring beneath us. And we know that they are not good chained comfortable beasts that come to our call and work in our service. Sometimes our hair stands on end as we listen, in a night's dark loneliness, to their unchained prowling, the scuffle of great pads, the rasp of breath coming out of hot red throats, and we picture their eyes lifted to their ceiling, which is our frail floor: the light green or golden pitiless eyes shining over the jaws that drip hungrily. Sometimes in dream the floor dissolves, and we are the beasts and the beasts are we, and all is chaos. And those who have known only this latter half of what has been my life think with envy of that first half, seeing it as green pastures and tranquil waters and talking of the long opulent Victorian afternoon and golden evening.

It wasn't so. The beasts were there then. The beasts are always there. Always our loft is perched between them and the stars, that seem to look implacably down on them and us, as if serenely and indifferently expecting the moment when the fools in the loft will become so heavily embroiled that they will smash the floor beneath their feet.

They were always embroiled, but they go on adding to the weight of their embroilment; and the only question is whether they will stop or whether the weight will become too much.

They were always embroiled. I have lived long enough to have no illusions about that. I am nearing my ninetieth year as I write this. I was born in a time when my living eyes could look at the Dook who had been at Waterloo. And then I watched the great glass bubble go up and heard the talk of peace on earth. And then I saw the Crimean men, legless and armless and eyeless and hopeless, sitting under the railings of Hyde Park, holding out their tin mugs for coppers, as we rode inside the Park and Mama bowed or did not bow, and Papa became a knight because he had helped to win the war. And I loved Lord Burnage who had ridden in the desperate moment of that war, and I had stroked the flank of the lovely beast that helped Tennyson to make the poem that moved us all to pride and wonder. And there had been the savage horror of mutiny in India; and I had watched my half brother Justin drive away, through the soft airs of a Cornish morning, because they were still embroiled, and he had never come back, and already that was so long ago that the moment when the path was empty and we turned back into the renovated house seemed, as the century ended, a moment lost in the mists of dream.

There had been embroilment in China, and Gordon had died at Khartoum, and the Boers had swept us off the hill at Majuba; and I had seen wooden ships with sails become ironclads with boilers, and rifles become machine guns, and cannon balls become explosive shells; and finally, at the turn of the century, the little soldier on the gray horse whom Nika had excitedly watched leading the grand parade to St. Paul's on Diamond Jubilee day had led a grand parade to Oom Paul, and many who went with him did not come back, and among them were Richard and Trimmer and poor Tom Chadderton.

And this was the long Victorian afternoon and golden evening.

—HOWARD SPRING, *The Houses In Between*

In reading the essays of professionals, it is helpful to develop a sensitivity to various techniques of transition from paragraph to paragraph. "How has he connected these parts?" can be our repeated question—and sometimes we will find that he has not connected them as well as he might. Similarly, when writing our own compositions, we can develop a critical awareness of paragraph sequence. Fairly early in the development of one's reading skill, and eventually in the development of proficiency in writing, this awareness of how paragraphs can be linked together becomes almost automatic. Finally, weaknesses in paragraph structure can usually be improved during revision—a process we shall be considering in our next chapter.

E X E R C I S E S

EXERCISE 1, SENTENCE ORDER. *The following paragraphs are composed with a scrambled order of sentences. In each case, re-order the sentences so as to make a paragraph with the best possible internal organization. Do not rewrite any sentence. You will probably find the paragraphs increasing in complexity as you proceed.*

1. Another is to outlaw trucks during daylight hours. At any rate, most solutions are either inadequate or impossible. Some have suggested a more drastic alternative—to forbid passenger cars inside the city limits. One is to enforce the speed and parking laws. There are several ways of dealing with the city traffic problem.

2. The gigantic range of the Alps separates it from France, Switzerland, Austria, and Yugoslavia. The Mediterranean Sea borders Italy on the other sides. Nature, which lavished so much beauty on this country, has also given it majestic and precise borders, separating it from the rest of Europe by the Alps and the sea. Italy is a peninsula in southern Europe, jutting into the Mediterranean Sea, toward Africa, and practically dividing that sea into two parts, the Western and Eastern Mediterranean. It has the characteristic form of a boot.

3. You will acquire knowledge and understanding which are not given to all but are reserved for the few who have earned them. Foreign-language study offers another great advantage. It places you in direct contact with another people—their history, their past and present achievements in science and the arts, in a word, their civilization. The study of any foreign language, either ancient or modern, is first of all a splendid training for the mind. It has often been stated that a good knowledge of a foreign language gives a double value to one's life. It teaches you to organize facts and trains you in clear, logical reasoning.

4. The child who is unusually sensitive or who has not found his place in the outside world may need just as much protection as the average small child. Generally speaking, jealousy of the baby is strongest in the child under five, because he is much more dependent on his parents and has fewer interests outside the family circle. Being pushed out of the limelight at home doesn't hurt so much. He, too, needs consideration and visible reminders of love from his mother, particularly in the beginning. It would be a mistake, though, to think that jealousy doesn't exist in the older child. The child of six or more is drawing away a little from his parents and building a position for himself among his friends.

5. The best-known of these, and in some ways the most interesting, are the trilobites, which are generally ranked as a distinct class. In many places their remains are very abundant, and they are familiar to every collector of fossils. They died out, as far as we know, at the close of the Palaeozoic era. Among the animals whose remains are found as fossils in the older rocks of the geological series there are many arthropods which differ greatly in structure and appearance from any now living. Whether this be so or not, they are among the very oldest animals of which we have any definite knowledge, some of them being found in rocks of the Lower Cambrian age, at the very beginning of the geological record. They are interesting because they come nearer than any others to what we suppose the primitive Arthropoda to have been like, and they have been regarded as the ancestral stock from which many, possibly all, of the existing classes have been derived.

EXERCISE 2, INTRODUCTORY PARAGRAPHS. *Look through an anthology of modern essays, noting the introductory paragraphs. Find a paragraph stating a thesis to be argued, one telling an anecdote, and one offering a definition. Find one using a combination of these methods. Find one that fits none of these categories. Can you invent a useful fourth category to contain it?*

EXERCISE 3, WRITING INTRODUCTORY PARAGRAPHS. *Write three possible opening paragraphs for an essay on "The Role of the American College President." Use each of the three approaches outlined in the first part of this chapter.*

EXERCISE 4, TONE. *Rewrite your three paragraphs, drastically changing the tone in each case.*

EXERCISE 5, PARAGRAPH VARIETY. *Locate examples of the following:*

1. A paragraph with a topic sentence at the end.
2. A paragraph used as a transition between two topics of an essay.
3. A paragraph with a light tone on a heavy subject.
4. A paragraph within which the tone shifts.
5. A paragraph summarizing a section of an essay or chapter.

EXERCISE 6, REVISING A PARAGRAPH. *In the following passage, revise and combine the sentences, inserting transitions where necessary, in order to produce a logical and readable paragraph:*

Students of the English language have divided its historical growth into three main periods; the Old English Period, from 450 to 1100, was the first one. The Middle English Period lasted from 1100 until 1500. The Modern English Period began in 1500 and lasted up to the present time. The people of England did not stop speaking one kind of language and begin speaking another in any one year. The change was gradual. There were definite historical events occurring at the times mentioned which caused a more rapid change in the language of the people of England. The Angles, Saxons, and Jutes invaded England in 449. The Norman Conquest occurred in 1066. The English Renaissance began about 1500.

(*After you have finished this exercise, you might turn to page 6 in this book to see one way of solving these problems.*)

5 THE PROCESS OF PLANNING AND WRITING

PROBLEMS OF SUBJECT AND FOCUS

Selecting a Subject

Many of the papers that you will write in college will be on subjects prescribed by the occasion, or chosen by some person such as your instructor in history, political science, or sociology. Some of your papers will be summaries or reports based on assigned reading. Some will be brief discussions in answer to examination questions. Conditions such as these will place their own limitations on what you will say, how you will organize your material, and what attitude you will adopt toward your material.

Frequently, however, especially in a course in English composition, you will be given a broad or general subject that you must narrow down to a usable topic, or you will be assigned a type of writing to experiment with, such as a personal essay, a narrative sketch, or a pattern of structure. The choice of specific subject will be left to you.

Preliminary Planning. The planning of your paper begins when your instructor tells you that you are to write, let us say, an eight-hundred-word theme on some local custom, on some new development of science, on the author of the book you happen to be reading—whatever the particular subject may be. You begin by thinking in terms of the space you have to fill, just as the professional writer begins to plan when his editor asks him to write a five-hundred-word piece on a new grass for shady lawns, a two-thousand-word article on the local tourist industry, or a six-thousand-word article on the commercial uses of radar. You begin to think of space to fill and readers to interest. What do you have to say that is new, that has not been said over and over again, and, most important at the moment, that can be effectively said in eight hundred words? This process of thinking in terms of a limited space to fill is what is called "limiting the subject."

Limiting the Subject. The natural tendency of the apprentice writer is to think of subjects in the large. Subjects like "Home and Friends," "Amusements," "Politics," "Reading," or "Vacations" are not subjects for short papers; they are warehouses of subjects. Each contains the materials for innumerable essays, articles, anecdotes, descriptions, whatever you wish to write. The larger the subject, the more hopeless it seems and is. It must be narrowed, cut down, limited to usable size.

Let us illustrate the general principle of limiting a subject by using an example. Let us say that you are interested in antiques, a general subject about which many books have been written. You know something about antiques because your mother and your older sister have several cupboards filled with early American glass. You too have a few choice pieces as the beginning of a collection. Your subject is already beginning to limit itself. What can you tell your reader—in eight hundred words—that is not old and general? Your answer may be the natural result of your own experiences: you decide to give point and direction to your article by concentrating on a single objective, on the idea that an amateur collector of glass develops through three stages. State this objective in the form of a thesis or summarizing sentence: "An amateur collector of early American glass develops through three stages: first, he buys everything in sight; second, as his knowledge and taste grow, he discards all except a few of his choicest pieces; third, he begins to trade in a discriminating way with other collectors." There you have a target to shoot at, a rough plan of operations, and some idea of the ammunition you are going to use. Up to this time most of your planning has been done in your head. Now jot down your main ideas on a sheet of paper, write down under each main head a few of the details as they occur to you, and you have a working plan.

You will probably change your plan as you proceed, but every writer must do that. Change will improve your finished product so long as you keep to your main objective and your first general plan. Your paper will have direction, purpose, organization, and clearness.

Some Types of Subjects. Perhaps you will get a better idea of how various kinds of subjects can be limited by examining the lists under the following fairly simple categories. These are limited subjects derived from larger units, though many of these limited subjects are susceptible to much closer subdividing as you proceed.

GENERAL SUBJECT: HOME AND FAMILY LIFE

1. Space problems in an apartment house
2. Feeding the baby
3. I am an only child
4. Father comes home at night
5. The dinner hour in Suburbia
6. The well-planned kitchen
7. Papering a room
8. Sister falls in love
9. Nostalgia in an attic
10. Short-order cooking

GENERAL SUBJECT: HOBBIES

1. Hunting birds with a camera
2. The fascination of old guns
3. Indian relics in my community
4. The sports car club
5. Collecting antique glass
6. Keeping a journal
7. Wood carving
8. Remaking old cars
9. Photographing flowers in color
10. The rock hunter

GENERAL SUBJECT: TRAVEL

1. Bicycle trips on Cape Cod
2. Exploring in a canoe
3. A strange place I have slept in
4. Touring with a trailer
5. Glacier Park trails
6. Bus versus car travel
7. Plane versus ship travel
8. A day in Rome
9. A walking trip in England
10. The trouble with sleeping bags

Much of your writing in college, of course, will be of a more academic sort than these topics suggest. Some of your more ambitious papers will involve gathering materials from your reading and organizing them into a coherent and serious argument. This kind of project will be considered in detail in our next chapter. For the present we are concerned with types of subjects that depend largely on your own experience or on sources readily available to you. The further suggestions that follow are designed to help you explore the various resources at your command, by presenting examples of various types of writing often assigned to students.

Autobiographical Materials. "The Story of My Life" is of course a favorite topic that our natural egotism rather enjoys. But there are dangers. Beware of writing a narrative account of your life, listing in chronological order such items as when and where you were born, who your parents were, where you went to school, and so on. Instead, try telling about the development of your interest in music, about your religious life, about your attitude toward a life work. Better yet, concentrate on the development of a dominant trait in your character or personality. You could bring out a dominant trait most effectively, probably, by means of a typical incident, as in the following example.

I was a shy infant and, alas, was frightened by my father, who was the most gentle and tender of men. Something about his black mustache alarmed me. Far from running to meet him on his return, I avoided him and turned away my head when my mother brought me to him. This grieved him deeply, and after seventy years I am still enraged with myself whenever I think of it.

Otherwise I seem to have been a well-behaved child, generally quiet and obedient, giving little trouble. So the only anecdote which came down to me from these years of my early childhood is quite surprising. (My friends say it throws definite light on my subsequent character.) One morning at breakfast, when I started to get down from my high chair, my mother turned to me and said, "Baby, you must say, 'Please excuse me.'" And I replied, "I won't." So my mother of course said, "Then you may not get down until you say 'Please excuse me.'" But I resolutely refused.

There was great agitation in the household. Everyone tried to persuade me. My brother Harry, who loved me dearly, especially begged me to be good. My nurse wept. My high chair was moved from the breakfast table over to a corner, and there I remained sitting. My father said, "That child should be punished," put on his hat, and went out of the house. It was a Sunday morning but no one went to church. After some hours the family gave in. I was removed from the high chair and allowed to go about my daily routine.

The following morning when I had finished my breakfast, no one said anything to me at all. My mother made no suggestions, but I turned to her gravely and said, *"Now* I will say 'Please excuse me.' " It was, I suppose, my mother's use of the word "must" that Sunday morning that touched some chord in my infant disposition. Apparently I was quite willing to do anything that seemed reasonable and proper, but, however reasonable it might be, not to do it under any kind of pressure. All my life this latent quality has continued to exist. Any kind of pressure or threat stirs up some mulish trait in my disposition.

—Virginia C. Gildersleeve, *Many a Good Crusade*

As the foregoing passage may demonstrate, a single memorable incident is often a better choice as a subject than a number of events in your life sketchily treated over a longer space of time. And you should be wary of the obvious incidents everyone has talked about: the camping trip, the auto accident, the big fire downtown. Much more effective is some apparently minor incident, so developed with concrete detail that it acquires importance in the telling.

There were the annual excitements, too, of Chautauqua and the Champaign County Fair. My clearest memory of the fair I have preserved in the story "Dollar Bill," where a boy who accurately corresponds to me teases his mother for money with which to go to the grounds on a day when the rest of the family have not planned to go. She gives him a dollar, the smallest amount she can find in her purse, and presses upon him the importance of his bringing half of it back; admission for him as a child will be a quarter, and with the other quarter he can buy good things to eat and drink. He goes at last, a little ashamed of having teased her into consenting, but comforted by the prospect of the lemonade and hamburgers he can buy with the second quarter. But a scoundrel at the window, pretending not to notice he is under age, gives him an adult ticket with only half a dollar in change, so that he enters the grounds not merely in shame but in despair. He tries to get interested in the free exhibits; smells hamburgers cooking; decides that one such indulgence will be forgiven by his mother; goes up to the counter; is given a sandwich; and before he can eat it hears the man telling him his half-dollar is counterfeit. I do not tell in the story how my father, when we all went the next day, passed the bad coin in the same window and heard nothing further from it. I looked at the implements and animals again, and in the grandstand saw pacing and trotting races. There was no horse like Dan Patch, the world's champion pacer whom we had read about and admired; but the sulkies, the drivers with their silk caps, the starters and the judges, not to speak of the horses themselves, so gaily harnessed and at the finish line so dark with sweat, were a spectacle of which I could never get enough.

—MARK VAN DOREN, *The Autobiography of Mark Van Doren*

You can always find material for descriptive or expository papers in your home life—anything from short profiles of your father or your mother to longer discussions interpreting your family life in terms of its relation to American social history. Or you can take a single brief incident out of your home life and make it interesting and significant. Such home-grown materials can also provide a basis for the actual writing of fiction.

First Impressions of College. Instructions to record one's first impressions of a brave new college world have been familiar in freshman composition courses for a long, long time. The following, done by a great artist, will show what can be done with such materials.

In order to place this question fairly before you, I will describe, for memory has kept the picture bright, one of those rare but, as Queen Victoria would have put it, never-to-be-sufficiently-lamented occasions when in deference to friendship, or in a desperate attempt to acquire information about, perhaps, the French Revolution, it seemed necessary to attend a lecture. The room to begin with had a hybrid look—it was not for sitting in, nor yet for eating in. Perhaps there was a map on the wall; certainly there was a table on a platform, and several rows of rather small, rather hard, comfortless little chairs. These were occupied intermittently, as if they shunned each other's company, by people of both sexes, and some had notebooks and were tapping their fountain pens, and some had none and gazed with the vacancy and placidity of bull frogs at the ceiling. A large clock displayed its cheerless face, and when the hour struck in strode a harried-looking man, a man from whose face nervousness, vanity, or perhaps the depressing and impossible nature of his task had removed all traces of ordinary humanity. There was a momentary stir. He had written a book, and for the moment it was interesting to see people who have written books. Everybody gazed at him. He was bald and not hairy; he had a mouth and a chin; in short he was a man like another, although he had written a book. He cleared his throat and the lecture began. Now the human voice is an instrument of varied power; it can enchant and it can soothe; it can rage and it can despair; but when it lectures it almost always bores. What he said was sensible enough; there was learning in it and argument and reason; but as the voice went on attention wandered. The face of the clock seemed abnormally pale; the hands too suffered from some infirmity. Had they the gout? Were they swollen? They moved so slowly. They reminded one of the painful progress of a three-legged fly that has survived the winter. How many flies on an average survive the English winter, and what would be the thoughts of such an insect on waking to find itself being lectured on the French Revolution? The enquiry was fatal. A link had been lost—a paragraph dropped. It was useless to ask the lecturer to repeat his words; on he plodded with dogged pertinacity. The origin of the French Revolution was being sought for —also the thoughts of flies. Now there came one of those flat stretches of discourse when minute objects can be seen coming for two or three miles ahead. "Skip!" we entreated him—vainly. He did not skip. There was a joke. Then the voice went on again; then it seemed that the windows wanted washing; then a woman sneezed; then the voice quickened; then there was a peroration; and then—thank Heaven!—the lecture was over.

—Virginia Woolf, *The Death of the Moth and Other Essays*

The Narrative Incident. Have you ever been called on the carpet by an outraged parent? Then the following incident will appeal to you. Study this for the author's use of concrete details.

But there, alas, was the rub—as Morison himself would ruefully admit. He was himself such a mad, scape-grace sort of fellow that his acts sometimes passed all the bounds of decorum and propriety, and for that reason "the governor" was always "having him in upon the carpet."

There, in fact, was the whole setting. The governor existed for the sole purpose of "having him in upon the carpet"—one never saw them in any other way, but when Morison spoke about it one saw them in *this* way with blazing vividness. And this picture—the picture of Morison going in "upon the carpet"—was a very splendid one.

First, one saw Morison pacing nervously up and down in a noble and ancient hall, puffing distractedly on a cigarette and pausing from time to time in an apprehensive manner before the grim, closed barrier of an enormous seventeenth-century door which was tall and wide enough for a knight in armor to ride through without difficulty, and before whose gloomy and overwhelming front Morison looked very small and full of guilt. Then, one saw him take a last puff at his cigarette, brace his shoulders in a determined manner, knock on the panels of the mighty door, and in answer to a low growl within, open the door and advance desperately into the shadowed depths of a room so immense and magnificent that Morison looked like a single little sinner walking forlornly down the nave of a cathedral.

At the end of this terrific room, across an enormous space of carpet, sat "the governor." He was sitting behind a magnificent flat desk of ancient carved mahogany; in the vast shadowed depths behind him storied rows of old bound volumes climbed dizzily up into the upper darkness and were lost. And men in armor were standing grimly all around, and the portraits of the ancestors shone faintly in the gloom, and the old worn mellow colors of the tempered light came softly through the colored glass of narrow Gothic windows which were set far away in recessed depths of the impregnable mortared walls.

Meanwhile, "the governor" was waiting in grim silence as Morison advanced across the carpet. The governor was a man with beetling bushy eyebrows, silver hair, the lean, bitten and incisive face, the cropped mustache of a man who had seen service in old wars, and commanded garrisons in India, and after clearing his throat with a low menacing growl, he would peer fiercely out at Morison beneath his bushy brows, and say: "Well, young man?"—to which Morison would be able to make no answer, but would just stand there in a state of guilty dejection.

And the talk that then passed between the outraged father and the prodigal son was, from Morison's own account, astonishing. It was a talk that was no talk, a talk that was almost incoherent but that each understood perfectly, another language, not merely an economy of words so spare that one word was made to do the work of a hundred, but a series of grunts, blurts, oaths and ejaculations, in which almost nothing was said that was recognizable as ordered thought, but in which the meaning of everything was perfectly conveyed.

The last outrageous episode that had brought Morison into his present position of guilt "upon the carpet" was rarely named by name or given a description. Rather, as if affronted decency and aristocratic delicacy could not endure discussion of an unmentionable offense, his fault was indicated briefly as "that sort of thing" (or simply "sort of thing," spoken fast and slurringly)—and all the other passions and emotions of anger, contrition, stern condemnation and reproof, and, at length, of exhausted relief and escape, were conveyed in a series of broken and jerky exclamations, such as: "After *all!*" "It's not as if it were the first time you had played the bloody fool!" "What I mean to say is!" "Damn it all, it's not that I mind the wine-woman-song sort of thing—young myself once—no plaster saint —never pretended that I was—man's own business if he keeps it to himself—never interfered—only when you do a thing like this and make a bloody show of yourself—you idiot!—sort of thing men can understand but women!—it's your mother I'm thinking of!" and so on.

[117]

Morison's own speech, in fact, was largely composed of phrases such as these: he blurted them out so rapidly, scarcely moving his lips and slurring his words over in such a broken and explosive way, that when one first met him it was hard to understand what he was saying:—his speech seemed to be largely a series of blurted-out phrases, such as "sort of thing," "after *all*," "what I mean to say is!" and so on. And yet this incoherent and exclamatory style was curiously effective, for it seemed to take the listener into its confidence in rather an engaging manner which said: "of course there's no need to go into detail about all this, because I can see you are a man of the world and the same kind of fellow as I am. I know we understand each other perfectly, and the truth of what I am saying must be so self-evident that there's no point in discussing it."

—THOMAS WOLFE, *Of Time and the River*

Descriptions. Most of the description that you read consists of brief pictures so interwoven with narrative that it is impossible to say what is description and what is incident. Occasionally, however, a writer presents a larger picture, in which we may point out a few general principles. If a writer sets out to describe for us a visual scene, he again must establish his point of view —that is, he must tell the reader where he is when he views the scene. If he changes his position, he must inform the reader of the change. He may unify his picture by means of a summarizing statement, or by expressing a dominant and consistent attitude toward the images he is describing.

Do you have a favorite brook or river? You could make a list of the changes in its moods, and then a list of the characteristic things that happen along its banks, morning, daytime, evening and night. There is your material for a descriptive sketch like this one of the Carmel River:

The Carmel is a lovely little river. It isn't very long but in its course it has everything a river should have. It rises in the mountains, and tumbles down a while, runs through shallows, is dammed to make a lake, spills over the dam, crackles among round boulders, wanders lazily under syca-mores, spills into pools where trout live, drops in against banks where crayfish live. In the winter it becomes a torrent, a mean little fierce river, and in the summer it is a place for children to wade in and for fishermen to wander in. Frogs blink from its banks and the deep ferns grow beside it. Deer and foxes come to drink from it, secretly in the morning and evening, and now and then a mountain lion crouched flat laps its water. The farms of the rich little valley back up to the river and take its water for the orchards and the vegetables. The quail call beside it and the wild doves come whistling in at dusk. Raccoons pace its edges looking for frogs. It's everything a river should be.

—JOHN STEINBECK, *Cannery Row*

Sometimes an effective general description of a complex scene can be clarified by emphasizing contrasts between the present occasion and some former time more familiar to the reader. Here a journalist describes the look of a modern army camp by using this device of contrast:

From the road, the camp seemed quiet, clean, almost deserted. Gone were the tent cities, the mud roads, the steam locomotive acting as a temporary boiler plant for a new hospital. The white barracks of World War II were still there, but alongside them now were the brick barracks, built to house a whole company instead of a platoon.

And indoors things had changed. Instead of a single room filled with cots, walls now gave each set of four bunks almost the privacy of a room. Instead of bare chairs in a day room, this one had the soft chairs and the relaxed look of a recreation room at a resort hotel. Instead of long wooden tables in a drab mess hall, it had separate tables, each seating four soldiers. There were tablecloths, curtains, photomurals in color, and the word was out that china dishes would soon replace metal trays. But the new pressed meat tasted like the old Spam, and the G. I. coffee had aged, but not changed.

—RALPH G. MARTIN, *"An Old Soldier Looks at the New Army"*

Occupations. The work you have done during your vacations, the job that you have while attending college, the profession you expect to enter after you leave college—all offer material for interesting discussion. Probably the last named topic, however, is the most difficult and dangerous. Most students, even if they have determined on a future occupation, necessarily speak of it in vague terms because they have experienced so little of its details and complexities. A general rule: it's hard to write about what you don't know about.

One familiar decision that faces many students seeking a profession is whether to concentrate on the scientific and engineering

[119]

side of life or on those occupations that do not involve such technical training. The relation here with immediate choices in undergraduate education is of course obvious. Anyone facing such decisions, and trying to write about them, might ponder the following defense of the humanistic side of things. It was written, needless to say, by a nonscientist!

The scientist indeed may be less qualified than the nonscientist to talk outside his field, for his education is likely to have become rigorously narrow. Unless he has had the good fortune to attend an old-fashioned liberal arts college, he will have had the most superficial and hurried contact with the social sciences and humanities. If he has gone to one of the larger colleges of engineering, many of which are now turning out scientists as well as engineers, his contact may well have been nonexistent, for many such schools design special humanities and social-science courses which have been dehydrated of their most vital content. He will not know the facts and concepts of history or sociology or the ideas and values of literature or philosophy. Even if the scientist's undergraduate studies were sufficiently humane and liberal, the world he moves in makes for narrowness and, except in his own discipline, for shallowness. A physical chemist, lamenting his restricted focus, once complained to me in desperation that he can scarcely keep up with the work being done in his particular specialty, let alone in physical chemistry itself; he long ago gave up hope of keeping up with the whole of chemistry. His only reading outside chemistry since his one undergraduate course in humanities was for an inter-disciplinary honors class he was assigned to for one year.

—MORRIS FREEDMAN, *Confessions of a Conformist*

The Profile. A profile is a short biographical sketch that depends for its effect on a few well-chosen, vivid facts and details. The subject of a successful profile need not be famous—or notorious; as a matter of fact, the writer of a profile often takes some totally obscure person and tries to make the reader feel that that person is worth knowing. On the other hand, many profiles, like some of those in *The New Yorker*, are of celebrities. You may take your choice.

One possible project is to write a profile of a distinguished citizen in your community, one whom you have known fairly well. Select one you have liked and admired. Go to the library and consult some local "who's who" for background facts. Then organize your profile on the basis of a number of the following divisions.

    I. An interview, in which you introduce your subject and give us a quick picture of his appearance
   II. A glimpse of him at work
  III. A transition to the facts about his career, education, and so on
  IV. His dominant traits
   V. A typical professional performance (your big scene)
  VI. What others say about him

You need not use all of these divisions, but if you want to compress, remember that I, III, and V are essential.

If you want to do a more ambitious biographical piece, one that will take you to some of the reference books in the library, try writing a biographical sketch of (1) the author of a book you are reading; (2) a pioneer of your locality; (3) the man who represents you in Congress; (4) a well-known scientist who is connected with your college or university. You will find more detailed assistance for writing such papers in Chapter 6. Be careful to give all your borrowed information in your own words!

When Senator John F. Kennedy, shortly before he became president, wrote his book about several distinguished members of the Senate over the years, he called the book *Profiles in Courage*, and he was using the word *Profiles* in this more ambitious sense. Here is a passage from his profile of Senator Robert A. Taft, in which you will note the combination of incidents, quotations from others, and personal testimony from the writer's own experience that can make a persuasive piece of writing in this genre.

So Bob Taft, as his biographer has described it, was "born to integrity." He was known in the Senate as a man who never broke an agreement, who never compromised his deeply felt Republican principles, who never practiced political deception. His bitter public enemy, Harry Truman, would say when the Senator died: "He and I did not agree on public policy, but he knew where I stood and I knew where he stood. We need intellectually honest men like Senator Taft." Examples of his candor are endless and startling. The Ohioan once told a group in the heart of Republican farm territory that farm prices were too high; and he told still another farm group that "he was tired of seeing all these people riding in

Cadillacs." His support of an extensive Federal housing program caused a colleague to remark: "I hear the Socialists have gotten to Bob Taft." He informed an important political associate who cherished a commendatory message signed by Taft that his assistant "sent those things out by the dozen" without the Senator ever seeing, much less signing them. And a colleague recalls that he did not reject the ideas of his friends by gentle indirection, but by coldly and unhesitatingly terming them "nonsense." "He had," as William S. White has written, "a luminous candor of purpose that was extraordinarily refreshing in a chamber not altogether devoted to candor."

It would be a mistake, however, to conclude from this that Senator Taft was cold and abrupt in his personal relationships. I recall, from my own very brief service with him in the Senate and on the Senate Labor Committee in the last months of his life, my strong impression of a surprising and unusual personal charm, and a disarming simplicity of manner. It was these qualities, combined with an unflinching courage which he exhibited throughout his entire life and most especially in his last days, that bound his adherents to him with unbreakable ties.

—JOHN F. KENNEDY, *Profiles in Courage*

The Brief, Informal Book Review. If your instructor wishes you to produce a formal analysis or critical interpretation of a piece of literature, he will probably give you explicit directions to follow. But there is another sort of informal report, based on reading, that is enjoying increasing popularity in our time. More and more in recent years, the tempo of book publication has increased to the point where no one can expect to read all the new books, even those restricted to a particular field of interest. Readers therefore must depend on the reports of others in order to select the particular books they may want to buy and read. To meet this demand for quick and ready information, there has developed in newspapers and magazines a special kind of review: a very short, informal description of a book, with some brief information about the author, and at least an implied evaluation of his work. You will find such brief reports in *Time,* in *The New Yorker,* and in several other magazines and newspapers that are likely to reach serious readers of books.

Sometimes such an informal review can be accomplished—or at least attempted—in a single paragraph. In the example below you will note the almost breezy tone adopted by the anonymous reviewer. Thus he speaks of armies being "licked" instead of defeated, and he humorously speaks of Russia as an "amoeba" that "doesn't mind amputations." But beneath the informality there is much serious purpose, and much important information is presented in quick and palatable form.

> Seven Roads to Moscow, by Lieutenant-Colonel W. G. F. Jackson (Philosophical Library). This is an interesting study of all the invasions of Russia, written by a British Army officer who has taught at the Royal Staff College and at Sandhurst. During the Middle Ages, Russia was successfully invaded a few times, but in the eighteenth, nineteenth, and twentieth centuries, Charles XII of Sweden, Napoleon, and Hitler all tried it and were licked. The story of their campaigns, which Colonel Jackson tells in considerable detail, is an awe-inspiring record of military ineptitude. The invaders lopped off huge stretches of territory and only then discovered that Russia, like an amoeba, doesn't mind amputations. The Russian armies retreated, wondering why they had not been able to stop the enemy at the border; these confused retreats later looked like wisdom, because by the time the Russians were ready to counterattack, the invaders were exhausted from chasing them. Since the French imagined they could avoid the mistakes that the Swedes had made, and the Germans were certain they would avoid the mistakes that the French had made, and none of them did anything except make mistakes, Colonel Jackson's moral—don't invade Russia—seems unimpeachable.[1]
>
> —*The New Yorker*, January 24, 1959

In attempting such a brief review yourself, you should keep in mind at least three purposes. First, you should indicate something of the author's reputation or qualifications. Second, you should carefully but in large strokes sketch the contents of the book. Third, you should indicate by some evaluative remark your notion of the author's success. In the review above, for example, it is clear from some of the adjectives ("an interesting study," "seems unimpeachable") that this is a favorable judgment.

Directions, Processes, Organizations. The "how to do it" and "how it was done" literature of America is impressive in extent, and some of it, at least, is impressive in literary quality. The ability to give accurate directions is extremely important and should be cultivated just as strictly as the more "creative" kinds of writing. Here are a few suggestions that you may find useful:

---

[1] Reprinted by permission. Copr. © 1959 The New Yorker Magazine, Inc.

1. Take two points rather far apart in your city, such as your home in the suburbs and a downtown theater. Write a short paper of directions in which you tell a total stranger to the city how to reach your home by starting from the point downtown. Do *not* once use any of the directions of the compass—north, east, south, west—in your explanation. Depend entirely on an accurate record of landmarks and distances.

2. Explain to an unmechanical friend how to start and drive a farm tractor. Do not use a single technical term without explaining it in clear, untechnical language.

3. Tell one of your younger friends what he is to do to register in college. Take him from one building to another, and explain every step of the procedure in words that he cannot fail to understand.

An explanation of a process is not necessarily a set of directions to be followed by someone. Thousands of such explanations are written merely because there are people who like to know how things work. If you try one of the following subjects, you might try making it an interesting explanation as well as a set of directions to be followed:

1. Measuring wind velocity	6. Format in the school paper
2. Photographing children	7. How to model clothes
3. Coming about in a sailboat	8. Operating an elevator
4. How to use a fly rod	9. Transplanting wild flowers
5. Making Christmas cards	10. Making a banana split

An explanation of an organization calls for somewhat more extensive treatment, in many cases, than an explanation of a process. It is a particularly effective device for practicing outlining techniques, for you must be careful that your divisions are coordinate and that they are mutually exclusive and not overlapping. Here are a few topics that you might use:

1. A military unit	6. Camp Fire Girls or Girl Scouts
2. Your fraternity or sorority	
3. The Department of State	7. The 4-H clubs
4. An army induction center	8. A consumers' cooperative
5. A city police department	9. A county fair
	10. An insurance company

One world of activity in which "how to do it" writing plays an important role is sports. Here the problem of expressing in precise language just what one does with one's own body is crucial. Following are some directions for performing the flutter kick in swimming:

In the flutter, the water is squeezed, thrust, and kicked away, imparting a forward drive. It is most effective when the power comes from the hips and thighs, the rest of the legs controlled but relaxed, the knees slightly bent, the ankles loose. The ankles may be turned slightly inward in pigeon-toed fashion and should be completely relaxed so that they flop loosely, the toes pointed to eliminate resistance.

The kick is, of course, a series of beats, the legs moving alternately up and down. As it is lifted toward the surface, the leg is relaxed at the knee and bends slightly, the bend increasing until the leg is near the surface. The downward thrust is a whiplash motion in which the whole leg is straightened, imparting a snap to the lower leg and the ankle. The effect is to drive the water down along the thighs and snap it away; or, to look at it in another way, the legs both in the upward and in the downward beat catch hold of the water and drive the body forward.

The first rule for practicing the flutter kick is to make the thighs do the lifting and thrusting. If those big muscles in the thighs and lower back do the work, the kick will not be as tiring as it would be if it were primarily a knee kick, incorrectly used by many swimmers. By applying force from his thighs, the swimmer will give an undulating movement to his legs somewhat like that of a piece of rope when one end of it is snapped. At first there should be little, if any, bending of the knees. The swimmer can let his legs twist inward slightly, rolling the knees closer together and pointing the toes inward and downward.

—HAROLD S. ULEN AND GUY LARCOM, JR., *The Complete Swimmer*

A good test of a "how to do it" article is this: can you, from reading it, put the process into operation yourself? Can you, in a word, *do* it? This test is particularly appropriate when you are reading an account of a process that is utterly unfamiliar to you.

Here is Vilhjalmur Stefansson's explanation of the method used by Eskimos in catching fish under ice:

In getting ready to fish through ice you fasten your floats to one edge of the net and your sinkers to the other, so that one edge of the net shall be held at the surface of the water and the other down vertically. Then you cut two holes in the ice about forty feet apart (for that is a common

[125]

length for Eskimo nets) and each a foot or eighteen inches in diameter. Between these two holes you cut a series of smaller holes just big enough to stick your arm into the water, and perhaps six to eight feet apart. Next you take a stick of dry, buoyant wood that is eight or ten feet long. You shove it down through one of the end holes until it is all in the water, when it floats up and rises against the ice. You have a string tied to the stick and this stick you fasten to one end of the net. Then you lay the string so that, while one end is still visible at your hole, the other end is visible below the next hole six or eight feet away. You now go to the second hole, put your hand into the water and slide the stick along under the ice until you can see it through the third hole. The stick, of course, pulls the string in after it and by the time you have worked the stick along to the furthest hole your net is set. You now take a rope that is about ten feet longer than the net and tie each end of the rope to one end of the net so as to make an "endless chain," the net being under the water and the rope on top of the ice.

During the night the holes all freeze over. You allow the small holes to remain frozen permanently but each time you go out to tend the net you open the two end holes and pull the net out of one of them. As you pull the net out the rope part of your endless chain is pulled into the water. When you have picked all the fish out of the net, you pull on your rope and thus drag the net back into the water.

—Vilhjalmur Stefansson, *Hunters of the Great North*

As we have said, a complex operation can be described with the purpose of putting the reader into a position to perform it himself. That is the implication in Stefansson's account, as his repeated *you* suggests. Often, however, and especially in cases involving modern pieces of machinery, a description is written not for the user, but for the layman, to give him at least some sense of how a complicated mechanism operates. In the following description of a space suit by an astronaut, observe how the language is addressed not to fellow-astronauts, but to you and me. How would the language be different if this were an official manual to be used for training purposes?

Normally, unless the cabin pressure fails and we are threatened with a case of the bends—which would almost certainly be fatal—the suit serves mainly to keep us ventilated and provides us with a constantly refreshed supply of oxygen to breathe. It is a beautifully contrived mechanical environment. A steady stream of pure oxygen—which emanates from one of the two volleyball-size flasks we have mentioned earlier—enters the suit through the inlet valve near the waist. We plug this valve in as soon as we enter the capsule. The oxygen then circulates through the entire suit and reaches all of our extremities to cool them off. A series of waffle-weave patches on our long-john underwear helps to keep the oxygen moving. The oxygen finally makes its exit through an outlet located near our right ear near the helmet. As it flows out, the oxygen takes with it whatever body odors, perspiration, carbon dioxide, water and other waste matter—like nasal discharge or bits of hair—it has picked up on its tour. The water and CO_2, of course, are normal by-products of the pilot's metabolism. The system dumps all of this into a marvelous bit of plumbing which traps out the waste and uses an electric fan to push the tired gas over a bed of activated charcoal. This filters out the odors and then the gas goes on through two tanks of lithium hydroxide to remove the deadly carbon dioxide. When it has been thoroughly cleaned, the oxygen then goes into a cooling device which removes the excess heat which it has picked up from our bodies. The hot gas is cooled by conduction in a heat exchanger. Here water takes up much of the heat, which is then discharged out of the capsule in the form of a puff of steam. One of the many things we have to worry about on a flight, incidentally, is making sure that this steam duct does not freeze up because of excess water flowing through the system. If that happened, the water would not get converted readily into steam, the steam duct would clog up and cease functioning, and so would the delicate systems which keep the Astronaut and his cabin cool. A device which Rube Goldberg himself would be proud of takes care of droplets of water which collect in the suit circuit at this point. The drops are soaked up by a little sponge which is struck by a small piston every thirty minutes to squeeze the water out and dump it into a storage tank. This, incidentally, is our emergency supply of drinking water. As soon as the oxygen has been purged of water, waste, odors, and carbon dioxide, it flows back into the suit and starts the same tour all over again. While all this is going on, a much simpler process is taking place in the separate atmosphere of the cabin. Here, a fan and a heat exchanger keep the cabin ventilated and cool. If the oxygen should start leaking from the cabin system, it can be replenished from the oxygen in the suit—after the Astronaut has had a chance to breathe it first.

—WALTER M. SCHIRRA, JR., *We Seven*

Local Color. The literature of travel, describing places unknown to the reader, has a long and distinguished history. Related to it is the growth of local-color writing, in nineteenth-century America, when people came to realize that their own communities were exotic and interesting in their own right. Now every section of America has its literature of praise and interpretation. But works of travel and local color have had to change their emphasis in our own time, when increased mobility, general education, movies, and television have brought vividly to our senses the scenes of places formerly unknown. As a result, much writing about local color must now assume a considerable factual knowledge on the part of the reader, and the author nowadays may try instead to give his reader some special sense of the *feel* of the place. That at any rate is the way the well-known New York writer, E. B. White, goes at a description of his favorite city:

There are roughly three New Yorks. There is, first, the New York of the man or woman who was born here, who takes the city for granted and accepts its size and its turbulence as natural and inevitable. Second, there is the New York of the commuter—the city that is devoured by locusts each day and spat out each night. Third, there is the New York of the person who was born somewhere else and came to New York in quest of something. Of these three trembling cities the greatest is the last—the city of final destination, the city that is a goal. It is this third city that accounts for New York's high-strung disposition, its poetical deportment, its dedication to the arts, and its incomparable achievements. Commuters give the city its tidal restlessness; natives give it solidity and continuity; but the settlers give it passion. And whether it is a farmer arriving from Italy to set up a small grocery store in a slum, or a young girl arriving from a small town in Mississippi to escape the indignity of being observed by her neighbors, or a boy arriving from the Corn Belt with a manuscript in his suitcase and a pain in his heart, it makes no difference: each embraces New York with the intense excitement of first love, each absorbs New York with the fresh eyes of an adventurer, each generates heat and light to dwarf the Consolidated Edison Company.

—E. B. WHITE, *Here Is New York*

There is always one's home town, a subject of infinite possibilities. You could investigate the history of your community and write a paper on some phase of it, such as the pioneer days, the coming of the railroad, Civil War days. You could investigate local science—geology, botany, and so on—and write an article on the geologic structure of the region, the birds of the region, or the characteristic vegetation. Or, as in the passage you have just read, you could assume much of this information on the part of your reader and try for something more literary.

Here are some further suggestions for the writing of compositions about one's community:

1. Cultural resources
2. The teen-agers
3. What people do for a living
4. Contact with the past
5. Politics and government
6. The school system
7. Recreation: parks, etc.
8. Industrial domination
9. Commuters .
10. Relation to other urban centers

The Personal Essay. A good deal of the reading and writing we have to do in this world, as every student knows, seems to be terribly serious, solemn, and pretentious. Every textbook (including this one) conveys the depressing implication, "Now this is important—you must *get* it!" But it might be wholesome to conclude this collection of various types of writing by offering another kind of tone altogether. Here is a light personal essay, which, if it is out to prove anything at all, is doing so with considerable ease and good humor. The process of composing such a piece, though, is just as difficult and disciplined an activity as any other composing.

Ladies on the Highway

That men are wonderful is a proposition I will defend to the death. Honest, brave, talented, strong and handsome, they are my favorite gender. Consider the things men can do better than women—mend the plumbing, cook, invent atom bombs, design the Empire waistline and run the four-minute mile. They can throw a ball overhand. They can grow a beard. In fact, I can think of only two accomplishments at which women excel. Having babies is one.

The other is driving an automobile.

Don't misunderstand me. Some of my best friends are male drivers. And they seldom go to sleep at the wheel or drive 90 on a 45-an-hour road or commit any other of the sins of which statistics accuse them. But insurance companies have been busy as bees proving that I don't get around among the right people.

New York State—where I live—has even made it expensive to have sons. Car insurance costs much more if there are men in the family under

25 driving than if there are only women. Obviously the female of the species make the best chauffeurs.

They ought to. They get the most practice. Aside from truck- and taxi-drivers, it is women who really handle the cars of the nation. For five days of the week they are in command—slipping cleverly through traffic on their thousand errands, parking neatly in front of the chain stores, ferrying their husbands to and from commuting trains, driving the young to schools and dentists and dancing classes and Scout meetings. It is only on Saturdays and Sundays that men get their innings, not to speak of their outings, and it is over week ends when most of the catastrophes occur.

Not that men are responsible for *all* the accidents. Some are caused by women—by the little blonde on the sidewalk at whom the driver feels impelled to whistle. Or by the pretty girl sitting in the front seat for whom he wants to show off his skill, his eagle eye, and the way he can pull ahead of the fellow in the red sports car.

But it isn't caution and practice alone which make the difference between the sexes. It's chiefly an attitude of mind. Women—in my opinion —are the practical people. To them a car is a means of transportation, a gadget more useful, perhaps, than a dishwasher or a can opener, but no more romantic. It is something in which we carry the sheets to the laundry, pick up Johnnie at kindergarten and lug home those rose bushes.

Men, the dear, sentimental creatures, feel otherwise. Automobiles are more than property. They are their shining chariots, the objects of their affections. A man loves his car the way the Lone Ranger loves his horse, and he feels for its honor on the road. No one must out-weave or out-race him. No one must get off to a better jack-rabbit start. And no one, but no one, must tell him anything while he's driving. My own husband, ordinarily the most good-tempered of men, becomes a tyrant behind the wheel.

"Shouldn't we bear south here?" I inquire meekly on our Saturday trips to the country. Or, "Honey, there's a gray convertible trying to pass."

"Who's driving!" he snarls like Simon Legree, veering stubbornly north or avoiding, by a hair, being run into.

Women drivers, on the other hand, *take* advice. They are used to taking it, having had it pressed on them all their lives by their mothers, teachers, beaus, husbands, and eventually their children. And when they don't know their routes exactly, they inquire at service stations, from passers-by, from traffic officers. But men hate to ask and, when they are forced to do so, seldom listen.

Have you ever overheard a woman taking down directions on the phone? "Yes," she says affably. "I understand. I drive up that pretty road to the Danbury turn-off. Then I bear left at the little antique shoppe that used to be a barn—yellow with blue shutters. Then right at a meadow with two beech trees in it, and a couple of black cows. Up a little lane, just a tiny way beyond a cornfield, and that's your place. Yes. With a Tiffany-glass carriage lamp in front. Fine. I won't have any trouble." Nor does she.

A man has too much pride to take such precautions. "O.K." he says impatiently. "Two point seven miles off the Post Road. A left, a rotary, another left. Six point three to—oh, never mind. I'll look it up on the map."

When they don't insist on traveling by ear, men travel by chart. I've nothing against road maps, really, except the way they clutter up the glove compartment where I like to keep tissues and sun glasses. But men have a furtive passion for them.

When my husband and I are planning a trip, he doesn't rush out like me to buy luggage and a new wardrobe. He shops for maps. For days ahead of time he studies them dotingly; then I am forced to study them en route. Many a bitter journey have I taken past the finest scenery in America with my eyes glued to a collection of black and red squiggles on a road map, instead of on the forest and canyons we had come all the way across the country to behold.

"Look!"I cry to him as we rush up some burning autumn lane. "Aren't the trees glorious!"

"What does the map say?" he mutters. "I've marked a covered bridge about a quarter of a mile along here. That's where we turn."

If we should ever approach the Pearly Gates together, I know exactly how the conversation will run. "See all the pretty stars," I'll be murmuring happily. "And, oh, do look over there! Isn't that the City of Gold?"

"Never mind your golden cities," he'll warn me sternly, as he nearly collides with a meteor. "Just keep your eye on the map."

—Phyllis McGinley

PROBLEMS OF WRITING AND REVISING

Nature of the Plan or Outline

Every paper written needs a plan, although some plans spend their life cycles in the heads of the writers without ever emerging on paper in the form of outlines. Some plans take the form of a series of notes on the back of an old envelope. The experienced writer may plan almost subconsciously; some writers say that they do all their outlining in their heads, whereas others say that they write out elaborate outlines on paper. But the inexperienced writer has everything to gain by using paper and pencil to record and clarify the planning that goes on in his head. Even when a paper is written offhand, as the outpouring of an inspired idea, an outline of the finished paper is an excellent check for organization and logic. If there are flaws in the product of the writer's inspiration, an outline may reveal them.

The Informal Outline.   A short paper should have a short outline. In fact, a few notes on a scrap of paper might do well enough. Let us illustrate: You plan to write a thoughtful little essay on childhood memories. You decide to begin by commenting on the difficulty of remembering things that at the time must have been very vivid to you. Then you go as far back as you can into your childhood and tell a few of the things you remember. You close with a paragraph of comment on the possible reasons why those things and not a million others have remained in your memory. A very poignant and appealing little essay may be written in this way—and yet what slaughter of wistful details could result if this material were forced into a formal outline!

The Process of Synthesis.   Making an outline is often spoken of as a process of dividing a subject. It is assumed that the thought mass exists in its entirety in the writer's mind, and in preparing it for the market he methodically slices it up into pieces called topics and subtopics. That may be true for some. For most of us outlining is a process of synthesis, not division. We usually begin with a problem and the necessity of doing something about it. Our first suggestion may be an ill-favored and disreputable little idea. We pull it out and look it over. It seems promising—possibly. But then we look about again—by thinking, by reading, by observing—and pull out other ideas to add to it. We jot down these ideas on paper. Some writers use file cards, which they can later organize in coherent order. Pretty soon, if we are fortunate. we have enough, or perhaps more than enough for our purpose. Then and only then can we begin to select and arrange and divide.

Let us remind ourselves here that in this process of writing a paper or a speech many things go on at the same time. We do not select a subject first, limit the subject second, plan next, outline next, and so on. We may think of a good illustration—and write it down quickly before it fades away; we are conscious of the persons who will read what we say; we have a sudden inspiration of a clever opening paragraph; we think of another important idea that just has to have a place somewhere; we add another thought brick to the structure. And so our essay grows. But the process cannot be explained in that way.

Order of Presentation. The order in which you present your material to your reader will depend partly on what you have to say and partly on the sort of reader you are addressing. The following paragraphs will suggest four among many possible ways of constructing order.

The Chronological Order. If you are telling how something is made, how a game is played, how a system grew or developed in the course of time, you will naturally use the order of happening, called the chronological order. In topics such as the following the chronological order is inherent in the material: how to clean a rifle, how to organize and manage a formal dance, how to prepare for a final examination, how to operate a bulldozer, the history of tennis, the development of consumers' cooperatives, learning how to tap-dance. When a subject does not naturally call for chronological order, you can often achieve a clearer presentation by changing your approach so that you can use the order of time.

The Inductive Order (Order of Easy Acceptance). Occasionally you may gently lead your reader toward an unpalatable idea by starting with a presentation of a number of facts, instances, or observations that support your main idea. This technique may be used where it is necessary to prepare a reader's mind for a new idea, but inasmuch as most articles are read quickly, the device of surprise has limited uses. It can be tried, however. For instance, if you are advocating the adoption of an honor system in your school, you may get a more favorable response from your readers if you convince them first that a system of strict, paternalistic supervision has resulted in widespread dishonesty. If you are urging the establishment of teen-age night clubs, you can begin by picturing the existing undesirable conditions.

Order of Enumeration. If you can divide your subject into several parts of equal importance, you may indicate the division in your opening paragraph and then discuss the parts one by one. We shall call this an order of enumeration. "Communism differs from socialism in four important aspects," you begin. "Before the Diesel engine could be used in light motor cars, automotive engineers had to solve the following three problems." You can see from such examples how a considerable number of subjects will adapt themselves to this sort of treatment. You must remember, however, that a formal enumeration of parts implies a serious and formal treatment of the subject.

Order of Easy Comprehension. If your subject is an organization, or a complicated piece of machinery, or an idea hard to grasp, you may start with the simple elements of the subject and gradually work toward those more difficult to understand. This could be called an order from easy to hard, or from known to unknown.

Beginnings and Endings

Every writer faced with the task of setting his ideas down on paper is conscious of the overwhelming importance of an effective beginning. It is like first meetings—the first interview with your employer, the first introduction to your mother-in-law. There is something terrifying about it simply because it must be got over with first. In writing, students spend entirely too much time getting started.

"The best way to begin is to begin. Do not write introductions. Just plunge in." All this is sound advice, but not very helpful to the beginner. One might as well tell him to learn to dance by plunging in—some persons do dance that way, after all. One needs to know what to do after he plunges in. Another piece of advice, possibly more helpful, goes this way: "Just write down anything about your subject. Keep going until you get well into your first main topic. Then in revision cross out the first two paragraphs."

There are, however, a number of specific devices that a writer may use to introduce his subject appropriately and interestingly, just as there are similar devices for the easier task of appropriately ending his paper. Anyone glancing over a recent file of a serious magazine in which various kinds of articles appear—*Harper's*, for instance—is sure to find repeated examples of particular techniques for beginning as well as for ending. As the following selections will show, there is usually a close logical and rhetorical relation between the two. The moral for the student is clear: he who ends his paper without some kind of reference to his beginning is likely to give his reader a scattered or diffuse impression of his argument. To connect your beginning and ending is one obvious way to give your paper *organization*.

Eight possible ways to begin (among many) are illustrated below.[2] In each case the author's ending is also quoted. Their relation is worth study. As always, your choice of any particular technique depends not only on personal taste, but on the kind of article you are writing and the kind of reader you are addressing. In studying these illustrations, note how the various beginnings and endings are in part responses to the particular subject and tone that the author has chosen.

The Dramatized Example or Incident. A familiar opening is a dramatized example or incident from which a larger generalization is to emerge. Here is a case of such an introduction, in the first few sentences of an article on the status of women in Japan.

> On every floor of Tokyo's crowded department stores, near every escalator, a graceful Japanese girl in a crisp, white-collared uniform stands and bows to customers as they ride up. Hour by hour she bows and murmurs polite greetings—several thousand times a day.
> The Japanese take such girls' jobs for granted.

The author then proceeds to argue, from this and other evidence, that the status of women in Japan leaves a good deal to be

[2] All selections are from *Harper's Magazine*, January–October 1963. See also the discussion of introductory paragraphs in Chapter 4.

desired. She concludes, after summarizing a few changes during Japan's recent past, by returning to her thesis.

But so far, there are still very few cracks in the established order. And in my opinion, until the old order changeth, Japan is no place for a woman.

—MAYA PINES, "Lucky American Women"

The Anecdote.   A related technique is to begin with an anecdote, true or fictitious, but told in the manner of the story-teller. Here is a case where an anecdote, presumably factual, introduces the very serious argument the author is about to make.

Not long ago, Hans Thirring, the eminent Austrian physicist, made a $1,000 wager with Fred L. Whipple, the equally eminent American astronomer, on the chance of man's reaching the moon during the 1960s. Thirring, normally an optimist, bet he wouldn't.

The author goes on from this introduction to issue a warning against a hasty and dangerous race to the moon. He concludes by repeating his point about the perils of such a race.

In the meantime, it would be folly if we let the pressures of the moon race needlessly endanger the lives of brave men.

—CARL DREHER, "Martyrs on the Moon"

The Autobiographical Incident.   A similar opening technique is the exemplary incident taken from a moment in the author's own life. Here a writer conducts a discussion of modern Alaska by using the framework of a day's travel by dog-sled in which he personally participated.

One winter morning, Eelyoopuk—my Eskimo companion—and I finished a hefty breakfast of oatmeal porridge and tea at his house in the village of Kivalina on the northwestern coast of Alaska. The sun was still below the horizon when we went out into the half-light of the Arctic dawn and slid the twelve-foot freight sled into position for loading.

Retaining this framework of the day's journey, the article ends with nightfall, still in the first person.

Conversation in the tent finally died and we were nodding over our empty tea-mugs. We buttoned up the camp for the night, then wriggled into our sleeping bags. Tomorrow, weather permitting, we would reach our destination.

—William O. Pruitt, Jr., "Arctic Trails"

The Stereotype Refuted. A common device for opening an essay is to summarize stereotyped beliefs about a given subject, beliefs that the author is about to refute. Here is a typical gambit of this sort.

We in the West cherish our myths about the Arabs. One favorite is of the Bedouins, the Noble Savages of a considerable literature produced by European romantics who took spiritual refuge among them as the coal dust thickened over northern skies and the blunt yeomen of Europe transformed themselves into drab factory hands.

Go visit a Bedouin today on his native ground. . . .

The author then proceeds to demolish this myth, and to describe the Bedouins as (in his judgment) they really are. He ends by returning to his initial reference to our inadequate stereotypes, but now he somewhat qualifies his attack.

Reality is always complex, and stereotypes capture quite a lot of it. But they are never the whole story.

—Keith Williams, "The Real Arabs"

The Shock Opening (Solemn). A variation on the use of the stereotype is to begin an essay with a surprising or even shocking statement, one that is distinctly *not* a stereotype. Sometimes such a beginning may take the form of open hostility toward some public official or other authority, by making an unexpected charge, as in this case.

This spring Congressman Wayne N. Aspinall of Colorado intends once more to use his position as Chairman of the Committee on Internal and Insular Affairs to frustrate the expressed will of the American people.

Then, having lured us into his argument with this shocker, the author must document his charges, and he concludes by reminding us again of the importarce, in his eyes, of the sin being committed—in this case the threatened loss of public forest lands. He does so by the familiar device of the rhetorical question, which can be answered only one way.

Piecemeal action now is inevitably too little and too late. We need an overall wilderness system such as the Wilderness Bill would provide. Are we going to be deprived of it by another parliamentary trick?

    —PAUL BROOKS, "Congressman Aspinall Vs. the People of the United States"

The Shock Opening (Not So Solemn). Another kind of shock opening, far less brassy in tone, can be achieved by putting forward an argument that is absurd on the face of it. Can he mean it? we ask. Here is a woman suggesting, with apparent seriousness, that the raccoon should be a national emblem, right alongside the eagle!

People who have studied raccoons—and there are very few of them —have proposed that this animal join the eagle as an American emblem. Why not a national mammal as well as a national bird? Raccoons certainly qualify.

But as the author goes on with this proposition, she comes to her senses and ends her essay by refuting the argument she started with. Since the argument was, we realize, impractical if not absurd anyway, the turnabout is perfectly acceptable.

Coons remain hillbillies at heart and will never make a respectable national emblem. For there is in them a note of wild laughter and tall talk (you can see it in their faces), of joyous, anarchic liberty which may turn out to be more American than any eagle's pomp.

    —POLLY REDFORD, "Our Most American Animal"

Questions to Be Answered. We spoke previously of the rhetorical question, the question with only one possible answer, as an ending technique. It is also familiar as a beginning. But even more familiar, and clearly appropriate for many kinds of serious analytical essays, is to begin by asking questions that do not have easy answers. The effort to provide answers, then, becomes the central concern of the essay. Here is an example, in the complex fields of politics and economics.

What is fast becoming a traditional American rite—the periodic hassle over steel prices—has again brought into the open some of the most troubling questions that American businessmen have to face. How can an executive—with the best will in the world—be sure that he is acting in the public interest? How can he tell what it is? And what should he do if his duty to the public conflicts with his idea of his duty to his stockholders?

In this case the author proceeds to make a number of suggestions that in his opinion would improve the situation. He concludes, in rather too complex a sentence, as follows.

Some new arrangements like these will have to be devised if the lighting that perfect competition once provided for economic decisions is to be restored to those areas of concentrated power that cannot and should not be broken up.

—BERNARD D. NOSSITER, "The Troubled Conscience of American Business"

The Appeal of Importance. In all the beginnings we have discussed, it has been the author's responsibility to convince his reader that the article will be worth his time, that it is important or significant or amusing. Sometimes, instead of asking questions or telling stories to lure his reader in, an author may simply *tell* his reader that his subject is important.

Few scientific developments could surpass in importance a determination of how the brain achieves its remarkable results. A detailed explanation is undoubtedly many years away. However, in the laboratories of life scientists and the operating rooms of brain surgeons, important discoveries are beginning to penetrate the mystery.

After arguing that our subjective sensations may turn out to be determined in a predictable way by the brain's physical conditions, the author ends his essay by again overtly reminding us of the importance of what he is telling us.

It would be hard to imagine a development of more far-reaching importance to science and philosophy. Yet it could come as a consequence of research on memory and the brain.

—DEAN E. WOOLDRIDGE, "Man's Mysterious Memory Machine"

Writing the Paper

After you have thought your subject through, worked it over in your mind, laid out your general plan, and supplied as many details as you can, you will probably want to write rapidly without pausing too often to ponder over the perfect sentence or the exact word. Write rapidly if that is the way you write naturally. Write slowly and carefully if slow and careful writing is your best method. Among professional writers no two work alike. Some write fast and revise slowly, changing words and phrases, crossing out and rewriting, copying the revised manuscript and then rewriting again, sometimes as many as fifteen times. Some chisel out every word in creative agony in their first draft—and never revise.

Although no two writers use an outline alike, the apprentice writer can profit, here as elsewhere, by observing the practice of the skilled writer. A short outline for a short paper is probably so well fixed in the writer's mind by the time he has finished it that he can give it a quick survey, lay it aside, and proceed to write his paper from memory. In the composition of a long paper with a complex outline, especially when the writing is done from notes, it is well to study the notes and the section of the outline dealing with a small unit, lay both aside for the time, and write from memory. The writer does go back—and should, too—for a recheck of his material before his revision of his first draft. There is such a thing as an outline-ridden paper. A writer gives himself freedom to add illustrations, examples, and typical cases that do not show in the outline. He should also have the freedom to cut if that seems best in the writing.

Proportion. The amount of space that you give to each of the topics in your paper will depend on what you have to say and on your purpose in writing.

In general, certain things are unimportant. Long, rambling beginnings, formal conclusions, and digressions from the central idea should be severely pruned or grubbed out entirely.

As for the rest, the principle is simple. Keeping in mind the old rule of "an interesting beginning and a strong ending," you will give relatively more space to the important topic that you have saved for the end of your paper. That topic is the fact or idea that you want to stress, both by placing it at the end and by saying more about it. You may, of course, introduce your last topic by some such phrase as, "And, finally, the most important . . . ," but telling your reader that an idea is most important is not the same as making him think and feel that it is. (We have suggested this difference in our example number 8 in "Beginnings and Endings.") You need concrete details. You need evidence. And you also need to allow a certain amount of time for the idea to sink into your reader's mind.

Substance: Use of Details.   To reach the mind of your reader, then, to make him understand and to persuade him to accept, you must usually be specific and concrete. Generalities seldom convince. A vague essay on the need for international understanding and cooperation may earn a reader's passive mental agreement, but a concrete picture in terms of someone's actual experience will win him more directly. A lecture on man's inhumanity to man is one thing; a newsreel showing the inside of a concentration camp is something different. Your outline and much of your note-taking are often a series of generalities. They are the skeleton of your paper, with all the emotional appeal, the personality, and the warmth of a skeleton. You must cover the skeleton with living flesh. Explanations, specific details, instances, illustrations, concrete examples—out of these you build your finished essay.

One way of placing yourself in a better position to put substance into your writing is to keep substance in mind from the beginning, during your preliminary note taking and outlining. Be specific from the start. Actually few ideas come into your mind as abstractions unless you are merely pushing other people's words around like so many billiard balls. Abstractions usually start with an actual event of some sort. An abstraction such as the need for international understanding is likely to mean, if it means anything at all to you, something that *happened* in your experience. Perhaps it was a conversation with a South American; perhaps it was something you read in a foreign book; perhaps you saw a French movie. Whatever it was, your notion of a need for international understanding was a logical connection you made between all the pious and abstract talk you have heard on this subject and something definite that was part of your own life. When you begin your note-taking and outlining, do not forget this connection. We all know the sort of note or outline heading that means almost nothing and that gives the writer almost no help for proceeding. "Need for international understanding vital." What can you do about that except repeat it in other and even duller words? But suppose your notes read something like this: "Conversation with Juan, acquaintances from Cuba. Passionate defense of Castro's policies. 'You don't understand Cuba,' he says. Does he understand America? And what do we mean by 'understand'?" This is only a beginning, but it is promising. Obviously, abstract terms and headings are always necessary to hold an argument together and give it direction. But when your abstractions become disembodied from the drama and experience of the daily events that gave them birth, you are on your way to writing mush.

Preparing the Final Draft: Revising, Proofreading. In Section 7 of the Handbook you will find detailed instructions on the mechanical preparation of a manuscript: proper size of paper, width of margins, and so on. You will also find suggestions for correcting a manuscript, particularly after your instructor has seen it. For the present, we shall summarize some procedures in preparing your final draft by revision and by proofreading.

Many students, perhaps most students, do not know how to revise. Of all writing performances, revising is probably the least teachable, the most difficult to master. Too many young writers revise by simply copying over the ill-conceived sentences they have already perpetrated. Here is one down-to-earth suggestion. Try to complete a draft of a paper at least a day or two before it is due. (This alone is no easy task!) Then select, out of the remaining time, an hour or two when you are at your most alert, when you are feeling brisk and efficient. Pick up your manuscript and begin to read. As you do so, try to *pretend it was written by somebody else*. In your role as just another reader of this document, make quick notes in the margin of everything that makes you hesitate, for any reason. You could ask yourself, How can I tell that this essay was written by an amateur, not a professional? Here are some of the kinds of evidence you might notice: weak transitions between sentences, loose logical connections between ideas, inexact use of certain words, a vague pronoun or two (*it* and *this* are the common examples), a nonstop sentence, a collection of very short sentences sounding like baby talk, a failure after all to organize the whole essay around a single theme. The list is almost endless. After you have made what notes you can of this sort, take steps to correct all these weaknesses, using your dictionary and this handbook as you need to. Then try reading your paper again, but this time read it *aloud*, and listen to yourself. You should be able to pick up still more troubles: harsh sound effects, awkward repetition of words, clauses that breed other clauses that breed still more clauses. When you have done everything you can of this sort, you are ready to begin making your final draft.

It is unwise, while typing or writing this final copy, to make serious changes, though you may notice one or two additional details for improvement and you should stay alert for them. If you have carried out your rereading and revising process thoroughly, additional changes of a drastic sort while copying will do more harm than good. But your final act of *proofreading* is absolutely essential. Now you are on the lookout, not for the logic and phrasing of your argument, but for those tiny mechanical details that can so irritate and distract a reader. Now is the time to make final corrections of punctuation, spelling, placing of quotation marks. To many students such things seem trivial, and in a way they are, but, unfortunately, to ignore them is suicidal. For the plain fact is that no matter how clever your words may be, if you spell them badly your reader will assume that you are ignorant and illiterate. He may be wrong but he cannot help himself. You would assume the same thing, about someone else's sloppy manuscript.

Finally, it is a fine thing to be proud of what you do. Consider the satisfaction the football player feels when he makes a clean, solid block. He knows he has done it well. Is it inconceivable to feel a similar satisfaction in handing in a clean, solid composition? It is not inconceivable, but it doesn't happen often enough.

CONVENTIONS OF THE FORMAL OUTLINE

There are a number of conventions governing the formal outline which the student should observe:

1. The parts of the outline, heads and subheads, should be labeled by alternating figures and letters as follows: I, II, III, and so on; A, B, C, and so on; 1, 2, 3, and so on; a, b, c, and so on. Periods, not dashes, should be placed after these numbering figures and letters.

2. No punctuation is needed after the topics in a topic outline. In a sentence outline, each sentence should be punctuated in the conventional manner.

3. The heads in any series should be of equal importance. That is, the heads numbered I, II, III, IV, and so on, should actually be divisions of the whole paper; heads numbered with capital letters should be coordinate divisions of heads numbered with Roman numerals; and so on.

4. Coordinate heads should be expressed in parallel form—that is, in a given series, nouns should be made parallel with nouns, adjectives with adjectives, and so on. But although parallel structure is desirable and logical, clearness and directness should never be sacrificed on the altar of strict parallelism. There are times when nouns and gerunds can live side by side in a formal outline.

5. In a topic outline, all heads and subheads must be topics. In a sentence outline, all heads and subheads must be sentences. Sentences should not run over from one head to another.

6. Each head and subhead should be as specific as it is possible

to make it in an outline. Vague topics and sentences are bad because they tend to hide flaws in the logic or organization of the outline.

7. Using such headings as "I. Introduction, II. Body, III. Conclusion" is unnecessary and undesirable. Such divisions do not indicate correctly the structure of most essays or articles. Many papers written by students are too short for a formal introduction or conclusion. In most long papers the conclusion is simply the main topic which the writer wants the reader to hear about last —for reasons explained elsewhere. Separate introductions are used more often than separate conclusions in essays of six thousand words or more, but in the outline it is better to use a topic that tells what is said in the introduction than to use the vague "Introduction" itself.

8. Since an outline represents a grouping of parallel parts, it is illogical to have a single subhead under any head. A single subhead can usually be combined with its head with benefit to the logic and organization of the outline.

Finally, let us illustrate two kinds of conventional outline by examining a subject for a paper that might emerge out of our treatment of occupations, in the first part of this chapter.

TOPIC OUTLINE

Choices—In College and After

Thesis: The decisions I have to make in choosing college courses depend on larger questions I am beginning to ask about myself and my life work.

I. Two decisions described
   A. Art history or chemistry?
      1. Professional considerations
      2. Personal considerations
   B. A third year of French?
      1. Practical advantages of knowing a foreign language
      2. Intellectual advantages
      3. The issue of necessity
II. Definition of the problem
   A. Decisions about occupation
   B. Decisions about a kind of life to lead

III. Temporary resolution of the problem
    A. To hold open a professional possibility: chemistry
    B. To take advantage of cultural gains already made: French

A sentence outline is similar in organization to a topic outline. It differs from a topic outline in that every topic and subtopic is translated into a complete sentence, stating the central idea of the particular topic. The sentence outline has two advantages over the topic outline: (1) it forces the writer to study his material carefully so that he has something specific to say for each head and subhead, and (2) much more than the topic outline, it is able to convey information in logical sequence to the reader. The topic outline merely states a series of subjects, rather like titles, which the writer intends to say something about. The sentence outline actually summarizes what he has to say.

Here is an example of a sentence outline, based on the topic outline we have just examined:

SENTENCE OUTLINE

Choices—In College and After

Thesis: The decisions I have to make in choosing college courses depend on larger questions I am beginning to ask about myself and my life work.

   I. I have two decisions to make with respect to choosing college courses in the immediate future.
     A. One is whether to elect a course in art history or in chemistry.
       1. Since at one time I planned to be a chemical engineer and still have this career much in mind, professional considerations would indicate the choice of chemistry.
       2. On the other hand I enjoy art and plan to travel to see more of it; I need training in art history if I am going to be more than just another ignorant museum-goer.
     B. The second decision is whether to continue for a third year of French, beyond the basic college requirement.
       1. French might be practically useful to me, both in business (including engineering), and in the travel I hope to undertake.
       2. Furthermore I am eager to put to actual use, in the reading of good books, the elementary French I have already mastered.

3. But how necessary are these considerations in the light of other courses I might take instead?

II. My problem can be put in the form of a dilemma involving larger questions about my whole future.

A. On the one hand I want to hold a highly-trained position in a lucrative profession.

B. On the other hand I want to lead a certain kind of life, with capacities for values not connected with the making of money.

III. I will have to make a decision balancing the conflicting needs I have described.

A. I will hold open the professional possibilities by electing chemistry.

B. I will improve and solidify what cultural proficiency in another language I have already gained, by electing French.

EXERCISES

EXERCISE 1, TOPIC OUTLINES. *Select a subject from each of the three lists on page 112 and prepare a topic outline to show how a composition might be written on this subject.*

EXERCISE 2, AN AUTOBIOGRAPHICAL ESSAY. *Reread the section called "Autobiographical Materials." Take preliminary notes on three incidents in your life that could be interpreted as expressing a dominant trait in your character. Write a five-hundred word essay based on one of these.*

EXERCISE 3, VIEWPOINT. *Describe an incident in which you met a friend at an airport or railroad station. Tell it from the point of view of yourself. Then rewrite the incident, telling it from the imagined point of view of the other person.*

EXERCISE 4, DESCRIPTION. *Describe a scene that has changed dramatically since you first knew it—a neighborhood, a building, a room. Use contrast in the manner of the "old soldier" on page 119.*

EXERCISE 5, THE BOOK REVIEW. *Try in a single page to give a fair description of the last book you read. With what kinds of book is this particularly difficult? With what kinds is it relatively easy?*

EXERCISE 6, DIRECTIONS. *Make a list of some operations you believe you can perform better than your English teacher. (Examples: throwing a curve, repairing a buttonhole, using a microscope.) Give directions for one of these, so clearly that even your teacher might be able to perform it adequately.*

EXERCISE 7, STYLE. *Find a short, serious essay written in formal style. Try rewriting it in the breezy manner of Miss McGinley (page 129). Is the essay still serious? And just what do you mean by "serious" here?*

EXERCISE 8, BEGINNINGS. *Select a subject that you want to use for an essay. Write four beginnings for it. With the help of your instructor pick out the most promising one and use it in writing your paper.*

1. Begin by using an imagined incident which illustrates the point of your paper or out of which a discussion may seem to arise.
2. Begin with evidence of the importance or the timeliness of your subject.
3. Begin with a shock opening.
4. Begin with a question or a series of questions.

EXERCISE 9, PROOFREADING. *Make a list of the errors you catch in your proofreading. Compare it with a similar list of corrections made by your instructor on your paper. Does this comparison suggest some hints for future proofreading? Are you missing something?*

EXERCISE 10, WHEN TO OUTLINE. *For a fairly ambitious writing assignment, compose a formal outline before beginning to write. Then, on your next writing assignment, ignore outlining altogether until just before your final draft. Which procedure seems more useful to you? Why?*

6 WRITING THE LIBRARY PAPER

IMPORTANCE OF THE LIBRARY PAPER

Almost every class that you attend in college demonstrates the importance of knowing how to prepare a paper based on printed materials that may be found in a library. The lecture on the causes of World War I in your history class, the analysis of the European Common Market in your economics class, the talk on Gregor Mendel's principles of hereditary phenomena in your biology class—these and hundreds of thousands of other class lectures are all "papers based on research in a library." Outside the classroom—and as a part of your professional and social life when you are no longer a college student—countless numbers of papers written to be read before clubs, civic groups, study organizations, and so on, are "library papers."

You may, of course, have occasion later in your life to prepare a paper based on original experiments, on some special type of work that you have been engaged in, on travel or explorations on ocean bottom or in outer space, or even on the study of original documents in the British Museum. If that time comes, you will remember the first rule of scholarship: "Before you begin writing, first learn what has already been done and written about in your field." In other words, go to the libraries.

There are many values and skills to be got from writing a library paper:

1. You will get practice in preparing the term papers that will be required in many of your college courses.

2. You will acquire a great deal of interesting and perhaps useful information about a special subject.

3. You will increase your ability to distinguish between facts and opinions.

4. You will increase your ability to judge material as well as to find it, to evaluate its worth, to organize it, and to present it in attractive form.

Those are skills that will be useful to you some day, whether you compose a talk for your club meeting, for a professional or scientific group, or write an article for your company journal or for *Publications of the Modern Language Association*.

THE USE OF THE LIBRARY

Although we must always take into account differences in size and organization of different libraries, a study of the resources of a library can still be taken up under three main headings: (1) the card catalog, (2) the general reference library, and (3) the guides and indexes to periodicals and bulletins.

The Card Catalog: Basic Guide to the Library

The starting point for your exploration of the library is, logically, the card catalog, for this is a collection of cards listing every book (including reference books), bulletin, pamphlet, and periodical that the library owns.

The cards are arranged alphabetically according to authors, titles, and subjects. In other words, a large and complete library will have every book listed on at least three separate cards. You can therefore locate a book if you know the author's name, or the title, or the subject with which it deals. Magazines and bulletins are usually listed by title—that is, the card catalog will tell you whether or not the library owns a certain magazine or series of bulletins. The card for a given magazine or bulletin will tell you which volumes are bound and shelved (and usually the call number to be used in asking for them), and which are stacked unbound in a storeroom. In most libraries there will be a duplicate list of periodicals for use in the reference library room. For detailed information about the contents of periodicals, bulletins, and newspapers you will have to consult the periodical indexes. These are listed and explained on pages 160–162.

Let us examine a typical library card.

RA569   Calder, Ritchie, 1906-
C3

          Living with the atom. [Chicago] University of Chicago Press [c 1962]

          275 p. illus. 23cm.

          1. Nuclear engineering—Safety measures. 2. Radioactive waste disposal. 3. Radioactivity—Safety measures. I. Title.

---

1. RA569.C3 is the call number, according to the Library of Congress system. (See pages 153–154.)

2. "Calder, Ritchie, 1906–" is the author's name and date of birth, last name given first. The date of the author's birth (and death) may or may not appear on a card.

3. "Living with the atom. . . . [c 1962]" tells you the title of the book, the place of publication, the publisher, and the date of copyright.

4. The next line tells you that the book contains 275 pages, that it is illustrated, and that the shelf size (height on a shelf) of the book is 23 centimeters.

5. The titles at the bottom of the card tell you under what subjects the book may be found in the catalog. You can find this book by looking under: Nuclear engineering—Safety measures; Radioactive waste disposal; Radioactivity—Safety measures; and under the book title.

The card just examined is an *author* card. A *title* card is just like an author card, except that the title is typewritten at the top.

A *subject* card is an author card with the subject typed, usually in red, above the author's name at the top.

European War, 1914-1918--Campaigns--Western

D530   Tuchman, Barbara (Wertheim)
T8
         The guns of August. New York, Macmillan, 1962.

         511 p. illus. 24^{cm}.

         1. European War, 1914–1918—Campaigns—Western. I. Title.

   D530.T8   940.421   62–7515

      Library of Congress   [62k260]

On the card just illustrated you may have noticed two or three items not found in the specimen author card.

1. Both the Library of Congress and the Dewey Decimal call numbers are listed: D530.T8 and 940.421. (Both numbering systems are described in the section that follows.)

2. "Library of Congress" indicates that the Library of Congress has a copy of the book.

3. The two numbers at lower right on the card are for the use of librarians in ordering copies of this card. They are of no interest to the general user of the card catalog.

On the following page is a card showing that the library has a certain periodical.

Call Numbers. In most libraries, before you can take a book out you must fill out a call slip. On this call slip you write down the "call number" of the book, the name of the author, and the title of the book. Then you sign your name and add whatever identification your library requires.

H1   **Political** science quarterly, a review devoted to the historical,
P8   statistical and comparative study of politics, economics and
       public law . . . v. 1–75

       Mar. 1886–1960

       Boston, New York, Ginn and Company, [etc., etc.] 1886–
       1960 v. tables, charts, maps, 24cm

       Vols. 1–23 (1886–1908) edited by the Faculty of political
    science of Columbia university; v. 24–date (1909–date) edited for
    the Academy of political science in the city of New York by the
    Faculty of political science at Columbia university.

    Managing editors: 1886–93, Munroe Smith.—1894–1903, W. A.
    Dunning.—1904–13, Munroe Smith.—1914–1916, T. R.
    Powell.

H1.P8

(continued on next card)

A call number is a symbol or group of symbols used by libraries to designate any particular book. The call number of any book is typed in the upper left-hand corner of the card-catalog card, on the spine or bound end of the book, and usually on the inside of the back or front cover as well. Books are arranged on shelves according to their call numbers. Call numbers usually consist of two parts: the upper part is the classification number, and the lower part the author and book number.

For the ordinary undergraduate, a knowledge of the systems used in devising call numbers is relatively unimportant. To satisfy a natural curiosity on the part of many students and to make library work a little more interesting, the following brief explanation is given.

Two classification systems are used by libraries in this country: the Library of Congress system and the Dewey Decimal system.

The Library of Congress System. The Library of Congress system, found more frequently in college than in public libraries, uses the letters of the alphabet, followed by additional letters and Arabic numerals, as the basis of its classification.

A	General works	N	Fine arts
B	Philosophy—Religion	P	Language and literature
C	History—Auxiliary sciences	Q	Science
D	History and topography	R	Medicine
E and F	American history	S	Agriculture
G	Geography—Anthropology	T	Technology
H	Social sciences	U	Military science
J	Political science	V	Naval science
K	Law	Z	Bibliography and library
L	Education		science
M	Music		

The following table shows the larger subdivisions under one of these main classes:

G Geography—Anthropology

G	Geography (General)
GA	Mathematical and astronomical geography
GB	Physical geography
GC	Oceanology and oceanography
GF	Anthropogeography
GN	Anthropology—Somatology—Ethnology
	Ethnogeography (General)

	51–161	Anthropometry—Skeleton—Craniometry
	400–499	Customs and institutions (Primitive)
	537–686	Special races
	700–875	Prehistoric archeology
GR	Folklore	
GT	Manners and customs (General)	
GV	Sports and amusements—Games	
	201–547	Physical training
	1580–1799	Dancing

The Dewey Decimal System.   The Dewey Decimal system, devised by Melvil Dewey, uses a decimal classification for all books. The entire field of knowledge is divided into nine groups, with an additional group for general reference books. Each main class and subclass is shown by a number composed of three digits.

[154]

000	General works	500	Natural science
100	Philosophy	600	Useful arts
200	Religion	700	Fine arts
300	Sociology	800	Literature
400	Philology	900	History

The following table shows the first subdivision under the literature class and the beginning of the intricate system of further subdividing under the 820 group.

```
800  Literature
     810   American
     820   English
           821   English poetry
           822   English drama
                 822.3   Elizabethan drama
                         822.33   Shakespeare
     830   German
     840   French
     850   Italian
     860   Spanish
     870   Latin
     880   Greek
     890   Minor literatures
```

The Reference Library

The reference library consists of all the general reference works, such as encyclopedias and dictionaries, and collections of pamphlets, bibliographies, guides, maps, pictures, and the like, which are to be consulted for some specific information rather than to be read in their entirety. Reference books ordinarily cannot be taken from the library. The following list of reference books should be a starting point for your exploration of the library. It is well to know what they are, where they are shelved, and how they can be used to the best advantage. The date given is usually the date of the latest revision. In this changing world, the date of publication may be very important in a reference book.

[155]

The General Encyclopedias. A student using the *Britannica,* the *Americana,* and the *New International* should consult the annual supplements, the *Britannica Book of the Year,* the *Americana Annual,* and the *New International Year Book,* for additional information.

Encyclopaedia Britannica. 24 vols. Chicago: Encyclopaedia Britannica Company. Since 1940 the *Britannica* has been kept up to date by continuous revisions. Hence a date is necessary with a reference to any printing or revision of the work since 1940. For editions before 1940, give the number of the edition.

Encyclopedia Americana. 30 vols. New York: Americana Corporation. Like the *Britannica,* the *Americana* is now kept up to date by continuous revision. Hence the date is necessary with any reference to it.

Collier's Encyclopedia. 24 vols, 1963. New York: Crowell-Collier Publishing Co. Continuously revised. Although written in a popular style, for the general reader rather than the scholar, it is objective and authoritative.

New International Encyclopedia. 23 vols. plus 4 supp. vols. New York: Dodd, Mead and Company, 1902–1930. It has not been revised recently.

The Special Encyclopedias. A special or limited encyclopedia is available for almost any subject of importance that you can think of. You may find a long list by looking under "encyclopedias" in the most recent annual volume of the *Cumulative Book Index.* Many of these special encyclopedias, once useful and authoritative, have not been revised recently. The information they contain is now dated. Others are valuable as historical records. Here are a few examples of this type of reference book:

The Catholic Encyclopedia. 16 vols. New York: The Gilmary Society. Supp. I, 1922. Supp. II, 1950–1954. Although this work deals primarily with the accomplishments of Roman Catholics, its scope is very general. It is useful for subjects dealing with medieval literature, history, art, and philosophy.

The Jewish Encyclopedia. 12 vols. New York: Funk & Wagnalls Co., 1925.

McGraw-Hill Encyclopedia of Science and Technology. 17 vols. incl. yearbooks. McGraw-Hill Book Co., 1960, 1963.

Van Nostrand's Scientific Encyclopedia, 3rd ed. D. Van Nostrand Co., 1958.

The Yearbooks. In addition to the general yearbooks listed here, there are yearbooks for many specialized fields. See the *Cumulative Book Index* or *Books in Print*.

Britannica Book of the Year. Chicago: Encyclopaedia Britannica Company, 1938 to date.

Americana Annual. New York: Americana Corporation, 1923 to date.

New International Year Book. New York: Funk & Wagnalls Company, 1907 to date.

World Almanac and Book of Facts. New York: The New York World-Telegram and Sun, 1868 to date.

Information Please Almanac. New York: The Macmillan Company, 1947–1959; McGraw-Hill, 1960; Simon & Schuster, 1961 to date.

Economic Almanac. New York: National Industrial Conference Board, 1940 to date.

Statesman's Year-Book. London: Macmillan & Co., Ltd.; New York: St. Martin's Press, 1864 to date.

Guides to Reference Books. The following are the principal bibliographies of reference texts.

Winchell, Constance M. *Guide to Reference Books*, 7th ed. Based on Isadore Gilbert Mudge's *Guide to Reference Books*, 6th edition. Four supplements to June, 1962. Eighth edition in preparation. Chicago: American Library Association, 1951.

Cumulative Book Index (called *United States Catalog* up to 1928). New York: H. W. Wilson Company, 1928 to date. This is a catalog of books issued in any given year. It is invaluable for checking exact titles, author's names, dates of publication and revisions, and so on.

Murphey, Robert W. *How and Where to Look It Up*. New York: McGraw-Hill Book Company, 1958.

Shores, Louis. *Basic Reference Sources*. Chicago: American Library Association, 1954.

Biographical Information. Biographical information can also be secured through the aid of various periodical indexes and in very compressed form in your own desk dictionary.

Dictionary of American Biography. 21 vols. New York: Charles Scribner's Sons, 1928–1943.

Dictionary of National Biography. 22 vols. London: Oxford University Press, 1885–1949. The word *national* is sometimes confusing to students; it refers to the "nationals" of the British Empire, more recently known as the British Commonwealth of Nations.

Current Biography: Who's News and Why. New York: H. W. Wilson Company, 1940 to date. Published monthly, with six-month and annual cumulations.

Webster's Biographical Dictionary. Springfield, Mass.: G. & C. Merriam Company, 1943. A one-volume pronouncing biographical dictionary of over 40,000 names. It includes living persons.

Who's Who in America. Chicago: A. N. Marquis Company, 1899 and biennially to date.

Who's Who. London: A. & C. Black, Ltd.; New York: The Macmillan Company, 1849 to date.

Biography Index. New York: H. W. Wilson Company, 1947 to date. This is a guide to biographical information in books and magazines.

Dictionaries and Books of Synonyms.   For other books dealing with the English language, see the bibliography at the end of Chapter 1.

Webster's Third New International Dictionary. Springfield, Mass.: G. & C. Merriam Company, 1961.

New Standard Dictionary. New York: Funk & Wagnalls Company, 1935 to date.

New Century Dictionary. 3 vols. New York: The Century Company, 1927–1933. Based on the original *Century Dictionary,* 12 vols., 1911.

Oxford English Dictionary. New York: Oxford University Press, 1933. A corrected reissue of *A New English Dictionary on Historical Principles,* 1888–1933. The purpose of this work is to give the history of every word in the English language for the past 800 years. It contains many quotations illustrating meanings of words in various periods and full discussions of derivations and changes in meanings and spellings.

Dictionary of American English on Historical Principles. 4 vols. Chicago: University of Chicago Press, 1936–1944. This is especially useful to the student who wishes to learn the historical changes in the use and meaning of words in American English.

Webster's Dictionary of Synonyms. Springfield, Mass.: G. & C. Merriam Company, 1942. A dictionary of discriminated synonyms with antonyms and analogues and contrasted words.

Gazetteers and Atlases.   In a world of quickly changing national boundaries and of former colonies emerging as independent nations, gazetteers and atlases are out of date almost as soon as they are printed. Most of the following, however, are kept up to date by reasonably frequent revisions. Look for the date on the book that you are using.

The Columbia Lippincott Gazetteer of the World. A revision of *Lippin-cott's Gazetteer* of 1905. New York: Columbia University Press, 1952.

Rand McNally Commercial Atlas and Marketing Guide. Chicago: Rand McNally and Company.

Encyclopaedia Britannica World Atlas. Chicago: Encyclopaedia Britannica Company. Revised annually.

Webster's Geographical Dictionary. Springfield, Mass.: G. & C. Merriam Company, 1949.

Books on Literature.   The following are standard chronological accounts of literature in the English language. For current writing, see references to periodicals such as the *Readers' Guide.*

Cambridge History of English Literature. 15 vols. Cambridge University Press, 1907–1927.

Cambridge History of American Literature. New York: The Macmillan Company, 1933.

Literary History of the United States. 3 vols. Ed. R. E. Spiller, *et al.* New York: The Macmillan Company, 1948; 3rd ed. 1963.

Books of Quotations.   When you are in doubt about the source or wording of a passage which you can only partially recall, you may often find the complete passage in the book of quotations. These volumes are thoroughly indexed by key words.

Bartlett, John. *Familiar Quotations.* Boston: Little, Brown and Company, 1955.

Mencken, H. L. *A New Dictionary of Quotations on Historical Principles from Ancient and Modern Sources.* New York: Alfred A. Knopf, 1942.

Stevenson, Burton. *The Home Book of Quotations.* New York: Dodd, Mead and Company, 1956.

Books on Mythology, Classical Literature.   A classical dictionary is a necessity for serious students of literature. Here are three good ones.

The *Oxford Classical Dictionary*. Oxford: Clarendon Press, 1949.
Hamilton, Edith. *Mythology*. Boston: Little, Brown and Company, 1942.
Bulfinch, Thomas. *The Age of Fable*. Various publishers and dates.

Guides and Indexes to Periodicals and Bulletins

Magazines and Bulletins. Indexes to magazines, bulletins, and newspapers are usually shelved in the reference room of the library.

When you wish to find something published in a magazine, you need to know two things: (1) Does the library subscribe to that periodical? (2) In what issue was the article published? The answer to the first question is on a card, found in either the general catalog or an additional special card file in the reference room. For an answer to the second question you must look into a periodical index.

Bulletins are listed in most indexes. In compiling your bibliography you must remember that a bulletin is treated as a periodical if it is published at regular intervals (that is, as a series), and as a book if it is a separate, single publication.

There is a special index for material published in newspapers. See pages 161–162.

Poole's *Index to Periodical Literature*, 1802–1881, and supplements from 1882 to 1906. To be able to use this index intelligently, you must know that it is a subject index only; it has no author entries; all articles having a distinct subject are entered under that subject; materials such as poems and stories, which do not lend themselves to subject classification, are entered under the first word of the title; no date is given with an entry, only volume and page, but not inclusive paging; the periodicals indexed are principally of a general nature. Users of this index will find occasional errors in it.

Readers' *Guide to Periodical Literature*, 1900 to date. The special features of this index are that the entries are under author, title, and subject; it gives volume, inclusive paging, date; it indicates illustrations, portraits, maps, and so on; it indexes book reviews up to 1904; it has a list of 597 books in the second and third cumulated volumes. Since for the average student this is the most important of the indexes, a sample of its entries follows: [1]

[1] Reproduced by courtesy of The H. W. Wilson Company.

ASH, Volcanic. See Volcanic ash, tuff, etc.
ASHMORE, Harry Scott
  Our footloose correspondents. J. Bainbridge.
  il New Yorker 39:105-6+ N 9 '63
ASPIRIN
  Aspirin. H. O. J. Collier. Sci Am 209:96-104+
  bibliog(p 187) N '63
ASSOCIATION for supervision and curriculum
  development
  Current curriculum developments; with list
  of books. W. M. Alexander and H. Heffer-
  nan. NEA J 52:47-8 N '63
ASTRONAUTS
  Astronaut and investor; Alan Shepard turns
  banker. U S News 55:16 N 4 '63

           Clothing

  Hamilton standard starting manned tests of
  advanced Apollo suit design prototypes. D.
  E. Fink. il Aviation W 79:48-9+ O 28 '63
  Man in the moon suit. T. Alexander. il Es-
  quire 60:104-5+ N '63
ASTRONOMICAL photography
  Catch a falling star? B. Hering. il Pop Sci
  183:118-21+ N '63
  New look in eclipses. H. Keppler. il Mod Phot
  27:93 N '63

Specialized periodical indexes include the following:

International Index to Periodicals, 1907 to date. This is the best index to the scholarly journals. It also indexes some foreign-language journals, especially German and French.

Agricultural Index, 1916 to date. A subject index to periodicals, bulletins, books, and documents.

Art Index, 1929 to date. Author and subject index.

Dramatic Index, 1909–1960. An annual subject index to articles on drama, the theater, actors and actresses, playwrights and plays.

Education Index, 1929 to date. Author and subject index.

Engineering Index, 1892–1906. *Engineering Index Annual*, 1906 to date. A classified subject index from 1906 to 1918, and an alphabetical index from 1919 to date.

Experiment Station Record, 1899 to date. A record and digest of current agricultural literature.

Index to Legal Periodicals, 1908 to date.

Industrial Arts Index, 1913 to date.

Public Affairs Information Service, 1915 to date. Indexes periodicals, books, documents, and pamphlets relating to political science, sociology, and economics; the best source of last-minute information on subjects in these fields.

Quarterly Cumulative Index Medicus, 1927 to date. *Index Medicus*, 1879–1926. An author and subject index to 1,200 periodicals in the field of medicine, and to books and pamphlets.

Index to Newspapers. Although the following is an index to *The New York Times*, it can be used as an index to any daily newspaper in the United States, since the same major news stories will probably be found in all daily papers on the same day they appear in the *Times*.

New York Times Index, 1913 to date.

THE LIBRARY PAPER

Again, the library paper, variously known as the *investigative theme*, the *term paper*, or the *research article*, is an exposition, based on research in a library, that aims to present the results of careful and thorough investigation of some chosen or assigned subject. You will no doubt also have occasions to write term papers that are based not on library research but on laboratory experiments, questionnaires, or your own critical reactions to something that you have read; papers of that sort are organized and written like any other expository paper. Some English departments, too, require a long analytical discussion based on material collected and printed in what is often known as a *source book* or *casebook*. This type of paper, which is sometimes called the *controlled-research* or *controlled-sources* paper, solves certain problems inherent in this type of assignment and saves wear and tear on valuable reference books and on librarians' nerves by omitting the investigation in the library. Where the controlled-sources method is used, the instructor's directions should be followed exactly. The information that follows applies primarily to papers based on library material.

Let us summarize here the values or purposes of the library paper:

1. It will teach you how to use the library efficiently.

2. It will acquaint you with the methods of scholarly documentation—that is, the use of bibliography and footnotes.

3. It will increase your ability to take usable notes.

4. It will teach you how to organize and combine material from a number of different sources.

5. It will give you practice in presenting material in a way that will appeal to your readers.

The library paper can be a project full of frustrations, however, unless you follow orderly procedures. It might be well to review here the steps ahead of you, so that you will proceed without too much loss of time.

1. Deciding on a general subject or field of investigation.
2. Making a preliminary check of the library and doing some general reading.
3. Limiting the subject.
4. Preparing a working bibliography.
5. Reading and note taking.
6. Preparing the final outline.
7. Writing a first draft of the paper.
8. Writing a final draft with footnotes.
9. Preparing a final bibliography.

Deciding on a General Subject or Field of Investigation

As soon as the library paper is assigned, many students will ask themselves: "Now what subject do I know something about?" A major in English may want to investigate some author or literary movement. A student in forestry may be especially eager to investigate the new uses of forest products. A student of home economics may wish to write on nutrition or antique furniture. In some ways this attitude is commendable; it approaches in method the theory of the "honors course" now so popular in colleges—the independent investigation in depth of some special field related to a student's major interest. But in other ways this attitude is a mistake. A student should indeed be interested in the subject of his investigation, but his interest may as well bring the thrill of exploring a field entirely new to him.

Of course, if the subjects are assigned by the instructor or the department, the problem of choice does not exist. If the student has a choice, either unrestricted or limited, his choice must be based on a knowledge both of what is desirable and what must be avoided. The following kinds of subjects are *not* satisfactory; they lead only to frustration and unhappiness:

1. Subjects that are too broad. Broad or general subjects are starting points. They must be limited or narrowed to usable dimensions.
2. Subjects from the writer's own experience, or those based on interviews or experiments. Material of this sort, however, may be used to supplement information got from reading.
3. Subjects on which little has been published anywhere.
4. Subjects on which the local library has little material.
5. Subjects that are so technical that the writer cannot understand his material, much less present it intelligibly to others.
6. Events so recent that only newspaper comments are available.
7. Subjects that are too narrow or too trivial for a paper of the suggested length.

It is impossible to list all the general interests that will appeal to students everywhere. The lists given here are merely suggestive:

1. Something related to the course you are taking or expect to take in college, such as literature, history, medicine, and so on.
2. Something coming out of your experience, such as your work during your summer vacations, your military service, your travel or life in a foreign country, the occupations of your parents. But remember that this is but the starting point for your library work.
3. Something related to your hobbies, your special talents, or your reading interests, such as photography, archaeology, exploration, sports, aviation.

The advice of your instructor may be the last word on your choice of subject. If you have freedom of choice, however, or if you are urged to present several choices for his approval, the following list of general fields may help:

1. Archaeology	5. Drama
2. Art	6. Exploration
3. Aviation	7. History
4. Biography	8. Language and literature

9. Medicine
10. Music
11. Mythology
12. Nature
13. Photography
14. Psychology

15. Sciences
16. Sports
17. The theater
18. Utopias
19. The Vatican
20. Warfare

Making a Preliminary Check of the Library and Doing Some General Reading

Before you make your final decision on the general subject, it might be well for you to spend an hour or two browsing in the library to see whether your general subject will be satisfactory and to get an idea of how it can be limited. First look in the card catalog. Then check through some of the periodical indexes to ascertain the extent of the published material in your selected field. Notice in what types of periodicals your information is found, and make a preliminary check, either through the general card catalog or through a special list of periodicals, to see which of the sources are available in your library. Look in the *Britannica* to see what it has on your topic. After you have made this preliminary survey, you are ready to limit your subject.

Limiting the Subject

After you have indicated your general field of interest, you will, with the help of your instructor, select some part or aspect of it that can be effectively presented in the given space and time. If you are interested in American literature, you may decide to write about Robert Frost or Carl Sandburg. You may find it convenient to limit your subject still further and investigate the early poems of Frost, or Sandburg's stories for children. These are merely suggested topics. The variety of possible topics is vast. The manner in which you limit a broad subject depends partly on the time or the space that you have to fill, partly on the purpose of your paper, partly on the extent of available material. A scholarly probing of a very minor area is one thing; a more general presentation of facts, such as could be read before a club or a study group of adults, is another thing. In choosing your subject, always remember that you cannot narrow or limit a subject by excluding details. A research article should be interesting. Interest comes from the concrete details, the examples, and the imaginative touches that you can give your writing.

Now let us take two or three of these general fields and suggest in each one of them several topics narrowed down to what you could present adequately in the time and space at your disposal:

GENERAL SUBJECT: ARCHAEOLOGY

1. Mycenaean culture
2. Mayan pyramids
3. Pueblos of the Southwest
4. The Rosetta stone
5. Pictographs
6. The site of ancient Troy
7. Stonehenge
8. Easter Island statues
9. Cave paintings
10. Earliest man

GENERAL SUBJECT: SCIENCES

1. Ocean currents
2. Strontium 90
3. Smog control
4. Rockets to the moon
5. Artificial diamonds
6. Making weather maps
7. Sonar
8. Sunspots
9. Animal luminescence
10. The Sargasso Sea
11. The uses of atomic tracers
12. Hurricane tracking
13. Hibernating animals
14. The sense of smell
15. Psychology of learning
16. Mathematical sets
17. Operation of heat pumps
18. Migrating butterflies
19. The Dead Sea scrolls
20. Meteors

Preparing a Working Bibliography

A bibliography is a list of books, articles, bulletins, or documents relating to a given subject or author.

When you begin working on a library paper, it is wise to arm yourself with a supply of 3×5 cards or slips of paper. On these cards you will make a list of references—one and *only one* to each card—that you hope will be useful to you. You will collect your references from the card catalog, the encyclopedias, and the periodical indexes. Since there is always a great deal of wastage and frustration in this sort of project, you should take out insurance by getting more references than you expect to use. As you proceed with your reading, you will constantly upgrade your bibliography by adding new references and by discarding those that you find useless.

Bibliographic Forms. It is unfortunate that bibliographic forms have not been standardized as completely as have the parts of an automobile. Recently, however, the Modern Language Association has moved in the direction of standardization in the general field of literature, language, and the social sciences. The result of the move has been the publication of *The MLA Style Sheet*. Although this pamphlet concerns itself primarily with the preparation of *"learned articles* in humanistic fields," it has been "increasingly recommended to undergraduate and graduate students as helpful in the preparation of term papers and theses." [2] The forms of bibliographies and footnotes used here are based on *The MLA Style Sheet*, insofar as the recommendations of the MLA are applicable to undergraduate work.

There are other forms used for bibliographies and footnotes, however, and your instructor may well recommend modifications of the MLA style. Use the form that your instructor recommends.

Every bibliographic reference consists of the three parts necessary for a complete identification of the printed work used, and these parts are generally arranged in this order:

1. *The author's name.* (Write the last name first only where lists are to be alphabetized. If an article or pamphlet is unsigned, begin with the title.)
2. *The title.* (If it is a book, underline the title. If it is an article, essay, poem, short story, or any subdivision of a larger work, enclose it in quotation marks.)
3. *The facts of publication.*
   a. For a book, give the place of publication (with the abbreviated state, if needed for clarity, as *Garden City, N.Y.*), the name of the publisher in full, and the date. (The current MLA style permits omission of the publisher's name.)
   b. For a magazine article, give the name of the magazine, the volume number, the date, and the pages.

[2] *The MLA Style Sheet*, Supplement, p. 24.

c. For a newspaper article, give the name of the newspaper, the date, the section if the sections are paged separately, and the page.

The sample bibliography cards that follow illustrate the arrangement of items and the punctuation in various types of references.

ARTICLE IN AN ENCYCLOPEDIA
Initials of author identified in vol. I. Date of copyright from back of volume. Title of article in quotes. Underline title of reference book.

Atkinson, Richard J. C.

"Stonehenge." Encyclopaedia Britannica, 1958, XXI, 440-441.

BOOK BY A SINGLE AUTHOR
Copy call number. Underline title of book.

818   White, E. B.
W5818s

The Second Tree from the
Corner.

New York: Harper & Brothers,
1954.

BOOK BY TWO OR MORE AUTHORS
All names after the first are in normal order.

QC173   Bethe, Hans Albrecht, and
B4   Philip Morrison.

Elementary Nuclear Theory.

New York: John Wiley & Sons,
1956.

**BOOK BY A NUMBER OF AUTHORS OR BY
A NUMBER OF EDITORS**

Et alii ("and others") abbreviated *et al.* (do not underscore).

> PS92   Spiller, Robert E., et al.,
> L5   3 vols.
>
> <u>Literary History of the United
> States</u>.
>
> New York: The Macmillan Com-
> pany, 1949.

BOOK EDITED

> 811   Millay, Edna St. Vincent.
> M611x
>
> <u>Collected Poems</u>. Ed. by Norma
> Millay.
>
> New York: Harper & Brothers,
> 1956.

SIGNED MAGAZINE ARTICLE

STONEHENGE, England
New, exciting discoveries at mysterious Stonehenge. J. Stern. il House &
Gard 112:52+ S '57

> Stern, J.
>
> "New, exciting discoveries at myste-
> rious Stonehenge."
>
> <u>House and Garden</u>, CXII (Sept. 1957),
> 52+.

UNSIGNED ARTICLE

STONEHENGE, England
Mystery in stone. il NY Times Mag p84 S 7 '58

> "Mystery in Stone."
>
> <u>New York Times Magazine</u>, Sept. 7,
> 1958, p. 84.

NEWSPAPER ARTICLE
(From *New York Times Index* for 1958.) Neuberger, (Sen) Richard L.:
Article in Defense of the Politician; illus. N2, VI, p 13

```
Neuberger, Senator Richard L.

"Article in Defense of the Politi-
cian."

New York Times, Nov. 2, 1958, Sec.
VI, p. 13.
```

Bulletins are treated like books if they are occasional, and like
magazine articles if they are issued periodically (at regular intervals).

OCCASIONAL BULLETIN
Parker, William Riley. *The MLA Style Sheet.* New York: Modern Language Association, 1951.

PERIODICAL BULLETIN
"Amazing Gibberelic Acid," *Agricultural Research*, USDA, V (Sept.
1956), 12–13.

Reading and Note Taking

It is assumed that before you begin to read and take notes, you
have collected a few fairly promising bibliography cards. Take
your cards with you to the library. Look up several of your references. You might start with the encyclopedia articles. Your purpose is to make a preliminary exploration of your field. Read for
general information. While you are exploring, make a note of
each of the most important topics that seem to be related to your
particular project. These topics, properly arranged, will become
your first rough trial outline. They will be the headings you will
use on your note cards when you begin to take notes.

Reading and Skimming. The frustrations of research plague
everyone, but there will be fewer frustrations and less wasted time
if you remember that what you have learned about writing must

apply also to your reading. In your writing course you have learned to organize your papers so that their contents may be comprehended by your reader easily, quickly, without confusion, without wasted effort. Those who write books, chapters, essays, or articles in magazines employ the same principles of writing that you have learned—so that *you* may get the information you want, easily, quickly, without confusion, without wasted effort. Let us review these aids to quick reading and comprehension:

1. In a book you examine first the table of contents, the index (if it has one), the chapter headings, and the topics of the lesser divisions.

2. In an essay or article you look for a formal statement of plan or purpose at the beginning. Then if it is a longish essay or article —one of those five-part essays used by magazines for serious discussions, for example—look at the beginning of each part for a hint of the contents.

3. Then you glance through the essay, reading a topic sentence here, another one there, until you come to what you want. This process is called *skimming*.

Evaluating Your Sources. To expect a college freshman writing his first research paper to have the experience that will enable him to evaluate all his sources is not exactly fair or reasonable. But any college student can learn to use a few hints or signs that will help him to distinguish the totally unreliable from the probably reliable. The student should first arm himself with the knowledge that not all that gets into print is true. Some—perhaps most—of it is as true and as reliable as honest and informed men can make it. Some of it is mistaken or biased opinion. The following suggestions will help you to evaluate your sources:

1. The first aid you should use is the date of publication of the book or article. In some fields, such as chemistry, physics, and medicine, information even a few months old may be highly misleading or false. Try to get the most recent facts possible.

2. To a certain extent, try to judge the information by the authority of the publication in which it appears. The *Britannica*, for instance, selects its authors with more care than does a newspaper—if we can cite two extremes as a fair example.

3. A long, thorough treatment of a subject is probably more accurate than a short treatment of it, or a condensation.

4. Finally, if it is possible, you should find out something about the reputation of the author. Obviously a careful checking of authorities is a necessity in a scholarly thesis written for publication, and a desirable but often unattainable ideal in a freshman term paper. In practice, however, if you distinguish as much as you can between reports of facts and expression of opinion, you can usually trust that a college library has winnowed out most of the chaff before it buys.

The Preliminary Outline.   After your preliminary exploration of your field you will be ready to construct a topic outline of your paper. This topic outline will be based partly on what you have learned about your subject and partly on what you think any intelligent and mature person would want to be told if he were reading an article about your subject. Do not underestimate the value of this second source of your preliminary outline. A writer must always keep his reader in mind. It is a mistake to assume that all available material on your subject must become a part of your paper. On the other hand, it is also a mistake to assume that everything that a reader would like to know about your subject must be included in your paper. If the information on a given topic is not available, it just is not available; you merely discard that topic. Your working outline is subject to this sort of pruning until your paper is set in its final form. You add and you discard, as every professional writer must do, until your paper is completed; but in the main you will keep most of your original topics as a necessary guide for your note taking.

Use of Note Cards.   When you go to the library you should have with you a generous supply of note cards. These may be either the 3×5 cards that you use for your bibliography or some slightly larger, such as the 4×6 size. If you cannot obtain cards, you may cut notebook paper into quarters to make slips approximately 4×5 inches in size. It is not good practice to copy your notes into your notebook, because then they will be difficult to rearrange.

Methods of Identifying Notes. Notes must be identified if you are to avoid utter confusion later on. Two very simple and easy methods of identifying notes are presented here:

1. As you take notes, you write at the top of your card the topic under which the information falls. At the bottom of the card you write an abbreviated reference to the source of your information. This reference may consist of the author's last name, an abbreviated title, and the exact page reference.

2. The second method—a very simple one to use if you understand it—is to number all of your bibliography cards. Any number will do, just so you do not duplicate numbers. Then instead of the reference at the bottom of the note card, you write the number of your bibliography card and the page number. Of course, whichever method you use, you must always assign each note card to a topic in your working outline.

Be sure to use the method that is recommended by your instructor.

The Form of Notes. Sample note cards are given below, but before you study them, you should review the following well-defined principles of note taking:

1. Most of your notes will be in the form of a condensed summary. Get what is essential and get it accurately, but do not waste words. In order to avoid any chance of inadvertent plagiarism, try to paraphrase what you read—that is, try to *use your own words, not the words of your source.* But dates, figures, and such matters must obviously be quoted accurately.

2. If you wish to quote the exact words of an author, copy your material in the form of direct quotations. Ordinarily you should not use direct quotations from your sources if a summary will serve. But if you wish to preserve the words of your source because of unusually apt or precise language, or for some other adequate reason, quote your source exactly. If you leave out a part of a quoted sentence, indicate the omission by means of spaced periods (. . .) called *ellipsis periods* or *suspension points.*

Use three spaced periods, leaving a space between the word and the first period, if you omit words within the sentence, and four spaced periods (which include the period ending the sentence) if your omission follows a complete sentence.

3. Let your first unbreakable rule be "One topic to a card." Do not include in your notes on the same card material relating to two or more topics. You may have as many cards as you wish relating to the same topic, but you must label each card and give the exact source of your notes on each card.

4. Make your notes so accurate and so complete that they will make sense to you when they become cold.

5. Use headings or topics that represent actual divisions of your outline, as closely as it is possible for you to anticipate the outline you will use. Too many topics will merely result in confusion.

6. And finally, remember that every note card must have three pieces of information: (a) the heading or topic, which shows you where the information belongs; (b) the information itself (in quotation marks if you use the words of your source); (c) the exact source of your material (including page reference).

Plagiarism. In writing a paper based on research, it is very easy for a student to fall into unintentional plagiarism if he does not follow the procedure outlined in this chapter. If he is not careful about rephrasing the author's material in his own words, if he merely alters a word here and there, he will carry over into the final paper much of the language of his sources. That he must not do. The place to rephrase and summarize is in his notes. He will naturally do more rephrasing when he writes his first draft and then his final draft and thus avoid the danger of copying. As any student realizes, it is only honest and decent to give proper credit for borrowed words and ideas. Borrowing without giving proper credit is *plagiarism*, which is a very serious offense.

Sample Note Cards. If you follow the instructions on pages 170–174, you will have little trouble in taking usable notes. These samples are summaries. No sample cards are necessary for anything as obvious as a direct quotation.

II, C. Underlying causes of problems — spiritual vacuum.

Character of American occupation must be understood. Occupation policies generally "benevolent, constructive, sound." Gen. MacArthur's character and leadership served as symbol of Western ideals. Japanese deeply moved by the "sincerity and intensity of his idealism" and the "sureness of his touch." Actions of thousands of GI's also important in shaping Japanese attitude.

Kawai, *Japan's American Interlude*, pp. 11-13

I, C. High rate of suicide.

Manifestation of social confusion. Significant that Japan has highest suicide rate among modern nations. Largest cause of death among young people, ages 15 to 24. Idea of suicide rooted in tradition and mores. Perhaps felt as survival of influence of Buddhism.

Seidensticker, pp. 79-80.

Preparing the Final Outline

For the typical student, the final outline he hands in is not the one he writes the paper from. In other words, the outline is usually in a state of flux until the paper itself is finished. It is subject to change until the last moment. If something that looked good to you at first later seems to be out of place, throw

[175]

it out and improve the outline. The outline is your working blueprint, a simplified diagram of your paper, a help to you and to your reader, but it is no help to anyone if it forces you to construct something that at the last moment you feel is wrong. Change it if it needs changing.

For the conventions of the formal outline, turn back to Chapter 5. Then examine the outlines preceding the sample research paper in this chapter.

Writing a First Draft of the Paper

In the process of writing a paper based on research in the library, most writers—whether students or professionals—work up the outline slowly and gradually as they collect notes. The whole process is one of synthesis, of gradual putting together, of sifting and rearranging, which of course includes throwing away unusable material as well as filling in unexpected gaps. By the time you are ready to write, you have a pretty good idea of the limits or the extent of your paper. You have worked out your approach to your subject and perhaps to your reader. It may be that you even have thought of an interesting beginning. So you take your note cards and your outline, and on the table in front of you, you spread out your note cards for your first section. You read them over to freshen in your mind the sequence or flow of thought—and then you are on your own.

As you write, whenever you come to borrowed material, either quoted or paraphrased, you should include the reference in parentheses in the right place in the text. Later you will copy your footnotes, in the approved form, at the bottom of each page as you prepare the final draft of your paper.

When you quote verse, you may run two lines together in your quotation if you indicate the separation by a slash (/), but if you quote more than two lines you should center the quotation on the page. If you quote prose of some length, you should separate the quotation from your text by indention. No quotation marks are used when quotations are marked by indentions. Single spacing is customary. Study the sample research paper for examples of these conventions.

[176]

Writing a Final Draft with Footnotes

The Final Draft. You should go over your first draft carefully before you supply the footnotes and copy it for final submission. The following are major factors to keep in mind: (1) unity and direction of the paper as a whole; (2) interest, supplied by fact and example; (3) organization of the paper as a whole and of the separate paragraphs; (4) correctness of sentence structure; and (5) correctness of punctuation and spelling.

Footnotes: Where Needed. Whether in a college term paper or in a scholarly research article, footnotes are required:

1. To acknowledge and identify every direct quotation. Quoted material, as we have indicated earlier, should always be quoted exactly, word for word, and either enclosed in quotation marks or indented and single spaced. Footnotes are not used, however, with familiar sayings or proverbs; everyone knows that these are quoted.
2. To acknowledge and identify all information that has been used in the paper or thesis in paraphrased, reworded, or summarized form. Of course, facts of general knowledge need not be credited to any one source.
3. In graduate or professional work, to define terms used in the text, to give additional information that does not fit into the text, and to explain in detail what has been merely referred to in the text. A number of professional fields are discouraging this use of the footnote.

Numbering and Spacing Footnotes. To indicate to the reader that a footnote is being used, place an Arabic numeral immediately *after* the material referred to and a little above the line. Do not put a period after the number, either in the text or with the footnote at the bottom of the page. Place the same number *before* and a little above the line of the note at the bottom of the page.[3] Each note should be single-spaced, and there should be one line of space between notes.

[3] *The MLA Style Sheet,* p. 12.

Footnotes should be numbered consecutively, starting from 1, in a paper intended for publication; in a typed or handwritten paper, however, it is often required that they be numbered beginning with 1 on each page. You should use the style that your instructor recommends.

The Form of Footnotes. The first time that you use a footnote to refer to any source, you should give the same information that is given in the bibliographic entry, plus the exact page from which your information is taken: the author's name (but in the natural order, *not* with the last name first), the title of the work, the facts of publication, and the exact page reference. The punctuation in the footnote is changed in one important aspect—instead of periods, as in the bibliography, commas and parentheses are used to separate the three parts of the reference. Later references to the same source are abbreviated. If only one work by an author is used in your paper, the author's name with the page reference is enough. If more than one work by the same author is used, the author's name and a shortened form of the title (with exact page reference, of course) will suffice. Book publishers' names are given in the shortest intelligible form—*Macmillan,* not *The Macmillan Company*—when they are included.

The forms illustrated here are those recommended by *The MLA Style Sheet,* with the addition of the publishers' names. For scientific papers the forms are slightly different, and the student who writes papers for publication in scientific journals must be governed by the rules set up by those journals.

FOOTNOTE—BOOK BY ONE AUTHOR

[1] E. B. White, *The Second Tree from the Corner* (New York: Harper, 1954), p. 36.

[2] Bertrand Evans, *Shakespeare's Comedies* (Oxford: Clarendon Press, 1960), p. 328.

FOOTNOTE, LATER REFERENCES

[3] White, p. 38. (The MLA recommends use of *p.* or *pp.* only with works of a single volume.)

[4] Evans, *Comedies,* p. 123.

[178]

FOOTNOTE FOR A BOOK WITH TWO OR MORE AUTHORS
5 Hans Albrecht Bethe and Philip Morrison, *Elementary Nuclear Theory* (New York: Wiley, 1956), p. 32.

FOR AN EDITED BOOK
6 Emily Dickinson, *Bolts of Melody*, ed. by Mabel Loomis Todd and Millicent Todd Bingham (New York: Harper, 1945), p. 207.

According to the principles set forth in *The MLA Style Sheet*, which are widely used in the fields of language, literature, and the social sciences, and which have been officially approved by a large number of university presses, Roman numerals are used for volume numbers and Arabic numerals for page numbers. Roman numerals, often as unfamiliar to college freshmen as the Roman language itself, are briefly explained below.

FOOTNOTE FOR A TRANSLATED WORK OF TWO OR MORE VOLUMES
7 H. A. Taine, *History of English Literature*, trans. H. Van Laun (New York: 1889), IV, 296.

FOR AN ARTICLE IN A COLLECTION OF ARTICLES
8 W. A. Shaw, "The Literature of Dissent," *Cambridge History of English Literature* (New York: Macmillan, 1917), X, 422.

FOR AN ARTICLE IN AN ENCYCLOPEDIA
9 Richard J. C. Atkinson, "Stonehenge," *Encyclopaedia Britannica* (1958), XXI, 440.

FOR A SIGNED MAGAZINE ARTICLE
10 H. Keppler, "New Look in Eclipses," *Modern Photography*, XXVII (Nov. 1963), 93.

FOR AN UNSIGNED MAGAZINE ARTICLE
11 "Better a Free World," *Newsweek*, XXXVII (March 19, 1951), 60.

FOR A SIGNED NEWSPAPER ARTICLE
12 Sen. Richard L. Neuberger, "Article in Defense of the Politician," *New York Times*, Nov. 2, 1958, Sec. VI, p. 13.

For an unsigned newspaper article, simply begin with the title. Bulletins are to be treated either as books, if published occasionally, or as magazine articles, if published regularly or as a series.

[179]

Roman Numerals. Because Roman numerals have a restricted use, students are sometimes unfamiliar with them. The following brief explanation may be helpful:

The key symbols are few in number: $1 = I$, $5 = V$, $10 = X$, $50 = L$, $100 = C$, $500 = D$, $1,000 = M$.

Other numbers are formed by adding or subtracting. The three main principles involved are as follows: (1) A letter following one of equal or greater value is added value; (2) A letter preceding one of greater value is subtracted value; (3) When a letter stands between two of greater value, it is subtracted from the last of the three and the remainder is added to the first. Try this explanation with the following examples:

RULE 1

$2 = II$	$20 = XX$	$200 = CC$
$3 = III$	$30 = XXX$	$300 = CCC$
$6 = VI$	$60 = LX$	$600 = DC$
$7 = VII$	$70 = LXX$	$700 = DCC$

RULE 2

$4 = IV$	$40 = XL$	$400 = CD$
$9 = IX$	$90 = XC$	$900 = CM$

RULE 3

$19 = XIX$	$59 = LIX$	$1,900 = MCM$

Abbreviations in Footnotes. Although the number of abbreviations used in research papers at the graduate-school level is large—and often confusing to the lay reader—only a few are of immediate concern here.

anon.   Anonymous.

c., ca.   *Circa*, "about." (Used with approximate dates.)

cf.   *Confer*, "compare." (Should not be used when *see* is meant.)

ch., chap.   Chapter.

chs., chaps.   Chapters.

col., cols.   Column, columns.

ed.   Edited, edition.

e.g.   *Exempli gratia* [ĕg·zĕm′plī grā′shĭ·à], "for example."

et al.   *Et alii* [ĕt ā′lĭ·ī], "and others."

f., ff. And the following page (f.) or pages (ff.)

ibid. *Ibidem* [ĭ·bī′dĕm], "in the same place." (*Ibid.* refers to the note immediately preceding. *The MLA Style Sheet* recommends substituting either the author's name or an abbreviated title; either is unambiguous and almost as brief as *ibid.*)

i.e. *Id est,* "that is."

l., ll. Line, lines.

loc. cit. *Loco citato* [lō′kō sī·tă′tō], "in the place cited." (*Loc. cit.* refers to the same passage cited in a recent note. It is used with the author's name but is not followed by a page number.)

op. cit. *Opere citato* [ŏp′ĕ·rē sī·tă′tō], "in the work cited." (*The MLA Style Sheet* calls this "the most abused of scholarly abbreviations," and recommends instead the use of the author's name alone or with an abbreviated title.)

The Fair Copy. After you have finished your final draft, you should prepare a clean copy for submission. Section 7, in Part Two of this book, gives some general rules that you should follow unless your instructor has some other preference. The sample library paper at the end of this chapter will assist you, also.

Preparing a Final Bibliography

Your final bibliography should include all the articles and books cited by your paper in the footnotes, plus whatever additional materials your instructor specifies. After you have completed typing the final draft of your paper, you can prepare your bibliography quickly by simply going through your footnotes, pulling out the appropriate bibliographical cards, and then arranging alphabetically (in index, *not* dictionary, order) by author, or by title when no author is given.

To alphabetize titles in index order, you should remember that (1) initial articles (*a, an, the*) are disregarded and (2) alphabetization is by word, with short forms of the same word coming first no matter what letter the second word starts with. For instance, *Japan* always precedes *Japanese:*

Japan: Her Industry and Commerce.

Japan: The Coming of the Occupation. [Note that articles are considered after the first word.]

Japanese Customs.

A *Japanese Gardener*. [Note the disregarded article.]

To alphabetize names in index order, you will also need to bear in mind a few variations from dictionary order. *Mc-* and *M'-* are alphabetized as if spelled *Mac-*. When two authors have identical last names, alphabetize by first names first, second names next: *Norman, Marie B.* precedes *Norman, Mary A.* An initial takes precedence over a spelled name that begins with the same letter, and a last name followed by a single initial takes precedence over a last name followed by two initials: *Norman, M.* precedes *Norman, M. B.*, and both precede *Norman, Mary A.* Use the titles (or dates, if titles are identical) to alphabetize a number of works by the same author writing alone. When there are collaborators, you may use the following order: (1) single author; (2) author and collaborator; (3) author "et al."; (4) title; (5) date, with the earliest first:

Norman, A. B. *My Life and Opinions*. New York: The Macmillan Company, 1963.

―――― and Tom Wilson. *The Hoe and the Scythe*. New York: The Macmillan Company, 1954.

―――― et al. *Dogs*. New York: The Macmillan Company, 1954.

―――― et al. *Two Essays*. New York: The Macmillan Company, 1956.

―――― et al. *Two Essays*. New York: The Macmillan Company, 1963.

The form of the individual entries has of course already been treated on pages 167–170. See also the bibliography accompanying the sample paper that follows.

Sample Outlines and Library Paper

The following sample outlines and library paper are reproduced here, not as perfect models to imitate, but as examples of conscientious and competent work.[4]

―――――――――

[4] Reproduced by permission of the author, Barbara H. Teruya, a student at Lawrence University.

TOPIC OUTLINE

Modern Japan's Young People

Thesis sentence: Japan's defeat and rapid Westernization
have created a spiritual vacuum in the youth of Japan from
which they can recover if they learn to value the aspects of
their traditional culture that have the greatest significance in the modern world.

  I.   Symptoms of problem facing Japan's young people
       A.   Popularity of literature that expresses hopeless-
            ness and despair
       B.   Rise in political influence of religious sects
       C.   High rate of suicide
       D.   Participation in anti-American demonstrations
 II.   Underlying causes of problem
       A.   Anxiety about growing economic power
       B.   Challenge to traditional norms
       C.   Spiritual vacuum
III.   Possible solution to problem
 IV.   Extent of success so far

SENTENCE OUTLINE

Modern Japan's Young People

  I.   Symptoms of deep inner fear and confusion are seen in
       several aspects of Japanese life.
       A.   The younger generation prefers pessimistic reading
            material.
            1.   One of the more popular authors is Hermann
                 Hesse.

      2. The unique position of literature in Japanese life should be recognized.

  B. Another example of unrest is reflected in the growing political influence of two religious sects.

      1. Both are concerned with ethical and moral values.

      2. Their strong appeal suggests a yearning for such values.

  C. Japan's high rate of suicide is another manifestation of confusion and frustration.

  D. A fourth sign of stress is student participation in anti-American demonstrations.

      1. Observers such as the late John D. Rockefeller IV noted that participants were often not really anti-American.

      2. Many took part for the sake of being in a crowd.

      3. For others, participation gave vent to inner frustrations.

II. Japan's rapid industrialization seems to be the chief cause of this spiritual disease.

  A. The accompanying growth to power frightens the young Japanese, who react instinctively to power that they feel will destroy peace.

  B. Industrialization has also created confusion by challenging Japan's traditional norms.

      1. Sikoku-san's situation is an illustration of this confusion.

          a. The old industrial system with its con-

[184]

cepts of mutual obligation and clan loyalties is not flexible.

    b. The new young worker, like Sikoku-san,
finds that his talents are wasted or un-
recognized in the old system.

  2. The Emperor's public renunciation of his
divinity disrupted a whole way of life for the
Japanese.

C. In addition, the Japanese have lost a great deal
of faith they once had in the United States.

  1. During the American occupation, General Mac-
Arthur impressed the Japanese with his strong
leadership and guidance.

  2. Today, signs of America's own political
crisis, such as the unrest over race problems,
create feelings of anxiety and apprehension.

III. Japan's first step toward solving her problem is to
acquire a confidence in her own individual worth.

A. Interrelationships with the Western world may
develop national pride.

B. There are signs today that Japan can successfully
synthesize East and West.

  1. Her modern art work stands up to western
standards, yet maintains an essential Japanese
quality.

  2. Of significance in Japan's development is her
new awareness that she need not conquer to be
free.

IV. Japan's growing sense of national pride points to a
more spiritually unified nation.

Modern Japan's Young People

The young, educated people of modern Japan seem confused and plagued by a deep inner fear. They seem to be
reaching out for some value or standard to guide them, but
they find none. Aptly described by Peter F. Drucker as the
"baffled young men of Japan," these young people represent
the wide gap which has been created between the old generation and the new.

Symptoms of fear and confusion are seen in several
aspects of Japanese life. For example, consider the reading material of the young generation. Its literary taste
leans heavily towards novels which express depression, hope-
lessness, and self-pity. Characteristic of such novels are
the early works of Hermann Hesse, German-Swiss Nobel Prize
winner, who is one of the more popular authors in present-
day Japan.[1] To appreciate the import of this literary tendency, we should recognize the significance of literature in
Japanese life. Partly because of tradition and partly because of Japanese temperament, the daily life of the Japanese is inseparably bound up with art, poetry, novels, and
plays. To the Japanese these art forms are as much a part
of life as breathing.[2]

Another example of unrest is reflected in the growing
influence of two religious sects, "Ten Rikyo," the Japanese
Seventh Day Adventists, and "Soka Gakkai," a schismatic

---

[1]Peter F. Drucker, "The Baffled Young Men of Japan,"
Harper's, CCXXII (Jan. 1961), 73.

[2]Edward Seidensticker and the Editors of *Life*, *Japan*
(New York: Time, Inc., 1961), pp. 91-94.

Buddhist sect. Both sects are concerned with the "ethical, moral, and spiritual values of politics." In fact, "Soka Gakkai" may be translated as "creation of values." The "Ten Rikyo" sect, though it does not actively participate in politics, stresses voting for "what is right"; "Soka Gakkai," on the other hand is directly active and polled four million votes in the July Senate elections of 1962.[3] The "Soka Gakkai" has been criticized for being "fanatic and dangerous," for seeking world domination, and for playing upon human desires for material wealth and fame.[4] The Japanese Government and the major political parties are uneasy about its growing power.[5] Nonetheless, the strong appeal of these sects suggests a yearning for values, guidance, and direction.

Japan's high suicide rate is another manifestation of confusion and depression. Rooted in her traditional mores, suicide is an inextricable part of the Japanese way of life. However, there is no denying the fact that Japan's suicide rate is the highest in the world for young people. It is the largest cause of death among the young Japanese between the ages of fifteen and twenty-four.[6]

A fourth sign of stress is the participation of Japanese young people in the recent anti-American riots. In the demonstrations of 1960, staged in opposition to the defense treaty with the United States, observers, such as the late

---

[3]Peter F. Drucker, "Japan Tries for a Second Miracle," Harper's, CCXXVI (March 1963), 77.

[4]Richard Okamoto, "Japan," Look, XXVII (Sept. 10, 1963), 16, 23-24.

[5]Emerson Chapin, "Buddhist Faction Growing in Japan," New York Times (Nov. 17, 1963), p. 9.

[6]Seidensticker, pp. 79-80.

John D. Rockefeller IV, noted that the participants were often not really anti-American. Their reasons for taking part in the riots reflected their fear and insecurity. Many took part just for the sake of being in a crowd. In answer to questions posed by opinion pollers as to why they participated in the riots, many gave no better reason than that it made them feel good.[7] For others, participation gave vent to unrest and inner frustrations. As George Packard recognized, "Zengakuren," the Marxist student organization, attracts students more as an "outlet for emotions" than for any Marxist principles. The students see "Zengakuren" as a means of attaining "quick and absolute solutions to frustrating problems." "It represents an instinctive mistrust of the old order, the love of solidarity and comradeship in a divided and confused society."[8] Probably, participants in other demonstrations, such as the recent one outside the U.S. Air Force base in Yakota, in which 50,000 "leftists" protested the U.S. plan to have jet fighter-bombers there, are similarly attracted.[9]

These symptoms characterize a disease which is eating away at the spirits of the young Japanese. As a teacher in Japan, John Ashmead, Jr. was struck by the spiritual sickness evident in his students' pessimistic attitudes. Rather than commit himself to some guiding principle or belief, one student thought it was better "not to think seriously about anything." Another felt that the majority of college stu-

---

[7] "A Challenge to U.S. by Riotous Japanese," _Life_, XLVIII (June 20, 1960), 28.

[8] George Packard III, "Japan's New Nationalism," _Atlantic Monthly_, CXI (April 1963), 67.

[9] "Japanese Protest at U.S. Base," _New York Times_ (Jan. 27, 1964), p. 3.

dents were "hopeless in heart," despite a promising future.
A third aptly summed up the general feeling of his generation when he said, "Sometimes pessimistic ideas possess me
so violently,and I want to do nothing."[10] Other observers
use various epithets to describe this spiritual disease.
E. V. Kuehnelt-Leddihn noted the "despair and emptiness
among the youth."[11] Drucker pointed to the spiritual
"malaise" of the baffled youth.

What is behind this spiritual sickness? Ironically,
the root of Japan's problem seems to lie in her rapid and
successful industrialization. Since opening her gates to
the influence of foreign powers, she has made great strides,
advancing from a weak feudal nation to a powerful industrial
one. Particularly within the last twenty years, she has
shown a tremendous surge of energy and drive, emerging as a
leading economic power. In 1960 Robert Martin cited data to
illustrate Japan's new industrial status. Within a ten-
year span from 1950 to 1960, Japan's crude-steel production
increased from 4.8 to 18 million tons; her refined oil products from 1.7 to 2.2 million tons; her foreign trade from
820 million dollars to 3.5 billion.[12] In 1962 the _Atlantic_
report on Japan recorded a continuation of "record prosper-
ity."[13] As a matter of fact, Japan's consistently fast

---

[10]John Ashmead, Jr., "These Were My Japanese Students,"
Atlantic Monthly, CCIV (Sept. 1959), 58.

[11]E. V. Kuehnelt-Leddihn, "What Makes Japan Tick,"
National Review, XII (Feb. 13, 1962), 95.

[12]Robert P. Martin, "Japan After 15 Years: The American
Way--But Anti-American Violence," _U.S. News and World Re-
port_, XLVIII (June 20, 1960), 76-77.

[13]"The Atlantic Report: Japan: _Atlantic Monthly_, CCIX
(March 1962), 14.

growth is the cause of many of her present economic problems. At the end of the fiscal year 1963, despite efforts
to check her rapid economic growth, Japan's Gross National
Product was 61 billion dollars, a 13% rise since the previous year.[14]

As the young Japanese become more aware of their country's new and growing economic power, their fear grows
correspondingly. They sense enormous power growing within
their country and are overwhelmed. Part of this fear stems
from the tendency of the Japanese to underrate themselves
since their defeat in World War II.[15] Because of her proud
heritage, rooted in her isolationist past, Japan felt that
anything short of complete conquest was a disgrace—a "loss
of face" and pride. But more than a feeling of inferiority,
her fear is an instinctive reaction against power and success. Having lived through the horrors of a war, the Japanese have assimilated the effects of the A-bomb and Hiro-
shima as a part of their modern consciousness. Theirs is an
instinctive passion to remain neutral and in peace. Perhaps
fear of power is another explanation for participation in
mob riots, such as those staged against the Japanese-U.S.
Security Treaty of 1963.[16] Cries of "Yankee, Stay Away" are
really reactions of fear, for such treaties force Japan to
accept the responsibility of her power.[17]

------

[14]"Japan: Search for a Better Balance," Business Week
(Feb. 22, 1964), 69.

[15]Drucker, "The Baffled Young Men," 72.

[16]"Yankee, Stay Away," Newsweek, LXI (June 3, 1963),
43.

[17]Drucker, "The Baffled Young Men," 72. Cf. A. M.
Rosenthal, "The New Japan: Timid Giant Seeks Identity," New
York Times (June 24, 1963), p. 1.

Besides a fear of power, industrialization has created "the confusion of a society in transition," one in which no one is quite sure what the standards of behavior should be.[18] Confusion stems primarily from a clashing of old traditions with the new ways of life which have accompanied industrialization, a confusion intensified by the great rapidity with which industrialization has taken place. A tremendous gap between the old generation and the new has been created. It spans a space of time comparable to a hundred years in Western development.[19] As one would expect, such a gap would create a conflict between the ideas, values, and customs of the old tradition and the new industrial innovations; but the crux of Japan's problem seems to lie not so much in this conflict as in the lack of new standards to replace those outmoded by industrialization. "Indeed, it is the very absence of philosophical or spiritual foundations that defines the problem . . . of contemporary Japan."[20]

This confusion of a society in transition—a society in which the position of the young Japanese is like being "fixed in a fluid society"—is well illustrated in the example of Sikoku-san, a successful consultant on personnel training who is married to the daughter of the dean of one of the big universities. In terms of wealth and prestige, Sikoku-san is an ideal son-in-law. Yet his father-in-law disapproves of him for being too independent; he feels that

---

[18]Drucker, "The Baffled Young Men," 67.

[19]Rafael Steinberg, "Japan Today—The Paradox," *Newsweek*, LV (June 20, 1960), 52.

[20]"Japan: Of Dynamo and Destiny," *Saturday Review*, XLVII (May 9, 1964), 32.

Sikoku-san needs someone to tell him what to do. The irony of this is that Sikoku-san's father-in-law is one of the leading "liberals" of Japan.[21]

In this kind of society no one knows exactly what the rules are. For the most part, the old traditional standards are adhered to. For example, the bases for Japan's social system may be seen in employer-employee relations in which clan loyalties and a concept of mutual obligation and loyalty hold. If a man is hired for a job, he is really being "adopted into a clan." He does not expect to be fired, nor does his employer expect him to quit and leave for a better job. In effect, a life-time contract is made. As a result of this kind of social system, seniority, rather than merit or skill, is the basis for wages. In addition to their wages, employees benefit from the profits of the enterprise in an elaborate bonus system. Bonuses, however, are balanced by low wages, or "monthly salaries" which are traditionally based on the amount of rice a man needs for a month. Also, since the employer-employee relationship is essentially a family tie, an employee receives other benefits; for example, his employer is expected to pay his hospital bills, to support his widow and children in case of death, and even to help send his sons through college.[22]

How do the young educated Japanese fit into this system? Not very well! The educated professional youth in Japan has risen to positions of great responsibility through merit alone. In many cases he has achieved previously undreamed of goals. But the traditional social system has not

---

[21]Drucker, "The Baffled Young Men," 67-68.

[22]Ibid., 68.

been flexible enough to correspond with his rise in the world. His group is one of the poorest paid groups in modern Japan; he ranks too high to receive workers' benefits, yet is not old enough to benefit from seniority rights. Instead of cash, he is given the promise of a great future; instead of recognition for his merit, he is assured of seniority rights; instead of a challenge, he is given security; instead of being able to use his knowledge and abilities where they will be best recognized, he is limited to one employer and the limited opportunities offered by that employer.[23] In addition, his employer often looks down upon him as "unreliable, insincere, unpatriotic, undisciplined and lacking in the proper spiritual outlook to guide Japan's future wisely."[24]

And perhaps there is justification for being suspicious of the young generation's lack of "the proper spiritual outlook"; for one of the principal causes of the young people's malaise seems to be a spiritual vacuum. Of this void, Masamichi Royama, the president of Ochanomizu Women's College, said,

> In the first years after the war, the old culture was disrupted and "democracy" introduced. But "democracy" in Western terms was an abstraction not known to the Japanese. It was difficult to absorb—has not been absorbed. . . . In Japan today we have a spiritual vacuum.[25]

A more disquieting example was described by Ashmead. Once when teaching an advanced English class, he asked his stu-

---

[23]Ibid., 67.

[24]"A Challenge to U.S. by Riotous Japanese," 29.

[25]Steinberg, 52.

dents to write about what they remembered when they were
Huckleberry Finn's age, forgetting that at that time they
were experiencing the effects of the A-bomb. One boy wrote:

> As a child I was taught both at school and at home
> to live for the sake of the living God, or Emperor
> Hirohito. I fancied that I was ready to dash into
> flames in His place, if need be. . . . But our
> surrender ten years ago put an end to our dream,
> since the one in whom we put the most faith had
> proved to be a mere nothing. Now most of us
> haven't been able to find anyone or anything to
> heartily believe in. One may say I live just
> because I dare not kill myself.[26]

Indeed, that the Emperor symbolized a whole way of life for
the Japanese cannot be overemphasized. He was their God,
whose every word was to be reverently received and obeyed
unquestioningly. As a symbol of the nation, he represented
the unity of the people. Thus, when Emperor Hirohito was
compelled by the Peace Treaty to renounce publicly any claim
to divinity, "the U.S. Occupation untied the knot that had
bound the Japanese in a tight web of constraint; the whole
social fabric started to unravel."[27] A whole way of life
was changed, and with it came a loss of faith in the values
of old Japan and of those who had led their country into
war.

This spiritual vacuum may also be viewed as a let-down.
After the war the Japanese had some goal to work towards—
the restoration of their war-torn country. They concentrated all their energies on this one immediate task. But
now that it has been completed and the stability resulting
from it is gone, the Japanese seem lost.[28]

---

[26]Ashmead, 59.

[27]Steinberg, 52.

[28]Drucker, "The Baffled Young Men," 71.

Related to this feeling of purposelessness is the attitude of the young Japanese toward the United States. As Drucker suggests, young Japanese are too dependent on the United States. Ho-Itsy, a personal friend of Drucker, remarked to him that

> We are attracted to the United States. . . . You, in the United States, however, have been our light —and we worry lest it fail us just when we need light the most.[29]

To see why the Japanese feel such a dependence, it might be helpful to understand the character of the American Occupation, for it is here that the strong influence of the United States took hold. First, the Occupation policies were as a whole benevolent, constructive, and sound, which impressed the Japanese. In the second place, General MacArthur provided the Japanese with strong leadership at a time when, disillusioned by their own leaders who had led them into a disastrous war, they needed guidance most. They were deeply moved by the "sincerity and intensity of MacArthur's idealism"; and the "sureness of his touch" in delivering his speeches assured them that they were in good hands. Probably as important as General MacArthur's leadership, if not more so, were the countless American GI's who made up the Occupation forces.[30] In the following paragraph, Kazuo Kawai beautifully expresses the influence that these Americans had on the Japanese:

> Their exuberant good spirits came as a welcome release to the Japanese, who had long been re-

---

[29]Ibid., 74.

[30]Kazuo Kawai, <u>Japan's American Interlude</u> (Chicago: University of Chicago Press, 1960), pp. 11-13.

pressed by the humorless authoritarianism of their militarists. The enthusiasm with which the Japanese children waved and shouted at passing GI's had little to do with gifts of chewing gum and candy, which generally were quite unexpected. The children must have been unconsciously responding to a kindred spirit of unspoiled youthfulness in the Americans which they failed to find in their own elders and for which they were starved. The elders also, laughing at the good-natured antics of the GI's, were charmed into letting down their suspicions against American influence. The Americans acted as the Japanese themselves would have liked to act but could not because of their social inhibitions, and thus the Americans became envied, models of a desired conduct.[31]

If we contrast this image with the present situation in America, we get a good idea of why men like Ho-Itsy are apprehensive "lest America fail them." Today as the United States undergoes its own spiritual crisis, its guiding light no longer shines as brightly. Evidences of America's period of re-evaluation are omnipresent. Books, magazines, and newspapers are full of discussions about the changing values in America's attitude toward religion, marriage, and sex. Our American heritage, based upon the Declaration of Independence, the Emancipation Proclamation, Patrick Henry's stirring words of "Give me liberty or give me death," is undermined by racial conflicts. Probably most shattering for the Japanese was the recent assassination of President Kennedy, who was highly popular among the Japanese and admired as a "symbol of American vitality and for his political policies."[32] When news of the assassination broke, the Japanese had special reasons for echoing the anguished cry, "My God, what has this world come to?"

---

[31] Ibid., p. 14.

[32] Emerson Chapin, "Economic Question Now Left in Abeyance," New York Times (Nov. 24, 1963), Sec. IV, p. 4.

However, no matter what the world has come to, this is the world that the Japanese must live in, in which they must face up to their problem. How will they do so?

It seems that the first necessary step is to acquire a confidence in their individual worth, to find a successful answer to what was described by John W. Bennett and others as "a search for historical identity and cultural definition." Although Mr. Bennett and his colleagues came to no conclusion, their research suggests that an answer is being reached particularly through interrelationships with America. For example, a Japanese student studying in America expressed his new awareness that out of the midst of an industrial and westernized Japan, his country must remain essentially Japanese:

> It was important for me to learn that these old customs of ours were not so bad, that there was some reason to them. American ways are not everything.[33]

As evidenced by such tours as the trip to Japan made by Leonard Bernstein and the New York Philharmonic Orchestra, and Ed Sullivan's bringing over ancient theater to American audiences, a new interest in the culture of Japan—not the Americanized and commercial Japan, but the old Japan—may very well add to a growing sense of national pride. On January 25, 1962, the joint U.S.-Japan Conference on Cultural and Educational Interchange, the first of its kind in U.S.-Japanese history, had its first meeting at Tokyo.[34]

---

[33] John W. Bennett et al., *In Search of Identity: The Japanese Overseas Scholar in America and Japan* (Minneapolis: University of Minnesota Press, 1958), p. 142.

[34] "U.S. Delegation to U.S.-Japan Cultural Conference Meet," *Department of State Bulletin*, XLVI (Jan. 22, 1962), 142.

[197]

Other reinforcements may come from successful and worthy achievements in the musical, literary, and scientific fields. In the fashion world, the Japanese kimono has already found its place. California designer Kow Kaneko has adapted the "graceful and simple elegance" of the kimono for easy, contemporay at-home living.[35]

The Japanese have been known for their love of harmony, their desire to connect new ideas and developments with the old.[36] There are signs today that Japan can successfully achieve this desire. In this regard, the influence of modern art has been particularly important, for it embodies the ideas of individuality, eccentricity, and freedom.[37] That Japan is asserting her individuality is seen in her paintings, in which abstract works stand up to Western standards yet maintain an unmistakable Japanese quality. Similar accomplishments are being made in the movie industry, in architecture, and in literature.[38] Underlying such achievements has been a significant development in Japan's thought —an awareness that she need not conquer to be free. As one of the leading competitors in the economic world, Japan has experienced a tremendous liberation of mind in her realization that she can compete and survive without conquest.[39]

Paul Linebarger finds hope for Japan in her growing sense of national pride:

---

[35]Okamoto, 36.

[36]Seidensticker, p. 105.

[37]A. M. Rosenthal, "The New Japan: Nation Emerges from War Sharply Divided," New York Times (June 25, 1963), p. 12.

[38]Drucker, "Japan Tries for a Second Miracle," 78. Cf. Seidensticker, pp. 93-94.

[39]Rosenthal, p. 12.

[198]

There is a change in the underlying public philosophy of Japan. . . . Following the fire and humiliation of defeat and surrender, the Japanese have turned to another facet of their own traditional culture—the cultivation of inwardness, the understanding of a beauty which rests in sparseness and scarcity, the patriotism so deep that it rests on the awareness that there can be no other Japan.[40]

George R. Packard speaks of a "new nationalism," in which "everyone calls for harmony, solidarity, and a united front against the outside world."[41]

This awareness that there can be no other Japan is essential, for "no matter how Western her economy, how technically educated her people, how advanced her physicians and scientists—her roots of culture and history, art and religion, script, literature, and language are not European but Asian."[42] With this awareness, the Japanese can begin to work constructively toward building a more spiritually unified nation.

---

[40]Paul M. A. Linebarger, "The New Japan in a Troubled Asia," Current History, XLI (Dec. 1961), 356.

[41]Packard, 61.

[42]Drucker, "Japan Tries for a Second Miracle," 78.

Bibliography

Ashmead, John Jr. "These Were My Japanese Students."
    Atlantic Monthly, XXIV (Sept. 1959), 56-59.

"The Atlantic Report: Japan." Atlantic Monthly, CCIX
    (March 1962), 14-23.

Bennett, John W., et al. In Search of Identity: The Japa-
    nese Overseas Scholar in America and Japan. Minneap-
    olis: University of Minnesota Press, 1958.

"A Challenge to U.S. by Riotous Japanese." Life, XLVIII
    (June 20, 1960), 26-35.

Chapin, Emerson. "Buddhist Faction Growing in Japan."
    New York Times (Nov. 17, 1963), p. 9.

——————————. "Economic Question Now Left in Abeyance."
    New York Times (Nov. 24, 1963), Sec. IV, p. 4.

Drucker, Peter F. "The Baffled Young Men of Japan."
    Harper's, CCXXII (Jan. 1961), 65-74.

——————————. "Japan Tries for a Second Miracle."
    Harper's, CCXXVI (March 1963), 72-78.

"Japan: Of Dynamo and Destiny." Saturday Review, XLVII
    (May 9, 1964), 32-33.

"Japan: Search for a Better Balance." Business Week (Feb.
    22, 1964), 69.

"Japanese Protest at U.S. Base." New York Times (January
    27, 1964), p. 3.

Kawai, Kazuo. Japan's American Interlude. Chicago: Univer-
    sity of Chicago Press, 1960.

Kuehnelt-Leddihn, E. V. " What Makes Japan Tick." National
    Review, XII (Feb. 13, 1962), 95.

[200]

Linebarger, Paul M.A. "The New Japan in a Troubled Asia."
Current History, XLI (Dec. 1961), 355-359.

Martin, Robert P. "Japan After Fifteen Years: The American
Way—But Anti-American Violence." U.S. News and World
Report. XLVIII (June 20, 1960), 76-80.

Okamoto, Richard. "Japan." Look, XXVII (Sept. 10, 1963),
16, 23-24.

Packard, George R. III. "Japan's New Nationalism." Atlantic Monthly. XXXI (April 1963), 64-69.

Rosenthal, A. M. "The New Japan: Nation Emerges from War
Sharply Divided." New York Times (June 25, 1963),
p. 12.

——————————. "The New Japan: Timid Giant Seeks Identity." New York Times (June 24, 1963), p. 1.

Seidensticker, Edward, and the Editors of Life. Japan. New
York: Time, Inc., 1961.

Steinberg, Rafael. "Japan Today—The Paradox." Newsweek,
LV (June 20, 1960), 51-56.

"Yankee, Stay Away." Newsweek, LXI (June 3, 1963), 42-43.

7 *LETTER WRITING*

THE FORMAL LETTER AND ITS PARTS

There are many kinds of letters, and all of them are forms of composition. To some extent they are governed by the same considerations that govern other kinds of writing. But when you dash off a note to the milkman, you would be foolish to worry very much about your grammar and punctuation. Your first draft is probably adequate. On the other hand, a letter to a prospective employer may be the most important document you ever write, in which every detail may count. The variety of letters is enormous. In every letter you write, however, even the one to the milkman, you are explicitly expressing yourself to one other individual. A letter is not an essay intended for general interest; it is, usually, a private communication between you and another person. In no other letter writing, therefore, is the emphasis so heavily on the character of your reader, what you know and expect of him.

Your letter to the milkman probably needs no improvement; the only test is whether you get the milk you want and don't offend the milkman. Furthermore no one, not even an English teacher, should presume to tell you how to write your most personal correspondence. You know best what ought to go into it. (The history of literature, however, provides many a love letter composed with grace and style.) What a teacher *can* help you to write, and what this chapter undertakes to consider, are all those letters you write that are relatively formal—that is, letters addressed to individuals you don't know intimately, under circumstances in which you cannot use language in a loose or perfunctory way. These include not only letters of application and business letters, but all those letters you have to write to people, especially older people, with whom you are not on terms of easy social equality.

Formal letters, then, are governed by considerations similar to those you must have in mind for all compositions. You must be clear, well organized, coherent. You must be punctilious in spelling, grammar, and punctuation. But in addition to these familiar injunctions, there are certain other laws, or conventions, of usage that the letter writer cannot ignore. Let us see what they are.

These are the parts of a letter:

1. The heading.
2. The inside address.
3. The salutation or greeting.
4. The body of the letter.
5. The complimentary close.
6. The signature.

For each of these parts usage has prescribed certain set forms. These forms must not be ignored or altered, especially in business letters. Conformity, not originality, is a virtue here.

The Heading

The parts of a heading, written in the following order, are the street address, the name of city or town, the name of the state, the date. A printed letterhead takes the place of a typed address. On paper with letterheads, the writer types the date either directly under the letterhead or flush with the right-hand margin of the letter.

[Letterhead]

September 23, 1964 [or] September 23, 1964

A growing number of letter writers, influenced possibly by European practice, or by the military services, are writing dates with the number of the day first, the month next, then the year —all without punctuation—for example, 23 September 1964. There is a logic and simplicity to this form that may in time win universal acceptance.

On paper that does not have a letterhead, the writer types the heading at the right according to one of the following forms:

Block form with open punctuation—that is, end punctuation is omitted. This form is rapidly becoming almost universal.

> 327 East Walnut Street
> Springdale, Wisconsin
> September 23, 1964

Indented form, with closed punctuation. Final punctuation is usually omitted.

> 76 Belmont Street,
> Canton, Iowa,
> September 23, 1964

Whichever form he uses, the writer should be consistent throughout the letter—in the heading, the inside address, and in the address on the envelope.

The Inside Address

In a business letter the inside address is the address of the person written to. The purpose of repeating in this way is to be absolutely clear about the identity of the addressee, and to include this information on the carbon copy that is retained in the sender's files. In a personal letter the inside address is usually omitted, though it may be added at the bottom of a fairly formal personal letter, in the lower left-hand corner. The first line of the inside address should be flush with the left-hand margin of the letter. Either the block form or the indented form may be used.

```
Mr. H. G. Warren
Warren & Stacey, Builders
132 First Avenue
Ogden, Maine

Dear Mr. Warren:
```

or

```
Parr Oil Company,
   20 Main Street,
      Helena, Illinois

Gentlemen:
```

The block form, illustrated first, is preferred by a majority of letter writers for business purposes.

In a business letter it is always correct to use a personal title with the name of the person addressed. The use of a personal title is correct even when a business title follows the name. Correct personal titles are *Mr., Mrs., Miss, Dr., Professor, Messrs.* A business title, designating the particular office or function of the individual in his organization, should not precede the name. The business title may immediately follow the name of the person addressed if the title is short, or it may be placed on the line below if the title is long:

```
Mr. T. C. Howard, Secretary      Mr. William R. Jones
Pueblo Rose Society              Personnel Manager

Dr. James L. Pendleton           Mrs. Theodore Jackson
Director of Admissions           Treasurer, City Women's Club
```

The inclusion of a business title usually implies that the writer is addressing the reader in his capacity as holder of a particular office or authority. In such cases, answers may properly be made by an assistant who speaks for his superior, or by a successor, should the original addressee have left office for some reason.

The Salutation or Greeting

The following forms are correct for business and professional letters:

```
Gentlemen:                       Ladies:
Dear Sir:                        Dear Madam:
My dear Sir:                     My dear Madam:
Dear Mr. Jackson:                Dear Miss White:
```

The expressions *My dear Sir* and *My dear Madam* are a little over-formal nowadays, and to most people have an old-fashioned ring.

In personal letters the range of greetings is unlimited, but somewhere between the inappropriately formal *Sirs* or *Madam* at one extreme, and an inappropriately affable *Hi Fella* at the other, we may mention the following as usually appropriate:

```
Dear Jack,        Dear Mr. Howard,        Dear Miss Brown,
```

We also ought to be aware that a great deal of modern business is transacted on a first-name basis, even when the relations between the parties are entirely professional.

Correct usage in addressing government officials and other dignitaries will be found in a good desk dictionary such as *Webster's New World Dictionary*, the *American College Dictionary*, or *Webster's Seventh New Collegiate Dictionary*.

A colon is used after the salution in a business letter; either a colon or a comma may be used in a personal letter. A comma is considered less formal. A dash—appropriate enough for a letter to an intimate friend—should be avoided in formal letters.

The Body of the Letter

The composition of business letters is a subject much too complex to be discussed here except in a very introductory way. A good letter, again, obeys the principles of any good writing. It should be clear, direct, coherent, dignified, and courteous. A student who can write a good class paper ought to be able to write a good business letter. But there are whole college courses devoted to the subject, and the interested student should either enroll in such a course or consult one of the numerous special guidebooks available.

At its best, the efficient and graceful composition of a business letter is a genuine art that few have perfected. Much more flexibility is required than is generally understood. There are times when a letter must speak very formally, as if in the abstract voice of its letterhead, a large and impersonal corporation. There are other times when warmth and genial good fellowship are appropriate. The executive who can say no without hurting his reader's feelings is a valuable man to his company. But these skills, however interesting and important, are beyond the range of this handbook.

The Complimentary Close

Correct forms for the complimentary close of business letters are as follows:

```
Yours truly,            Faithfully yours,
Yours very truly,       Sincerely yours,
Very truly yours,       Yours sincerely,
Respectfully yours,     Cordially yours,
```

It is now considered bad taste to use a participial phrase in closing a letter, such as *Hoping you are well*. A comma is the usual punctuation after the complimentary close; only the first letter is capitalized. In ordinary formal business letters, *Yours truly* or *Yours very truly* is the accepted form. In business letters between men who know each other well, *Yours sincerely* and *Cordially yours* are used, or even, more informally, *Sincerely* and simply *Yours*.

The Signature

For the ordinary person it is correct to sign a business letter as he would sign a check. If possible, he should write his name legibly. But just to make sure, it is desirable to type the name under the signature.

Some of the conventions that govern the form of a signature are the following:

1. Neither professional titles, such as *Professor, Dr., Rev.,* nor academic degrees, such as *Ph.D., LL.D., M.A.,* should be used with a signature.

2. An unmarried woman should not sign herself as Miss Laura Blank, but she may place *Miss* in parentheses before her name if she feels that it is necessary for proper identification.

3. A married woman or a widow signs her own name, not her married name. For example, *Diana Holoday Brown* is her own name; *Mrs. George Brown* is her married name. She may place *Mrs.* in parentheses before her signature, or her married name in parentheses under it.

4. When a secretary signs her chief's name to a letter, she may add her own initials below the signature.

The following is an example of a business letter, of the type that might be written to a business organization from a private individual:

37 North Cove Road
Los Gatos, California
June 18, 1965

Acme Camera Shop
876 Fifth Street
Palo Alto, California

Gentlemen:

I am returning to you a lens which you sent me, on my
order, on June 16. The lens is a 35-mm F 2.5 (wide angle)
P. Angenieux Retrofocus, with a bayonet mount to fit the
Exacta camera. The number of the lens is 463513.

You will notice by holding the lens against a bright light
that there is a distinct scratch on the front element. As
the lens is guaranteed to be free from imperfections, I am
returning it to you for a replacement.

Will you kindly send me a new lens as soon as you can?
I must have it by June 25, as I am leaving then on a camera
trip to Utah.

You have my check for $120, dated June 12, in payment.

Yours very truly,

Martin H. Hanson

Martin H. Hanson

LETTERS OF APPLICATION

One of the most difficult and probably most important letters
that you will have to write is the letter of application for a job.
Of course it is impossible to say what will appeal to every employer, but certain general guides can be set up. It is true that
usually in applying for work you have to fill out a printed form.
Well, so will five hundred others applying for the same job. It is
the letter you write that will help you stand out in the crowd.

A letter of application should be direct, sincere, and informa-
tive. It must not be vague; it must not grovel in undue modesty
nor boastfully promise what cannot be delivered. It should not
include irrelevant personal information. Something is to be
gained, as it often is in other types of writing, by putting yourself
in the place of the person you are addressing. Suppose *you* were
a busy personnel manager, shuffling through dozens of letters of

application. What would attract you favorably? Obviously, long-windedness would not.

A typical letter of application contains the following components:

1. An introductory statement in which the writer states that he has heard of a possible vacancy.
2. Personal data.
3. Record of education.
4. Record of experience.
5. References.
6. Request for an interview.

Probably the most important section is the one in which the writer shows how his education or experience has a vital bearing on the job for which he is applying. This is hard to write, but you must try it. Your job depends on it.

37 Twenty-third Street
Corvallis, Oregon
April 10, 1964

Mr. F. C. McVey
Personnel Officer
Baird and Summers, Contractors
35 Division Street
Salem, Oregon

Dear Mr. McVey:

Mr. James Ryan, one of the engineers on your staff, has informed me that you will need several truck drivers for your road construction jobs early in June. I wish to apply for a job as gravel truck driver.

I am twenty years old, six feet tall, and I weigh 182 pounds. I am unmarried.

Two years ago, when I was eighteen, I graduated from Central High School, where I took the college preparatory course with emphasis on mathematics and physics. I also played football in my junior and senior years.

When I was in high school I spent my weekends and vacations working for Bert's Texaco Station and Garage, where I learned a great deal about the operation, service, and maintenance of various types of trucks. Mr. Bert Jenkins will write you about my work there.

Since then I have worked at various jobs to earn money for my college education. I am now finishing my first year

in the school of engineering at Oregon State College. After
I graduated from high school I spent a year working for the
Ochoco Ranch, near Knappa, Oregon, where I drove tractors,
trucks, cultivators, and harvesters. Last winter I drove
a bulldozer for Bruce & Stewart, clearing the old Camp Adair
site near Corvallis. Then last summer I had a job with
Pelican Builders of Klamath Falls, for whom I drove gravel
trucks and cement mixers. I believe that my experience
should qualify me for the job for which I am applying.

The following employers for whom I have worked have given
me permission to use their names as references:

Mr. H. D. Winslow
Ochoco Ranch
Knappa, Oregon

Mr. Edwin Stewart
Bruce & Stewart
Corvallis, Oregon

Mr. Karl Swensen
Pelican Builders
Klamath Falls, Oregon

I should appreciate an opportunity to call at your office
for an interview at any time that you designate. My telephone is Plaza 3-5948.

Yours very truly,

Henry Williamson

Henry Williamson

Sometimes a shorter letter of application, though for a more
permanent position, may be used as a supplement to other records—college grades, statements of recommendation—that are
forwarded to an employer by a placement service. Here is an
example of such a letter, in which it is wise not to repeat much
of the information that the employer already possesses in the
official dossier.

14 Riggs Avenue
Columbus, Ohio
14 May 1964

Dr. Leroy Faust
Superintendent of Schools
Shaker Heights, Ohio

Dear Dr. Faust:

I understand from our local placement office that a
position as third grade teacher is open for next fall in
your school system. I believe I am qualified for that

position. My record of training at the University School of Ohio State University is being forwarded to you, and as you will see, I maintained a "B" average at the University and completed all necessary requirements in teacher training. I hold a temporary teacher's certificate for the state of Ohio. This letter is meant to convey, in addition, my great enthusiasm for teaching and my personal interest in becoming a part of your much-admired system.

Though I have done no classroom teaching beyond that provided by my university courses, I believe my devotion to young people may in part compensate for inexperience. My enthusiasm for teaching those younger than I began early in my life, and was increased by my years as a leader in Girl Scout work. Summer jobs as a camp counselor, involving instruction in outdoor activities for young children, improved my confidence in handling the eight-to-ten age group. Considerable testimony from parents and from the children themselves convinced me that I have been successful in reaching these young people.

Naturally I am eager to become a part of a school system so well thought of as yours at Shaker Heights. I am available on short notice for interview, at your convenience.

Sincerely yours,

Mary A. Clark

Mary A. Clark

SOME FAMILIAR FAULTS TO AVOID

Do not omit pronouns, prepositions, and articles where they are grammatically necessary. If your letter should begin with *I* or *we*, begin with *I* or *we*.

BAD
Received your letter yesterday.
Am writing to you in reply . . .
Have not heard from you . . .

RIGHT
I received your letter yesterday.
I am writing to you . . .
I have not heard from you . . .

Do not close a letter with a sentence or a phrase introduced by a participle.

[211]

B A D

Hoping to hear from you soon . . .

Hoping for an early answer . . .

Thanking you again for your past favors . . .

Trusting to hear from you by return mail . . .

Do not write *yours, your favor,* or *your esteemed favor* for *letter.*

B A D

In reply to yours of the 20th . . .

Your esteemed favor at hand, and in reply . . .

Avoid certain trite and stilted expressions frequently used in business letters.

B A D

In reply would say . . .

Yours of the 10th inst. received . . .

And contents thereof noted . . .

Your valued favor . . .

And oblige, Yours truly . . .

Enclosed please find . . .

PUBLIC LETTERS

We have spoken of letters as, usually, private communications from one individual to another. The exception is the public letter in which the writer, while ostensibly addressing a single person, is in fact addressing a larger audience. An obvious example is the letter to the editor, in which the greeting *Dear Sir* might more accurately read *Dear Everybody* or *Dear World.* Many business letters, without being directed to the world, are intended for more than one reader—a committee, a sales force, a staff of officers. Modern duplicating methods are so cheap and efficient that any member of an organization may expect to find his semi-public report to a superior photocopied and scattered all over the office. When this happens, of course, his infelicities of expression, his misspellings and his vague logic, are photocopied too.

The composition of a public, or semipublic, letter requires a special kind of skill. When addressing a group of individuals—a committee for example—one must often be aware of the likes and dislikes of particular individuals among one's readers. Sometimes these likes and dislikes conflict. How can one persuade some of one's readers without offending others? What compromised expression of one's own view might win a majority approval, or at least acquiescence? These are serious matters. Some organization men report that every word they write is composed in balanced awareness of the varying possible responses among a number of specific readers whose prejudices may be in conflict. This sort of tight-rope act does not, of course, make for individual strength and verve of style. But it is a fact of organization life.

EXERCISES

EXERCISE 1, A LETTER OFFERING SUGGESTIONS. *Write a letter to the principal of your high school in which you suggest two or three specific ways students might be better prepared for your particular college.*

EXERCISE 2, A LETTER OF CORRECTION. *Write a letter to your college newspaper in which you correct a wrong impression produced by a news story that has just appeared in the paper. Make your letter courteous, dignified, and logical.*

EXERCISE 3, A LETTER REQUESTING A SPECIAL PRIVILEGE. *Write a letter to your dean in which you request permission to take your final examinations several days before the scheduled period. Give your reason clearly and convincingly.*

EXERCISE 4, A LETTER URGING ACTION. *As secretary of a student organization, write a letter to the members urging them to pay their dues.*

EXERCISE 5, A LETTER OF PROTEST. *As a member of the same organization, write a letter to its secretary protesting his undue anxiety about the members' dues.*

EXERCISE 6, A LETTER OF APPLICATION. *You plan to work at one of the national parks during the summer. Write a letter of application. Apply for some position that you could fill. Give adequate information about yourself and your qualifications.*

EXERCISE 7, A LETTER TO A CONGRESSMAN. Write to your congressman requesting an interview with him when you visit Washington in a month's time.

EXERCISE 8, A LETTER REQUESTING PAYMENT. A man for whom you worked last summer owes you thirty dollars. Write him a letter that will induce him to pay you what he owes you.

PART
TWO

A
HANDBOOK
OF
WRITING
AND
REVISION

GRAMMAR AND USAGE

§ 1. SENTENCE FRAGMENTS

Fragmentary sentences should be avoided in expository writing, in both formal and informal varieties of standard English.

A grammatically complete sentence is a pattern of communication in words that is based on a verb with its subject. That is the essential core of a complete sentence—at least one verb with its subject or subjects. Structurally the sentence must be an independent unit, capable of standing alone. This statement means simply that dependent units, such as phrases, clauses, appositives, and similar groups of words, are not sentences, and should not be written as sentences. When any one of these dependent units is written and punctuated as a sentence, it is called a *sentence fragment*.

Of course there are also nonconforming patterns in writing and speech—especially in informal speech—which we may call legitimate fragments, or non-sentences, or unconventional sentences, as we fancy. The exact naming is less important than your understanding of these patterns. They exist in our language, and their uses must be understood. In the kind of expository writing that you will do in college, however, they are usually objectionable. These patterns are discussed below.

The ineffective sentence fragment, a result of ignorance or carelessness, is the affliction of only the first few papers written in a college composition course, for sentence sense is something that is easily and quickly mastered. It must be mastered quickly, too, if you are to progress to more vital matters related to good writing. If at this stage of your education you still do not know what a sentence is, turn back to pages 48–62 and study the definitions, the examples, and the diagrams that you find there.

LEGITIMATE SENTENCE FRAGMENTS

Fragments of various kinds, verbless and subjectless sentences, with or without understood additions that would make them complete grammatically, are commonly used in speech. In narrative writing they are necessary to reproduce dialogue naturally. By some writers they are also used for special stylistic effects, especially in novels and short stories. In some of the fragments either the subject or the verb is understood; in others, no amount of ingenious interpretation will supply a subject or a predicate. We must accept them for what they are—language patterns correctly punctuated as sentences. Here are examples:

THE COMMAND
Drive your car to the last platform. Please drive carefully. Then stop your motor. Open the trunk and let me look into your suitcases. [The typical pattern of the imperative sentence omits the subject.]

THE QUESTION
Why the delay, officer? A wreck ahead? How bad? Anyone hurt? Two elderly women? Oh, not seriously.

THE EXCLAMATION
Another fumble! Oh, what luck, what awful luck. Three fumbles already and no recoveries.

BITS OF DIALOGUE
"Hi, Penny," he exclaimed. "Great game, isn't it?"
"Yes," said Penny, "depending on whose side is winning."
"You alone? Sit with me. Room enough here. And no books for us today."

SPECIAL EFFECTS — THE "POINTING-OUT" METHOD OF DESCRIPTION
Sam Clark's Hardware Store. An air of frankly metallic enterprise. Guns and churns and barrels of nails and beautiful shiny butcher knives.
Chester Dashaway's House Furnishing Emporium. A vista of heavy oak rockers with leather seats, asleep in a dismal row.
Billy's Lunch. Thick handleless cups on the wet oilcloth-covered coun-

ter. An odor of onions and the smoke of hot lard. In the doorway a young man audibly sucking a toothpick.

The warehouse of the buyer of cream and potatoes. The sour smell of a dairy.

—SINCLAIR LEWIS, *Main Street*

INEFFECTIVE SENTENCE FRAGMENTS

An ineffective sentence fragment may be revised by (1) attaching the fragment to the sentence from which it was split off, (2) completing its form by adding the necessary words, (3) rewriting the passage.

It will help you to write complete sentences if you know what the trouble spots are and what you should do about them. The four main types of ineffective sentence fragments are listed below and their corrections indicated by examples:

1a. A dependent clause should not be written as a complete sentence.

If you remember that a dependent clause usually begins with a connective that relates it to the main clause, you can guard against some types of fragments. For adjective clauses look for the relative pronouns *who, which,* and *that,* and the relative adverbs *when, where,* and *why.* For adverb clauses look for the subordinating conjunctions *after, although, as if, because, before, if, since, though, unless, when, where, while,* and some others. Noun clauses are almost never used as fragments. Another helpful fact to remember is that the fragment usually *follows* the main clause, to which it may be joined in correction.

FRAGMENT
He spent his life preaching social justice. *Which was a startling concept in his day.*

REVISION
He spent his life preaching social justice, which was a startling concept in his day. [Add fragment to main clause.]

FRAGMENT
The animosity that his ideas excited is incredible. *Although a few brave men praised him.*

[219]

REVISION

The animosity that his ideas excited is incredible, although a few brave men praised him. [Add clause to sentence.]

FRAGMENT

The officer came to the alley where the man was last seen. *And where the stolen gems were probably hidden.*

REVISION

The officer came to the alley where the man was last seen, and where the stolen gems were probably hidden. [The second *where*-clause also modifies *alley*.]

1b. A verbal or a prepositional phrase should not be written as a complete sentence.

FRAGMENT

The two boys took the first faint trail to their left. *Hoping it would take them to a river.*

REVISIONS

The two boys took the first faint trail to their left, hoping it would lead them to a river. [Join phrase to main sentence.]

The two boys took the first faint trail to their left. They hoped it would lead them to a river. [Supply subject and verb to make the fragment a sentence.]

FRAGMENTS

They plodded along the trail all day. *Without a rest. Without stopping to eat what food was left.*

REVISION

Without a stop to rest or to eat what food they had, they plodded along the trail all day. [You may also revise by putting the prepositional phrases after the main clause.]

FRAGMENT

The railroad made Virginia City a lumber center. *Its population leaping from three hundred to five thousand in three years.* [This is a participial phrase, of the special type called the absolute phrase. See page 53.]

REVISION

The railroad made Virginia City a lumber center. Its population leaped from three hundred to five thousand in three years. [Change the participle to a verb to make a complete sentence. You may also join the phrase to the main clause.]

1c. An appositive phrase should not be written as a complete sentence.

Guard against this fault especially when the phrase is introduced by such words as *namely, for example, such as,* and the like.

FRAGMENT
Some games are called contact sports. *Namely, football, basketball, and ice hockey.*

REVISION
Some games, namely football, basketball, and ice hockey, are called contact sports.

FRAGMENT
New problems face the girl entering college. *Such as budgeting her money and her time for study.* [*Budgeting* is in apposition with *problems.*]

REVISION
New problems, such as budgeting her money and her time for study, face the girl entering college. [Place the appositive near *problems,* not at the end of the sentence.]

FRAGMENT
We found him starving in his shack. A *development that completely puzzled us.* [*Development* is in apposition with the whole idea expressed in the main clause.]

REVISION
We found him starving in his shack, a development that completely puzzled us. [Add the appositive to the main clause.]

1d. Any verbless chip or fragment of a sentence, whether you can classify it or not, should not be allowed to stand as a sentence.

Some fragments are written because the writer was in too much of a hurry to think; others are written because the writer has carried over into writing the exclamatory nature of very informal speech. The following examples will make the points clear:

FRAGMENTS
Just a lazy weekend vacation. No work. No worries. That's what he promised me.

REVISIONS

Just a lazy weekend vacation with no work or worries—that's what he promised me. [The dash indicates a sharp break in the construction.]

What he promised me was a pleasant weekend vacation, with no work and no worries.

FRAGMENT

Unexpectedly I dropped in on her daughter. *Just a friendly call, no party.* [The writer of this was making note jottings, not sentences.]

REVISION

Unexpectedly I dropped in on her daughter. I intended this to be just a friendly, informal call. [Make a sentence out of the fragment.]

EXERCISES

EXERCISE 1, RECOGNIZING SENTENCE FRAGMENTS. *Copy the following sentences. Some of them are complete. Some are fragments. If a sentence is complete, underline its subject once and its verb twice. If the group of words is a clause, encircle the subordinating connective. If it is a verbal phrase, encircle the verbal.*

1. *Main Street* being Sinclair Lewis's first really important novel.
2. Although he had already published two or three full-length stories.
3. A native of Sauk Center, Minnesota, he wrote about the people he knew best.
4. At first, the natives of Sauk Center were very indignant.
5. Resenting his slurs against them and their way of life.
6. They insisted that his novel was not a true picture of their town.
7. That his characters were caricatures and his town a monstrosity.
8. Finding that his fame brought them notice and recognition.
9. Gradually capitalizing on their notoriety in profitable ways.
10. Merchants adopted "Gopher Prairie" as a sort of brand name for several of their commercial enterprises.

EXERCISE 2, ELIMINATING SENTENCE FRAGMENTS. *In some of the following word groups you will find sentence fragments. Eliminate each fragment either by joining it to the main clause or by rewriting it as a complete sentence. Be able to tell whether rule 1a, 1b, or 1c applies.*

1. Last summer, while on our way from New York to Denver, we stopped at State College, Pennsylvania, to visit a friend of ours. Whom we had not seen since our college days.

2. The college is now a state university, but the town is still State College. Names of towns not being subject to quick changes.

3. The town is not exactly inaccessible, as some say. Neither is it close to a modern turnpike or expressway.

4. The drive to the city took us across several ranges of hills. The road at times narrow and curving but never difficult to take at reasonable speeds.

5. I was amazed at the extent and attractiveness of the campus. Situated as it was in the beautiful Nittany Mountains.

6. We found our friend in the college infirmary, where he had his office. And where he has worked with the students for many years.

7. His face showed at once that he had aged and gained weight. And his hair, or what was left of it, having turned gray.

8. He said he could leave his office early, drive us about the campus, and then take us out to dinner. Which was an offer that we accepted with many thanks.

9. Talking with an old friend usually revives old memories. Such as college pranks, football games, and wartime experiences.

10. Leaving him the next morning, we felt that he had led a happy, useful, and rewarding life. A fact that we spoke of at odd moments most of that day.

§ 2. RUN–TOGETHER SENTENCES

When two or more complete sentences are combined in a single sentence, they must be properly separated from one another.

A sentence made up of two or more independent, coordinate clauses, properly joined and punctuated, is called a *compound sentence*. (See page 57.) The usual means of joining these independent clauses are (1) a semicolon, (2) a conjunction, (3) a comma and a conjunction, (4) a semicolon and a conjunction. (See also Sections 13 and 14.)

2a. The comma splice may be corrected in several ways.

The use of a comma to join independent, coordinate clauses (except in certain infrequent situations that will be discussed later) is called a *comma splice* or a *comma fault*. It should be avoided in college writing, especially in serious discussions of serious subjects. A comma splice may be corrected in one of the following ways. The student should choose the method of revision that produces the most effective sentence.

1. The comma splice may be corrected by subordinating one of the two independent sentences. (If the student puts both statements in the same sentence, he must believe that one is closely related to the other. A subordinate clause can express this relation specifically.)

SPLICE

We all went home after the picnic, it had started to rain.

BETTER

We all went home after the picnic because it had started to rain.

SPLICE

The food was fine except for the cake, I didn't like it.

BETTER

The food was fine except for the cake, which I didn't like.

2. The comma splice may be corrected by inserting a coordinating conjunction after the comma. (These conjunctions are *and, but, for, or, nor, yet.*)

SPLICE

We were looking for a shady spot, we couldn't find one.

BETTER

We were looking for a shady spot, but we couldn't find one.

3. The comma splice may be corrected by using a semicolon instead of a comma if the sentences are close enough in meaning to be combined into a compound sentence.

SPLICE
We finally found a satisfactory place, it was breezy but quiet.

BETTER
We finally found a satisfactory place; it was breezy but quiet.

If you wished to subordinate instead, however, then of course the sentence would look like this:

We finally found a satisfactory place, which was breezy but quiet.

4. The comma splice may be corrected by using a period to separate the two coordinate clauses. In simple examples, such as the ones we are discussing here, the danger of this alternative is a series of very short sentences that look choppy.

CORRECT BUT CHOPPY
We finally found a satisfactory place. It was breezy but quiet.

Note that your choice of a solution for the run-together sentence, like all your choices in writing, can affect the *tone* of your statement. Thus in the last revision above, the choice of two very short sentences produces a speaker who sounds close-lipped or laconic. The decisions you make about your grammar relate directly to the way your words are understood by your reader.

The use of a comma to join coordinate clauses is more common in novels, stories, and some types of journalistic writing than it is in serious expository prose. In any case the clauses so joined are likely to be short and simple.

LEGITIMATE COMMA JUNCTIONS

In serious discussions—with which we are primarily concerned here—the comma is used by most writers to join coordinate clauses in the following situations:

1. When the clauses are arranged in the "a, b, and c" order.

EXAMPLE
The shrubs were leafy and well-pruned, the walks had been scrupulously raked, and the fountain shone in the sunlight.

2. When the series of statements takes the form of a climax.

EXAMPLES
I came, I saw, I conquered.
The sun is growing warm, frogs are waking in the marshes, planting time will soon be here.

3. When the statements form an antithesis, or are arranged in the "it was not merely this, it was also that" formula. This is an effect particularly characteristic of traditional stylists.

EXAMPLES
It was more than an annoyance, it was a pang.

—WINSTON CHURCHILL

To allow the Mahdi to enter Khartoum would not merely mean the return of the whole of the Sudan to barbarism, it would be a menace to the safety of Egypt herself.

—LYTTON STRACHEY

You should guard against two familiar situations that especially invite the comma splice. One such danger point is immediately following tags such as *he said* in dialogue.

DIALOGUE
"That's right," said Paul. "I'd almost forgotten her name." [A period is the usual punctuation, although a semicolon is occasionally used.] "No one remembers the good things I have done," she complained; "no one ever does." [Semicolon used here.]
"Yes, I know, sir," said Jones. "I warned him to be careful." [Period used here.]

The other danger concerns conjunctive adverbs such as *however*, *moreover*, and so on.

ADVERBS
The prisoner told a long story of atrocities; however, his companion did not agree with his version of what had happened to them. [Use a semicolon before the conjunctive adverb. Better still, use a semicolon and hide the adverb within the second clause.]
When I registered for engineering, I had two high-school subjects to make up; moreover, I had forgotten most of the algebra I ever knew. [Use a semicolon before the conjunctive adverb.]

2b. The fused sentence may be corrected by the same methods as the comma splice.

The fused sentence is one in which two sentences are run together with no punctuation at all between them. It is an extreme example of the same kind of carelessness that produces the sentence fragment and the comma splice, and like those elementary errors, it should quickly disappear from college writing.

FUSED

At first I wondered if I should speak to her she seemed to be so wrapped up in her thoughts.

I almost decided to walk by and pretend I did not see her she might think I was intruding.

I was lonesome I decided to speak and I said hello in a weak voice.

UNIFIED

She seemed so wrapped up in her thoughts that at first I wondered if I should speak to her. [Subordination]

Fearing that she might think I was intruding, I almost decided to walk by and pretend not to see her. [Subordination]

As I was lonesome, I decided to speak to her, and I said hello in a weak voice. [Subordination]

If a student knows what a sentence is, he should not let carelessness of this sort destroy his writing. If he still finds it difficult to master elementary sentence sense—for example, to identify immediately the subject and verb of a main clause—then he must be helped with practice in analysis and diagraming.

EXERCISES

EXERCISE 1, SUBORDINATING CLAUSES. *Correct each of the following sentences by subordinating one or more of the run-together coordinate clauses.*

1. Some people like an ocean voyage in winter, they want to escape the frost and snow at home.
2. A few are likely to be bored on a ship it is such a closed-in community.

[227]

3. The weather may be fine for days, however, it may change abruptly, everyone gets seasick.
4. The food is usually rich and plentiful, it would be unfortunate not to enjoy it.
5. Deckchairs are the rule in sunny weather, in bad weather one stays below.
6. Who would not appreciate seeing the islands of the West Indies, we have heard so much about them?
7. The stewards on shipboard are uniformly pleasant and efficient, they have been so well trained, they know exactly what to do.
8. Vacations at sea are within the reach of many people today they were a luxury for a privileged class not so very long ago.
9. Air travel is much faster, of course, nevertheless a week on a ship can be far more restful.
10. Most people are glad to get home, however, you can tell by looking at their happy faces as they step ashore.

EXERCISE 2, SUBORDINATING WITH PHRASES AND APPOSITIVES. *Revise each of the following sentences by using subordination of a rank below that of a subordinate clause (a phrase or an appositive).*

1. Success in life, they say, requires two principal qualities, they are perseverance and innate talent.
2. This is like most such generalizations it is hard to put to practical use.
3. A man has perseverance, or he has innate talent, how can you distinguish?
4. Many people apparently have perseverance and talent, they still do not conspicuously succeed.
5. Such statements are misleading they are so simple, they are falsely profound.

EXERCISE 3, REVISING AN INFORMAL PARAGRAPH. *Here is a paragraph composed in extremely informal style. Rewrite it more formally by revising its fragments and run-together sentences in any way you think appropriate.*

I'm disgusted with him. The liar. Telling me all the time how honest he was, too. He wanted to borrow my car, I knew he didn't even have a license, his roommate told me that. I should have said no to him, I know I should. Right to his face. I'm rather soft-hearted, you know how I am. In spite of all past disappointments. I wonder where my car is, it's been quite a long time now. That robber.

Notice again, as you do this exercise, how the tone changes with the changes in grammar. Is the speaker in your revision more angry than the original speaker, or less? Is he closer to his listener, or further away?

§ 3. SUBJECT–VERB AGREEMENT

A verb must agree in number with its subject.

Actually there is nothing very difficult about the general principle that singular verbs should match singular subjects and plural verbs should match plural subjects. In simple sentences such as "The boys are playing in your yard," in which the verb stands next to the subject, no college student would be tempted to say, "The boys is playing . . ." Neither would he ever say, "The man were working." Difficulties arise when the sentences are not so simple as these. Problems in agreement can be listed under three main categories:

1. When several other words intervene between the subject and verb, or when the word order is unusual, the writer or speaker may forget for the moment just what the subject is and so make an error.

2. When the subject seems to be singular and plural at the same time—"everybody," "gymnastics," "the whole family," "either of us," "a group of people"—or when there seems to be a choice between one and the other, a writer can easily become confused as to what rule should apply.

3. Because usage differs according to situation or occasion, the writer may not know which rule best suits a given occasion. The forms recommended in this book, however, are appropriate and correct in all varieties of English—formal or informal, written or spoken. In very informal situations, other forms may *also* be current. Let us repeat—the forms given in this book are the language patterns of *general* English, proper in formal essays and

books, in college themes, in *Harper's, The New Yorker, Time, Life,* the daily newspaper, in formal and informal conversation.

It is often helpful for the student, especially the visual-minded one, to make a quick mental diagram of the grammatical subject and verb of a sentence.

3a. Plural words that intervene between a singular subject and its verb do not change the number of the subject.

EXAMPLES

The *racket* of all those engines *was* deafening. [*Racket was,* not *engines were.* "Of all those engines" is a phrase modifying *racket,* and this of course does not make *racket* plural.]

One of the many techniques he explained to us *was* that of flycasting. [*One* technique *was flycasting,* not all of them.]

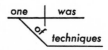

3b. When words are added to a singular subject by *with, together with, as well as, in addition to, except,* and *no less than,* the number of the subject remains singular.

EXAMPLES

The *teacher,* as well as his principal, *was* exonerated. [*Teacher was*]
The *boy,* together with three companions, *was* discovered the next day. [*Boy was*]

These expressions may be logically considered as introducing modifiers of the subject. They do not have the force of *and,* which is the word that compounds a subject and makes it plural. In informal speech, however, *with* and *together with* are sometimes felt to be conjunctions, not prepositions, making the subject plural. Usage, especially informal usage, sometimes disregards logic.

3c. In sentence patterns that depart from the typical subject-verb-complement order, watch especially for the following situations.

1. The Subject Following the Verb. Mental transposition into normal order will clarify agreement of subject and verb.

EXAMPLES
Scattered over the floor *were* the *remains* of the evening's feast. [*Remains were scattered*]
Browsing peacefully in her vegetable garden *were* a large *elk* and three mule *deer*. [*Elk and deer were*]

2. Introductory *It*. Introductory *it*, as in "It is the people who matter," is always followed by a singular verb, no matter whether the noun that follows is singular or plural. *It* in such cases is an expletive, often called the *dummy subject*, preparing the way for the real subject to come. Nevertheless it controls the verb. No one would say, "It are the people."

EXAMPLES
It is her *happiness* that we must consider. [*It is happiness.*]
It is the *colleges* that must take up the burden. [*It is colleges.*]

3. Introductory *There*. In present-day English, usage seems to be divided in regard to the number of the verb when the dummy *there* introduces a sentence.

In sentences in which the noun that follows the verb is plural, most writers and speakers will use a plural verb.

EXAMPLES
There *are*, if I counted right, exactly thirteen *persons* at this table. [*Persons are*]
There *are*, you must admit, several *degrees* of guilt. [*Degrees are*]

When the subject following the verb consists of a number of nouns, the first of which is singular, there is a definite tendency, in both speech and writing, to make the verb singular. Those who are strongly conscious of the requirements of grammatical

[231]

agreement, and who have time to plan their sentences, will doubtless use the plural verb in such cases.[1]

EXAMPLES

From Long Island to San Francisco, from Florida Bay to Vancouver's Island, there *is* one dominant race and civilization, one language, one type of law, one sense of nationality.

—FREDERIC HARRISON, *Memories and Thoughts*

At Valenciennes, where there *was* a review and a great dinner. . . .

—LYTTON STRACHEY, *Queen Victoria*

There *is* much manganese and chrome, and enough uranium in the slag heaps of the Johannesburg gold mines to make its extraction worth while.

—*Harper's Magazine*

3d. The verb agrees with its subject, not with its subjective complement.

If the difference in number between subject and complement produces an awkward sentence, it is better to rewrite.

RIGHT

The one last *object* of her love *was* three Siamese cats. [Not *object were*]

REWRITTEN

She had nothing left to love except her three Siamese cats.

RIGHT

Our *worry was* the frequent storms that swept the lake. [Not *worry were*]

REWRITTEN

We worried because storms frequently swept the lake.

3e. A compound subject joined by *and* takes a plural verb.

Again, do not be distracted by unusual word order or by intervening phrases.

EXAMPLES

The *rest* of the manuscript and the *letter* from Whitney *seem* to have been destroyed in the fire. [Not *seems*]

---

[1] Examples here used are quoted from David S. Berkeley's "An Agreement of Subject and Verb in Anticipatory *There* Clauses," *American Speech*, May, 1953. By kind permission.

A heavy *coat* or *windbreaker* and a fur *cap are* recommended as additional equipment. *Are* both an *overcoat* and a *parka* necessary? [Not *overcoat and parka is*]

When several singular subjects represent the same person or thing, however, or when they form one collective idea, a singular verb is used.

EXAMPLES
The *sum* and *substance* of the book *is* that all men are created equal.
The *tumult* and the *shouting dies*. . . .

—RUDYARD KIPLING, "Recessional"

Our *ally* and *neighbor* to the south, the Republic of Mexico, *maintains* a quiet border.

But notice the difference that an article (*a, an, the*) can make.

EXAMPLES
The blue and gold sweater is very becoming.
The blue and the gold sweaters are very becoming.
A red and white rose is in bloom.
A red and a white rose are in bloom.

3f. When subjects are joined by *neither—nor, either—or, not only —but also,* the verb agrees with the nearer subject.

It is obvious, then, that when both subjects are singular, the verb is singular, that when both subjects are plural, the verb is also plural. But when one subject is plural and the other singular, formal usage follows the rule, whereas in informal usage there is a tendency to make the verb always plural. One way to avoid an awkward sentence—as well as an awkward decision—is to recast the sentence entirely.

FORMAL
Neither the *students* nor their *teacher is* quite prepared.
Neither *you* nor *I am* going there now.

INFORMAL
Neither the *students* nor their *teacher are* quite prepared.
*You are*n't going there now and neither *am I*.

3g. After *each, every, each one, everyone, everybody, anybody, nobody, none, either,* and *neither* the singular verb is used in formal English.

EXAMPLES

Each of us *is* willing to pay *his* share of the expenses. [Note that *his*, referring to *each*, is also singular.]

Every American *knows his* duty.

Has anyone seen her.

I doubt that *anybody knows* who wrote the song.

The rule as stated here represents the practice of most writers. Exceptions can easily be found, both in formal and informal writing. In an attempt to interpret usage, it is said that the *intention* of the writer determines whether the singular or the plural is to be used. But that is a razor-edge distinction for a student to make. When you say *"Each* of the boys *tells* a different story," the choice is clear, but it is a choice between *"None* of the boys *is* telling the truth," or *"None* of the boys *are* telling the truth." You may justify the first as formal usage and the second as informal usage. The simplest solution is to say, "All the boys are lying."

3h. With a collective noun a singular verb is used when the group named by the noun is regarded as a unit; a plural verb is used when the noun is regarded as indicating the individuals of a group.

Common collective nouns that are troublesome are *class, band, number, data, family, group, public, committee.*

EXAMPLES

The *number* of failures *was* surprising. [*The number* is usually construed as a single unit.]

A *number* of boys *are* failing this term. [A *number* refers to individual items or members of a group and is therefore plural.]

The whole *family is* here. [The modifier indicates that *family* is considered as a single unit.]

The *family are* all attending different churches. [Here the reference is to the individuals of the family.]

Since there is considerable range for individual choice in the use of collective nouns, consistency must be the student's guide. Once he has spoken of a group as a single unit, he should not, without some explanation, refer to it as a plural.

EXAMPLES

The *platoon are* removing their knapsacks. *They are* getting ready for a mock charge.

The *class was* assembled promptly and proceeded with *its* assignment.

3i. When the subject is a title, the name of a book, a clause, a quotation, or some other group of words expressing a single idea, the verb is singular.

EXAMPLES

Bolts of Melody is a collection of Emily Dickinson's poems.

All men are created equal is a statement of dubious truth.

This rule also applies to expressions signifying number, quantity, distance, time, amount, or extent. When the subject is felt as a unit, the verb is singular.

EXAMPLES

Twenty years is a long time to wait for a sweetheart to make up her mind.

Five hundred words is plenty for most daily themes.

Thirty miles is a long day's walk.

But when the amount is meant to be made up of separate units, the plural verb is used.

EXAMPLES

The first *ten years* of every marriage *are* the hardest to endure.

There *are five hundred words* in his essay.

3j. Several words ending in -s are governed by special rules of usage.

A number of nouns ending in *-ics* are considered singular when they refer to a branch of study or a body of knowledge (*linguistics, physics, mathematics, civics, economics*), but are usually plural when they refer to physical activities, qualities, or phenomena (*acoustics, acrobatics, tactics, phonetics, athletics*).

Other words likely to cause trouble are listed below.

Usually singular: *news, measles, mumps, gallows.*
Usually plural: *scissors, tidings, riches, trousers, means, falls* [water].
Either singular or plural: *headquarters, politics, alms.*

3k. A singular verb is used with a relative pronoun referring to a singular antecedent, and a plural verb is used with a pronoun referring to a plural antecedent.

EXAMPLES
It is well to associate with *students who are* courteous. [*Who* refers to *students*, a plural noun.]
He is the only *one* of the family *who intends* to enter college. [*Who* is singular because it refers to *one*.]

Now notice the difference between the last example above and the following construction: "She is one of those girls who always get into trouble." If you shift this about to read, "Of those girls who always get into trouble she is one," you can see that *who* refers to *girls* and is therefore plural. But in practice the singular verb is very common, more so in speech than in formal writing: "She is one of those girls who always gets into trouble."

EXERCISES

EXERCISE 1, RECOGNIZING SUBJECTS AND VERBS. *Some of the difficulty with agreement, as we have seen, is simply a matter of making sure just what the subjects and verbs in sentences are. In the following sentences write S above each subject and V above each verb.*

1. As he said, there were a policeman and a crowd of people in front of our house.
2. The policeman, as well as most of the crowd, was looking up at the sky.
3. One of several things that I worried about was a fire.
4. Neither burglars nor a fire is ever far from a householder's thoughts.

5. Every one of my neighbors is worried about fires.
6. The sum and substance of it is that we have poor fire protection.
7. Smoke, as well as fire and water, causes much damage to a burning house.
8. Looking up toward the treetops in front of our house were three small boys.
9. The number of people inspecting our residence was growing steadily.
10. The news that finally reached us was reassuring; the excitement was about a kitten frantically trying to descend from its perch on a tall tree.

EXERCISE 2, CORRECTING ERRORS IN SUBJECT-VERB AGREEMENT. *Correct the errors in each of the following sentences. Tell what rule applies.*

1. The outcome of all those meetings and conferences were the appointment of a committee.
2. In colleges and in governments there is usually a type of person that love to serve on committees.
3. This committee, with the Dean of Administration, serve as a check on other committees.
4. There seems to be several explanations why this was called a standing committee.
5. If my mathematics is correct, this committee sat from two to six the first day.
6. Four hours are a long time for a standing committee to sit.
7. Each of the members have a different cause to champion.
8. Neither the dean nor the chairman admit saying, "A camel is a greyhound designed by a committee."
9. One man complained that the acoustics in the auditorium was poor.
10. The outcome of all their deliberations were that the questions under discussion should be referred to a new committee.

EXERCISE 3, RECOGNIZING AND CORRECTING ERRORS IN AGREEMENT. *Some of the following sentences contain errors; some are correct. Point out each mistake that you find, correct the sentence, and tell what rule applies.*

1. The teacher remarked that his use of slang expressions were unfortunate.
2. Either you or I am going to tell him to watch his language.

3. Linguistics are not exactly his strong point; he is much better at athletics.
4. Athletics, whether you believe it or not, do require some skilled teaching.
5. The salary of a football coach, fifteen thousand a year, is much more than the average professor earns.
6. There seems to be several reasons why this is so.
7. The public know that a good fullback is hard to find, and it is willing to pay the price required.
8. But many a good fullback were lost to the world because he could not pass his entrance examinations.
9. My uncle is one of those who do not believe that a knowledge of poetics is useful in a business office.
10. After his long career as a little-known author, one of his novels were made into a motion picture.

§ 4. PRONOUNS

Be careful to use the right form of the pronoun.

Nouns in modern English change their form for the plural and for the possessive. Plurals are discussed in section 21. The possessive forms are discussed in section 15. There are very few problems connected with the form changes of nouns.

Some pronouns, however, change their forms for person, number, and case, and thereby cause the student of the English language numerous difficulties. In English there are three cases: the *nominative* or *subjective*, the *possessive*, the *objective*. There are also three persons: the *first* person indicates the speaker; the *second* person indicates the one spoken to; the *third* indicates the one spoken about.

The forms of the personal pronoun are shown in the table below:

SINGULAR NUMBER

	FIRST PERSON	SECOND PERSON	Masc.	Fem.	Neuter
				THIRD PERSON	
Nominative:	I	you	he	she	it
Possessive:	my, mine	your, yours	his	her, hers	its
Objective:	me	you	him	her	it

PLURAL NUMBER

	FIRST PERSON	SECOND PERSON	THIRD PERSON
Nominative:	we	you	they
Possessive:	our, ours	your, yours	their, theirs
Objective:	us	you	them

The relative and interrogative pronoun *who* has only three forms:

Nominative:	who
Possessive:	whose
Objective:	whom

There are also a number of *indefinite* pronouns, such as *another, anybody, anyone, anything, both, each, either, everybody, everyone, everything, few, many, neither, nobody, none, one, somebody, someone.* Those that can be so used form the possessive by adding an apostrophe and *s.*

EXAMPLES
Somebody's hat was left behind.
Anybody's method is better than nobody's.

The intensive pronouns (used for emphasis) and the reflexive pronouns (used to point the action back toward the subject) are *myself, himself, herself, itself, yourself, yourselves, ourselves, themselves.*

INTENSIVE
The general *himself* gave the order. I *myself* will carry it out.

REFLEXIVE
"You can easily hurt *yourselves,*" I said, but they picked *themselves* up.

NOMINATIVE CASE

4a. The nominative case is used when the pronoun is the subject of a verb.

The student must watch out for three trouble spots in connection with the use of the nominative case:

1. A parenthetical expression, such as *they think, they say, we believe,* etc., between *who* (*whoever*) and the verb may confuse the writer.

EXAMPLES

Jones is one senior who we think could teach this class. [Not *whom we think,* but *who could teach*]

A young man who we believe was the driver of the car is being held.

Who did you say brought us these cherries? [Not *whom did you say*]

We agreed to accept whoever they thought was the best foreman. [Not *whomever*]

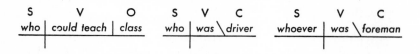

2. The fact that a *who* or *whoever* clause follows a preposition may confuse the writer into using the wrong case.

EXAMPLES

Send a card to *whoever* asks for one. [Not *to whomever.* *Whoever* may seem to be attracted into the objective case by its position after the preposition. But it is the subject of the verb *asks.* The whole clause is the object of the preposition.]

Every girl ought to dance with *whoever* asks her. [Not *with whomever,* but *whoever asks*]

3. In clauses of comparison, with *than* and *as,* the nominative is used with the implied verb.

EXAMPLES

She can usually see more in a painting than *I* [can see].

No one knows that better than *she* [knows it].

4b. In standard literary English, the nominative-case form is used when the pronoun is a subjective complement after the verb be.

In conversation, "it's me" is generally accepted, and in most conversational situations "it's I" or "it is I" would sound affected and silly. As for "it's *us*" or "it's *them,*" probably the best advice

—*in conversation*—is to follow your own ear and your own sense of propriety. You should do the same when writing dialogue. In standard written English, outside of quotation marks, however, the foregoing rule applies.

EXAMPLES
It is *we* who must bear the burden of the tax program, even though it was *they* who initiated it.

POSSESSIVE CASE

4c. The apostrophe is not used with personal pronouns to form the possessive case; the apostrophe is used, however, with those indefinite pronouns that can be used in the possessive.

The possessive forms of the personal pronouns are *my, mine, your, yours, his, her, hers, its, our, ours, their, theirs.*

The possessive forms of the indefinite pronouns are *anybody's, anyone's, everybody's, nobody's, no one's, one's, somebody's.*

WRONG
The furniture is *their's*, but the house is *our's*.
The bush is dying; *it's* leaves are covered with mildew.

RIGHT
The furniture is *theirs*, but the house is *ours*.
The bush is dying; *its* leaves are covered with mildew.

Note carefully the distinction between *it's*, which means *it is*, and *its*, which is the possessive form of *it*. Note also that when *else* follows the indefinite pronoun, such as *anybody, somebody, someone*, the apostrophe and *s* are added to *else*, not to the pronoun.

RIGHT
It's [contraction of *it is*] *anybody's* guess *whose* [possessive form of *who*] horse will win this race.
Would you like to ride in somebody *else's* car?
I wouldn't trust someone *else's* judgment.

4d. In standard English of the more formal varieties, the general practice is to use the possessive form of the pronoun when it precedes a gerund.

Please note that here we do not use *general* in the sense of *universal*. We mean, "Most do; some don't." It is easy enough to find exceptions in the writing of reputable authors.

EXAMPLES
I cannot understand *his refusing* to do that for me.
Her driving off so abruptly was most unfortunate.
I told them about *your resigning* from office.

In these sentences the verbals *refusing, driving, resigning* are gerunds. They are used as object, as subject, and as object of a preposition, in that order. When the verbal is a participle, however, the objective case is correct.

EXAMPLES
We saw *them waving* a flag. [Them in the act of waving]
I found *him using* my typewriter. [Him in the act of using]

With nouns introducing or modifying gerunds, usage varies. There are situations in which the possessive is desirable; there are others in which it is difficult or clumsy, and therefore it gives way to the objective.

EXAMPLES
The family resisted the idea of *Mary's leaving* home.
The prospect of *nations fighting* one another again is almost unthinkable.
It was hard to imagine so many *buildings being constructed*.

4e. Instead of the apostrophe-*s* form, the *of*-phrase may be used to show possession when the situation calls for it.

1. Ordinarily, the *of*-phrase is used for inanimate objects: "the back of the building," "the top of the totem pole," "the hem of the dress" (*not* "the dress of my sister"). However, notice such forms as "in an hour's time" and "a week's pay." In some cases either form may be used; in other cases only one form is possible.

2. The *of*-phrase may also be used to shift the position of a word so that it will stand closer to its modifier.

EXAMPLE
The trustworthiness of a man who never thinks twice is highly questionable. [Not "The man's trustworthiness who never thinks . . ."]

The double possessive is a construction long established in standard English.

EXAMPLES
friends of Jane's   that old sweetheart of mine   a colleague of his

OBJECTIVE CASE

4f. The objective case of the pronoun is used when the pronoun is the direct or indirect object of a verb or verbal.

DIRECT OBJECT
We liked *him*. Mother called *her*. Father tried to pay *him*. Punishing *him* did little good.

INDIRECT OBJECT
Mother served *them* their dinners. I agreed to read *him* a story.

No one is likely to make a mistake in the objective case of a pronoun when the pronoun immediately follows the verb or verbal of which it is the object. For instance, no one would say, "I saw *she* at the game," or "Father took *I* and Bob to the game." Difficulties do arise, however, in three types of constructions:

1. With *who* and *whom*, when these appear out of their normal subject-verb-object pattern. Here we have to distinguish between the more or less formal, literary pattern and the conversational, informal pattern. In questions, when *who* begins the sentence, *who* is used in informal speech for both the subject and the object forms.

CONVERSATIONAL
Who did you want to see?
I'd like to know *who* they're going to elect.

FORMAL

Whom can we trust at such a moment in history? [We can trust *whom*.]
He was the one *whom* they finally selected. [They selected *whom*.]

2. When the pronoun is the second of two objects connected by *and*.

EXAMPLES

Mr. Case told John and *me* to make the decision. [Not *John and I*]
Everyone was astounded when the association chose for membership both *her* and *me*. [Not *her and I*]

3. When the pronoun is the object of an implied verb, after *than* and *as* in clauses of comparison.

EXAMPLES

He always gave Jack more than [he gave] *me*.
Mary told me more about it than [she told] *him*.

By reviewing paragraph 3, Section 4a, you can observe the difference when the nominative pronoun is used as the subject of the implied verb in similar constructions:

EXAMPLE

Mary told me more about it than *he* [told me].

4g. The objective case form is normally used when the pronoun is the object of a preposition.

Here again trouble arises not when the pronoun immediately follows a preposition, as in "I said to *her*" [not, of course, *to she*], but when the pronoun comes before its preposition or when it is the second of two objects.

EXAMPLES

It is difficult to predict *whom* the electorate will vote for. [For *whom*]
Whom could we turn to at a time like this? [To *whom*]
There was some controversy between *him* and *me*. [Not *him and I*]

Informal, conversational usage accepts *who* as the objective form, especially in questions, in which the pronoun may begin a sentence or a clause, such as "*Who* did you call for?" or "*Who* are you talking to?" But it is *not* acceptable, either in speech or writing, to use a nominative pronoun linked with a noun in the objective case, as in "of we citizens" or "between we men and women."

4h. The objective case is proper when the pronoun is the assumed subject or the complement of the infinitive *to be*.

EXAMPLES

Everyone wanted *him* to be the leader of the movement.

The woman whom I thought to be *her* turned out to be someone else.

4i. A pronoun should agree with its antecedent in number, gender, and person.

The antecedent of a pronoun is the word or words to which the pronoun refers. If the antecedent is singular, the pronoun should be singular; if it is plural, the pronoun should be plural.

EXAMPLES

First one woman cast *her* vote.

Then three men cast *their* votes.

An old man cast *his* vote.

The man and his wife had left *their* house early.

The responsibility will probably fall to *me, who am* the oldest one present. [The awkwardness that agreement seems to cause here can be avoided by a simple revision: "since I am the oldest one present."]

We prefer to speak to *you, who are* the chairman.

Here as elsewhere, when questions of usage arise, we must distinguish between what is customary in formal usage and what is accepted, at least by a great many educated persons, in conversational, informal situations. We shall discuss the problems of agreement in terms of certain typical trouble spots that often require more than one kind of answer.

1. In situations that call for more or less formal English, it is customary to use a singular pronoun to refer to any of the following: *anybody, anyone, everyone, everybody, nobody, no one, somebody, someone, person.*

In informal English, especially in conversation, these words, although they take singular verbs, are quite generally felt to be collectives (plural in sense), and the pronouns referring to them are often plural. In addition, all sorts of special situations arise. For instance, *each, every, everybody, everyone* have a general meaning of "all, or a group, but taken individually." Apparently it is the "group" sense that is dominant in influencing the number of the pronoun referring to one of these words. In some cases, when the group consists of both males and females, the speaker uses the plural form because he feels that neither *his* nor *her* is quite accurate. Finally, in some situations, such as in this sentence, "Everybody started to laugh, but in a moment *they* realized that the speaker was not joking," the singular form just would not make sense.

FORMAL AGREEMENT
England expects every man to do *his* duty. [No question of gender here]
Everyone must do *his* part in this war.
Nobody has a right to think that *his* happiness is more important than the happiness of others.

OFTEN ACCEPTED IN CONVERSATION
Somebody must have left *their* coat here.
Everyone ought to feel that *their* vote really counts.

By "often accepted," however, we do not mean universally accepted, even in conversation, and in any case a stricter agreement is required in formal written English.

2. Either a singular or plural pronoun may be used to refer to a collective noun, depending upon whether the noun designates the group as a whole or the members of the group. Consistency is the governing principle. The construction should be either singular or plural, but not both.

INCONSISTENT
The cast *is* giving *their* best performance tonight. [The verb is singular but the pronoun is plural.]
The team *is* now on the floor, taking *their* practice shots at the basket. [Again, verb and pronoun indicate a shift in number.]

CONSISTENT
The cast *is* giving *its* best performance tonight.
The team *are* on the floor now, taking *their* practice shots at the basket.
[The team is thought of as being more than one person.]

3. Ordinarily one of the masculine pronouns, *he, his, him,* is used to refer to one of these "group taken individually" words, not *he or she, his or her, him or her.*

RIGHT
Every person in the audience was requested to sign *his* [not *his or her*] name to the petition.

4. In modern usage, the relative pronoun *who* is used to refer to persons and occasionally to animals, but *whose* may refer to persons, animals, or things, especially when *of which* produces an awkward construction. The relative pronoun *that* may refer to both persons and things. The relative *which* may refer to animals, things, and ideas.

EXAMPLES
My brother, *who* is an art critic, particularly admires modern painting. It is a taste *that* I cannot understand. He once gave me a painting, *which* I hung upside down in my room. It is a masterpiece *whose* meaning is obscure, at least to me. But my best friend, *whose* critical taste I admire, thinks it magnificent. The whole experience is one *that* I find most perplexing.

5. When *one* is the antecedent, American usage prefers *he* and *his* to the repetition of *one,* which is regarded as too formal.

TOO FORMAL
One must not lose one's temper when one is being criticized for one's conduct. [Most people would regard this as affected.]

ACCEPTED FORMAL ENGLISH
A person must not lose his temper when he is being criticized for his conduct.
If one were to read between the lines, he would quickly detect the irony in Swift's calm proposal.

The informal equivalent of these expressions is the second-person pronoun.

INFORMAL

You mustn't lose your temper when being criticized for your conduct.

6. Pronouns used in apposition are in the same case as their antecedents.

EXAMPLES

The reward was divided among us three, Smith, Jenkins, and *me*. [Not *I*]

They had told *us*—*him* and *me*—to report to headquarters immediately.

EXERCISES

EXERCISE 1, CASE OF PRONOUNS. *In the following sentences, tell whether each of the italicized pronouns is used as the subject of a verb, the complement of a verb or verbal, or the object of a preposition.*

1. *I* wonder whether *you* will walk downtown with Harris and *me*.
2. *We* men must visit a lawyer *whom* we talked to last week.
3. *I* usually try to bring along *whoever* wants to come, if *he* asks *me*.
4. *Neither* of *us* is quite sure what the lawyer wants *us* to do.
5. *Who* else do *you* suppose would care to come with *us?*
6. A woman can often be of assistance to *us* men in such cases if *she* wishes.
7. *It* was *she* who helped *us* last time.
8. *Everyone* knows a lawyer can be difficult for those of *us* who are unsure of *themselves*.
9. If *he* says, "Try to remember *whom* you met that day," I am likely to forget *whoever* it may have been.
10. *You* are more quick-witted than *I*, so come along.

EXERCISE 2, CORRECTING PRONOUN ERRORS. *Correct every error in the use of pronouns in the following sentences. Assume that your corrected sentences are to appear in a college theme, not in informal conversation.*

1. Thompson, who is more energetic than me, is the man they must have for the job of chairman.
2. We voters, of course, are the only ones who's preference matters.

3. Of all we men whom I think should be available for office, Thompson is the first who comes to mind.
4. But the whole question, as I say, is up to we voters, who will cast our ballots on Friday.
5. When a person casts their ballots, they have to consider very carefully who they should vote for.
6. At any rate Thompson is the man whom I feel sure will be most adequate to serve us all, and everybody will be pleased with their new leader.
7. If I were him I would be overjoyed at their showing so much confidence in me.
8. Yesterday a man said to Thompson and I that they would probably give him or me their vote.
9. You probably know to who I am referring.
10. No one could be more pleased by such information than me, who is always eager to serve.

EXERCISE 3, FORMAL AND INFORMAL ENGLISH. *For each of the following sentences, provide two versions, one of which can be, but need not necessarily be, the form given here. One version should be appropriate to conversational speech, and one appropriate to graceful, formal, written English. In some cases (as in the first sentence), you should revise wording that may be formally correct but that is awkward or stuffy. In some cases you may feel that your two versions should be identical; after all, good written prose and good conversation may employ in very many instances exactly the same language. Do not be afraid to remove pronouns altogether in the interests of realistic speech or graceful prose.*

1. It is I who am best prepared of all those whom you have available for the task which we have been discussing.
2. I wonder who he's talking to—me?
3. One should not exaggerate one's virtues in order to impress one's listener with one's superiority.
4. Who is it? It is I.
5. Some people whom I know intimately are likely to assert that which they know with altogether too much passion.
6. Everybody has their own opinion about that.
7. I wonder who he's going to call on next.
8. Somebody left their raincoat on this rack; he will have to come and get it.
9. Those to whom I have spoken on the subject which is before

us have made the point that all is lost which is not pursued vigorously, and I am bound to agree with their opinion.

10. Whoever I need, I get.

§ 5. ADJECTIVES AND ADVERBS

Distinguish between adjectives and adverbs and use the correct forms of each.

Adjectives modify nouns. Adverbs modify verbs, adjectives, other adverbs, or groups of words, such as phrases and clauses. One superficial sign of distinction between the two is that most adverbs end in *-ly*.

Some difficulty can arise because a few adjectives, such as *friendly, lovely, manly,* also have the *-ly* ending, and because a number of common adverbs, such as *fast, far, here, there, near, soon,* do not. Usually these are not hard to recognize.

ADJECTIVE
That's a *friendly* gesture.
It was a *manly* reply.
He is a *violent* man.
He is a *lazy* boy.

ADVERB
Butter it *only* on one side.
He learns *fast*.
I shook him *violently*.
He sat *lazily* in the sun.

Actually the difference between adjectives and adverbs depends not on a distinctive form or ending but on the way the words function in sentences. Thus a number of familiar words are used as either adjectives or adverbs, depending on function. In the list below, note that when the word modifies a noun, it is used as an adjective; when it modifies a verb, an adjective, or another adverb, it is used as an adverb.

EXAMPLES

	ADJECTIVES	ADVERBS
deep	We dug a *deep* well.	He dug down *deep*.
early	I am an *early* bird.	They sent us home *early*.
fast	He is a *fast* walker.	He walks much too *fast*.
little	It is a *little* book.	The book is *little* read.
right	I wish I had the *right* answer.	I wish I could do it *right*.

5a. The clumsy or awkward use of a noun form as an adjective should be avoided.

In our flexible language, as we have seen, words commonly used as nouns can also function as adjective modifiers, as in: a *bird* dog, a *house* cat, an *ivory* tower, an *iron* rod, a *silk* dress, a *flower* pot, the *city* streets, the *Chicago* fire. These are absolutely natural and legitimate uses. The objection is to awkward or ambiguous uses, as in the following examples:

AWKWARD
We heard a communism lecture.
It was really a heart attack sign.
Then we heard the governor of New York's speech.

BETTER
We listened to a lecture explaining communism.
It was a symptom of a heart attack.
Then we heard the speech made by the governor of New York.

5b. Use the adjective after certain linking verbs, such as *be, become, appear, seem, prove, remain, look, smell, taste, feel*.

A linking verb is completed by a subjective complement, either a noun or an adjective. The adjective complement describes the subject. Observe this fact in the following examples:

[251]

The girl was *quiet*. [The *quiet* girl]

girl | was \ quiet

The little boy appears *happy*. [The *happy* little boy]
Hyacinths smell *sweet*. [*Sweet* hyacinths]

hyacinths | smell \ sweet

This water tastes *bad*. [*Bad* water]

water | tastes \ bad

The report proved *true*. [*True* report]

With some of the verbs, when the word in the predicate refers to the manner of the action and not to the subject, it is, of course, an adverb, and the adverb form must be used.

EXAMPLES
The boy appeared *unexpectedly*.
The man felt *carefully* for the door.
She looked *quickly* at me.
We tasted the water *suspiciously*.

5c. Use the adverb form for a word that modifies a verb, an adjective, or another adverb.

ADVERB MODIFYING A VERB
He dresses *well* [not *good*], but his manners are poor.
During the summer I improved my golf game *considerably*. [Not *considerable*]
Although he talks *cleverly* [not *clever*], his arguments are shallow.

ADVERB MODIFYING AN ADJECTIVE
My uncle was *really* [not *real*] happy to see us again.
It was *awfully* [not *awful*] generous of you to help us out. [Informal usage]

ADVERB MODIFYING ANOTHER ADVERB
He slid down the hill *considerably* [not *considerable*] faster than he had crawled up.
He *almost* [not *most*] always takes a walk before breakfast.

Most of the difficulties here center in a few words, of which the following are typical: *bad—badly, good—well, sure—surely, real—really, most—almost, awful—awfully, considerable—considerably*.

The words *most* and *almost* are a special problem. In formal usage, *almost* is the accepted modifier in such expressions as: almost all were saved; summer is almost here; we almost never see him; almost everyone respects him. But in informal conversation, *most* is widely used in those situations, and occasionally it appears in writing of a serious character.

5d. Certain nonstandard uses of adjective and adverb should be avoided: *type*, *like*, *-wise*.

UNDESIRABLE
This *type* screw won't go into that *type* wood.

BETTER
This kind of screw will not go into that kind of wood.

UNDESIRABLE
I slid down the hill *like* and then I saw this sort of glow *like* in the sky.

BETTER
I slid down the hill and then I saw a glow in the sky.

UNDESIRABLE
Moneywise I was in favor of it, but *fraternitywise* I was against it.

BETTER
The proposal was good financially, but I disapproved of it in the interest of the fraternity.

5e. When an adverb has two forms (the short and the *-ly* forms), any difference in their use or meaning is determined by idiom.

The following adverbs—and a few others—have two forms:

bright—brightly	high—highly	near—nearly
cheap—cheaply	late—lately	right—rightly
close—closely	loose—loosely	tight—tightly
deep—deeply	loud—loudly	wrong—wrongly

The adverbs in these pairs are not always interchangeable. Nor is there any quick and easy way of learning how to distinguish them in meaning and function. Using them in sentences, as in the following, will help.

IDIOMATIC	NOT GOOD IDIOM
Lately the son has been staying out late.	Late the son has been staying out lately.
The dog crept close to me.	The dog crept closely to me.
Nobody was near.	Nobody was nearly.
He was highly respected.	He was high respected.
The boy slowly opened the door.	The boy slow opened the door.
Go slow. Drive slow.	
Go slowly. Drive slowly.	

5f. Use the correct form of the comparative and the superlative.

The positive form of an adjective or adverb assigns a quality to the word it modifies, as in "a *big* bed," "he walked *rapidly*." The comparative degree is formed by adding *-er* to the positive or by using *more* or *less* with the positive, as in "a *bigger* bed," "he walked *more rapidly*."

The superlative degree is formed by adding *-est* to the positive form, or by using *most* or *least* with the positive. The superlative degree ranks the modified word highest or lowest in a class. It implies that there are at least three things in a class: "a *big* bed," "a *bigger* bed," "the *biggest* bed." (See also Section 36.)

The comparative degree, then, is used when referring to two persons or things; the superlative degree is used when three or more persons or things are involved.

COMPARATIVE

He was *taller* than his brother.

Of the two boys, Penwick was the *more intelligent* and the *more cooperative*.

SUPERLATIVE

He was the *tallest* boy on the basketball team. [More than two]

Penwick was the *most intelligent* and the *most cooperative* boy in school. [Highest in a group consisting of more than two]

Some words are compared irregularly:

many	more	most	much	more	most
bad	worse	worst	good	better	best
little	less *or* lesser	least	well	better	best
little	littler	littlest			

Adjectives of more than two syllables rarely take *-er* and *-est* to form comparatives and superlatives. Forms such as *famouser* or *magnificentest* are not modern English. In formal writing, there is some objection to comparative or superlative forms of adjectives that name qualities thought of as absolute, such as *more perfect, most perfect, most unique;* but these forms, and others such as *straightest, blacker, most complete,* are found in both formal and informal English.[1]

Those who object to modification or qualification of *unique, perfect, complete, black,* and other words that express absolute states or qualities may use *most nearly unique, more nearly* or *most nearly perfect, most nearly complete, most nearly black,* and so on. When the makers of our Constitution wrote, "We the people of the United States, in order to form a *more perfect* union . . ." they may have had *more nearly perfect* in mind. Or they may have accepted usage without giving it much thought. In student writing this is a problem that does not occur frequently.

In modern English one does not combine two superlatives to form a kind of super-superlative. The same principle applies to comparatives.

WRONG

That is the *most unkindest* thing you could have said.

RIGHT

That is the *most unkind* thing you could have said.

[1] Bergen Evans and Cornelia Evans, A *Dictionary of Contemporary American Usage,* pp. 105–107.

WRONG

He finally reached the *more remoter* regions of the country.

RIGHT

He finally reached the *more remote* regions of the country.

EXERCISES

EXERCISE 1, RECOGNIZING ADJECTIVES AND ADVERBS. *Copy the following sentences. Underline each adjective once and each adverb twice.*

1. Her spirits were high because the sun shone bright on her wedding day.
2. You may be right, but the little boy does not appear lazy.
3. The elderly teacher was considerably provoked because the bright boys protested loudly against the assignment.
4. When he awoke after a deep sleep, he noticed that the cold morning air smelled fresh and sweet.
5. All decisions regarding high policy must be highly respected, whether they are right or wrong.
6. Then, too, a lively conversation with the kindly old man was an awfully pleasant price for a delicious dinner.
7. The room smells stuffy, the milk tastes sour, the oilcloth feels gritty, the toast appears sooty, and the prospect for a happy day looks poor.
8. The housekeeper is coming early, I am sure, for everything looks wrong in my room.
9. Really, I feel well, although I did not sleep well last night.
10. Things look bad everywhere today.

EXERCISE 2, CORRECTING ADJECTIVE AND ADVERB ERRORS. *Correct the error in the form or use of the adjective or adverb in each of the following sentences.*

1. In the window she saw a mink coat that was richer and luxuriouser than anything she could imagine.
2. His manners were courtly and he spoke friendly to me, but I could not trust him.
3. All the players felt unhappily after losing the game, and I sure felt bad about it too.
4. You have been so good to me that I feel cheaply because I cannot repay you.
5. Lately he has taken to driving his sports car real fast.

6. I am most ready; my paper is near finished.
7. There is considerable merit in your paper ideawise, but structurewise it is badly arranged.
8. When I compare it with the one written by Anne, it is real hard to say which is worst.
9. He held the bat closely to his chest and then batted the ball highly in the air.
10. Sit tight; the doctor is near ready to see you.

EXERCISE 3, CHOOSING CORRECT ADJECTIVE AND ADVERB FORMS. *In each of the following sentences select the correct form of the adjective or adverb.*

1. I was (really carefully, real careful, really careful) about mounting the horse.
2. In spite of his education, he still does not read (well, good).
3. We drove (slow and careful, slowly and carefully) over the icy roads.
4. When we lost our way, Tracy (sure, surely) felt (bad, badly).
5. Like most careful persons, he takes his driving (real serious, really seriously).
6. Eugene is the (tallest, taller) of the two forwards on the team.
7. Plambeck did (good, well) on his English test.
8. Plambeck is (carefuller, more careful) than Eugene.
9. Eugene's history essay was (more perfect, more nearly perfect) than Plambeck's.
10. Harriet looked (curious, curiously), but actually she was only amused.

§ 6. VERB FORMS

The appropriate form of the verb should be used.

A student who is uncertain about the right form of a verb turns to his dictionary for help. Let us see what he finds (omitting the guides for pronunciation):

lay, *v.t.* [LAID, LAYING]
lead, *v.t.* [LED, LEADING]
lie, *v.i.* [LAY, LAIN, LYING]
look, *v.i.*

These examples illustrate the fact that a dictionary gives what are known as the *principal parts* of a verb, or as many of them as are necessary. Verbs are *regular* or *irregular*, and this distinction controls the amount of information that the dictionary gives. The regular verbs form their past tense and their past participle by adding *-d, -t,* or *-ed* to the present: "I *looked*," "I *have looked.*" Therefore only one part (*look*) is sufficient. But the irregular verbs change the present stem form to make the past tense and the past participle: "I *lie* on the floor," "I *lay* on the floor," "I *have lain* on the floor." The dictionary gives us as many principal parts as we need to make all the forms of the verb—or its *conjugation.* In the case of *lie,* the dictionary lists all the principal parts—namely, the past tense, the past participle, and the present participle. When the dictionary does not list the past participle of an irregular verb, it is assumed that it is the same as the past tense, as in "I *lead*," "I *led*," "I *have led.*"

An abridged conjugation of the verb *take* follows. For other forms and their uses, see Section 6a. The principal parts of *take* are *take, took, taken, taking.*

INDICATIVE MOOD

ACTIVE VOICE / PASSIVE VOICE

PRESENT TENSE

Singular	Plural	Singular	Plural
I take	we take	I am taken	we are taken
you take	you take	you are taken	you are taken
he takes	they take	he is taken	they are taken

PAST TENSE

I took	we took	I was taken	we were taken
you took	you took	you were taken	you were taken
he took	they took	he was taken	they were taken

FUTURE TENSE

I shall (will) take	we shall (will) take	I shall (will) be taken	we shall (will) be taken
you will take	you will take	you will be taken	you will be taken
he will take	they will take	he will be taken	they will be taken

PRESENT PERFECT TENSE

I have taken	we have taken	I have been taken	we have been taken
you have taken	you have taken	you have been taken	you have been taken
he has taken	they have taken	he has been taken	they have been taken

PAST PERFECT TENSE

I had taken	we had taken	I had been taken	we had been taken
you had taken	you had taken	you had been taken	you had been taken
he had taken	they had taken	he had been taken	they had been taken

FUTURE PERFECT TENSE

I shall (will) have taken	we shall (will) have taken	I shall (will) have been taken	we shall (will) have been taken
you will have taken	you will have taken	you will have been taken	you will have been taken
he will have taken	they will have taken	he will have been taken	they will have been taken

IMPERATIVE FORMS: take, be taken
INFINITIVE FORMS: to take, to have taken, to be taken, to have been taken
GERUNDS: taking, having taken, being taken, having been taken
PARTICIPLES: taking, taken, having taken, being taken, having been taken

TENSES

6a. The correct tense forms of the verb should be used.

1. The Present Time. Present time may be expressed by three main verb forms. The simple present tense form usually expresses general or habitual action: "I *work*," "he *teaches*," "she *lives* in Albany," "they *drive* a Lincoln." To express action as going on at the present time we use the *progressive* form of the present: "I *am working*," "he *is teaching*," "she *is living* in Albany," "they *are driving* a Lincoln." There is also a "do" form, which is used for emphasis (I *do* work), for negations (she *does* not *teach*), and for questions (*does* she *live* in Albany?).

2. The Past Time. Past time is usually expressed by the past tense, as in "I *studied*," "she *played* the piano," "he *taught*," "I *worked*." Past time may also be indicated by the present tense form (called the *historical present*), as "The captain *looks* at me, and I *stare* back at him, and he *says* to me . . ." It is a device that can easily be abused in student writing.

3. The Perfect Tenses. The *present perfect* tense shows that an act has been completed prior to the present.

EXAMPLES
The men *have taken* all the tickets.
All the tickets *have been taken*.

The past perfect tense shows that an act was already completed before some specified or understood time in the past.

EXAMPLES
I *had heard* about the news before you told me.
He *had* already *paid* his respects to his hostess.

The future perfect tense, which is less common than the others, indicates a future act as having already taken place, in relation to some specified or understood time in the future.

EXAMPLES
He *will have counted* the money by the time you arrive to collect it.
By late this afternoon the money *will have been counted*.

4. The Future Time. Future time may be indicated in several ways. It may be indicated by the *present tense with an adverb or an adverbial phrase of time*.

EXAMPLES
We *arrive* in Chicago *in thirty minutes*.
Our wedding *takes* place *next June*.

The future may also be indicated by using *going to* or *about to* with the verb.

EXAMPLES

We *are going to stay* overnight in Chicago.

He *is about to declare* himself a candidate.

Shall—Will, Should—Would. Finally, and most obviously, the future may be indicated by using *shall* or *will* with the verb. Attitudes toward the use of *shall* and *will* have provoked controversy because the words are another illustration of the language in rapid change, and when usage changes quickly, tempers often rise. But the fact is that the distinction between *shall* and *will*, once considered vital to educated English, now no longer seems so important. In modern informal speech, most people use *will* and *would* (or the contractions *I'll, he'll, he'd, you'd*) for all expressions of the future, and many do the same in writing. Others, at least in writing, use *shall* and *should* for the first person, and *will* and *would* for the second and third persons. Once again, these seemingly trivial choices have their effect on tone: to maintain the *shall—will* distinction is to add a slight touch of traditional formality to the style.

Those who do maintain the distinction observe, in general, the following rules: for simple future, *shall* with the first person, *will* with the second and third persons; for the emphatic future, *will* for the first person, *shall* for the second and third persons.

EXAMPLES

I shall discuss the uses of verbs, and you will observe the appropriate forms.

You will have to study diligently if you are to put them to good use.

In asking questions, *shall* is ordinarily used with the first and third persons and *will* with the second person when a request for permission is implied: "*Shall* I wrap it up for you?" "*Shall* he take you home?" "*Will* you do it?" A note of formality may be implied to a question if the speaker uses the form that he anticipates in the answer: "*Shall* you be at the meeting?" "I *shall*."

To express habitual or customary action, *would* is used in all three persons.

EXAMPLES

He *would* read in the library instead of playing baseball with the boys.
She *would* sit in her rocker and knit all day long.

Should is often used in the sense of *ought*, although in some sentences *ought* may imply a slightly stronger sense of obligation.

EXAMPLES

He really *should keep* his mouth shut. [He *ought to* . . .]
The policy *should have been defined* long before this. [The policy *ought to have been defined* . . .]

Sequence of Tenses.   Use the tenses that show the correct relation of time between the main verb and the subordinate verb. When, for example, a verb indicates action that took place before the action of the main verb, and the main verb is in the past tense, then the subordinate verb must of course be past perfect.

EXAMPLE

After I *had talked* with him for a while, he *was* more agreeable.

Be careful to use the correct tense of infinitives and participles. Notice in the following examples that the time indicated by the verbal is always in relation to the time expressed by the main verb. That is, a present infinitive indicates the same time as the main verb, even when the main verb is past.

EXAMPLES

I was very pleased *to hear* from you. [Not *to have heard*]
He intended *to go* home, but he did not make it. [Not *to have gone*]

But in the case of participles, a past tense of the participle must be used to indicate a time previous to the main verb.

EXAMPLES

Having played tennis all day, we were tired. [Not *playing*]
Talking as we walked along, we soon arrived at the house. [Not *having talked*]

Careless Shifts in Tense.   In telling a story, it is undesirable to shift from past to present or from present to past unless there is a real change in time of the action being described. For this reason the use of the historical present must be undertaken warily. See also Sections 34 and 43.

EXAMPLE

I *went* out the door and *walked* steadily down the street, where the traffic *seemed* even more noisy than usual. Suddenly a man *approaches* me from an alleyway. "Look!" he *says*, and *thrusts* his face into mine, but when I *looked* at him I *saw* nothing. I *continued* my walk. . . .

THE SUBJUNCTIVE

6b. The subjunctive mood is still used in a number of special situations in literary English.

The following is a simplification of a very complex subject. As far as the form of the verb is concerned, we can say that for most verbs the subjunctive form of the verb differs from the indicative in only the third person singular of the present tense.

INDICATIVE		SUBJUNCTIVE	
I take	we take	if I take	if we take
you take	you take	if you take	if you take
he takes	they take	if he take	if they take

EXAMPLE

We recommend that he *take* the entrance examinations.

The verb *to be* is a special problem. The problem may be simplified by saying that the subjunctive of *to be* uses:

1. *Be* in all forms of the present tense.
2. *Were* in all forms of the past tense.
3. *Have been* in all forms of the present perfect tense.

The only uses of the subjunctive with which a student need concern himself in his speech and writing are as follows:

1. In *if*-clauses expressing doubt or impossibility of the condition (usually referred to as "condition contrary to fact").

If she *were* here, you would not say that.

Were he with us today, he would be gratified at this scene. [This word order now has a somewhat old-fashioned ring.]

Note that when the condition is *not* contrary to fact, the subjunctive is not used.

EXAMPLE
Either he was here or he was not. If he was here, then he must know what happened.

2. In *that*-clauses expressing a wish, request, or command.

EXAMPLES
The president has ordered that all prisoners *be* treated equally.

I desire that he *come* here at once. [Again, note the relative formality of these utterances using the subjunctive. *Compare:* I want him to come here at once.]

3. In main clauses to express hope, wish, or prayer, usually in traditional and stereotyped patterns.

EXAMPLES
God *be* with you.

Long *live* the King!

"The subjunctive *be* hanged!" exclaimed the weary student.

VOICE

6c. The passive voice of the verb should not be overused.

In most writing, and especially narrative and descriptive writing, the active voice is preferred as more direct, vivid, and emphatic. It is obviously simpler and usually better to say "I hit the man on the nose" than "the man was hit on the nose by me." But the passive voice has its legitimate uses, as the first sentence in this paragraph should testify. It is indispensable when the action of the verb is more important than the doer, when the doer of action may not be known, or when the writer may wish to place the emphasis on the recipient of the action rather than on the doer.

EXAMPLES

A sum of twenty thousand dollars was collected from a number of sources.
Another man was fired last night.
All the bridges were destroyed during the war.

It is not the passive voice in itself that is objectionable—it is the overuse or misuse of it. Constant repetition of passive verbs can give an effect of deadness to the action of the prose, as if no one were *doing* anything but simply waiting around *having* things *done* to them.

The passive voice becomes the scapegoat if not the actual culprit when there is a shift in point of view in a group of sentences. Notice what happens in the following sentences:

CONFUSED

One girl may be writing a letter; a book absorbs the attention of another. As usual someone sat in her chair sound asleep. Constant whispers could have been heard by the lecturer.

CONSISTENT

During the lecture, one girl is writing a letter; another is reading a book. As usual someone sits sound asleep. Several girls are whispering constantly.

The passive voice, on the other hand, may be useful in that it enables a writer to maintain his point of view through several sentences.

SHIFT IN POINT OF VIEW

She sat absorbed over her book. A frown could be seen on her face. Then a long whistle from outside interrupted her thoughts. She glanced in annoyance toward the window. Then she smiled as if what she saw there amused her.

CONSISTENT POINT OF VIEW

As she sat there frowning, absorbed over her book, her thoughts were interrupted by a long whistle from outside. Annoyed, she glanced through the open window. Then she smiled in amusement at what she saw there.

EXERCISES

EXERCISE 1, PRINCIPAL PARTS. *With the help of your dictionary if necessary, find the principal parts of the following verbs. List the form given, the past tense, the past participle, and the present participle or gerund: for example,* begin, began, begun, beginning.

bear	dive	know	raise	spring
blow	drink	lay	ride	sting
break	drive	lead	ring	swim
bring	eat	lend	rise	take
burst	get	lie	set	throw
buy	go	lose	shake	wake
choose	grow	prove	sink	write

EXERCISE 2, TENSES. *Make necessary corrections of tenses in the following sentences.*

1. I was eager to have learned German since I planned to go abroad.
2. I told everyone I bought my ticket two days before.
3. Learning the language in a few weeks, I was ready to go at last.
4. I should have purchased a round trip, but I failed to do so.
5. Will you be in Berlin at any time this summer?
6. The year before, I had traveled in England so that I could have spent some time with a friend of mine there.
7. Shall I try it once more?
8. By midnight we shall have reached our first destination.
9. I was pleased yesterday to have heard from you at last.
10. Knowing what a good correspondent you are, I look forward to hearing from you soon.

EXERCISE 3, THE SUBJUNCTIVE. *In the following sentences select the correct forms from those given in parentheses.*

1. I requested that an invitation (be, is, was) sent to them immediately.
2. We all wish we (are, were) with you at this time.
3. He demanded that their unruly behavior (cease, ceased, ceases) at once.
4. We suggested that he (withdraw, withdraws) these demands.

5. He looks as if he (is, were) angry, but one cannot be sure.
6. I know he (is, were) angry because I heard him swear.
7. My suggestion is that he (bring, brings) you along with him.
8. Finally someone made the motion that the whole discussion (is, be, was) dropped.
9. If Jack (is, were) here at last, you (should, would) not treat me so.
10. Since Jack (is, were) here at last, you will not treat me so.

MECHANICS

§ 7. MANUSCRIPT: FORM AND REVISION

7a. In the preparation of manuscript follow standard procedures and any special instructions given you by your English teacher.

1. *Use standard typewriter paper or, for handwritten papers, the 8½ x 11 ruled theme paper.* Most English departments require composition students to use regulation typewriter paper, unruled if the themes are typewritten, ruled if the themes are handwritten. Notebook paper, if its use is permitted, should not be ripped out of its notebook. No instructor will warm up to a student who uses narrow-ruled notebook paper for his themes. Material written on that sort of paper is extremely hard to read.

2. *Write legibly.* If you write by hand, make your writing easy to read. Write with a good pen and use black or dark blue ink. Do not use red, violet, or green ink. Form all letters distinctly, especially those that might be confused with other letters. Dot your *i*'s and cross your *t*'s. Do not decorate your letters with unnecessary loops and flourishes.

3. *Type legibly.* If you use a typewriter, see that the ribbon is fresh and the type clean. Adjust your margin properly. Always double-space your typing. Space five spaces for paragraph indentations, one space between words, and two spaces after the end punctuation of a sentence. If you must delete material in typing, type over it with a capital *M*. If you must cross out any considerable portion of your material, type your page over again. Never begin a line with a punctuation mark, such as a comma, a

period, a question mark, or an exclamation point, that belongs at the end of the preceding line.

4. *Label your themes correctly.* Use the method of labeling papers that is recommended by your instructor. Follow his instructions exactly. If the themes are to be handed in on flat, unfolded sheets of paper (the method preferred by all publishers), the correct place for the name, the page number, and the theme number is the upper right-hand corner of each page. Of course you should never write on the back of the paper. To a typesetter, paper has only one side.

5. *Be careful about the correct placement and capitalization of the title.* Write the title on the first line of the first page only, or about two inches from the top of the sheet. Center the title on the page. Capitalize the first word and all important words in the title. The usual practice is to capitalize all nouns, pronouns, verbs, adverbs, and adjectives, and all prepositions that stand last or contain more than five letters. Do not underline the title or enclose it in quotation marks. Of course when the title is a quotation, and for some reason you wish to emphasize the fact that it is quoted, you enclose it in quotation marks. Do not use a period after it, but you may use a question mark or an exclamation point if the sense of the title calls for either of these marks. Leave a space of about an inch between the title and the first line of your theme. Do not repeat the title on succeeding pages.

6. *Use proper margins.* Leave margins of an inch at the top and at the left of each page. Do not crowd your words at the right or at the bottom of the page. Some instructors like a wide margin at the right as well as at the left of the page so as to have room for comments and corrections. After the first page, begin writing on the first line.

7. *Indent properly to indicate paragraphs.* Indent five typewriter spaces for the first line of a paragraph.

If you are quoting verse—a fairly uncommon occurrence in composition—center your quotation on the page and follow the line arangement of the poem from which you are quoting. No quotation marks are needed. If the quotation does not end a para-

Why I Came

12   Why did I come to college. That is a hard question,
2 it cannot be answered in a few words. From one point of
20 view, it seems abserd that I should be here without know-
15/20 ing why I am here. Its true my parents allways wanted me
to go to college. They probably never quite analyzed
their reasons for wanting me to go. They wanted me to
1 better myself. To learn a profession or a trade. They
11 felt that a well educated man would be able to lead an
6/32/6 easier life than they lived. Knowing the hard life they
13 lived their attitude seems reasonable to me. From another
13 point of view however, it seems logical to me that I
should come to college to find out why I came to college.
I am not sure that I can find all the answers. My college
1 work may give me one answer to my question. Or maybe
44 several of the many possible answers. While I do not
expect to find all the answers, after four years here
20 I may know more definately what the question means.
29   I have talked with other freshmen about their reasons
20/22 for comeing to college. They have many solutions. Most
1 of them talk about economic security. Which of course is
a legitimate objective. Others talk about a life of serv-
26a ice to others. If you talk long enough about the subject,
you will hear about cultivation of the mind and the emotions. These are ideas I will try to discuss here.

Why I Came

Ques.   Why did I come to college/? That is a hard question,

RS ~~which~~ ~~it~~ cannot be answered in a few words. From one point of

Sp view, it seems ~~absord~~ *absurd* that I should be here without know-

Pn/ *Sp* ing why I am here. It's true my parents ~~allways~~ *always* wanted me

to go to college. They probably never quite analyzed

their reasons for wanting me to go. They wanted me to

PF better myself/ *by learning* ~~To learn~~ a profession or a trade. They

Pn felt that a well-educated man would be able to lead an

Tnse *Dng* *Tnse* easier life than they_∧ lived. *have* *Because 2 know* ~~Knowing~~ the hard life they_∧ *have*

C lived, their attitude seems reasonable to me. From another

C point of view, however, it seems logical to me that I

should come to college to find out why I came to college.

I am not sure that I can find all the answers. My college

PF work may give me one answer to my question/ *or* ~~Or~~ maybe

Gl several of the many possible answers. *although* ~~While~~ I do not

expect to find all the answers, after four years here

Sp I may know more *definitely* ~~definately~~ what the question means.

Sub ~~I have talked~~ *As 2 talk* with other freshmen about their reasons

Sp/Ex for ~~comeing~~ *coming* to college/, ~~They have many solutions.~~ *I encounter many ideas.* Most

PF of them talk about economic security/, *which* ~~Which~~ of course is

a legitimate objective. Others talk about a life of serv-

Wd *Rep* ice to ~~others.~~ *humanity.* If you talk long enough about the subject,

you will hear about cultivation of the mind and the emo-

tions. These are ideas I will try to discuss here.

graph, begin the next line of your composition flush with the left margin.

8. *Make deletions and corrections clearly.* Parentheses and brackets are never used to delete or cross out a word. These marks have other uses.

To delete material draw a horizontal line through it. In typing, material may be deleted by typing a capital *M* over it—if the section to be crossed out is not too extensive.

If you wish to insert a correction in your text, mark the point of insertion with a caret $(\wedge)$ and write the inserted material above the caret.

7b. Revise your manuscript carefully, both before you hand it in and after it has been returned to you for correction.

1. *Go over your paper carefully in first draft and copy it for final submission.* As an aid in revising your first draft, you should consider the following checklist:

a. Has the paper an objective, a central idea, a direction?
b. Is the content made interesting by facts and examples?
c. Is the organization, in the whole paper and in the separate paragraphs, as logical as I can make it?
d. Have I corrected obvious errors in sentence structure, such as the period fault, the comma splice, failure of verbs and subjects to agree?
e. Have I checked the punctuation and spelling?

There are other things to check for, of course, but if you keep these in mind as you revise, your paper will gain in clarity and force and correctness.

2. *Revise your paper carefully after the instructor has returned it to you.* Make every correction indicated or suggested by your instructor. If he refers you to a handbook section, first study the section carefully to see how it applies to your error. Then, in red ink, draw a horizontal line through the word or words you wish to cancel, and in the space above, between the lines, write the revised version.

On pages 270–271, you will find the process of correction and revision exemplified.

On page 270, there are two paragraphs of prose filled with elementary errors. The instructor has used section numbers to show the student where each kind of error is discussed and the correction explained. If the instructor had wished to be more explicit, he would have underlined the points of error.

On page 271, the same selection appears. This time the instructor has used correction symbols, according to the system indicated on the inside of the back cover of this book. The student has revised his sentences, in response to the instructor's corrections, by writing between the typewritten lines.

If your instructor indicates by a note or a comment in the margin that some part of your page is confused, undeveloped, or illogical, rewrite the section criticized. Whenever the revision is short, you may write between the lines. When you rewrite a number of sentences or paragraphs, however, you should first make your corrections in red ink on the face of your manuscript, and then recopy the entire page. You may recopy in black ink or type.

3. *If you rewrite or recopy a page or an entire theme, be sure to return both versions to your instructor.*

§ 8. CAPITALS

A capital letter is a kind of punctuation mark, designed to draw the reader's attention to itself for a particular reason. These reasons have been highly formalized in a pattern of standard practice. When you capitalize a word, know why you are doing so. Above all, do not overcapitalize.

8a. Capitalize the first word of every sentence, including fragments punctuated as sentences, and the first word of any group within a sentence that is understood as a sentence in its own right.

EXAMPLES
What now? Who knows? Nobody.
He replied, "There is little hope left."
The main question is, When do we eat?

Do *not* capitalize the first word of (a) an indirect quotation, (b) a direct quotation that is not a complete sentence or that is made a structural part of the new sentence in which it is quoted, (c) the part of a direct quotation that follows dialogue tags such as *he said*, unless this begins a new sentence.

EXAMPLES

Everyone said that the statement was untrue. [Indirect quotation. *Compare:* Everyone said, "The statement is untrue."]

Most people feel, like the speaker in Wordsworth's sonnet, that "we lay waste our powers." [Direct quotation made a structural part of the new sentence]

"I wish I could tell you," he added, "what I really mean about that."

In quoting poetry or any other document, follow the original exactly in respect to capitalization. For capitalizing the title of a student paper, see Section 7a, 5. The same procedure described there applies to titles of books, stories, essays, poems. For further information on the special problems of titles, see Section 10a.

8b. Proper nouns and adjectives are capitalized.

A proper noun names some particular person, place, or object; a common noun indicates one of a class of persons, places, or objects. In practice the distinction is usually not difficult.

Capitalize:

1. Names of persons, places, buildings, ships, and so on: John H. Farley, Wisconsin, the Washington Monument, the *Independence*, Middletown Township, Chinatown, North Vietnam.
2. Names of political and geographic divisions if they are part of a proper name: Union of South Africa, Northwest Territory, Dominion of Canada. [But *not:* a union of states, the territory toward the northwest]
3. Names of historic events or epochs: the Middle Ages, the Black Death, World War I, the Depression.
4. Names of nationalities, religious groups, and languages: Eng-

lish, Mormon, Slavic, Japanese. [Note that these can be used either as nouns or as adjectives.]
5. Adjectives derived from proper names: Byronic, Assyrian, Scottish. [A few such adjectives, used in special senses, such as *roman* or *italic* type, are often considered common rather than proper.]
6. Names of organizations: United States Steel, the Red Cross, Congress of Industrial Organizations, United Nations, Phi Beta Kappa.
7. Days of the week, names of the months and of particular holidays: Easter, Good Friday, Veterans' Day, the second Monday in March.

As a rule, difficulties arise only when the same word is used both as a proper noun and as a common noun; some of these difficulties are discussed in 8c and 8d below.

8c. Any title used preceding a name or as a substitute for the name is capitalized.

A title is always capitalized preceding a name; following a name, it is capitalized only to show particular respect or distinction.

EXAMPLES
Captain Townsend; Prince Philip; Pope Paul; Dean Rusk, the Secretary of State; *but:* D. H. Jones, the chairman of the committee.

Notice that these words are *not* capitalized when they are not used as a title for a particular, named person. The article *a* is usually a signal that a common noun follows.

EXAMPLES
A queen's consort is usually a prince.
He was promoted to captain.
When will they elect a new pope?

Abbreviations after a name, such as Esq., Ph.D., M.D., F.R.S., are usually capitalized and not spaced. The following, however, are correct either with or without capitals: Jr., jr., Sr., sr., (*and note also* No., no.; A.M., a.m.; P.M., p.m.). Be consistent.

8d. Common nouns are capitalized only when they are used in the sense of proper names.

1. Capitalize *North, South, East, West, Northwest, Far East* only when these words refer to specific geographical divisions. Do not capitalize when they refer to directions.

EXAMPLES

The South is gaining industrially at the expense of the Northeast.
I turned south at the crossroads.

2. Capitalize the words for educational and other institutions only when they are a part of some name, not when they are used as common nouns.

EXAMPLES

The school was near Memorial Hospital, not far from the University of Maryland.
I attended high school there. It was called Beaverbrook High.
Many universities are looking for a good president.
I should like to work for the Smithsonian Institution or the Metropolitan Museum, but not all museum work interests me.

3. Capitalize the names of particular courses of study, such as *Mathematics 42, Physical Education 485b*. But do not capitalize such terms when they are used to refer to general areas of learning: *mathematics, physical education, history, law*. Remember, however, that names of nationalities and languages are always capitalized: *French history, Russian literature, Mexican art*.

4. Capitalize words denoting family relationships (*mother, father, uncle, grandfather*) only when these words stand for an individual who is called by that name. Again, be alert for the signal of a common noun, such as an article or possessive preceding the word.

EXAMPLES

A mother is often a twenty-four–hour laborer. My mother was such a person. One day I said to her, "Do you work as hard as Grandmother did, Mother?" She only replied that mothers have always worked hard.

The dictionary can often be useful in determining standard practice of capitalization. But in most doubtful cases, as our examples have been illustrating, it is necessary to recognize just how you are using a word in a particular context.

EXERCISES

EXERCISE 1, SUPPLYING CAPITALS. *Copy the following sentences, supplying capitals where necessary.*

1. the new york central railroad serves many communities in upstate new york and the great lakes region.
2. there are a number of colleges and universities on its route, including syracuse and the university of buffalo.
3. syracuse is famous for courses in journalism, but it also offers programs in all the liberal arts studies including french, anthropology, history, physics, and so on.
4. the central, as the railroad line is called, runs along the mohawk river and the old barge canal toward lake erie.
5. it spans the whole northeastern part of the united states, connecting the new england states with the middle west.
6. everyone knows that this line played an important part in what is often termed "our western expansion."
7. the line's president was an important figure in american history, though airlines and truck companies have now reduced the central's commanding position in transportation.
8. as I have often said to my mother, "always travel on the central, mother, when you go west to chicago."
9. at grand central station they still spread a red carpet for passengers of the crack train, the twentieth century limited.
10. during world war II, as in all wars, the railroads performed great services in the nation's interest.

EXERCISE 2, SUPPLYING CAPITALS. *Here is a piece of administrative English, of the sort that might appear on a college bulletin board. Again, supply capitals where necessary, and only where necessary.*

registration for the fall term will take place in walker hall from monday at 9 a.m. till wednesday at 4 p.m. all students will bring high school records and identification cards with them. the following courses will not be offered this year: economics 13, english 5, french 15, chemistry 37. students expecting to major in

physical science should see professor adkins. those expecting to
enter law school must elect political science 43. please interview
without delay the professor who has been designated as your
adviser.

§ 9. ABBREVIATIONS AND NUMBERS

**9a. In ordinary writing, abbreviations are usually avoided (with a
few standard exceptions).**

The following are usually written out, although in footnotes,
bibliographies, tabulations, and addresses they may be abbreviated to conserve space:

1. Names of countries and states: Canada [not *Can.*], West Virginia [not *W.Va.*] North Dakota [not *N.Dak.*].
2. Names of the months and days of the week: September [not *Sept.*], Monday [not *Mon.*], Friday [not *Fri.*].
3. Christian names: Charles [not *Chas.*], Robert [not *Robt.*], Edward [not *Edw.*].
4. Names of college courses, titles of professors, and other words frequently abbreviated in campus conversation: professor [not *prof.*], educational psychology [not *ed. psych.*], political science [not *poli. sci.*].
5. The titles *The Reverend* [not *Rev.*] and *The Honorable* [not *Hon.*], at least in formal situations. These titles are used with the person's whole name, not with just the last name.
6. The following words: number, volume, chapter, page, and [not *&*], street, avenue, manufacturing, company, mountain, Christmas.

POOR

He was looking forward to Xmas vacation next Dec.

BETTER

He was looking forward to Christmas vacation next December.

POOR

This class meets on Tue., Thurs., and Sat.

BETTER
This class meets on Tuesdays, Thursdays, and Saturdays.

POOR
He worked in N.Y. for the Cohoes Mfg. Co.

BETTER
He worked in New York for the Cohoes Manufacturing Company.

POOR
Some day she hopes to be a prof. of home ec.

BETTER
Some day she hopes to be a professor of home economics.

POOR
Wm. and Chas. live on Jerome Ave., near Dilmore St.

BETTER
William and Charles live on Jerome Avenue, near Dilmore Street.

The following abbreviations are customary and appropriate:

1. Titles before proper names: Dr., Mr., Mrs., M., Messrs., Mme., Mlle.
2. Certain designations after names: Jr., jr., Sr., sr., D.D., M.D., Ph.D.
3. With dates only when necessary for clearness: A.D. and B.C. [Octavian lived from 63 B.C. to A.D. 14.]
4. Certain expressions usually abbreviated in informal and in technical writing, though written out when a more formal effect is desired: i.e., e.g., viz., etc. These actually stand for *id est, exempli gratia, videlicet, et cetera,* but they are written out as *that is, for example, namely, and so forth.*
5. Names of government agencies and certain other well-known organizations: TVA, CARE, NATO, WAVES. Note that the last three of these are pronounced as single words, rather than as series of letters. Note also the omission of periods. When in doubt about the punctuation, consult your dictionary.

Note that B.C. follows the date, A.D. precedes it. Observe, also that it is not customary to space after periods within most abbreviations, except that initials representing personal names *are* spaced: A. L. Jones.

9b. In ordinary writing, most numbers are written out whenever they can be expressed in one or two words, or in a simple phrase.

EXAMPLES

She is about twenty-five years old.

She earned nearly eight thousand dollars last year.

She was able to buy three and a half acres of land.

For the use of the hyphen with compound numbers see Section 11.

A number beginning a sentence is usually spelled out. If it cannot be easily written out, change the sentence so that the number does not stand at the beginning.

EXAMPLES

Thirty-five persons attended the ceremony. [Not *35 persons* . . .]

She paid a price of $4,550 for the property. [Not *$4,550 was paid* . . .]

9c. Figures are used for the following:

1. Dates: March 20, 1964; *not* March twentieth, nineteen hundred sixty-four.
2. Street and room numbers: 415 State Street; *not* four hundred fifteen State Street; Union Hall 216, *not* Union Hall two hundred sixteen.
3. Page numbers: page 334; *not* page three hundred thirty-four.
4. Decimals, percentages, mathematical and technical statistics.
5. Several numbers occurring in the same paragraph or section, if the numbers refer to different quantities of the same thing and if one of the numbers would ordinarily be given in figures.

EXAMPLE

These systems are at distances ranging from 100,000 to 1,500,000 light years, their diameters range from 4,000 to 45,000 light years, and the total luminosities from 20 to 500 million times the luminosity of the sun.

Notice in the last example that commas are used to separate the figures into groups, for clearness and convenience in reading.

Commas are not used, however, in dates, serial numbers, telephone numbers, or social security numbers. In some of these it is customary to use hyphens to divide complex numbers into groups.

EXERCISES

EXERCISE 1, CORRECTING ABBREVIATION ERRORS. *Correct the errors in the use of abbreviations in the following sentences.*

1. Our route took us through Mich., Wis., and Minn.
2. The Stoic philosopher, Seneca, lived from 4 B. C. to 65 A. D.
3. This author was not born until after 1917 A. D.
4. English lit and math are my best courses.
5. We were in Vt. and Mass. for the fall color festival.
6. Thos. Jones took me to the game with Hancock Hi.
7. I think that our chem labs are poorly designed.
8. One of the profs there said they were firetraps.
9. Professor L.B. White and Doctor A.G. Black are my lab assistants.
10. Rev. Holmes was our convo speaker.

EXERCISE 2, IDENTIFYING ABBREVIATIONS. *Identify each of the following abbreviations. Consult your dictionary.*

1. ad lib	6. ESP	11. UNESCO
2. ASCAP	7. f.o.b.	12. S.R.O.
3. BMR	8. q.v.	13. USAFI
4. CIO	9. TNT	14. NCAA
5. colloq.	10. S.J.	15. op. cit.

EXERCISE 3, SPELLING OUT NUMBERS. *In the following sentences encircle the numbers that should have been written out in words.*

1. He will inherit the estate when he reaches the age of 21.
2. The estate consists of a ranch, some stocks, and $35,600 in bonds.
3. Brenda was given an expensive car on her 18th birthday.
4. Her sister Diana, who is 16, is in love with a boy 3 inches shorter than she.
5. Margaret's birthday parties are awkward, for she was born on December 26, 1950.
6. Although a member of the 4-H Club for 6 years, she does not know what the four *H*'s stand for.

7. Timmy, an 8th grader, told her his scholastic average for 2 years is 86.55.
8. He has just bought a 90mm lens for his Exakta, which is a 35mm single lens reflex camera.
9. In 1940 McMillan and Abelson produced element 93, named *neptunium* after the planet Neptune.
10. 36 boys can be housed in the dormitory at 218 South 36th Street.

§ 10. ITALICS

Italics are used to set words apart in a variety of situations.

The word *italics* refers to print. In handwriting or in typing, if the writer wishes to direct the printer to set a word in italic type, he underlines it.

TYPEWRITTEN

In the March, 1959, issue of <u>Harper's Magazine</u> there is a review of Robert Payne's <u>The Gold of Troy.</u>

PRINT

In the March, 1959, issue of *Harper's Magazine* there is a review of Robert Payne's *The Gold of Troy.*

In business letters, instead of being underlined, the words are usually typed in capitals, as: HARPER'S MAGAZINE, THE GOLD OF TROY.

Usage varies greatly in regard to the use of italics. The principles or statements of usage in this section refer to more or less formal usage. Newspapers, as a rule, do not use italic type. The *New York Times Book Review* uses quotation marks for titles of books. The *Saturday Review* does the same thing, both for books and for musical compositions. *Harper's Magazine* italicizes the titles of books, magazines, and newspapers, but uses quotation marks for titles of musical compositions. *Time* uses italics for the titles of newspapers, magazines, books, motion pictures, and musical compositions. If you are writing for publication, the only sure guide is the style sheet of the magazine you are aiming at.

The following rules are usually observed in college papers of a formal nature.

10a. When referred to in formal writing, titles of books, plays, newspapers, magazines, musical compositions, works of art, and names of ships are usually underlined in manuscript and printed in italics.

EXAMPLES

Huckleberry Finn   *Scientific American*

Mozart's *Marriage of Figaro*   the Portland *Oregonian*

Michelangelo's *Pietà*   the *Queen Mary*

Quotation marks are generally used for titles of chapters or subdivisions of books, for titles of short stories, magazine articles, newspaper articles, and short poems. Also see Chapter 6, pages 169–170, for proper procedure in citing such sources.

EXAMPLES

The stories in Maugham's *East and West,* such as "Rain" and "The Letter," could have appeared in a magazine, such as the *Atlantic,* before being published in book form. Later, as a play, *Rain* enjoyed a long run.

The definite article *the* and the name of the city before the title of a newspaper are usually not italicized: the St. Louis *Post-Dispatch.* Some periodicals, however, prefer the italicized article: *The New Yorker.*

10b. Foreign words and phrases that are still not Anglicized are italicized (underlined) when used in writing.

A number of terms pronounced like foreign words are nevertheless considered so much a part of our language that italics are *not* used. Examples include: cliché, staccato, blitzkrieg. Some dictionaries will tell you if a word is still considered foreign and therefore must be italicized. Different dictionaries use different symbols for this purpose.

10c. In formal writing, words, letters, and figures, referred to as such, are usually italicized.

You have seen this procedure exemplified many times in this book, where italics have been used to mark off a word being discussed *as a word*. But in informal writing, quotation marks may be used for the same purpose. In definitions, the word to be defined is commonly set in italics (underlined) and the definition is enclosed in quotation marks.

FORMAL STYLE

We realize the humorous intention when somebody invents from the noun *swashbuckler* a verb to *swashbuckle*, or to *buttle* and *cuttle* from *butler* and *cutler*, but it is not so well known that the same process (probably with the same humorous intent behind it) gave us such sober words as *burgle, sidle, edit, grovel, beg,* and *greed*.

—OWEN BARFIELD, *History in English Words*

Thus words like *sapolio, oleomargarine, brillo,* a name for steel wool used in polishing, *fermillac,* fermented milk, *sozodont,* the name of a tooth powder, and dozens of others like these betray at least a moderate degree of familiarity with the classical languages.

—GEORGE P. KRAPP, *The Knowledge of English*

A nasturtium is a pretty flower, but the word *nasturtium* actually means "a nose twister." Few persons remember that *sabotage* means "throwing your wooden shoes into the machinery."

INFORMAL STYLE

Many people confuse "imply" and "infer."
The European "7" is written differently from ours.

10d. Italics may be used to give special emphasis to a word or phrase.

The use of italics or underlining for emphasis can be badly abused in formal writing, where it is likely to appear as a weak effort to give importance to words that ought to be important without such mechanical help. Furthermore, excessive underlining has associations with trivial dialogue, often of a feminine or juvenile flavor. ("My *dear,* you should have seen her *hair.* I mean you should have *seen* it. *Really!*") In a similar way, italics have been liberally used by some modern novelists, notably J. D. Salinger, to suggest the up-and-down stresses of emotional speech. "I was *born* here. I went to *school* here. I've been *run over* here—*twice,* and on the same damn *street.*"

But in formal exposition, it is conventional to use italics for emphasis far more sparingly, usually only when the sentence would not be immediately clear without them.

EXAMPLES

Emotions represented in literature are, neither for writer nor for reader, the same as emotions in "real life"; they are "recollected in tranquillity"; they are "expressed"—that is, released—by analysis; they are the *feelings* of emotions, the perceptions of emotions.

—RENÉ WELLEK AND AUSTIN WARREN, *Theory of Literature*

Every writer should be clear *who he is* for the purpose of writing—whether himself, or the representative of a point of view, or the spokesman of a particular group.

—ROBERT GRAVES AND ALAN HODGE, *The Reader over Your Shoulder*

E X E R C I S E S

EXERCISE 1, ITALICS AND QUOTATION MARKS. *Copy the following paragraph, underlining for italics and adding quotation marks where necessary. Use the formal conventions.*

Webster's New World Dictionary, like other such works, includes helpful lists of synonyms for many familiar words. Listed under crowd, for example, you will find throng, multitude, swarm, mob, host, and horde, with precise differences indicated. An introductory article called Guide to the Use of the Dictionary is of further assistance to the reader searching for a mot juste. A subsection of this article, titled The Synonymies, treats antonyms as well, and concludes: "the antonym sad heads a synonymy that includes melancholy, dejected, depressed, and doleful, all antonymous to happy."

EXERCISE 2, ITALICS AND QUOTATION MARKS. *Copy the following paragraph in the same way, underlining for italics where necessary and adding quotation marks in the proper places.*

Eliot's The Love Song of J. Alfred Prufrock has long since supplanted Hiawatha and the Gettysburg Address as a set piece for young elocutionists. Prufrock has become the poem of a whole generation born long after it was written, and no doubt Eliot's Collected Poems owes at least some of its success to the popularity of this one poem. His religious poems, such as Ash

Wednesday, and his plays, such as Murder in the Cathedral, are all very well, but apparently young people today prefer to think of themselves as junior Prufrocks.

§ 11. SYLLABICATION AND HYPHENS

11a. The awkward division of a word at the end of a line of hand-written or typewritten manuscript should be avoided.

In printed matter, where a perfectly even right-hand margin is mandatory, we have become accustomed to a number of word divisions at the ends of lines. In handwritten or typewritten papers, however, it is usually unnecessary to divide many words. An uneven right-hand margin is preferable to a large number of split words. For clearness and ease in reading, it is well to observe the following cautions about dividing words at the end of a line:

1. Never divide words of one syllable, such as *eighth, rhythm, signed, burned.* Note that the *-ed* ending in the past-tense form must not be split off as a syllable when it is not pronounced as a syllable.

2. Never divide a word so that a single letter is allowed to stand by itself, either at the end of a line or the beginning of the next line, as in *a-/mount, a-/round, e-/lope, greed-/y, read-/y.*

3. Try to avoid dividing proper names.

4. Try not to separate a name and the initials that go with it.

5. Try to avoid dividing the last word of a paragraph or a page. In print such a division is often necessary, but in manuscript it can be easily avoided.

11b. If a division of a word is necessary, the division should be made between syllables and a hyphen placed at the end of the line.

It may be helpful to assume that your reader is pronouncing your sentence aloud. Divide words so that both parts are pronounceable. Furthermore, you must divide correctly between syllables, and your best resource in doing so is your dictionary, where syllables are clearly indicated. The following cautions should be of additional help:

1. Divide compound words on the hyphen, and try to avoid a second hyphen: self-/evident, *not* self-evi-/dent; college-/trained, *not* col-/lege-trained.

2. In words with prefixes, divide on the prefix: non-/sensical, pre-/caution, ante-/diluvian. Note that these words are ordinarily written solid; they are not hyphenated compounds.

3. In words with suffixes, divide on the suffix: boy-/ish, dog-/like, youth-/ful, fall-/ing, yell-/ing.

4. As a rule, when a word contains double consonants, divide between the two consonants: ac-/com-/mo-/date, in-/ter-/ro-/ gate. Note, however, as in the examples *fall-/ing* and *yell-/ing,* that when the rule about double consonants conflict with the rule about suffixes, it is the rule about suffixes that you should follow.

11c. Two or more words forming a compound adjective before a noun are hyphenated.

EXAMPLES
A broad-shouldered, long-legged boy; a rough-looking fellow; ready-made opinions; a twin-screw engine; in up-to-date condition; a well-traveled highway; a two-thirds majority; an old-fashioned sermon; a pitch-dark night; the Russo-Finnish border.

When a compound modifier consists of two or more words with a common beginning, the following style is used: A three- or four-room addition, Anglo- and Franco-American, paid in five- and ten-dollar bills.

The following are usually not hyphenated: compound modifiers that follow the noun; compounds in which an adverb ending in *-ly* is used.

EXAMPLES
The man was well known for thievery. [We met a well-known poet.]
His information was up to date. [He planned an up-to-date revision of the book.]
It was a loosely worded statement. [His explanations were loosely worded.]

11d. Compound numbers from twenty-one to ninety-nine are hyphenated.

EXAMPLES
Twenty-seven dollars, thirty-four inches

Fractions, when used as modifiers, are hyphenated. When one of the terms of the fraction is already a compound, however, no additional hyphen is used, as in *four twenty-fifths, twenty-one fortieths*. Such simple fractions as *one half, two thirds*, and so on are often written without a hyphen.

EXAMPLES
The bill was finally passed by a two-thirds majority.
One half of the pie was already eaten.

11e. Hyphens are used with the following classes of words.

1. With prefixes *ex-* (in the sense of "former") and *self-*: ex-president, ex-minister, self-regard, self-help, self-pity.
2. When two functions that are usually distinct are united in one person or thing: cleaner-polisher, secretary-treasurer, publisher-editor, city-state.
3. To avoid doubling a vowel letter or tripling a consonant letter: re-echo, pre-enrollment, semi-invalid (*but* cooperate, coordinate).
4. With groups making or containing prepositional phrases: son-in-law, man-of-war, jack-in-the-pulpit.
5. To prevent confusion with similar words: re-form [to form again], reform [to change or amend]; re-count [to count anew], recount [to tell]; re-creation [a second creation], recreation [play, sport, diversion].
6. When the second element of a compound is a proper noun: anti-American, pro-Russian.

When in doubt as to the correct form of a compound, consult *Webster's New Collegiate Dictionary*, the *American College Dictionary*, or *Webster's New World Dictionary*. See also, for a general discussion of compound words, Bergen and Cornelia

Evans, A *Dictionary of Contemporary American Usage,* Random House, 1957, pages 108–110.

EXERCISES

EXERCISE 1, SYLLABICATION. *Indicate which of the following words you should* not *split at the end of a line. Show how you would split the others. Give your reason in each case.*

1. agreed	6. sorely	11. brushed
2. precedence	7. speedy	12. elect
3. pre-eminent	8. unit	13. bankbook
4. through	9. across	14. squeezed
5. thorough	10. action	15. stringy

EXERCISE 2, COMPOUND WORDS. *With the aid of a dictionary determine which of the following should be written solid, which with a hyphen, and which are separate words.*

1. air raid	16. good bye
2. air raid shelter	17. half brother
3. all inclusive	18. half crazed lion
4. all right	19. half written theme
5. ante date	20. partly written paper
6. ante bellum	21. in as much as
7. anti climax	22. infra red
8. any body	23. north west
9. basket ball	24. post office
10. book store	25. score board
11. by law	26. text book
12. by pass	27. inter collegiate
13. post Renaissance	28. under graduate
14. dining room	29. week end trip
15. every thing	30. well made car

PUNCTUATION

The purpose of punctuation is to help make clear the meaning of printed or written language.

To some degree punctuation symbolizes the pauses we make in our oral speech, but it does so crudely and artificially. It is still useful to read a sentence aloud with attention to its meaning, and punctuate the pauses you hear in your own voice. But correct punctuation has also come to reflect the grammatical structures of sentences, as well as the particular conventions of the age. Therefore a comma does not always represent a drop or pause in the speaking voice, and the various marks of punctuation do not consistently distinguish between the various subtle drops that our voices so naturally perform. Like most conventional patterns of behavior, the conventions of punctuation have to be learned.

The practice of writers has been codified into a number of rules or principles of punctuation. These rules or principles govern a very large number of typical situations in writing. At times, however, certain marks are optional, depending on the writer's particular attitude toward what he is saying, and on decisions of publishers. On the whole, nevertheless, a college student can get along pretty well if he follows codified usage. When in genuine doubt, he can usually resort to common sense.

Punctuation, then, is more than a series of rules: it offers one more way of clarifying expression. Even in the many situations where one has a choice—for example, to include a comma or leave it out—one's choice need not be arbitrary. The slowness or speed of one's prose style will be very largely controlled by the use or omission of punctuation marks where no rule clearly applies.

§ 12. END PUNCTUATION

THE PERIOD

12a. A period is used after a declarative or imperative sentence, or after an indirect question, but not after a direct question.

EXAMPLES

I had no idea where I had been or how I got there. [Declarative]

Always know where you are. [Imperative]

The woman asked where I had been. [Indirect question]

The woman asked, "Where have you been?" [Direct question, ending with a question mark]

Note the difference, in the last two examples, in the way the human voice is used. At the end of the indirect question there is a drop in voice level characteristic of all declarative sentences. But a rise in pitch at the end of a sentence—Where have you been?—is usually a sign of a question, to be symbolized by a question mark.

12b. Most of the common abbreviations require a period.

EXAMPLES

Mr., Mrs., Dr., St., Jr., a.m., B.C., Mass.

Increasingly, the period is not used with certain groups of letters standing for organizations or government agencies. Note that the letters are written without spacing.

EXAMPLES

UN, USSR, CIO, TVA, FCC, NAACP

Usage is divided in regard to some of the older abbreviations consisting of the initial letters of words, though the tendency is toward omitting the period. Consult your dictionary when in doubt.

EXAMPLES

Y.M.C.A. *or* YMCA; r.p.m. *or* rpm; A.M.A. *or* AMA

[291]

12c. Periods (ellipsis marks or suspension points, usually three within a sentence, four at the end of a declarative sentence) are used to indicate the omission of words from a quoted passage, or pauses or hesitation in dialogue.

EXAMPLES

We the People of the United States, in order to . . . secure the Blessings of Liberty to ourselves and our Posterity, do . . . establish this Constitution for the United States of America.

The souls of emperors and cobblers are cast in the same mould. . . . The same reason that makes us wrangle with a neighbor causes a war betwixt princes.

—MONTAIGNE

"Now let me think. . . . Yes. . . . I suppose so."

THE QUESTION MARK

12d. A question mark is used after a direct question but not after an indirect question.

Note the distinction in voice level discussed under 12a. Most of our problems in using the question mark are mechanical ones, involving other punctuation surrounding the mark in special cases.

EXAMPLES

What will I do if Miss Byrne is there? What will I say to her? she asked herself, but did not wait for an answer. [Quotation marks are sometimes omitted when unspoken thoughts are quoted.]

—MICHAEL McLAVERTY, *School for Hope*

Was it not Plato himself who said that he would never write a treatise on philosophy, that the latter must be acquired by conversation, the flame leaping from speaker to speaker "until the soul itself caught fire"? [Note relation of question mark to quotation marks when part of a phrase is quoted in a question.]

—IRWIN EDMAN, "Fashions in Ideas"

After we landed we learned, with a tremendous surge of pride, that as the waters rose around them, those green troops, soldiers from far northwestern states mostly, stood in ranks on the canted decks singing a popular song of the war, "Where Do We Go from Here, Boys?" [A question mark ends the sentence if the last part is a quoted question.]

—Irvin S. Cobb

Instead of asking "What would a good education consist of?" many professors of education are asking "What do most college students want?"; instead of asking "What books are wisest and best and most beautiful?" they conduct polls to determine which the largest number of students have read with least pain. [Some writers would have put commas after each *asking*. Note that a question mark is used with a title if it is a question.]

—Joseph Wood Krutch, "Is Our Common Man Too Common?"

A single question mark is used after a double question—that is, a quoted question following a question. (See also Section 16.)

EXAMPLES

Who wrote "Where are the snows of yesteryear?"
Why does he not simply ask, "Where do I go now?"

A question mark within parentheses may be used to indicate doubt or uncertainty as to the preceding figure or fact. This is a conventional practice in the case of a doubtful birth or death date.

EXAMPLE

Lucien Botha was born in 1779(?) and died in 1859.

But the use of a parenthetical question mark to indicate irony is the mark only of very juvenile writing.

POOR

We had a wonderful(?) time at that party.

A question mark is often used after commands or requests phrased as questions if a formal effect is desired, but a period is used for a less formal effect. A convenient test, once again, is to read the sentence aloud, checking for the rise in pitch characteristic of the last syllable of a question.

FORMAL

May I ask the entire staff to reassemble here at four o'clock?

LESS FORMAL

Will the whole staff meet here again at four o'clock, please.

THE EXCLAMATION POINT

12e. An exclamation point is customary after an expression of strong feeling.

The student's temptation often is to overuse the exclamation point, creating a breathless or overexcited style not unlike that produced by an overuse of italics. (See Section 10d.) Words such as *yes, no, oh, well, alas, surely,* when beginning a sentence, are usually followed by a comma. Actually it is well to avoid them in such constructions, except in dialogue. If *oh* introduces an expression of strong feeling, put the exclamation point at the end of the expression. Never use more than one exclamation point in a sentence.

EXAMPLES

"Good lord!" he shouted in consternation.

It is difficult to see how anyone in his right mind could have concluded *that!*

Oh, this is unpardonable!

The days wore on, and yet got nowhere. . . . Time had simply come to a standstill! He had never seen the like; this was worse than the deadest lay-up in Lofoten!

—O. E. RÖLVAAG, *Giants in the Earth*

EXERCISE

EXERCISE, END PUNCTUATION IN DIALOGUE. *In the following dialogue, supply commas, periods, question marks, and exclamation points where they are necessary. Be careful to place punctuation correctly in relation to quotation marks.*

1. "Did you know the ending would turn out that way" asked Dr Fisher
2. "No I didn't" she replied
3. The doctor asked her what other movies she had seen lately
4. "Oh not many" she said "Have you seen anything like this before"
5. "What makes you ask that" he replied
6. "Do you know who said 'Movies are getting better' " she asked

7. "Who was it that used to ask 'Why not try a good movie tonight' "
8. "Watch out" he shouted suddenly as they attempted to cross the street in front of the theatre
9. "Wasn't that Mr Wells in his MG Golly That was too close for comfort"
10. "I wonder" he observed "when the streets will ever be safe for pedestrians"

§ 13. THE COMMA

Of all the marks of punctuation, the comma has the widest variety of uses. Probably because the comma is used in so many situations, any attempt to codify the practice of writers and to state usage in terms of definite principles must give due weight to the exceptions. Yet, however important the differences of practice are, to the student the most important thing is that there is such a large area of agreement. Most of the uses of the comma can be stated in terms of principles, principles that reflect what most writers are doing.

The student should always remember, however, that these descriptions of usage must be interpreted with a little common sense. It is true, for instance, that writers place a comma after an introductory clause or phrase if they feel that this sentence element is not an integral part of the main clause—that is, if it is not closely restrictive— but no rule, only common sense, can tell a student when this clause stops being restrictive and becomes nonrestrictive.

In a general way, punctuation tends to be *close* (that is, using commas liberally) in serious or formal writing, where precision is vital. It tends to be *open* (that is, using a minimum of punctuation) in informal description and narration and in journalistic writing.

Although the primary function of punctuation is to help make meaning clear, punctuation has another function, a rhetorical one. The comma—and to a certain extent the semicolon—may be used to indicate the degree of pause or emphasis or rhetorical balance or contrast of ideas. The important fact still remains, however, that before a writer can make punctuation an artistic resource he must first become familiar with the general practice of writers.

Because of its wide variety of uses, the comma may appear to some a subject of puzzling complexity, although at times it is hard to see why eager young men of eighteen, who speak familiarly of isotopes and engage to pilot Comet jets, should be bowled over by so simple a thing as a comma. At any rate, it is possible to simplify a simple subject further by dividing all comma uses into two groups. In one group we have the *to separate* uses; in the other group we have the *to enclose* uses. A picture of the whole thing makes it still simpler and clearer.

A TABLE OF COMMA USES

Usually to Separate		Usually to Enclose	
13a.	main clauses	13h.	nonrestrictive clauses
13b.	elements in series	13i.	parenthetical elements
13c.	coordinate adjectives	13j.	absolute phrases
13d.	words that may be misread	13k.	appositives
13e.	introductory modifiers	13l.	words in direct address
13f.	transposed elements	13m.	dialogue guides
13g.	mild exclamations, etc.	13n.	dates and addresses

13a. A comma is ordinarily used to separate coordinate clauses joined by *and, but, for, or, nor*, except when the clauses are short and closely related in meaning.

A writer is safe to apply this rule rather strictly in formal writing and to relax its application progressively as the level of writing becomes more and more informal. If he does so, he will not be wrong. At the same time he must know that the use of a comma to separate main clauses has become almost optional. Journalistic writing discards the comma in this situation except to prevent misreading. At the formal level, the general practice is to omit the comma when the subject of the sentence does not change after the first clause. If there is any other clearly defined practice to help the beginning student, it is that the comma is obligatory before *for* (to prevent confusion with the preposition *for*) and recommended before *but*.

Marco Polo, the Italian explorer, visited the island of Sumatra in 1292, and in 1509 Portuguese traders established commercial stations there.

For the boundary between sea and land is the most fleeting and transitory feature of the earth, and the sea is forever repeating its encroachments upon the continents. [Note, as in this sentence, that the conjunctions *but* and *for* are often used to begin independent sentences.]

—RACHEL CARSON, The Sea Around Us

The brilliance of a nova at its peak is usually not sufficient to make it visible to the naked eye, but supernovae surpass in brilliance the brightest of ordinary stars and some of them can be observed in full daylight. [Note that no comma is used before *and* because the subjects of the last two clauses are felt to be closely related.]

In a sense, the processes of fission and fusion are similar, for they both are used to convert mass into energy in an amount given by Einstein's equation. [Note comma before *for*.]

—DONALD J. HUGHES, "Atoms, Energy, and Peace"

They [the buildings of architecture] may be sophisticated, worked out with the greatest intellectual subtlety, designed like the Parthenon by known architects of genius; or they may, like some old stone barn in Pennsylvania, be the naïve, natural legacy of half-understood tradition, put up by an anonymous builder. [Note the semicolon before *or* in a compound sentence with a number of commas. See Section 14 for further discussion.]

—JOHN E. BURCHARD, "Architecture and Building"

13b. Commas are used to separate words, phrases, or clauses in a series.

A series must have at least three members; usually the last two are joined by *and* or *or*. It is at this point, the point of the conjunction, that usage differs. Although the comma is generally used here in most formal writing,[1] some writers do omit it. In informal writing there is a progressive tendency to discard the comma before the conjunction, except for clearness, as the writing grows less formal. In journalistic writing, the comma is regularly omitted.

Men, women, and children enjoyed the happy, carefree, and refreshing outing. [Nouns and adjectives in series] The boys stopped, looked, and then darted for cover. [Series of verbs]

---

[1] In the MLA *Style Sheet*, the only comment on commas is "Use them before 'and' and 'or' in a series of three or more." P. 9.

In scarlet and blue and green and purple, three by three the sovereigns rode through the palace gates, with plumed helmets, gold braid, crimson sashes, and jeweled orders flashing in the sun. [Series of nouns]

—Barbara W. Tuchman, *The Guns of August*

They may stay fifty years, they may love, marry, settle down, build houses, raise families, and die beside the Potomac, but they usually feel, and frequently they will tell you, that they are just here for a little while. [Series of predicates]

—Allen Drury, *Advise and Consent*

What is the nature of man's consciousness, his feelings, his hopes and aspirations, his personality, his learning, logic, and memory?

—Harold G. Wolff, "The Mind-Body Relationships"

It was an extraordinary mind put to extraordinary uses. No one can read a page of Shaw's prefaces, his journalism, his letters, or his better plays without feeling its lunge, its force, magnificence, sparkle, and originality. [Series with *or* and series with *and*]

—John Mason Brown, "GBS, Headmaster to the Universe"

Here is an example from serious writing in which the author omits the comma:

To be courageous, these stories make clear, requires no exceptional qualifications, no magic formula, no special combinations of time, place and circumstance.

—John F. Kennedy, *Profiles in Courage*

In the following sentence observe not only the omission of the final comma in a series but also the use of the semicolon before *but* in a compound sentence.

An unstable society, with extremes of poverty and wealth, but with easy access to riches and a quick turnover in the composition of the aristocracy, might produce a brief, frenetic and opportunistic radicalism; but it was not likely to produce a radicalism which was serious, unbridable and consistent.

—Arthur M. Schlesinger, Jr., *The Age of Jackson*

13c. Commas are used to separate consecutive adjectives preceding the noun they modify when the adjectives are coordinate in meaning.

The comma is correct only when the adjectives are coordinate —that is, when each of the adjectives refers directly to the noun.

When an adjective modifies the whole idea that follows it, it is not separated from it by a comma. If you can substitute *and* for the comma, the comma is correct. Note in the following examples that *and* would be a natural substitute for each comma used:

with slow, powerful strokes ... these cold, treeless heights ... the still, dimly lighted street ... this bold, gleaming structure ... his exuberant, energetic brother ... their dull, inglorious lives ... the muddy, tired, discouraged men

A safe practice is to omit the comma with numerals and with the common adjectives of size and age:

the little old lady ... a lazy old fellow ... the spreading chestnut tree ... a large red-haired girl ... four tiny black dots
But predominant among all this music of early summer there was that sweet, minor, infinitely moving lament, that voice of the north woods, the unhurried song of the little white-throated sparrow.

—EDWIN WAY TEALE, *Journey into Summer*

13d. The comma is used to separate words and phrases that might be incorrectly joined in reading.

This rule applies to the following situations:
1. When the conjunctions *for* and *but* might be mistaken for prepositions.

The men all waited in anxious silence, for the messenger seemed to be in a desperate hurry. [Waited in anxious silence for the messenger?]
All the men slid down the ropes, but one sailor seemed to be caught in the rigging. [All slid down the ropes but one sailor?]

2. When a noun might be mistaken for the object of a verb, verbal, or preposition before it.

After washing, the men filed into the dining tent. [Not After washing the men]
Before starting to eat, Father bowed his head in prayer. [Not Before starting to eat Father]

Above, the sun burned a dull red; below, the sand radiated heat like a furnace. [*Not* Above the sun . . . below the sand]

When we left, the boys were still playing their endless game of one old cat. [*Not* When we left the boys]

13e. Ordinarily, a comma is used to set off a modifier which precedes a main clause, especially when the introductory element is long and not closely connected with the main clause in meaning.

In punctuating modifiers that precede the main clause you must depend on your good sense as well as on rules. You must decide whether the sentence will be clearer with the introductory modifier or not. Length of clause alone will not tell you when to use a comma and when not to use it. Frequently very short clauses are set off for emphasis. In general, if you feel that the introductory element is not restrictive, put a comma after it. The following distinctions will help you:

1. Use a comma when you begin with a fairly long nonrestrictive adverbial clause:

When it came to the actual count, every measure against the Americans passed Parliament by large majorities.

—CATHERINE DRINKER BOWEN, *John Adams and the American Revolution*

Because the powerful beams that attract the insects are directed low over the river, they do not lead birds to their death as airport ceilometer lights, pointing straight up, sometimes do.

—EDWIN WAY TEALE, *Journey into Summer*

If a language is spoken by at least two people, then there are always some differences of usage which an observer can detect if he looks closely enough.

—CHARLES F. HOCKETT, *A Course in Modern Linguistics*

2. Use a comma to set off a beginning participial phrase modifying the subject or an absolute phrase before the subject:

Stopping often to gaze back or to browse in ripe raspberries hanging beside the trail, we ascended to the top. [Phrase modifies *we*.]

—EDWIN WAY TEALE, *Journey into Summer*

The excitement being over, the students returned to the classroom. [Absolute phrase]

3. Set off short introductory prepositional phrases only when they are definitely nonrestrictive, such as transitional phrases.

NO COMMA
Up to this point we are on safe ground.
During the ceremony a dog strayed into the room.
In the spring the ground is covered with poppies.

COMMA USED
In addition, such experiences are educational.
Of the small islands, the nearest is heavily timbered.
In the first place, his idea is not new.

Long introductory prepositional phrases may be set off if the writer believes that a comma is an aid to clearness:

In addition to the picture information it sends out, a television station also transmits sound.

—LOUIS N. RIDENOUR, "Electronics and the Conquest of Space"

In the biological and physical as well as the sociological sciences, statistics have become, as they never were before, the most important tool of investigation.

—JOSEPH WOOD KRUTCH

4. A short introductory clause is usually not followed by a comma. It may, however, be set off for greater emphasis or for clearness.

When he gives us a test he usually leaves the room. [Informal]
If the boy comes I shall tell him to look for you in the shop. [Informal]

13f. A comma, or commas, may be used to indicate transposed or contrasting sentence elements.

EXAMPLES
A boy, thin, ragged, and terribly frightened, had wedged himself behind the crate. [*Note:* A thin, ragged, and terribly frightened boy had . . .]
Inequality, by arousing jealousy and envy, provokes discontent. [*Not transposed:* Inequality provokes discontent by arousing jealousy and envy.]
He [Shakespeare] knew that Hamlet's dilemma, between the flesh and the spirit, was at the heart of every human being's private tragedy, and he

made Hamlet so terrifyingly real, with his courtesy and his violence, his intelligence and his self-hatred, his inconsistencies and his terrors, that every generation since has been able to recognize in him its own image. [Note here how commas set off balanced elements.]

—Marchette Chute, *Shakespeare of London*

She insisted on blue, rather than white, candles. [Contrasting sentence elements]

13g. Commas are used to set off mild exclamations, sentence adverbs, and the responsives *yes* and *no* when they begin a sentence.

EXAMPLES

Yes, he assigned another essay for Friday.

Evidently, you will not have it ready for him.

Unfortunately, I shall have to stay up all night to write it.

Mary said, "Well, what excuse can I give him?"

Oh, you will think of something to say before Friday.

13h. Commas are used to set off nonrestrictive clauses. They are not used to set off restrictive clauses.

If the distinction between restrictive and nonrestrictive clauses is not already clear to you, think of restrictive clauses as "identifying" or "pointing-out" clauses. A restrictive clause helps to locate or identify its antecedent. It says to the reader, "I mean this particular person or object, and no other." It is close to its antecedent in meaning, so close that it cannot be separated from it by a comma. A nonrestrictive clause does not point out or identify; it merely gives additional information about its antecedent.

RESTRICTIVE CLAUSES

The board decided in favor of another candidate, one *who has had more experience.* [Not just another candidate, but one with more experience]

The boy *who has a hobby* will never be lonely. [Not any boy, but that particular kind of boy]

Please bring me the book *that you see lying on the table.* [That particular book and no other]

NONRESTRICTIVE CLAUSES

The board decided in favor of Mr. Rossi, *who has had more experience*. [The name identifies the person; the clause does not need to identify or point out.]

Fenwick Jones, *who has a hobby*, will never be lonely. [The name identifies him.]

Please bring me Ryan's *The Longest Day*, *which you see lying on the table*. [The title identifies the book.]

Astronomy, *which is the study of heavenly bodies*, is a fascinating subject. [*Astronomy* identifies itself. It does not need a clause to tell which particular astronomy.]

My father, *who had not heard the question*, shook his head in silence. [A person has only one father. The clause cannot help identify him.]

Participial phrases may be either restrictive or nonrestrictive, depending on the meaning intended.

RESTRICTIVE

The boy *standing near the door* is waiting to register. [That particular boy]

A book *written by that author* is sure to be interesting. [Phrase points to a particular kind of book—one written by that author.]

NONRESTRICTIVE

Henry Black, standing there by the door, is waiting to register. [Name identifies him.]

Raising his rifle quickly, he fired at the moving object. [Nothing in the phrase helps to identify the person.]

13i. Commas are used to set off parenthetical elements (inter- rupters), or words, phrases, and clauses used to explain, to qualify, or to emphasize.

In a sense, several of the sentence elements discussed under other rules are "interrupters" in that they tend to break or interrupt the normal flow of a sentence, but strict classification is not here important. The parenthetical elements dealt with here may be classified as follows:

1. Conjunctive adverbs such as *however, therefore, moreover, furthermore*, when they are used within the clause. These words are more appropriate in a formal than in an informal style. And

in any style, an epidemic of *moreover's* and *furthermore's* is as bad as a plague of *and's* and *but's*.

EXAMPLES

An institution, *therefore*, may fail because its standards are too high.
In truth, *however*, it was probably not known until after the French Revolution.

2. Directive and qualifying words and phrases. Some of the most common of these, such as *also, perhaps, indeed, too, at least*, may, in informal writing, be considered as close modifiers and therefore not set off by commas. Others are usually set off.

EXAMPLES

All of this, *of course*, is theory.
My theory, *unluckily*, was disproved by the events that followed.
He would become, *in short*, a problem child of the worst kind.
Indeed, two of them actually did escape from the island.

3. Parenthetical phrases and clauses. Most of these are parenthetical comments, but some are adverbial clauses that break into the sentence flow.

EXAMPLES

This, *I suppose*, is the essence of morality.
Our interpretation of his motives is, *I think*, totally unfair.
If you must take risks on the lake, see to it that, *whenever storm warnings are up*, you at least have a life preserver with you.

It must be noted here that three types of punctuation are used with parenthetical elements. Parentheses are used for the most distant interrupters, dashes for something a little less distant, and commas for interrupters most closely related to the rest of the sentence. For a further discussion see Sections 17 and 18.

EXAMPLES

The Silent Generation (*loquacious enough among its contemporaries*) holds its tongue because it cannot both explore itself and explain itself.
—THORNTON WILDER, "The Silent Generation"

In music, *especially slow music*, a given tone is held for an appreciable length of time. This means that reverberation adds to the power of a given tone resulting in a desirable (*to the bathroom tenor, at least*) expansion in volume.

—WILLIAM C. VERGARA, Science in Everyday Things

Finally—*and this is true both for storable and perishable products*—were there a good way of disposing of inventories there would be far less need to worry about production control.

—J. KENNETH GALBRAITH, "Why Be Secretary of Agriculture?"

13j. Commas are used to set off absolute phrases when they occur within the sentence.

EXAMPLES

A great dam came into view, *water boiling from its curved rank of spillways.*

—ANDREW H. BROWN, National Geographic

She stood there, *her damp face glowing with happiness,* and asked us all to be seated.

13k. Commas are used to set off appositives.

An appositive, or a word in apposition, is used to limit or qualify the meaning of another word, to stand for it, to add to its meaning, or to emphasize it. The name *appositive* refers to the fact that a word and its appositive stand side by side. Most appositives—with the exception of the types listed below—are to be set off by commas.

EXAMPLES

Mr. Perkins, the *foreman* of the plant, was hurt yesterday. [Appositive with modifiers]

Other animals, such as the giraffe, camel, and brown bear, use a different type of locomotion. [Appositive introduced by *such as*]

—WILLIAM C. VERGARA, Science in Everyday Things

As he neared Fourth Street, another man, *a new one,* sprang up suddenly before him, *a short, heavy-set fellow,* stepping out of the shadows and striding directly toward him. [Notice how the use of appositives may add to sentence variety.]

—ROBERT M. COATES

Cooper, *an aristocrat in temper,* was a stickler for his social rights, *the rights to consideration, privacy, respect,* and he was often at war with him-

[305]

self, for his tastes and prejudices were by no means in harmony with his conscience and convictions.

—VAN WYCK BROOKS

But do *not* use commas with many common expressions in which the appositive and its substantive are so close that they are felt as a unit:

Jack the Ripper, Jack the Giant-killer, Henry the Eighth, my son Harold, William the Conqueror, the word *appositive*, the novelist Hawthorne.

Participles and occasionally adjectives may be placed for greater emphasis or for variety after the words they modify. When so placed they are said to be in the appositive position and are therefore set off by commas. See also Section 13f.

EXAMPLES
During an interval of quiet, one of the younger animals, *endlessly curious*, came running up and peered into the hole. . . .

—EDWIN WAY TEALE

A growl, *low and distant like the roll of a train on a faraway bridge*, began to stir in his throat.

—WOLCOTT GIBBS

This style, *so elegant and so simple*, was to mark all of Irving's work, *the sign of his cheerful good nature and transparent good taste.* . . . [Adjectives in the appositive position and then a substantive appositive]

—VAN WYCK BROOKS

Appositives may also be enclosed in parentheses or set off by dashes to indicate a greater degree of separation, if such a distinction is desired. (See Sections 17 and 18.) Sometimes dashes are used because of the presence of several commas.

EXAMPLES
It follows that every policy of the West that contradicts these fears—every Marshall Plan, every extension of economic aid to backward areas, every increase in social economic opportunity, every act of justice and reconciliation—breaks with the Communists' fundamental gospel—the fatality of history—and restores, triumphantly and creatively, the freedom of the West. [Note here not only the two appositives set off by dashes

but also the use of two adverbs *triumphantly* and *creatively,* in an unusual position.]

—BARBARA WARD, *Policy for the West*

The city is always full of young worshipful beginners—young actors, young aspiring poets, ballerinas, painters, reporters, singers—each depending on his own brand of tonic to stay alive, each with his own stable of giants.

—E. B. WHITE, *Here Is New York*

Appositives are sometimes introduced by such words as *that is, namely, such as, for instance, for example,* and the like. In long, formal sentences these words may be preceded by a colon or a semicolon. In ordinary writing, both formal and informal, *namely, that is, for example,* and *for instance* are usually preceded and followed by commas. *Such as* is not followed by a comma.

EXAMPLES
Short prepositions, such as *in, on, to, for,* are not capitalized in titles.
We know that white light—light from the sun, for example—is really a mixture of light of all colors.
There is only one proper thing for a driver to do when the army mule dies, namely, cut the harness and pull the cart himself.

13l. Commas are used to set off substantives used in direct address.

EXAMPLES
Professor Holmes, your lectures are a constant delight to your class. [To begin a sentence]
Read the poem, *my dear fellow,* and tell me if it means anything to you. [Within the sentence]
"*Please change places with me, Helen,*" I requested. [With quotation marks]

13m. An explanatory clause such as *he said* (a dialogue guide), when it breaks into a sentence of dialogue, is set off by commas.

EXAMPLES
"For your next project," said the teacher, "you will write an essay about the Blarney Stone."

Sean McCarthy raised his hand and said, "Did you know that Cormack MacCarthy, one of my ancestors, built Blarney Castle in 1602?" [Dialogue guide begins sentence.]

"Most tourists," explained Eric Swensen, "do not know that the real Blarney Stone is impossible for them to reach."

"They are allowed to kiss a substitute stone," he added. "It works just as well." [Dialogue guide at end of one sentence and before the second sentence]

Also see Section 16 for placing of quotation marks in relation to commas.

13n. Geographical names, dates, and addresses are set off by commas.

EXAMPLES

Miss Mercy Stockwell, 214 Union Street, Fairview, Vermont; Mr. D. C. Ulin, 522 Northwest 32nd St., Stockton, Ohio. [The form of a street address depends on the locality, but in any case the parts are separated by commas for clearness.]

Granville Stanley Hall was born in Ashfield, Massachusetts, on February 1, 1844, a farm boy who attended the district school, the local academies, and finally was graduated from Williams College, in 1867, with the conviction that he belonged in the ministry.

—OSCAR CARGILL, *Intellectual America*

The standard form for dates is "March 20, 1964," but there is a growing tendency among many people to write "20 March 1964." Both forms must be considered correct. Some publications also omit the comma when the day of the month is not used, as "March 1964."

EXERCISES

EXERCISE 1, NONRESTRICTIVE CLAUSES. *Punctuate each nonrestrictive clause in the following sentences.*

1. I remembered that this was the day when every man was to be only his better self.
2. Every year we have a homecoming day when everybody tries to impress parents and other visitors.
3. I awakened Toby Blair who was my roommate so that he would have time to dress a trifle less disreputably.

4. His everyday garb which consists of white jeans and a sweater seemed hardly appropriate.
5. His father and mother of whom he was very proud were coming to visit us.
6. We found them a room at the Green Mountain Inn where most of the alumni liked to stay.
7. I did not think that my parents who were vacationing in Mexico would come for the reunion.
8. I am happy to have a roommate whose parents adopt me on occasion.
9. I know one boy who gets letters and checks from two sets of parents.
10. This week end which we spent with Toby's parents was very happy for us.

EXERCISE 2, USING COMMAS AND SEMICOLONS. *Punctuate each of the following sentences. Decide whether to use a comma, a semicolon, or no mark at all. Be able to justify your decision.*

1. I have considered going into social work but my mother has tried to discourage me.
2. My mother is a practical person and she thinks that I am too young to know my mind.
3. I know something about the work for I have studied sociology and made trips to the state institutions.
4. During the summer I worked in the Red Cross office and I enjoyed the work.
5. A friend of mine is a social case worker and I have occasionally gone with her on her trips.
6. Her work is very interesting for it introduces her to all sorts of people.
7. She visits needy families but she does not actually take them baskets of food.
8. Sometimes she comes home very angry for she has no patience with drunken husbands.
9. She makes a careful study of each case and then she recommends the most suitable kind of assistance.
10. At times the Red Cross gives immediate help and then the happiness of the needy family is a welcome reward to the case worker.

EXERCISE 3, WORDS IN SERIES. *In the following sentences insert commas where they are necessary.*

1. Mark Twain was a journeyman printer a Mississippi River steamboat pilot and a famous writer and lecturer.

2. Few could compete with him in the ability to capture the lusty humor the spirit and the idiom of nineteenth-century America.

3. His humor his zest for life and his ability to see the ridiculous in everyday things endeared him to his readers.

4. Mark Twain was born in the Middle West lived in the Far West and died in New England.

5. He knew Bret Harte a poet short-story writer college professor and editor.

6. From his boyhood in Hannibal he found the materials for such characters as Tom Sawyer Huckleberry Finn and Becky Thatcher.

7. Mark Twain's best work reveals his genuine love of humanity his impatience with sham his irreverent lusty humor and his hatred of all pretense and deceit.

8. During his stay in San Francisco he associated with Bret Harte and Artemus Ward and other pioneers of the new literature of America.

9. He was attracted to Charles Farrar Browne, who was a humorist specializing in original spelling homely philosophy and shrewd comments on human nature.

10. As a tall imposing white-haired and white-garbed celebrity he was well known in his later years through his popular appearances on the lecture platform.

EXERCISE 4, INTRODUCTORY ELEMENTS. *In each of the following sentences decide whether the introductory phrase or clause is to be followed by a comma or not.*

1. If a blind poet had not written a long poem about it few modern readers would have heard about the Trojan War.

2. Because the wife of a Spartan king ran off with a young Trojan many good men perished before the walls of Troy.

3. Although the Homeric account may be the romantic version of the story the real cause of the war may have been political and economic rivalry.

4. After the sudden elopement of Helen and Paris the friends of King Menelaus of Sparta assembled to avenge the insult.

5. Having discovered a just cause to do what they liked to do even without cause the Greek heroes assembled at Aulis for the expedition.

6. Excited by hopes of an easy victory and thoughts of rich plunder the avengers gathered 100,000 men and 1186 ships.

7. Unlike modern wars in which everybody loses ancient wars could often be profitable to the victors.
8. Ten long years having been frittered away before the walls of Troy both sides were willing to try any stratagem to win or call the war off.
9. Deciding to put their faith in trickery instead of bravery the Greeks built a large hollow horse and pretended that it was an offering to their gods.
10. Convinced by a Greek spy that the horse would make them invincible the Trojans dragged it into the city and with it enough armed Greeks to open the gates of the city to the invaders.

EXERCISE 5, DATES AND ADDRESSES. *Copy the following sentences. Insert commas where they are needed.*

1. Our friends used to live at 826 Elm Drive Harris Junction Illinois but they recently moved to 230 Warren Street Duluth Minnesota.
2. Elinor Wylie was born in Rosemont Pennsylvania in 1887 and died in London England on December 16 1928.
3. Stephen Crane was born in Newark New Jersey on November 1 1871 and died twenty-nine years later on June 5 1900 at Badenweiler in the Black Forest.
4. Mary's new address is 722 East McMillan Street Rosemont Indiana.
5. All inquiries should be addressed to 38 Oak Street Southwest Fargo Texas.

EXERCISE 6, COMMAS AND RULES. *Copy the following sentences. Supply every missing comma and tell what rule of usage applies.*

1. If you have never heard of Phineas Barnum you have missed knowing what naïve curious gullible America will believe.
2. In 1842 Barnum opened the American Museum which housed an exhibit of wild animals freaks and curiosities.
3. Although many of his freaks were ordinary persons decked out to fool the public some we must admit to his credit were real celebrities.
4. Phineas Barnum an American showman was born in Bethel Connecticut.
5. Many of us still remember paying to gape at the tattooed

lady the wild man of Borneo the sword swallower and the fire eater.

6. In 1871 having failed in a bid for Congress Barnum organized his famous circus publicized as "The Greatest Show on Earth."

7. Many years earlier he had publicized General Tom Thumb a dwarf whose real name was Charles Sherwood Stratton.

8. Stratton strange to say was a normal child of normal parents but at a very early age for reasons never known to medical science he seemed to stop growing.

9. Barnum who believed that you could fool all of the people all of the time depended on an extravagant flamboyant type of advertising new at that time but now general in the show business.

10. Barnum internationally famous as a showman was also interested in serious affairs; in 1850 for example he brought to this country Jenny Lind the famous Swedish soprano.

EXERCISE 7, ALL USES OF THE COMMA. *Punctuate the following sentences. Tell what rule or principle of usage applies to each comma that you use.*

1. At the desk sat a slender red-haired girl who gave us more cards to fill out.

2. As we watched the girl reached for the telephone dialed a number and asked for somebody named Monty.

3. Her soft pleading voice dripping with honey she spoke words that would have melted a traffic policeman's heart.

4. My companion Henry Biggs a graduate of M.I.T. knew her for they had worked at the same summer resort in Vermont.

5. Vermont with hills lakes and rolling rocky New England scenery is a famous vacation region.

6. As he confided to me in whispers they had picnicked swum hiked and ridden horseback together over the famous Long Trail but their bridle paths as he said never became a bridal path to the altar.

7. Monty an elusive sort of character if we might judge from the overheard conversation finally agreed to some tentative arrangement.

8. The crisis having been postponed for the time the girl turned her attention to us and to her work.

9. She accepted our cards and with a fluttery momentary smile tossed them into a box.

10. "If you should ask me which I hope you don't" said Biggs "I would tell you that our applications will never reach the boss."

§ 14. THE SEMICOLON

14a. A semicolon is used between the main clauses of a compound sentence when they are not joined by one of the coordinating conjunctions.

In weight, or length of pause, a semicolon is more than a comma and less than a period. The period separates sentences. The semicolon separates main clauses within a sentence. Its frequent use marks a dignified formal style, implying relatively long, balanced sentences, and for this reason an abundance of semicolons in a light, informal paper should be viewed with suspicion. On the other hand the semicolon provides an excellent substitute for weak conjunctions between coordinate clauses, and it can often strengthen structures that are clearly parallel, and it is in general an important device in making a firm, economical style. (Rewrite that last sentence, removing the *and*'s, and you will see the point.)

Ordinarily a semicolon should not be used to cut off a phrase or a dependent clause from the main clause.

EXAMPLES OF INCORRECT USE
In these days, as writing grows increasingly brisk if not downright journalistic; one sometimes wonders what has happened to the good old semicolon.
She was habitually critical of me; because my manners, she said, were crude and my habits inconsiderate.

Notice, however, that substituting the semicolon for the subordinating conjunction, when the relationship between the clauses is implicit, can afford stylistic advantage.

EXAMPLE
She was habitually critical of me; my manners, she said, were crude and my habits inconsiderate.

[313]

OTHER EXAMPLES OF CONVENTIONAL USE

And there you have the whole secret of Beethoven. He could design patterns with the best of them; he could write music whose beauty will last you all your life; he could take the driest sticks of themes and work them up so interestingly that you find something new in them at the hundredth hearing: in short, you can say of him all that you can say of the greatest pattern composers; but his diagnostic, the thing that marks him out from all the others, is his disturbing quality, his power of unsettling us and imposing his giant moods on us.

—G. B. Shaw

The frontier has been a predominant influence on the shaping of the American character and culture, in the molding of American political life and institutions; the frontier is the principal, the recurring theme in the American symphony.

—Clyde Kluckhohn

This does not mean, of course, that the people are happy; the society to whose traditions they are adjusted may be a miserable one, ridden with anxiety, sadism, and disease.

—David Riesman

When the busman takes his proverbial holiday he takes a bus; when a sailor gets a holiday he hires a rowboat; when an anthologist has a holiday he thinks of another anthology.

—Louis Untermeyer

Often the verb in the second or third clause may be unstated, but understood to be the same as the verb in the first clause.

EXAMPLE

The humanist dismisses what he dislikes by calling it *romantic*; the liberal, by calling it *fascist*; the conservative, by calling it *communistic*.

—Robert Gorham Davis

14b. A semicolon is used between the coordinate clauses of a compound sentence with one of the following adverbs: *therefore, however, hence, accordingly, furthermore, nevertheless,* and *consequently.*

In modern prose, however, it is more usual to place the adverb within the second or third clause, enclosed in commas, rather than to use it as a conjunction at the beginning.

EXAMPLES

He had worked in the foreign service for two years without leave; hence he was tired almost beyond endurance.

He had worked in the foreign service for two years without leave; he was, therefore, tired almost beyond endurance.

14c. A semicolon is used in place of a comma when a more distinct pause than the comma would give is desirable.

In the following examples you will see uses of the semicolon that violate Rule 14a above. They should be studied as examples of unconventional placing; yet such uses of the semicolon are actually frequent in modern prose. (Observe that last sentence, for instance.) Obviously such uses should be imitated with caution by the beginning writer.

EXAMPLES

No man was less of a literary aesthete than Benjamin Franklin; yet this tallow-chandler's son, who changed world history, regarded as "a principal means of my advancement" that pungent style which he acquired partly by working in youth over old *Spectators*; but mainly by being Benjamin Franklin.

—F. L. LUCAS

This, then, is what I mean by "form"; but what is meant by calling such forms "expressive of human feeling"?

—SUSANNE K. LANGER

We allow our ideas to take their own course and this course is determined by our hopes and fears, our spontaneous desires, their fulfillment or frustration; by our likes and dislikes, our loves and hates and resentments.

—JAMES HARVEY ROBINSON

Most men have learned to read to serve a paltry convenience, as they have learned to cipher in order to keep accounts and not be cheated in trade; but of reading as a noble intellectual exercise they know little or nothing; yet this only is reading, in a high sense, not that which lulls us as a luxury and suffers the nobler faculties to sleep the while, but what we have to stand on tip-toe to read and devote our most alert and wakeful hours to.

—HENRY DAVID THOREAU

E X E R C I S E S

EXERCISE 1, FASHIONS IN THE USE OF SEMICOLONS. *Look through a few pages of a standard 19th-century essayist, and collect the first ten examples you see of the use of the semicolon. Classify these uses according to (a), (b), and (c) of this section. Then do the same for a modern essayist. Which took you longer to assemble? What can you conclude from this evidence about differences in the use of the semicolon in modern prose? Can you account for these differences?*

EXERCISE 2, COMMAS VERSUS SEMICOLONS. *In the following sentences, determine appropriate punctuation to be used in the places marked by brackets. Would you use commas, semicolons, or no punctuation at all?*

1. His hair was white and stood up wildly on his head [ ] nevertheless I was struck by a singular neatness in his appearance.
2. It was due, I suppose [ ] to his lofty stature and immaculate dress [ ] no doubt he has a careful wife looking after him.
3. Like all distinguished men in political life [ ] he spoke with assurance, even with arrogance [ ] yet I could not help sensing a touch of anxiety in his behavior.
4. I walked up to him then [ ] and stretched out my hand [ ] but he evidently failed to recognize me.
5. When a man has the weight of nations on his shoulders [ ] he may be forgiven for overlooking individuals [ ] but I confess I was angry.
6. It is one thing to be dignified and detached [ ] it is quite another to be downright rude.
7. I had arrived early [ ] as was my habit [ ] I therefore felt privileged to take my leave without delay.
8. The affair was not the worst I have ever endured [ ] but it was nearly so [ ] at such times one wishes one could escape at any cost.
9. Once I had arrived at the entrance [ ] however [ ] there was no turning back.
10. When I go to a place like that [ ] I go gladly [ ] when I I return [ ] I come home even more gladly.

§ 15. THE APOSTROPHE

15a. An apostrophe and -s are used to form the possessive of a noun, singular or plural, that does not end in -s.

EXAMPLES

A boy's will, women's hats, children's toys, a dog's life, the sun's rays, the earth's surface, Irene's husband, my mother-in-law's jewels.

When two or more names joined by *and* are represented as joint owners of something, in ordinary usage the last name alone takes the apostrophe.

EXAMPLES

Meier and Frank's store, Swenson and Carmody's Machine Shop, Nancy and Sally's mother, Larson, Jones, and Marshall's antique shop.

But when separate ownership is meant, the apostrophe follows each noun. Of course, when both nouns and pronouns are used, the pronouns take the possessive-case form.

EXAMPLES

Nancy's and Sally's clothes are strewn all over the bedroom.
Mr. Marshall's and Captain Ford's cars were badly damaged in the collision.
Mr. Danby said that his, his wife's, and his daughter's possessions were saved before the ship sank.

Usage sanctions such group possessives as *the Queen of England's hats*, but sometimes it is better to dodge an awkward construction by rewriting it. The double possessive or genitive is established usage, as in "some relatives of Mother's," "that old car of ours," "a friend of theirs," "that red coat of hers." [Note here that the *of*-phrase is used to indicate the possessive.]

15b. The apostrophe alone is used to form the possessive of a plural noun ending in -s.

EXAMPLES

Ladies' hats, three months' wages, girls' dresses, the Smiths' house, foxes' tails.

15c. The apostrophe with -s is used to form the possessive of singular nouns ending in -s, if the resultant form is not unpleasant or difficult to pronounce.

EXAMPLES

James's hat, Keats's poems, Jones's office; *but:* for goodness' sake, for conscience' sake, Demosthenes' orations.

15d. An apostrophe with -s is used to form the possessive of certain indefinite pronouns.

EXAMPLES

Anybody's game, somebody's hat, everybody's business, one's ideas, somebody's coat, another's turn.

The apostrophe should not be used with personal pronouns to form the possessive.

EXAMPLES

If this coat isn't yours [not *your's*], it's probably hers [not *her's*].
The decision is ours [not *our's*].
The two dogs are theirs [not *their's*].
It's only a little dog; its [not *it's*] bark is worse than its [not *it's*] bite.

15e. An apostrophe is used to indicate the omission of letters or figures.

EXAMPLES

Hasn't, doesn't, weren't, o'clock, it's [it is], I'll, class of '45.

15f. An apostrophe and -s are used to form the plurals of figures, letters, and words referred to as words.

EXAMPLES

You have not dotted your *i*'s or crossed your *t*'s.
Your *m*'s, *n*'s, and *u*'s look alike.
He used too many *and*'s and *but*'s in his paper.
Be careful not to make your 3's look like 8's.

Some publications omit the apostrophe in these situations, but there may be confusion in a sentence like this: In his handwriting the *is* and *us* are but a wavy line.

15g. The apostrophe is often omitted in titles.

EXAMPLES

The Authors League, Farmers Market, Kansas State Teachers College, Home Economics Teachers Association.

EXERCISES

EXERCISE 1, USE OF THE APOSTROPHE. *Copy the following sentences. Insert an apostrophe wherever it is correct.*

1. "Its almost ten oclock," said Toms cousin, "and hes not in in sight yet."
2. "I shouldnt worry," replied Maries mother. "Theyre very busy now at Smith and Eberlys Department Store this season."
3. "Were hungry, Mom," said little Edie. "Arent you going to make us a sandwich?"
4. "Mind your *p*s and *q*s, young lady, and youll earn your As and Bs," remarked Marie apropos of nothing.
5. "If Dads not here pretty soon," said Tom, "hell be here in time for tomorrows breakfast."
6. "Its all in the days work. Once he took the Smiths pet pooch to the doctors and decided to sit up all night with it," said Marie.
7. "Youre joking, of course," replied Tom. "You know that its leg was broken."
8. "Well, for Petes sake," exclaimed Maries mother, "it was somebodys responsibility, wasnt it?"
9. "Mother, did you say 'for Keats sakes' or 'for Keatss sakes'?" asked Marie. "Theres a fine difference, you know."
10. "I think everybodys so hungry hes getting silly," said Tom. "Whos going to make some hamburgers for us?"

EXERCISE 2, POSSESSIVE FORMS. *Write the possessive singular and the possessive plural of each of the following. Example:* child, child's, children's.

1. boy
2. baby
3. Smith
4. mother-in-law
5. he

6. goose
7. it
8. woman
9. Williams
10. Allen

11.	attorney	16.	Berry
12.	fox	17.	writer
13.	wolf	18.	she
14.	Powers	19.	sailor
15.	wife	20.	kangaroo

§ 16. QUOTATION MARKS

16a. Double quotation marks are used to enclose a direct quotation in dialogue and in reproducing passages from other writers.

EXAMPLES OF DIALOGUE

Jogging along in the hack along the Polifly Road they passed one of the brownstone farmhouses of the early settlers.

"Now, that's where I'd like to live," said Olga, the fat auntie.

"Is that so?"

"They're beautiful."

"You can have them," replied her sister Gurlie, Flossie's mother. "They're damp in summer and—cold in winter. And what are you going to do with the second floor? They never have room enough there to stand up in."

"They had to have it that way to keep warm."

"And they were always cold or too hot."

—W. C. WILLIAMS, *The Build-Up*

Note that in dialogue a new paragraph is used with every change in speaker.

The writer must be careful not to leave out one set of quotation marks. Quotation marks come in pairs, one set at the beginning and one set at the end of every quoted part.

WRONG

"I have no relish for the country, said Sydney Smith. It is a kind of healthy grave."

RIGHT

"I have no relish for the country," said Sydney Smith. "It is a kind of healthy grave."

A familiar student error in citing passages from others is to begin a quotation that never ends. By failing to close the quotation with the appropriate second set of marks, the passage from the quoted author and the comment by the student writer can become thoroughly muddled.

WRONG
Sydney Smith once remarked, "I have no relish for the country. It is a kind of healthy grave. This remark has often fascinated his admirers.

If a quotation consists of several sentences, the quotation marks are placed at the beginning and at the end of the entire quotation, not at the beginning and end of each separate sentence in that section.

"You'd have had your stomach full of fighting, young man," added Colonel Williams, "if Squire Sedgwick had not taken them just as he did. Squire," he added, "my wife shall thank you that she's not a widow when we get back to Stockbridge. I honor your courage, sir. The credit of this day is yours."

—EDWARD BELLAMY, *The Duke of Stockbridge*

If a quotation consists of several paragraphs, quotation marks are placed before each paragraph but at the end of the last paragraph only. This convention applies to a continued speech by one speaker. If the speaker changes, his words are placed in a new paragraph or paragraphs. Short descriptive, narrative, or explanatory passages may be paragraphed with dialogue, especially if they are placed between sentences of dialogue spoken by the same person.

A quoted passage of several lines of prose or poetry—not a part of dialogue—may be indicated by indention. In typing it is often typed single-spaced. In print it may be set in smaller type than the rest of the text. No quotation marks are needed when indention is used.

No quotation marks are used with an indirect quotation.

DIRECT
"Yes," I said to him, "it's all right."
"I am relieved to hear it," he replied.

[321]

INDIRECT

I told him it was all right.

He said he was relieved to hear it.

16b. Single quotation marks are used to enclose a quotation within a quotation.

EXAMPLES

"Finally," she said, "I just turned to him and shouted, 'Leave me alone, won't you?' " [Note the position of the quotation marks in relation to other marks.]

"If the good Lord should tell me that I had only five minutes to live," said Justice Oliver Wendell Holmes, "I would say to him, 'All right, Lord, but I'm sorry you can't make it ten.' "

—CATHERINE DRINKER BOWEN, *Yankee from Olympus*

16c. Quotation marks are used to enclose quoted titles of stories, poems, chapters, and other subdivisions of books, and, in newspaper style, the titles of books. (See Section 10.)

16d. Quotation marks are used to enclose words spoken of as words.

Italics are used for this purpose, however, when the style is formal, though writers are not consistent in this practice. In informal writing, quotation marks are usually more common. See Section 10c.

EXAMPLE

What I had to overcome was the traditional attitude toward such scare words as "socialization," "socialism," and "subsidization."

—HARRY S. TRUMAN, *Memoirs*

16e. Quotation marks are used to enclose words used in a special sense.

Often quotation marks are used to indicate to the reader that the writer, in repeating someone else's words, is opposed to their use, takes no stock in the manner in which they have been used, and is about to offer his own contrary views.

EXAMPLES

National greed has disguised itself in mandates to govern "inferior" races. [The writer does not think these races are inferior.]

How wrong-headed and time-wasting are the "refutations" of hedonism that spot and blot the pages of the history of ethics! [They are not refutations at all, according to the writer.]

—Wilmon S. Sheldon

The student is cautioned against the overuse of quotation marks in an apologetic or self-conscious way, enclosing slang or other expressions that he uneasily feels may be inappropriate. If they are inappropriate, he should find better ones. If they are appropriate, they need no apology.

16f. Quotation marks are often used to enclose the definitions or meanings of words spoken of as words.

EXAMPLE

Miscellaneous further illustrations of elevation are *pretty* from an early meaning "sly," through "clever," to something approaching "beautiful"; *nice* from an etymological meaning "ignorant," through its earliest English sense "foolish," and later ones like "particular," to its present broad and vague colloquial meaning of "pleasant" or "acceptable"; and *fond* from "foolish" to "affectionate."

—Stuart Robertson, *The Development of Modern English*

See also Section 10c.

16g. Commas and periods are always placed inside quotation marks.

This rule is a printers' convention. The period and the comma are the two marks that occupy the lower half of a line of print; all other marks—the colon, the semicolon, the question mark, and the exclamation point—stand the full height of the line. To have a comma or a period trail out beyond quotation marks looks bad. Remember the convention: periods and commas are *always* placed inside quotation marks. See Section 16b for examples.

16h. The question mark, the semicolon, and the exclamation point go inside quotation marks if they belong to the quoted part. They go outside if they do not belong to the quoted part.

EXAMPLES

Did you hear him say, "I won't go"? [The question mark belongs to the main clause, or the entire sentence. Hence it stands at the end. But notice that no period is used in addition to the end punctuation.]

"Well, I like that!" she exclaimed in anger.

"It is as much of a trade," says La Bruyère, "to make a book as it is to make a clock"; in short, literature is largely a matter of technique. [Note that the semicolon is not a part of the quotation. It belongs to the whole sentence.]

—IRVING BABBITT

16i. For dialogue guides (such as *he said*) with quoted dialogue, use the punctuation which the structure of the sentence calls for.

EXAMPLE

"The price is not a matter of profit," he said, stiffly; "it is a matter of principle." [Notice the semicolon to separate coordinate clauses in a compound sentence of dialogue. Most writers use a period and a following capital letter instead of a semicolon in this sort of construction. See 16a for other examples of punctuating dialogue.]

The general practice is not to use a comma before a quoted part that is woven into the sentence or before a title. This is logical enough: note that the voice makes little or no pause before reading such quotations.

EXAMPLE

It was tariff policy which seemed to him [Cordell Hull] "at the very heart of this country's economic dilemma." He saw in the expansion of foreign trade not only the "path to recovery" but the means of escape from regimentation and the road to world peace.

—ARTHUR M. SCHLESINGER, JR., *Triumph of the New Deal*

It is doubtful if adolescents since the time of Byron have repeated any poems (without compulsion) as frequently or as enthusiastically as the youth of the 'twenties recited "My candle burns at both ends" and "Safe upon the solid rock . . ."

—OSCAR CARGILL, *Intellectual America*

EXERCISES

EXERCISE 1, COMPOSING A PARAGRAPH WITH QUOTATIONS. *Copy out a paragraph of formal prose that seems to you interesting, for any reason. Then write your own paragraph of comment, in which you quote three or four short phrases from the original, punctuating properly as you do so.*

EXERCISE 2, QUOTATION MARKS AND PARAGRAPHING. *Copy the following, punctuating and paragraphing correctly.*

The father caught his son's eye at last, and gave him a mild, responsive smile. I am getting on very well, he said. Have you drunk your tea? asked the son. Yes, and enjoyed it. Shall I give you some more? The old man considered, placidly. Well, I guess I will wait and see. He had, in speaking, the American tone. Are you cold? his son inquired. The father slowly rubbed his legs. Well, I don't know. I can't tell till I feel. Perhaps some one might feel for you, said the younger man, laughing. Oh, I hope some one will always feel for me! Don't you feel for me, Lord Warburton? Oh yes, immensely, said the gentleman addressed as Lord Warburton, promptly. I am bound to say you look wonderfully comfortable. Well, I suppose I am, in most respects. And the old man looked down at his green shawl, and smoothed it over his knees. The fact is, I have been comfortable so many years that I suppose I have got so used to it I don't know it. Yes, that's the bore of comfort, said Lord Warburton. We only know when we are uncomfortable.

§ 17. COLON AND DASH

THE COLON

17a. The colon is used to introduce a long and formal quotation, an enumeration or a list of particulars, or a formal explanation.

The colon is a formal mark. It should not be used before a series introduced informally. In ordinary formal context, writers usually hold to the rule that what precedes the colon must be a grammatically complete clause or statement, but in lists and tabulations the colon is used after the verb introducing the list. In other words, a comma or no mark at all is used before a series if the series is part of a sentence.

POOR
My favorite amusements are: dancing, golfing, and attending movies.

RIGHT
My favorite amusements are dancing, golfing, and attending movies.

POOR
Then he shouted: "Eureka! I have found it."

RIGHT
Then he shouted, "Eureka! I have found it."

After a colon it is customary to use a capital letter when the list that follows consists of a complete sentence or several sentences; a small letter is used when what follows the colon is a part of the same sentence. Here are several examples of complete sentences introducing long quotations:

He adds, by way of parenthesis: [Seven quoted sentences follow.]

The following notes are purely personal: [Three quoted paragraphs follow.]

I add a few notes on minor irritations: [Three quoted paragraphs follow.]

The following are more general: [Several quoted paragraphs follow.][1]

Moreover, this author was somehow reassuring; he told the Province what it longed to hear: that its most fervent protests against Parliament were no new thing, no shocking innovation.

—CATHERINE DRINKER BOWEN, *John Adams and the American Revolution*

He must, we are sure, feel and know the steady progress of the morning: a crosstown car establishing its characteristic crescendo, a hose being played in a doorway after a hot summer night, the eight-o'clock greeting of a saw in a picture-framer's shop nearby.

—*The New Yorker*, "City Rhythms"

---

[1] These examples, typical of the formal use of a colon to introduce long quotations, are from *Opinions of Oliver Allston*, by Van Wyck Brooks, published by E. P. Dutton and Company in 1941.

17b. A colon may be used between main clauses when the second clause amplifies and interprets the first.

EXAMPLES

It is a good thing to be old early: to have the fragility and sensitivity of the old, and a bit of wisdom, before the years of planning and building have run out. [The second element here takes the form of an appositive.]

—MARTIN GUMBERT, *You Are Younger than You Think*

This is one of the difficulties about reading Greek and Latin, and, for that matter, Hebrew also: it is awfully hard to tell how the ordinary people spoke to one another, since almost all we have is literature, gracefully or powerfully stylized, far above the level of daily conversation. . . .

—GILBERT HIGHET, *A Clerk of Oxenford*

Some writers use the colon where others would use a semicolon. Since most writers distinguish between the colon and the semicolon, however, the practice of the majority is here recommended to college students. An example or two will show what is meant:

The great, the trusty educator of mankind was matter: and matter, in ladies' minds, was entirely veiled in a mist of words. And not in ladies' minds only. Most schoolmasters were people who had failed in the world, or who feared to fail in it: they knew matter only by the terror which they felt of it: yet even that indirect acknowledgment was better than a bland innocence. . . .

—GEORGE SANTAYANA, *The Last Puritan*

THE DASH

17c. The dash is used to indicate a sudden, abrupt break in thought or structure.

EXAMPLES

My first sight of him—if a new boy may look at a monitor—was on my rather wretched second day at a Public School. . . . He seemed to me of a fabulous height—about five feet ten, I suppose; thin and bolt upright. He had a stick-up collar—'barmaids' had not yet come in—but not a very high one, and his neck was rather long.

—JOHN GALSWORTHY, "The Man Who Kept His Form"

[327]

"I wish—I wish you'd let him know—please do—it was an accident."
[In dialogue to give the effect of hesitation]
"I don't know whether she would like—" [Speech abruptly broken off]

17d. The dash is used for an explanatory or parenthetical phrase or clause that breaks into the normal flow of the sentence.

Three kinds of marks may indicate parenthesis—the comma, the dash, and marks of parenthesis. The degree of separation indicated by these marks varies from the lightest, for which commas are used, to the most definite and the most formal, for which parentheses are used.

EXAMPLES
There may be lovelier country somewhere—in the Island Vale of Avalon, at a gamble—but when the sunlight lies upon it and the wind puts white clouds racing their shadows the Shenandoah Valley is as good as anything America can show.

—BRUCE CATTON, *A Stillness at Appomattox*

Like the British paratroopers to the east, the Americans—in humor, in sorrow, in terror and in pain—began the work they had come to Normandy to do.

—CORNELIUS RYAN, *The Longest Day*

17e. The dash is used to introduce or to set off a long, formal appositive or summary.

EXAMPLES
There is no substitute and there never can be any substitute for *men* in the process of education—for earnest, enthusiastic, capable men in the faculty and in the student body. [Introducing an appositive]

—WILLIAM BENNETT MUNRO, "Quack-doctoring the Colleges"

These obstacles—jagged triangles of steel, saw-toothed gatelike structures of iron, metal-tipped wooden stakes and concrete cones—were planted just below high- and low-tide water marks. [To set off long appositive]

—CORNELIUS RYAN, *The Longest Day*

The dash may occasionally be found before such words as *namely* and *that is* introducing an appositive. See also Section 13k.

EXAMPLES

Also you will find out about the queer fade-away, the slow curve, the fast in- and out-shoots that seemed to be timed almost as delicately as shrapnel, to burst, or rather break, just when they will do the most harm— namely, at the moment when the batter is swinging.

—PAUL GALLICO

A dash may be used before such words as *all* and *these* introducing a summary, or summarizing appositive, after a series. The occasions for this use of the dash are infrequent.

EXAMPLES

Teas, dances, new clothes, blind dates—all these should be a part of your freshman year.

Regional survey and regional service—these are the chief ingredients for a reasonable citizenship. . . .

—LEWIS MUMFORD

Caution: The dash must not be used indiscriminately for all other marks of punctuation. It should be saved for its special function, so that it will be intelligible when it is used.

§ 18. PARENTHESES AND BRACKETS

PARENTHESES

18a. Parentheses are used to enclose material that is supplementary, explanatory, or interpretive.

In theory, the general principle is that commas set off material that is fairly close to the main meaning of the sentence (see Section 13i); dashes set off material more distant in meaning (Section 17e); and marks of parenthesis are used to indicate the most distant parenthetical relation. In practice, however, there is considerable variety among modern writers in the way parentheses are used. One traditional function is to enclose an explanation, a definition, or a set of examples to clarify a particular reference.

EXAMPLES

The book, V-2, by Von Braun's superior at Peenemunde (the German rocket-testing station), General Walter Dornberger, sustains this particular and astonishing complaint throughout its length. . . .

—Morris Freedman

Many things may be legitimately inferred to exist (electrons, the expanding universe, the past, the other side of the moon) from what is observed.

—Sidney Hook

A less conventional function of parentheses favored by contemporary novelists is to enclose remarks that come as from another voice than the speaker's—remarks that may inject a critical note as if one were whispering something rather impolite behind one's hand.

EXAMPLE

Ideally bald, sun-tanned, and clean shaven, he began rather impressively with that great brown dome of his, tortoise-shell glasses (masking an infantile absence of eyebrows), apish upper lip, thick neck, and strongman torso in a tightish tweed coat, but ended, somewhat disappointingly, in a pair of spindly legs (now flanneled and crossed) and frail-looking, almost feminine feet. His sloppy socks were of scarlet wool with lilac lozenges; his conservative black oxfords had cost him about as much as all the rest of his clothing (flamboyant goon tie included).

—Vladimir Nabokov

Sometimes parentheses may be used to introduce a comment by the author about what he is doing, drawing the reader's attention to some particular device of style.

EXAMPLE

Almost every high-school graduate "knows" (I put quotation marks around the word) that air is primarily a mixture of oxygen gas and nitrogen gas. . . .

—James B. Conant

Finally, journalists are prone to enclose whole parenthetical sentences inside other sentences, sometimes at awkward points in the structure.

EXAMPLE

The major surprise in the hop-skip-and-jump came when Vilhjalmur Eirnarsson of Iceland (his fellow undergraduates at Dartmouth called him Willie) sailed out 53 feet 4 inches for second place.

—JOHN KIERAN

BRACKETS

18b. Brackets are used to enclose corrections, interpolations, and supplied omissions added to a quotation by the person quoting.

Here is an example from a passage that has already been used (in Section 16i) for another purpose.

It was tariff policy which seemed to him [Cordell Hull] "at the very heart of this country's economic dilemma." [The reader would have no idea what person the author was talking about if we had not added the bracketed explanation.]

—ARTHUR M. SCHLESINGER, JR.

In this book you will find many examples of conventional use of brackets, like the one just above, where they set off comment about a quoted passage in such a way that the reader cannot confuse the comment with the passage itself.

EXERCISES

EXERCISE 1, THE COLON AND THE SEMICOLON. *Copy out from any sample of formal modern prose five sentences in which colons are used. In which of these sentences could semicolons be used instead? What effect would such a substitution have on the meaning or the tone of each sentence?*

EXERCISE 2, THE COLON. *Write out three sentences of your own illustrating the use of the colon as a formal introduction, in the manner described in 17a. Then write out three others in which the colon is used to separate independent clauses (17b).*

EXERCISE 3, PARENTHESES, BRACKETS, DASHES. *From one of your textbooks copy five sentences in which parentheses or brackets are used. Try substituting dashes for the parentheses and brackets. What is the effect on meaning and tone?*

EXERCISE 4, THE DASH.   *Try writing a letter in which you use no punctuation at all except dashes. What is the effect on tone: that is, what kind of voice do you hear uttering these words? What kind of person speaks in this way?*

§ 19. TOO MUCH PUNCTUATION

19a. Superfluous commas should be avoided.

Fundamentally, the purpose of punctuation is to facilitate the communication of thoughts, ideas, or information by means of the printed or written language. But what writers—and readers—think is necessary to achieve clear and quick communication depends on the practices of the age in which they live. Many years ago, writers used much punctuation; at present we use as little punctuation as possible, especially in informal writing.

Journalism may have gone too far in eliminating punctuation marks, as many an irritated reader of inadequately punctuated newspaper writing can testify. There is a middle ground that we must take—always enough punctuation for clearness, no matter what the general tendency of the time is.

The following are typical situations in which unnecessary commas should not be used in short, simple sentences that would be clear without the commas:

1. *Commas should not be so used as to separate a subject and its verb, a verb and its object, a preposition and its object, an adjective and its noun.*

WRONG

My father's investments and savings, provided for my education.

RIGHT

My father's investments and savings provided for my education. [Subject and verb]

WRONG

We were told, that there were no fish in the pond.

RIGHT

We were told that there were no fish in the pond. [Clause as object of verb]

WRONG
Their warehouses held large stocks of, flour, packaged cereals, canned vegetables, dried fruits and other foods.

RIGHT
Their warehouses held large stocks of flour, packaged cereals, canned vegetables, dried fruits, and other foods. [Preposition and objects]

WRONG
He was a tall, lanky, shy, awkward, boy of fourteen.

RIGHT
He was a tall, lanky, shy, awkward boy of fourteen. [Adjective and noun]

2. *No comma should be used after a coordinating conjunction joining two clauses.*

WRONG
We tried to see him, but, he was not at home.

RIGHT
We tried to see him, but he was not at home. [Since both clauses are short, omission of both commas would also be correct.]

WRONG
Let me sit down, for, I am tired.

RIGHT
Let me sit down, for I am tired.

3. *No comma is used after a coordinating conjunction that* begins *a main clause.*

WRONG
But, I never learn anything from these discussions.

RIGHT
But I never learn anything from these discussions.

4. *No comma is used before a coordinating conjunction joining two words, two simple phrases, two subjects, or two predicates.*

POOR
Demeter, he explained, was the goddess of the earth, and of agriculture.

BETTER

Demeter, he explained, was the goddess of the earth and of agriculture.

POOR

Before the girl left the room, she stopped to powder her nose, and to pat her hair.

BETTER

Before the girl left the room, she stopped to powder her nose and to pat her hair.

Exception: Compound elements of a sentence, such as compound subject, compound predicate, compound direct object, and so on, if long and variously modified, may be separated by a comma for the sake of clearness.

A man walked into the lobby of the hotel that stands on the corner of Main Street and Seventh Avenue at four o'clock last Thursday afternoon, and with an air of secrecy approached a group of men who were sitting in the corner around a table that was covered with books and papers.

5. No comma is used to set off short introductory phrases or clauses that are not clearly parenthetical.

UNNECESSARY

In the south, the land consists of fertile plains.

BETTER

In the south the land consists of fertile plains.

UNNECESSARY

Later that spring, I applied at another college.

BETTER

Later that spring I applied at another college.

UNNECESSARY

After they are dry, they must be packed in peat moss.

BETTER

After they are dry they must be packed in peat moss.

6. Commas are not used to set off closely restrictive elements, such as clauses, appositives, and phrases. See Section 13h for a more complete discussion.

WRONG
Every boy, who enters the contest, will get some prize.

BETTER
Every boy who enters the contest will get some prize.

UNNECESSARY
My sister, Eileen, is coming here next year.

BETTER
My sister Eileen is coming here next year.

WRONG
A man, trained in research, will head the laboratory.

BETTER
A man trained in research will head the laboratory.

19b. Periods are not used in the following situations:

1. *Most contractions:*

Aren't, I'll, haven't, couldn't, won't, wasn't, isn't.

2. *Government agencies:*

TVA, CARE, UNESCO, USAFI.

3. *Roman numerals after names:*

Henry VIII of England, Louis XVI of France, King Edward VII of England.

4. *With another period or question mark as end punctuation:*

She said, "Stop writing." [*Not* "She said, "Stop writing.".]
Did she say, "Stop writing"? [*Not* "Did she say, "Stop writing."?]

19c. Question marks are not used after indirect questions or to indicate irony or sarcasm.

WRONG
The teacher asked whether we had finished writing? [Use a period.]
We spent an exciting(?) Sunday afternoon. [Omit the question mark. If the irony can't stand on its own feet, don't prod it.]

19d. A double or triple exclamation point should not be used for greater emphasis.

POOR

"Remember," she said. "This is the last time!! Positively!!!" [Use only one exclamation point at a time.]

19e. Quotation marks should not be overused.

Quotation marks should not be used for literary allusions that have become common property or for proverbs—even for clichés. In informal writing there is little need for enclosing slang in quotation marks, but in formal writing you are ordinarily expected to do so. Quotation marks with slang are a form of apology. But if you have too many occasions to say, "Excuse it, please," perhaps you should stop doing that for which you must apologize. In general the apologetic quotation mark is going out of favor.

19f. Dashes must not be used to replace all other marks of punctuation, not even in informal letters.

19g. Apostrophes are not used to form the plurals of either common or proper nouns.

WRONG

The Hedrick's, the Jones', the Smith's, and the Williams's were all at the Iowa picnic.

RIGHT

The Hedricks, the Joneses, the Smiths, and the Williamses were all at the Iowa picnic.

SPELLING

§ 20. THE SPELLING PROBLEM

As everyone knows, many words in English are not spelled the way they are pronounced. That is why spelling our language is so difficult.

Consider the problem of the foreigner who runs up against the various pronunciations of just one small group of letters: *-ough* in *cough, dough, rough, bough, through*. His problem is illustrated by the story of the exchange student from France, coming to America to improve his English accent, who on landing in New York saw a headline on the front page of a newspaper: EXHIBITION PRONOUNCED SUCCESS. "Ah, this fantastic language!" he exclaimed in utter discouragement.

There was a time, several centuries ago, when a writer gave little thought to using the right letters in his words. Some writers, Shakespeare for instance, appear to have spelled their own names in several different ways without a pang of remorse. Our modern attitude toward standardized spelling, however, is very different. Almost everyone—not just your English teacher—takes spelling seriously, perhaps too seriously. One reason is that, unlike most matters of language, spelling is an area where there is usually a Right or Wrong, and it is tempting to make much of someone else's errors when you know they are really errors. There is even an economic importance in trying to learn to spell; employers everywhere assume that poor spelling is a sign of stupidity or illiteracy. Perhaps they reason, rightly or not, that carelessness in spelling is a visible, measurable sign of carelessness in other, more important things. Spelling is something that shows.

And because it does show, because it can be easily seen and easily judged, it has become one of the first tests of a person's education and his fitness for a job.

How Spelling Got to Be a Problem.   Historically, spelling became a problem because the spelling of words jelled into a fixed form while the pronunciation of words went right on changing. Most of the weird spellings in our language, like *rough, dough, bough,* represent long-lost pronunciations that people once actually used in something like the way the words are still spelled. The growth of printing had much to do with this fixing of spelling conventions. A word in print, sent from one part of England to another, looked the same and stayed the same; pronunciation of that word continued to be affected by regional differences, and kept on changing with the passing of time. Further spelling difficulties we inherited with the influx of words from different languages, or even from different dialects of our own language, and our troubles were not lessened when foreign visitors, like the Norman French, began to remake the home language according to their lights. And finally, we simply do not have enough letters in our alphabet for the number of vowel and consonant sounds in our language. Some of our letters will always have to stand for several different sounds.

How the Student Got to Be a Problem.   Spelling is not difficult for everyone. Some young people master spelling easily, almost unconsciously, by the time they reach college, just as they learn table manners or driving a car. For others, spelling difficulties may be traced to the way they read. Many people read by words instead of by letters to such an extent that they scarcely notice the arrangement of letters in a word. Some minds have never been trained to focus on letters. And there are some whose minds —often very good minds—work in ways not particularly adapted to learning how to spell. Finally, some fail to learn spelling simply because in youth there never was sufficient motivation for doing so. They were just as successful in the things that mattered to them, and life was just as interesting without their knowing how to spell as it would have been with it.

What to Do About the Problem. There are almost as many schemes for teaching spelling as there are teachers. Some college teachers say, "So you never could spell! Well, it's important to learn here and now. So you just buckle down and learn it, just as you learn anything else in college." Much success has come from this method. Any scheme that manages to encourage, or force, the active cooperation and interest of students is a good scheme.

Analyzing words helps. It increases the student's awareness of words if he knows something about prefixes and suffixes and roots and stems. A study of word derivation helps. Dividing a word into syllables helps. Any scheme that makes a student focus on the letters of a word helps.

Systematic study of words in spelling lists, daily spelling drills, and keeping a record of misspelled words all help a great deal. The spelling list does contain many of the words usually misspelled; its chief value, however, is that through its use the student is made aware of words as composed of letters. Spelling rules help, too, in that they introduce at least some system into the seemingly hopeless snarl of English spelling.

The Value of Proofreading. And finally, even if a student finds it impossible to remember how all the words he uses are spelled, he can always proofread his written work, in the manner described in Chapter 5. The college student can use his dictionary. He can check every word he is not sure of. That is what many college teachers, stenographers, editors of newspapers—in fact, all who write or deal with words for a living—have to do. To proofread a theme before it is handed in is an obligation. To make your English teacher act as your proofreader for you is an insult that he may very properly resent.

20a. The following list of words often misspelled by college students is to be used as the instructor thinks necessary.[1]

1. abbreviate
2. absence
3. absorption
4. absurd
5. accidentally
6. accommodate *
7. accompanying
8. accomplish
9. accumulate
10. accustom
11. achievement *
12. acknowledge
13. acquaintance
14. acquire *
15. acquitted
16. across
17. additionally
18. address
19. aggravate
20. all right
21. always
22. almost
23. although
24. altogether
25. amateur

26. among *
27. analysis
28. analyze
29. annual
30. answer
31. apartment
32. apology
33. apparatus
34. apparently *

35. appearance
36. appropriate
37. arctic
38. argument *
39. arising
40. arrangement
41. ascend
42. association
43. athlete
44. athletics
45. attendance
46. audience
47. auxiliary
48. awkward
49. bachelor
50. balance

51. barbarous
52. becoming
53. beginning *
54. benefited *
55. biscuit
56. boundaries
57. brilliant
58. bureau
59. business *
60. cafeteria
61. calendar
62. candidate
63. career
64. carburetor
65. category *
66. certain
67. changeable
68. changing

69. characteristic
70. chosen *
71. commission
72. committed
73. committee
74. comparative *
75. competitive

76. compulsory
77. conceivable
78. conference
79. conferred
80. conqueror
81. conscience *
82. conscientious *
83. conscious *
84. continuous
85. convenient
86. courteous
87. criticism *
88. criticize *
89. curiosity
90. cylinder
91. dealt
92. decision
93. definitely *
94. describe *
95. description *
96. despair
97. desperate
98. dictionary
99. dilapidated

100. disagree
101. disappear

[1] Please pay particular attention to the words marked *. Vice President Thomas Clark Pollock of New York University has made a study of over 30,000 misspellings in the writing of college students. The words starred here are the words, or belong to the word-groups, that he found misspelled most often. The authors are grateful to Dr. Pollock for permission to use his findings.

102. disappoint
103. disastrous *
104. discipline
105. dissatisfied
106. dissipate
107. doctor
108. dormitory
109. eighth
110. eligible
111. eliminate
112. embarrass
113. eminent
114. environment *
115. enthusiastic
116. equipment
117. equivalent
118. erroneous
119. especially
120. exaggerated
121. exceptionally
122. exhaust
123. exhilarate
124. existence *
125. experience *

126. explanation *
127. extraordinary
128. extremely
129. familiar
130. fascinate *
131. February
132. foreign
133. frantically
134. fraternities
135. generally
136. government
137. grammar *
138. guard
139. guidance
140. height *
141. hindrance
142. humorous
143. illiterate
144. imaginary *

145. imagination *
146. immediately *
147. impromptu
148. incidentally
149. incredible
150. indefinitely

151. indispensable
152. inevitable
153. infinite
154. intellectual
155. intelligence *
156. intentionally
157. interesting *
158. irrelevant
159. irresistible
160. knowledge
161. laboratory
162. legitimate
163. lightning
164. literature
165. loneliness *
166. maintenance
167. maneuver
168. marriage
169. mathematics
170. miniature
171. mischievous
172. necessary *
173. nevertheless
174. noticeable *
175. nowadays

176. oblige
177. obstacle
178. occasion
179. occasionally *
180. occurred *
181. occurrence *
182. opportunity
183. optimistic
184. original *
185. outrageous
186. pamphlet

187. parallel
188. particularly
189. pastime
190. permissible
191. perseverance
192. perspiration
193. physically
194. picnicking
195. politics
196. practically
197. precedence
198. preference
199. preferred
200. prejudice *

201. preparation
202. prevalent *
203. privilege *
204. probably *
205. professor *
206. prominent *
207. pronunciation
208. prove
209. quantity
210. recognize
211. recommend
212. reference
213. referred *
214. repetition *
215. regard
216. representative
217. restaurant
218. rhythm *
219. rhythmical
220. ridiculous
221. sandwich
222. schedule
223. secretary
224. separate *
225. siege

226. similar *
227. simultaneous
228. soliloquy

229. sophomore	237. thorough *	244. undoubtedly
230. specifically	238. throughout	245. unnecessarily
231. specimen	239. tragedy	246. village
232. speech	240. tries *	247. villain
233. strictly	241. truly	248. weird
234. surprise *	242. Tuesday	249. whether *
235. temperament	243. unanimous	250. writing *
236. temperature		

20b. The following spelling rules will help you to remember how certain words are spelled.

1. A word ending in silent -e generally drops the -e before a suffix beginning with a vowel letter . . .

DROP -e

admire	+ ation	= admiration	desire	+ ous	= desirous
admire	+ able	= admirable	dine	+ ing	= dining
allure	+ ing	= alluring	explore	+ ation	= exploration
arrange	+ ing	= arranging	fame	+ ous	= famous
arrive	+ ing	= arriving	imagine	+ ary	= imaginary
believe	+ ing	= believing	imagine	+ able	= imaginable
care	+ ing	= caring	love	+ able	= lovable
come	+ ing	= coming	lose	+ ing	= losing
deplore	+ able	= deplorable	move	+ able	= movable

but it retains the -e before a suffix beginning with a consonant letter.

RETAIN -e

arrange	+ ment	= arrangement
care	+ ful	= careful
force	+ ful	= forceful
hate	+ ful	= hateful
like	+ ness	= likeness
move	+ ment	= movement

But after c *or* g, *if the suffix begins with* a *or* o, *the -e is retained to indicate the soft sound of* c *or* g.

RETAIN -e

advantage	+ ous	= advantageous
change	+ able	= changeable

courage	+ ous	= courageous
notice	+ able	= noticeable
outrage	+ ous	= outrageous
peace	+ able	= peaceable
service	+ able	= serviceable

2. *In words with* ie *or* ei *when the sound is long* ee, *use* i *before* e *except after* c.

i BEFORE e

achieve	cashier	piece	shriek
apiece	field	pierce	siege
belief	fierce	priest	thief
believe	frieze	relieve	wield
brief	grief	retrieve	yield
besiege	niece	reprieve	
chief	pier	shield	

EXCEPT AFTER C

ceiling	conceive	deceive	receipt
conceit	deceit	perceive	receive

Exceptions: either, neither, financier, weird, species, seize, leisure.

These may be remembered by arranging the words in a sentence: "Neither financier seized either species of weird leisure."

The so-called "seed" words can be easily remembered. For those who cannot memorize, a careful scrutiny of the list will suffice:

1. Only one word ends in -*sede:*   supersede

2. Three words end in -*ceed:*   exceed
   proceed
   succeed

3. The rest end in -*cede:*   accede
   cede
   concede
   intercede
   precede
   recede
   secede

3. In words of one syllable and words accented on the last syllable, ending in a single consonant letter preceded by a single vowel letter, double the final consonant letter before a suffix beginning with a vowel letter.

Now this looks like a formidable rule to unravel. Let us see what it involves. In the first place, it applies to short words such as *get*, *swim*, *drop*, *drip*. In the second place, it applies to longer words in which the accent is on the final syllable, such as *refer*, *begin*, *equip*. Examine the illustrations below to see what happens:

drop [word of one syllable] + ed [suffix beginning with a vowel] = dropped.

control [accented on the last syllable] + ed [suffix] = controlled.

benefit [not accented on last syllable] + ed [suffix] = benefited.

confer [accented on last syllable] + ed [suffix] = conferred.

confer [notice the shift in accent] + ence [suffix] = conference.

defer [accented on last syllable] + ed [suffix] = deferred.

defer [notice the shift in accent] + ence [suffix] = deference.

SUFFIX BEGINS WITH A VOWEL

One Syllable

brag	—bragging	man	—mannish
cram	—cramming	plan	—planning
drag	—dragging	snap	—snapped
din	—dinning	sin	—sinning
drop	—dropped	stop	—stopped
cut	—cutting	quit	—quitting
bid	—bidding	rob	—robbed
flag	—flagged	stab	—stabbed
get	—getting	whip	—whipped
clan	—clannish	glad	—gladdest

Accent on Last Syllable

admit'	—admitted	equip'	—equipped
begin'	—beginning	commit'	—committee
commit'	—committed	occur'	—occurrence
concur'	—concurring	submit'	—submitted
confer'	—conferring	compel'	—compelled

Not Accented on Last Syllable

prefer	—preference	benefit	—benefited
refer	—reference	profit	—profitable
happen	—happened	marvel	—marvelous

SUFFIX BEGINS WITH A CONSONANT

glad	—gladness	sin	—sinful
fat	—fatness	equip	—equipment
man	—manhood	profit	—profitless

4. A *noun ending in* -y *preceded by a consonant forms the plural in* -ies; *a verb ending in* -y *preceded by a consonant forms its present tense, third person singular, in* -ies.

ENDING IN -*y* PRECEDED BY A CONSONANT

baby, babies	sky, skies	fairy, fairies
marry, marries	copy, copies	fly, flies

ENDING IN -*y* PRECEDED BY A VOWEL

attorney, attorneys	valley, valleys	delay, delays
destroy, destroys	enjoy, enjoys	chimney, chimneys

Note: Some other rules for forming plurals are as follows:

5. *For most nouns, add* -s: boys, girls, houses, ideas, aches, pains.

6. *For nouns ending with a sound similar to* s, *add* -es: birches, foxes, boxes, classes.

7. *For nouns ending in* -f, -fe, -ff, *use* -s *or* -ves: chief, chiefs; staff, staffs, staves; wife, wives; sheriff, sheriffs; elf, elves.

8. *For nouns ending in* -o, *add* -s *or* -es: solo, solos; echo, echoes; potato, potatoes; motto, mottos, mottoes; tomato, tomatoes; alto, altos.

9. *Some nouns have irregular plurals:* foot, feet; mouse, mice; goose, geese; ox, oxen; woman, women; axis, axes; basis, bases; datum, data; locus, loci; formula, formulas, formulae.

But Mr. and Mrs. Berry are *not* "the Berries," but "the Berrys"; and Mr. and Mrs. Wolf are *not* "the Wolves," but "the Wolfs."

EXERCISES

Rewrite the following paragraphs, correcting the misspelled words.

EXERCISE 1.

It has often occured to me that any foreign environment begins to look familiar after sufficient experiance. In the begin-

ning one may believe that a foriegn land is wierd or even bar-
berous. But it is noticable that in the end one usally consedes
the virtues of strangeness. What is outragous is to persist in
repititions of embarassing criticisms that are definitly eroneous.

EXERCISE 2.

One chilly Febuary day, three sophmores were sitting in their
dormitery discussing one of their most prominant proffessors.
They sprawled on separate bunks in their room, occassionally
engaging in arguement about the professor's appearance and
achievments.

"I went to see his secretery last Tuesday," one boy remarked.
"I think she's more intelactual than he is."

"I disagree," said another. "But why is he so predjudiced
against fraternities?"

"Anyway," said the third, "I've always prefered a conference
with the secretary. It's a priviledge to talk to her."

EXERCISE 3.

The most interesting knowlege is likely to seem irrevalent on
its first occurence. Many have benefitted from explanations that
at first seemed throughly and unnecessarily ridiculous. I reco-
mend that you sieze consiously every ocasion for learning, even
if your committment to grammer may be comparitively un-
enthusiastic.

§ 21. SIMILAR FORMS

**Distinguish between words similar or identical in sound but different
in meaning.**

The list below is merely a check list for quick reference. If you
need more than this list can give you, refer to your dictionary.

accent. Emphasis or stress; to stress. [You accent the wrong syllable.]
ascent. Climbing; a way up. [The ascent of the cliff was difficult.]
assent. To agree; agreement. [He finally gave his assent to the plan.]

accept. To take something offered; to agree to; to approve; to believe. [He
　　accepted the gift. I accept your interpretation.]
except. To leave out; to exclude. [All except the cook were rescued.]

admittance. Permission to enter a place. [The sign read, "No admittance."]
admission. Admitting to rights and privileges; the price of being allowed to enter. [No admission was charged.]

affect. To influence; to pretend; to assume. [His threats do not affect me.]
effect. To perform; make happen. [The attorney effected a reconciliation.]

all ready. Everyone is ready. [They were all ready.]
already. By this time. [They had already eaten breakfast.]

altar. Place of worship. [They knelt before the altar.]
alter. To change. [Do not alter any part of my criticism.]

ante. Before. [This piece is of ante-Victorian design.]
anti. Against; opposed to. [I poured some antifreeze into the radiator.]

breath. Air drawn into lungs. [We need a breath of fresh air.]
breathe. To take a breath. [We cannot breathe in this room.]

capital. Chief; important; leading city; resources. [London is the capital city of England. That's a capital story. Invest your capital.]
capitol. The state building. [We shall meet on the capitol grounds in Albany.]

censure. Blame; condemn; criticize severely. [They voted to censure the general.]
censor. To oversee morals and conduct; to examine and make changes. [Three women will censor all motion pictures.]

charted. Mapped or diagramed. [The Arctic is still not fully charted.]
chartered. Hired; granted certain rights. [We chartered a boat.]

choose. To pick out, select. [Will she choose me again?]
chose. Past tense of *choose*. [They chose a new secretary.]

cite. To quote or use as example. [Did he cite any authorities?]
site. Location. [This is a good site for our church.]
sight. Vision; to see. [His sight was keen. At last we sighted land.]

coarse. Rough; crude. [coarse food; coarse manners; coarse sand]
course. Direction; path; series; order. [a course of study; of course]

complement. That which completes. [a subjective complement]
compliment. Praise; a polite and flattering lie. [He paid her a compliment.]

consul. Government official appointed to look after foreign business interests.
council. A group; an assembly. [We shall call a council of the elders.]
counsel. Advice; one who advises; a lawyer. [Give her good counsel. The accused has a right to counsel.]

detract. Take away. [Her hair detracts from her beauty.]
distract. Draw away; disturb. [The noise distracts me. Do not distract my attention.]

eminent. Distinguished. [The eminent statesman spoke briefly.]
imminent. About to happen. [War seems imminent.]

fain. Eager; willingly; pleased. [I would fain stay with you.]
feign. Pretend. [She feigned complete surprise.]

formally. In a formal manner. [He was formally welcomed by the mayor.]
formerly. In the past. [Formerly, no one had greeted him.]

hoards. Stores; collections. [The police found hoards of stolen jewels.]
hordes. Crowds; groups of nomads. [the barbarian hordes; hordes of tourists]

imaginary. Existing in the imagination. [Her life is full of imaginary troubles.]
imaginative. Having imagination; able to imagine. [She is a very imaginative girl.]

implicit. Absolute, implied. [implicit obedience to orders; an implicit displeasure]
explicit. Distinctly stated; definite. [He gave us explicit directions.]

incredible. Unbelievable. [Your story is incredible.]
incredulous. Unwilling to believe. [He was incredulous when I told my story.]

irrelevant. Not to the point. [His question is irrelevant.]
irreverent. Lacking reverence or respect. [His action was irreverent.]

loose. Not fastened; careless; not confined. [Tie up your loose apron strings. There is too much loose talk here. Your dog is loose again.]
lose. To mislay; to fail to win; to waste. [She lost her keys again. We may lose this game yet. Put your loose cash away or you will lose it.]

principal. Chief; most important; chief person; chief teacher. [the principal of a school; the principal actor; the principal occupation; paying something on the principal as well as the interest]
principle. A truth; a belief; a scientific rule. [He is a man of high principles.]

rend. To tear apart; to disturb. [The silence was rent by a frightening roar.]
render. Make; give; represent; play or sing. [You will render a service. The judge rendered his decision. She will render a selection.]

respectfully. With respect. [Speak to your teacher respectfully.]

respectively. Each in turn or in order. [His three sons, Igor, Dmitri, and Ivan, were 18, 21, and 25 respectively.]

stationary. Not movable; not changing. [a stationary engine; a stationary enrollment; a stationary income]

stationery. Writing materials. [Please let me have some stationery; I wish to write a few letters.]

straight. Not curved; upright; continuous; direct. [The road is straight. Come straight to the point.]

strait. Narrow; strict; restricting. [a strait jacket; a strait passage; the Straits of Magellan; the Straits of Gibraltar]

WORDS AND PHRASES

§ 22. EXACTNESS AND THE USE OF THE DICTIONARY

Use words that convey your meaning exactly and idiomatically.

If a word always stood for only one thing or only one idea, communication would be simple indeed. But words have a way of acquiring many meanings through their use by different people at different times under different conditions. Some of the most common words of everyday living, such as *get, give, hard, take, run, read, stand, shoot,* have dozens of meanings each. As an illustration of the complexity and multiplicity of meanings that a word can acquire, let us take the first in the list—*get.*

He got a reward. I'll get home early. Did you get him on the phone? Can you get Dallas on your set? Go get your coat. Can you get him to eat? Get going. Get the supplies to them. He got six months for that. He's got the habit. Drink will get him. Did you get the wig she was wearing? You'll get caught in the storm. Get it?

We speak of the *denotation,* or the exact, literal meaning of a word, and of the *connotation,* or associated meaning of a word. If we wish to be more exact, we have to point out that literal meanings and associated meanings blend and merge, and change with time and circumstance, and to some extent differ with every different person using these words. Let us take a very common noun —*dog.* How did so many opposite associated meanings attach themselves to this poor animal?

Faithful as a dog. He dogged her footsteps. They showed dogged courage. He's a lucky dog. He's going to the dogs. It's a dog's life. It's dog eat dog with him.

Many words—and very important ones too in the work of the world—seem to live perpetually in a fog, because there is nothing touchable or visible for which they stand, to which you can point with your finger and say, "This is it. This is what I mean." When you say *dog* or *chair* or *book*, you can, if it is important enough, find some dog or chair or book to point to and say, "This is it." But when words stand for ideas, such as *temperance* or *democracy* or *security*, your problem is much harder. Then all you can do is to qualify and define, or point to a person who is temperate, a state that is democratic, a social system that provides security. Such vagueness is not a very satisfactory state of affairs, it is true, but it is the best we have. When we do not choose our words with care, when we do not define, or point to examples, we may be talking about one thing and our listeners may be thinking another thing. And that is a worse state of affairs.

To make the art of exact communication by words even more difficult, some people seem to use words in devious ways. Words have always been used by some people to conceal meaning, not to reveal it. When you deal with those people, it is supremely important to be exact, to define and to use examples. With other people, some of these abstract words have only one real meaning—and that is the meaning that *they* have assigned to it. A difference of opinion as to what a word means does not always imply dishonesty or evil intent. Profoundly honest people may differ in their understanding of words, depending on differences in their background, their training, their temperament, and so on. In the minds of some honest persons, the meaning of a word changes under the stress of emotion, or even under the stress of political campaigns and elections. Such words as *creeping socialism, free enterprise, extravagance, bureaucracy* mean one thing to members of a political party when it is in office and another thing when it is out of office.

22a. Key words that may be understood in more than one sense should be carefully defined.

Most of the words that you use in your writing or speaking will do well enough without being defined. The least tricky words are the names of specific persons or objects, such as *General Grant, laboratory,* the *White House,* an *Exakta camera,* although, to be sure, each may arouse emotional reactions that color the meaning of the word. A trifle more tricky are the words that refer to things or qualities that have been a part of the daily life of many generations, such as *dog, cat, war, generous, honest, selfish,* and so on. Usually the meaning of the word is defined well enough by the context in which it is used. Nothing of vast importance has been lost through a lack of exact communication. But something of vast importance *is* involved when people use such words as *radicals, education, liberals, realistic, democratic people, peace-loving, aggression, freedom of speech.* Terms such as these must be defined.

22b. Words used in an inexact sense should be checked and re-studied with the help of a dictionary.

The point of this statement can be understood if we first take a quick look at the ways in which we usually acquire our stock of words. We grow up with most of the common ones; very few of those will bother us much. Some of the more difficult ones we learn in connection with our high-school studies, through our general reading, through listening to such things as radio talks, television newscasts, lectures, or the talk of others, and, when curiosity or necessity lead us there, by looking up unfamiliar words in a dictionary. Most of us learn new words as we need them, without much help from vocabulary improvement schemes. All of us depend very much and very often on the context, on approximations, for meanings. Here and there we miss the point—sometimes by a narrow margin, sometimes by a mile. So here and there someone catches us up.

The word you have missed—the one marked by your instructor—is a good word in its place, but it does not mean quite what you think it means. Maybe it is a word that you have picked up recently and are trying out. Maybe it is a word that you did not quite hear when it was spoken or did not quite see when you read it. Now you confuse it with another word that sounds like it but which means something else. And maybe you just guessed at its meaning because it made sense that way in its context—and you guessed wrong. See what your dictionary says about it. It would be naïve to assert that a dictionary can solve all your problems of controlling the meanings of words. But here are a few examples to show how a dictionary can serve you:

Mr. Barfoot said he was going out to *titivate* his garden. [Did he mean that he was going to tickle it? Well, that sounds reasonable—if you think of it figuratively. But see what a dictionary says about the word.]

The doctor decided to try an *explanatory* operation first. [That again sounds reasonable, but is that what he actually decided to try?]

The music served to *diverge* my thoughts to more pleasant things. [Here the writer was trying for a word that sounded like this one, and, in a vague way, meant something like it.]

She was listening *intensely* to the lecture. [The word you want here is *intently*.]

22c. Vague, blanket words should be replaced with more precise words.

This statement refers primarily to such words as *deal, factor, line, point of view, angle, proposition.* It refers also to any word that you have used not because it expresses your idea precisely and cleanly, but because you were in a hurry and it was easier to use a vague word than to think of a more exact one.

INEXACT AND WORDY
Did you *get his deal* about wanting to go into something *along the line* of engineering?

BETTER
Can you understand why he wants to study engineering?

INEXACT
An exciting *factor* of our summer vacation was a trip to Japan.

BETTER
An exciting event of our summer vacation was a trip to Japan.

INEXACT
I never could decide what his *angle* was from the *point of view* of making high grades.

BETTER

I never could decide what his thoughts (ideas) were about making high grades.

22d. A writer should guard against the right word taking an unintended meaning in the context.

A serious writer, that is, should guard against unintentional humor or boners. Boners, either the natural or the synthetic variety, are of course the stock in trade of the gag writer or the television comedian. Here are some examples of unintentional boners:

BONER

The writer made the poem more effective by the use of metaphors and illusions.

CORRECTION

The writer made the poem more effective by the use of metaphors and allusions.

BONER

Finally, at midnight, I sat down to learn my history.

CORRECTION

Finally, at midnight, I sat down to study my history assignment.

BONER

She lives by a schedule; for instance on Tuesday she always has her hair.

CORRECTION

She lives by a schedule; for instance, every Tuesday she has an appointment with her hairdresser.

EXERCISES

EXERCISE 1, ASSOCIATED MEANINGS. *In the following groups of words, which words suggest an unfavorable attitude and which a favorable attitude?*

1. Teacher, tutor, pedagogue, counselor.
2. Policeman, cop, flatfoot, traffic officer.
3. Dainty, fragile, delicate, weak, flaccid, spineless.
4. Womanly, womanish, effeminate, feminine, unmanly.
5. Mixture, mess, jumble, patchwork, blend, alloy.

EXERCISE 2, EXACTNESS. *Point out every instance of inexact use of words in the following sentences and suggest a revision.*

1. The long arm of television permeates all of the civilized world.
2. In this poem the author tells about England's downfall from a leading country.
3. Judge Brand ordered the man to disabuse his wife and children.
4. The effect of the poem depends on what the reader divulges from it.
5. In order to solve their curiosity they must read the story to the end.
6. He quickly built a shelter to shed the rain off his precious equipment.
7. He describes in a realistic way about the things he has experienced in the slums.
8. My problems are more of an uncertainty, like being able to place a comma in this place or a semicolon in that place.
9. My hobby includes time, work, and expense.
10. As I am a seldom reader of poetry, I did not enjoy this book.

22e. Information found in a dictionary will help a student use words more exactly.

A dictionary lists the words of a language, in alphabetical order, and gives information about their meaning, their spelling, their use, their pronunciation, their history, and so on; the degree of completeness of this information depends on the size and purpose of the dictionary. The information found in a dictionary is based on an extensive study of the language in action; for every word listed, a great mass of information has been collected, classified, filed, and studied by a trained staff and, where necessary, by consultants from special fields in which the word is used. All information in a reliable dictionary is based on a study of usage. A dictionary reflects usage; it does not prescribe it. It is an authority only insofar as it accurately reflects usage.

The various dictionaries of the English language fall into the following classes:

1. The monumentally complete ones, in which a word gets full historical treatment, with quotations illustrating its use from the time of its birth to the date of completion of the dictionary:

The New English Dictionary, in 10 vols. and a supplement, 1888–1928, reissued in corrected edition as *Oxford English Dictionary,* 12 vols., 1933 (also known as *N.E.D., O.E.D.,* the *Oxford,* and *Murray's*). In the *N.E.D.* there are 1,827,306 quotations of usage.

The Century Dictionary, 10 vols., 1901, vols. 11 and 12 added in 1909; the *New Century,* in 3 vols., 1948. This new edition has 160,000 entries and 12,000 illustrative quotations.

2. The one-volume unabridged dictionaries, which you find in schoolrooms and libraries for reference use. They are usually kept up to date by spot revisions and by "New Word Sections." The *New International,* however, has been entirely rewritten.

Webster's Third New International Dictionary. Springfield, Mass.: G. & C. Merriam Company, 1961.

New Standard Dictionary. New York: Funk & Wagnalls Company.

3. The one-volume, desk-size dictionaries, one of which almost every college student buys as a part of his working equipment. Each one of these listed here is well worth the cost; the choice is usually governed by the recommendation of the student's English instructor.

Webster's New World Dictionary, College Edition. Cleveland & New York: The World Publishing Company, 1964.

Webster's Seventh New Collegiate Dictionary. Springfield, Mass.: G. & C. Merriam Company, 1963.

American College Dictionary. New York: Random House, 1963.

Standard College Dictionary, Text Edition. New York: Funk & Wagnalls Company, Inc., 1963. Text edition published by Harcourt, Brace & World, Inc.

The following kinds of information may be secured from a desk dictionary:

1. The Meaning of a Word. As you can see by examining the various excerpts from dictionaries that are reprinted here, a dictionary uses several methods of clarifying the meaning of a word. First, it uses phrases of definition, and it often follows the definition with illustrative examples. Second, it uses synonyms, either immediately after the defining phrase or in a group below, where the synonyms are compared and contrasted. Then, at times, it may present a special list of idiomatic phrases using the word.

Finally, a dictionary classifies the different meanings a word may have, numbers them, and if a word has special technical uses, it labels these uses and explains them. Some dictionaries list the oldest meanings first; others begin with the most commonly used meanings. You can see that it is important to know which method your dictionary uses. It is important, moreover, to read *all* the definitions of a word before deciding to use the word in a certain sentence.

In the selection from *Webster's New World Dictionary*,[1] note that the most recent, the most commonly used sense of the word is given first. The thirteen different uses of *pull* as a transitive verb (*v.t.*) are given in order, numbered, and where necessary labeled, as: 6. [Dial. or Rare]; 7. [Colloq.]. The definitions of *pull* as an intransitive verb and as a noun follow.

> **pull** (pool), *v.t.* [ME. *pullen;* AS. *pullian,* to pluck, snatch with the fingers; ? akin to MLG. *pull, poll,* a husk, shell < IE. base **bol-, *bul-,* a lump, knob, seen also in L. *bulla,* a bud; etc.; basic sense would then be "to pluck (fruit, etc.)"], **1.** to exert force on in such a way as to cause to move toward or after the source of the force; drag, tug, draw, attract, etc. **2.** *a)* to draw, or pluck, out: as, he had two teeth *pulled.* *b)* to pluck and gather: as, she *pulled* several roses. **3.** to draw apart; rip; tear: as, the seam of her dress is *pulled.* **4.** to stretch (taffy, etc.) back and forth repeatedly. **5.** to stretch or strain to the point of injury: as, he *pulled* a muscle in the game. **6.** [Dial. or Rare], to draw the entrails from (a fowl). **7.** [Colloq.], to put into effect; perform; do: as, the police *pulled* a raid. **8.** [Colloq.], to hold back the force of deliberately; restrain: as, he's *pulling* his punches. **9.** [Slang], *a)* to arrest (someone). *b)* to make a police raid on. **10.** in *baseball, golf,* etc., to hit (the ball) so as to cause it to curve to the left or, if the player is left-handed, to the right. **11.** in *horse racing,* to rein in, or restrain (a horse), to keep it from winning. **12.** in *printing,* to take (a proof) on a hand press. **13.** in *rowing, a)* to work (an oar) by drawing it toward one. *b)* to transport by rowing. *c)* to be rowed normally by: as, this boat *pulls* four oars. *v.i.* **1.** to exert force in or for dragging, tugging, or attracting something. **2.** to take a deep draft of a drink or puff at a cigarette, etc. **3.** to be capable of being pulled. **4.** to move (*away, ahead,* etc.). *n.* **1.** the act, force, or result of pulling (in various senses); specifically, *a)* a dragging, tugging, attracting, etc. *b)* the act or an instance of rowing. *c)* a drink. *d)* a puff at a cigarette, etc. *e)* the effort used in climbing, etc.; hence, *f)* any difficult, continuous effort. *g)* in *sports,* the act or an instance of pulling a ball. **2.** something to be pulled, as the handle of a drawer, etc. **3.** [Slang], influence or special advantage.
> **pull apart,** to find fault with; criticize.
> **pull down, 1.** to tear down, demolish, or overthrow. **2.** to degrade; humble. **3.** to reduce.
> **pull for,** [Colloq.], to cheer on, or hope for the success of.

[1] From *Webster's New World Dictionary of the American Language,* College Edition. Copyright 1964 by The World Publishing Company.

pull off, [Colloq.], to bring about or accomplish.
pull oneself together, to collect one's faculties; regain one's poise, courage, etc.
pull over, [Colloq.], to move to or toward the curb, as a motor vehicle.
pull through, [Colloq.], to get through or over (an illness, difficulty, etc.).
pull up, 1. to uproot. **2.** to bring or come to a stop. **3.** to move ahead.
SYN.—**pull** is the broad, general term of this list, as defined in sense 1 of the *v.t.* above; **draw** suggests a smoother, more even motion than **pull** (he *drew* his sword from its scabbard); **drag** implies the slow pulling of something heavy, connoting great resistance in the thing pulled (he *dragged* the desk across the floor); **tug** suggests strenuous, persistent effort in pulling but does not necessarily connote success in moving the object (he *tugged* at the rope to no avail); **haul** implies sustained effort in transporting something heavy, often mechanically (to *haul* furniture in a truck); **tow** implies pulling by means of a rope or cable (to *tow* a stalled automobile).—*ANT.* push, shove.

You will notice here and in the excerpt from the *Standard College Dictionary* [2] how carefully the various synonyms are illustrated and discriminated. These illustrations and discriminated synonyms are a valuable help to the student in his efforts to find and use the exact word.

calm (käm) *adj.* **1.** Free from agitation; still or nearly still. **2.** Not excited by passion or emotion; peaceful. — *n.* **1.** Lack of wind or motion; stillness. **2.** *Meteorol.* A state in which there is little or no wind. See BEAUFORT SCALE. **3.** Serenity. — *v.t. & v.i.* To make or become quiet or calm: often with *down.* [< MF *calme,* orig., quiet, stillness < Ital. *calma* < LL *cauma* heat of the day < Gk. *kauma* heat; with ref. to the midday siesta] — **calm′ly** *adv.* — **calm′ness** *n.*
— **Syn.** (adj.) *Calm, tranquil, placid, serene, quiet,* and *still* denote freedom from violent movement or emotion. *Calm* describes a present state that may be transient; *tranquil* suggests a more enduring condition: a *calm* sea, a *tranquil* life. A *placid* person is regarded as temperamentally stolid; a *placid* lake is always peaceful and untroubled. Things elevated above earthly turmoil are *serene*: a *serene* sky, a *serene* smile. *Quiet* and *still* imply absence of noise as well as of bustle; of the two, *quiet* is more relative, while *still* verges on the absolute: a *quiet* meeting, *still* waters.
cal·ma·tive (kal′mə·tiv, kä′mə-) *adj.* Having a soothing effect; sedative. — *n.* A sedative or tranquilizer.

2. The Spelling of a Word. As a rule you can check your spelling of a word by looking it up in your dictionary, although if you do not know the first letter or two of a word you may be in trouble. For example, if your instructor has marked *rythem* as being misspelled, you may have trouble finding *rhythm*. Ordinarily, however, your use of the dictionary to check your spelling will be routine. A few words have variant spellings. Where these are indicated, you will be safe in using the first one listed. On the following page are some of the ways in which variant spellings are listed in dictionaries.

[2] By permission. From p. 194, *Funk & Wagnalls Standard® College Dictionary,* Copyright 1963 by Funk & Wagnalls Company, Inc.

AMERICAN COLLEGE DICTIONARY

color: Also, *Brit.*, colour
theater: Also, *esp. Brit.*, theatre
check, n: Also, *Brit.*, cheque

STANDARD COLLEGE DICTIONARY

color: Also *Brit.* colour
theater: Also *esp. Brit.* theatre
glamour: Also *U.S.* glamor

WEBSTER'S NEW WORLD DICTIONARY

aesthete: Also spelled esthete
connection: connexion, British spelling

WEBSTER'S SEVENTH
NEW COLLEGIATE DICTIONARY

pyjamas: *chiefly Brit var of* PAJAMAS
theater *or* theatre

3. The Pronunciation of a Word.

The pronunciation of a word is usually indicated by respelling it with diacritical marks and symbols or respelling it in some form of a phonetic alphabet. The method used is explained in detail at the front of every dictionary. A study of these explanations is worth while. In addition to these explanations, you will see a brief summary of the symbols used at the foot of every page or every two pages facing each other in the dictionary proper. Where two pronunciations are current, the dictionary will give both. Observe carefully the respelling, the variant accent, the pronunciation symbols, and the stress or accent points in the following from the *New Collegiate:* [3]

> **for·mi·cary** \'fȯr-mə-,ker-ē\ *n* [ML *formicarium,* fr. L *formica*]
> **:** an ant nest
> **for·mi·da·bil·i·ty** \,fȯr-məd-ə-'bil-ət-ē\ *n* **:** formidable quality
> **for·mi·da·ble** \'fȯr-məd-ə-bəl *also* fȯr-'mid-\ *adj* [ME, fr. L *formidabilis,* fr. *formidare* to fear, fr. *formido* fear; akin to Gk *mormō* she-monster] **1** **:** exciting fear ⟨a ~ prospect⟩ **2** **:** having qualities that discourage approach or attack **3** **:** tending to inspire awe or wonder — **for·mi·da·ble·ness** *n* — **for·mi·da·bly** \-blē\ *adv*

Each dictionary has its own set of pronunciation symbols and its own way of indicating accents. Observe these symbols carefully in the dictionary you own and use.

4. Labels: Subject, Geographical, Usage.

Every dictionary uses geographical and subject labels to show that a word in the sense indicated is characteristic of a region or language or that it has a special meaning in connection with a certain subject. To understand this more clearly, you might check the labels used with the following words: *pone, jollity, Erse, tot, trauma, suture, kirk, syne, cannikin.* You will find some of these words with a subject

[3] By permission. From *Webster's Seventh New Collegiate Dictionary*, copyright 1963 by G. & C. Merriam Co., Publishers of the Merriam-Webster Dictionaries.

label in one dictionary and without any label in another. A similar lack of agreement exists in connection with usage labels. *Webster's New World Dictionary* uses the following where in the judgment of its editors these labels are called for: *colloquial, slang, obsolete, archaic, poetic, dialect, British. Webster's Seventh New Collegiate* uses "status labels" instead of "usage labels." These are *obsolete, archaic, slang, substandard, nonstandard, dialect.* The "regional labels"—*dial Brit, New Eng, chiefly Scot,* and other similar ones—are classified under status labels. The *Standard College Dictionary* uses "restrictive labels," as follows: *illit., slang, dial., informal,* and other labels indicating regional or national divisions, such as *Southern U.S., Brit., Scot.* The *American College Dictionary* lists the folowing usage labels: *archaic, colloq., humorous, obs., slang, poetic, obsolesc., rare, Scot., Scot and N. Eng., South African, U.S.* Note that neither the *New Collegiate* nor the *Standard* uses *colloq.* All of the four still use *slang* as a label. Note the various usage labels in the following two excerpts, the first shown being from the *American College Dictionary.*[4]

cheek·y (chē′kĬ), *adj.,* **cheekier, cheekiest.** *Colloq.* impudent; insolent: *a cheeky fellow, cheeky behavior.* **—cheek′i·ly,** *adv.* **—cheek′i·ness,** *n.*

cheep (chēp), *v.i.* **1.** to chirp; peep. **—***v.t.* **2.** to express by cheeps. **—***n.* **3.** a chirp. [imit.] **—cheep′er,** *n.*

cheer (chĭr), *n.* **1.** a shout of encouragement, approval, congratulation, etc. **2.** that which gives joy or gladness; encouragement; comfort. **3.** state of feeling or spirits: *what cheer?* **4.** gladness, gaiety, or animation: *to make cheer.* **5.** food; provisions. **6.** *Archaic.* expression of countenance. **—***v.t.* **7.** to salute with shouts of approval, congratulation, etc. **8.** to inspire with cheer; gladden (often fol. by *up*). **9.** to encourage or incite. **—***v.i.* **10.** to utter cheers of approval, etc. **11.** to become cheerful (often fol. by *up*). **12.** *Obs.* to be in a particular state of spirits. [ME *chere,* t. OF: face, g.LL *cara*] **—cheer′er,** *n.* **—cheer′ing·ly,** *adv.*
—Syn. 8. CHEER, GLADDEN, ENLIVEN mean to make happy or lively. To CHEER is to comfort, to restore hope and cheerfulness to (now often CHEER UP, when thoroughness, a definite time, or a particular point in the action is referred to). (Cf. *eat up, drink up, hurry up*): *to cheer a sick person; soon cheered him up.* To GLADDEN does not imply a state of sadness to begin with, but suggests bringing pleasure or happiness to someone: *to gladden some one's heart with good news.* ENLIVEN suggests bringing vivacity and liveliness: *to enliven a dull evening, a party.* **9.** exhilarate, animate. **10.** shout, applaud, acclaim. **—Ant. 8.** depress. **9.** discourage.

Now look for various usage labels in the excerpts from dictionaries reproduced on pages 357 and 358 (*Webster's New World* and the *Standard*), and then examine carefully the

[4] Reprinted from *The American College Dictionary* (Copyright 1947, © copyright 1964) by permission of Random House, Inc.

selection below, which is quoted from *Webster's Seventh New Collegiate Dictionary*.[5]

¹stiff \'stif\ *adj* [ME *stif*, fr. OE *stif*; akin to MD *stijf* stiff, L *stipare* to press together, Gk *steibein* to tread on] **1 a :** not easily bent **:** RIGID **b :** lacking in suppleness ⟨~ muscles⟩ **c :** impeded in movement — used of a mechanism **d :** DRUNK **2 a :** FIRM, RESOLUTE **b :** STUBBORN, UNYIELDING **c :** PROUD **d** (1) **:** marked by reserve or decorum **:** FORMAL (2) **:** lacking in ease or grace **:** STILTED **3 :** hard fought **:** PUGNACIOUS, SHARP **4 a** (1) **:** exerting great force **:** STRONG ⟨~ wind⟩ (2) **:** FORCEFUL, VIGOROUS **b :** POTENT ⟨a ~ dose⟩ **5 :** of a dense or glutinous consistency **:** THICK **6 a :** HARSH, SEVERE ⟨a ~ penalty⟩ **b :** ARDUOUS, RUGGED ⟨~ terrain⟩ **7 :** not easily heeled over by an external force (as the wind) ⟨a ~ ship⟩ **8 :** EXPENSIVE, STEEP (paid a ~ duty) — **stiff·ly** *adv* — **stiff·ness** *n*
syn STIFF, RIGID, INFLEXIBLE, TENSE, STARK mean impossible to bend. STIFF may apply to any degree of this condition; RIGID applies to something so stiff that it cannot be bent without breaking; INFLEXIBLE stresses lack of suppleness or pliability; TENSE suggests a straining or stretching to a point where elasticity is lost; STARK implies a stiffness associated with loss of life or warmth
²stiff *adv* **1 :** STIFFLY **2 :** to an extreme degree **:** INTENSELY ⟨bored ~⟩
³stiff *n* **1 :** CORPSE **2 a :** BUM, TRAMP **b :** LABORER, HAND
¹stiff–arm \'stif-,ärm\ *vb* **:** STRAIGHT-ARM
²stiff–arm *n* **:** STRAIGHT-ARM

5. Derivation of a Word. As you know, our words have come from many languages, and some have undergone many changes in form and meaning. A daisy, for instance was a "day's eye," a nasturtium was a "nose twister," our common dandelion was once a "lion's tooth." And would you believe that our word *emerald* had an ancestor that in Latin was once *smaragdus* and in Greek *smaragdos*? The Roman Emperor Nero once used a polished *smaragdus* as a lens in front of his near-sighted eye. So you see that the derivations of words are interesting in themselves, and they might enrich your understanding of words.

The following words have unusually interesting origins: *bedlam, boycott, broker, calico, curfew, dollar, exhume, lunacy, panic, sandwich, sinister, saxophone, tawdry, thug, vandal.*

6. Grammatical Information. A desk-size dictionary gives adequate information about plurals of nouns and the principal parts of verbs. Inflectional forms are usually given only when they are irregular or when they present difficulties of spelling or pronunciation. For example, no plurals are given for *book, chair, handkerchief* because it is assumed that these nouns, and all others like them, form their plurals in the regular way. But after *index* you find two plurals: *indexes, indices;* after *deer* you find the in-

---

[5] By permission. From *Webster's Seventh New Collegiate Dictionary*, copyright 1963 by G. & C. Merriam Co., Publishers of the Merriam-Webster Dictionaries.

formation that the plural is also *deer* (occasionally *deers*); after *ox* you find the plural is *oxen* (rarely *ox*). Similarly, no principal parts are given after regular verbs, especially when no special problems are involved: see *talk, walk*. But note that *study* is followed by *studied, studying* to show what happens to the ending in the formation of the past tense and the present participle and gerund. Then look up the verb *lie*, which has two main meanings, and note that the principal parts are necessary to distinguish between the two meanings: *lie* [recline], *lay, lain, lying; lie* [prevaricate], *lied, lying*. The last example also illustrates the fact that when the past tense and the past participle have the same form, it is given only once:

lie: He *lied*. I had *lied* about it. [lie, lied, lying]
bring: He *brought* it. I had *brought* it with me. [bring, brought, bringing]
ring: He *rang* the bell. I had *rung* it a minute earlier. [ring, rang, rung, ringing]

7. Idiomatic Phrases. Many of the simple, everyday verbs of the language, through many years of various uses and associations, have acquired special meanings in phrases that we call *idioms*. Notice the quotation from *Webster's New World Dictionary*, page 357, to understand what is meant by an idiom: *pull apart* [to criticize], *pull down* [degrade, humble], *pull for* [to cheer on], *pull off* [accomplish], *pull oneself together* [to regain poise], *pull over* [to drive to the curb], *pull through* [to get over an illness], *pull up* [to uproot, to come to a stop, to move ahead]. Anyone can see that these are not literal meanings of the verb. Here are a few more examples of idioms, from various dictionaries: *give ground, give tongue, take amiss, take stock, take the floor, have it in for, have it out, run out of, do away with, do for*. See Section 24 for a fuller discussion of idiomatic speech.

8. Synonyms and Antonyms. Pairs of words that have exactly the same meaning—literal and associated—are none too common in the English language, but words may have approximately the same meaning, or approximately the same meaning in certain uses. Examine the excerpts from dictionaries listed here and study the synonyms under *cheer, calm, pull, stiff.* Note that synonyms are used in illustrative phrases and then sometimes in a separate list where they are compared and contrasted. Antonyms are listed less commonly than synonyms.

EXERCISES

EXERCISE 1, DEFINITIONS. *Look up the meanings of each of the following words. List at least two very different meanings for each.*

intern	aggravate	irony	criticize
propaganda	fellow	nice	curious

EXERCISE 2, SPELLING. *Look up each of the following words. Decide whether both spellings are used in your locality, or whether one is more common than the other.*

adviser, advisor	glamorize, glamourize	sulfur, sulphur
although, altho	night, nite	theater, theatre

EXERCISE 3, PRONUNCIATION. *Look up the pronunciation of the following words. Notice where the accent is placed in each word. Where more than one pronunciation is listed, try pronouncing the word in each way. Which form do you use in your own conversation?*

acumen	data	Don Quixote	inquiry
adult	decade	exquisite	irreparable
aspirant	decadence	finance	lamentable
combatant	despicable	formidable	preferable
culinary	Don Juan	gondola	superfluous

EXERCISE 4, STATUS OR USAGE LABELS. *What usage or status label—if any—follows each of the following words?*

alarum	coulee	hunk	lulu
belike	enthuse	hunky	petrol
bozo	goober	jalopy	scram

EXERCISE 5, DERIVATION. *From what language did each of the following words come?*

banjo	lava	prairie	rodeo
chinook	mosquito	rebus	sapphire
ersatz	pongee	riata	soprano

§ 23. APPROPRIATENESS

Use words that are in keeping with the subject of your paper, with the occasion, and with the readers you are addressing.

Many of the papers that you write for your college courses are formal; some are informal. You must always remember that the terms *formal* and *informal* are relative—not absolute. Each covers a wide range. Obviously, you will probably never try to write with the formality of Oliver Wendell Holmes, or Learned Hand, or Winston Churchill addressing Parliament; you may, however, approach the style of a present-day historian or critic or essayist. Examples of each are to be found in the first chapter of this book.

When you write a serious discussion of a serious subject, you should use language that is dignified though not pretentious or affected. If your occasion is informal, you write in an informal, easy manner—remembering always that as there are degrees of formality so are there degrees of informality. The informality that runs into sloppiness has little place in your college work. We have mentioned before, in Chapter 1, the analogy of varieties of writing with manners or dress. Every intelligent person has different styles of writing at his command just as he has clothes appropriate for different occasions. He does not attend a formal dinner in sweater and slacks, or a football game in a tuxedo, unless he is determined to make a spectacular and probably unfavorable impression. There *are* rules and conventions in the use of language, just as there are conventions and decencies governing social behavior everywhere else—at a dinner table, at a football game, on a street corner, anywhere. A writer's good sense, wide awake to the situation around him, is his best rule of conduct.

Here are a few examples of failure in appropriateness (in the first two examples, the italicized words do not appear in the originals):

INAPPROPRIATE IN FORMAL WRITING
When Roosevelt took office on March 4, 1933, thousands of American banks *were going broke*. [The original has the more appropriate *verged on insolvency*.]

—WILLIAM MILLER, *A New History of the United States*

There is no doubt that a *whole batch* of new mathematical techniques will have to be *cooked up* before it will be possible to solve satisfactorily *a lot of* scientific problems that today can only be tackled empirically or experimentally. [The original has the more appropriate *variety . . . invented . . . innumerable.*]

—Mario G. Salvadori, "Mathematics, the Language of Science"

The State Department's difficulty was that it had failed to find any device for ensuring that the press would *keep mum* on the new international agreement. [Say *remain silent.*]

INAPPROPRIATE IN INFORMAL WRITING

I certainly hope you are having a good time at college this year *and realizing your potentiality for intellectual growth and development.* [Say *and getting a lot out of it.*]

He told me what to do and *I accomplished the operation.* [Say *I did it.*]

23a. In serious writing inappropriate slang should be avoided.

Slang has often been defined as a kind of made-to-order language, characterized by extravagant or grotesque fancy or humor. This is by no means a complete or all-inclusive definition of slang, nor is an all-inclusive definition important in this book. Not even the editors of our excellent dictionaries agree on what is slang and what is not. *Webster's Third New International Dictionary* lists the following, among others, as examples of slang: rod [revolver, pistol], rap [to arrest, hold; to swear or testify falsely], long green [paper money, cash], mazuma [money], savvy [understanding, to understand], square [having conservative tastes], vamoose [to depart quickly], baloney [pretentious nonsense], big cheese [a person of consequence]. In other dictionaries you may find other words listed as slang, words that the unabridged lists without any usage labels.[1]

Slang is usually inappropriate in serious or formal writing, but some writers use it with telling effects. Students who avoid slang in college papers may still err by using stilted, general, vague, and pompously bookish words under the impression that a simple and direct style is not good enough for important ideas.

[1] A collection of critical reviews of *Webster's Third New International* may be found in James Sledd and Wilma Ebbit, *Dictionaries and That Dictionary* (Chicago: Scott, Foresman, 1962).

23b. A mixture of the colloquial and the formal styles is usually inappropriate in serious writing.

Most dictionaries—with the notable exception of *Webster's Third New International*—use *colloq.* as a usage label for certain words and phrases. *The New International* uses status labels, such as *slang, substandard, nonstandard,* but not *colloquial. Colloquial* means informal, or characteristic of a conversational style, as opposed to a formal, literary style. In the past, many people believed that *colloq.* implied a condemnation of a word or phrase, in spite of the fact that editors of dictionaries were careful to define the word correctly in the vocabularies and in the explanatory notes. Scholars, lexicographers, and linguists have pointed out that every educated person uses colloquial English, and, what is important to remember, he uses it correctly if he uses it in appropriate situations.

In the writing of college students the importance of the problem of colloquialism has been greatly overrated. If a student suspects some word or phrase in his more formal papers, he can check it through his desk dictionary. The dictionary will usually supply a more formal equivalent.

EXERCISES

Exercise 1, Appropriateness. *Some of the following italicized expressions are appropriate in serious writing; some are not. With the help of your dictionary, decide which are more appropriate in colloquial than in formal situations.*

1. We are determined to *face up to* this monstrous foe with all our hearts.
2. Finally, after many years of service, the one-horse shay *gave out.*
3. The trusted servant, we discovered, had *made off* with our two cameras.
4. He was to board a plane at ten, but none of his friends were there to *see him off.*
5. The man was instructed to *sing out* if he saw any prowlers.
6. Within a year the young man *had run through* his inheritance.

7. At the end of the year he felt that it was not easy to *take leave of* his new friends.
8. The principal was trying to find out who had *put him up to it*.
9. His arrogance was something no one was willing to *put up with*.
10. Nobody expected her to *take on so* when she heard that her daughter had eloped.

EXERCISE 2, FORMAL AND INFORMAL EXPRESSIONS. *Give the formal equivalent of each of the italicized expressions.*

1. to *back down*
2. to *beat down the price*
3. to *go him one better*
4. *How come?*
5. He was *let out* when the company went broke.
6. You'll *get your cut!*
7. He *gave* the new girl *a rush.*
8. That music really *sends* me.
9. Give him his *walking papers.*
10. *Stick around* for a while.

§ 24. IDIOMS

24a. The habit of using idiomatic English should be cultivated.

An idiom is an expression peculiar to a given language. Therefore it usually cannot be translated word-for-word into another tongue, though its sense can often be rendered by another idiom native and natural to that tongue. Created out of the day-to-day living of ordinary people, idioms are often irrational, racy, and lively with images. Many of them have originated in someone's clever and original metaphor, which then became "dead" as it was repeatedly used by other people. "You said a mouthful." "He was beside himself with worry." "Who slipped up?" "Water off a duck's back." As these examples suggest, idioms are often colloquial or slang, though not necessarily so.

Americans have been particularly fertile in producing an idiomatic language, and many volumes have been written on the subject of American word-making. Mitford M. Mathews' *Dictionary of Americanisms* (Chicago: Chicago University Press, 1951) is a special collection devoted to American inventions, including thousands of native idioms. Students interested in pursuing the history of a particular idiom should consult this work or the *New English Dictionary*. (See the further listing under "Dictionaries and Books of Synonyms" in Chapter 6.)

Even more than other elements in the language, idioms change status constantly as they come into or go out of fashion, or as they become respectable in formal English or fall into disrepute. In fact such change has become so rapid and complex in our time that the editors of the latest unabridged *Webster's* have dropped most of their notations of *Slang* and *Colloq.* Even your desk dictionary, however, can be very useful in listing the various idioms formed from ordinary single words. Many idiomatic phrases have grown up around the verbs of everyday living—*go, do, catch, make, take,* and so on.

The student's difficulties in handling idioms are likely to be of two kinds. First, he may have trouble sensing the status of a particular idiom for a particular purpose. He might, for instance, go so far as to write, in a formal essay, and with no humorous intention, "This sent me!" In this case, of course, he has failed to recognize the highly colloquial and ephemeral quality of that expression. Or the student might say, in a serious descriptive essay, "It rained cats and dogs," thus failing to recognize that this particular idiom has long been a very tired cliché. (Clichés are treated more fully in Section 27.) The best guard against errors of this kind is constant reading, writing, and listening, with an awareness of how different kinds of expressions are acceptable in different situations.

A second source of student difficulty with idioms might be called a failing of the ear—that is, the student may forget just how an idiom is said in English, and the fact that there is seldom much rhyme or reason to the phrasing of idioms makes his difficulties the greater. The problem is most severe in the case of prepositions, as the subsection immediately following will show.

Students whose native language is not English have far more serious problems with idioms, of course, just as native speakers of English have troubles with idioms in French or German or Russian.

24b. Observe the idiomatic use of prepositions after certain verbs, participles, adjectives, and nouns.

The following list will not take the place of an unabridged dictionary. It will serve merely as a check list to put you on your guard. Consult the dictionary for more complete information.

abstain from	distaste for
accede to	empty of
acquiesce in	envious of
acquit of	expert in
addicted to	foreign to
adept in	guard against
adhere to	hint at
agree to (a thing)	identical with
agree with (a person)	independent of
agreeable to	infer from
angry at (a thing)	initiate into
angry with (a person)	inseparable from
averse to	jealous of
capable of	obedient to
characteristic of	oblivious of
compare to (for illustration)	preparatory to
compare with (to examine qual-	prerequisite to
ities)	prior to
concern in (interest in)	proficient in
concerned for (troubled)	profit by
concerned with (involved)	prohibit from
concur in (an opinion)	protest against
concur with (a person)	reason with
desire for	regret for
desirous of	repugnant to
desist from	sensitive to
devoid of	separate from
differ about	substitute for
differ from (things)	superior to
differ with (a person)	sympathize with
different from	tamper with
disagree with	unmindful of
disdain for	vie with
dissent from	

It is characteristic of English that an idiom may have several meanings, and that it may shift into a new part of speech. The professor *makes up* a roster of students, and the *makeup* of the class displeases him. A lady *makes up* her face, which is to say she applies *makeup*. I *make up* a fairy story, which then appears *made-up*. Idioms such as these, composed originally of a verb plus an adverb, quickly become nouns in our language, as the following short list will suggest:

blowout	run-in
carryover	runaround
cookout	runaway
countdown	turnover
drive-in	upkeep

This process of word formation is one of several such shifts peculiarly in motion in our own time. Many nouns so formed are obviously of recent origin: *cookout, countdown, drive-in*. The student should not hesitate to make use of such new terms, in spite of their predominantly informal quality. In the list above, for example, almost every term is at least conceivably appropriate in almost any context.

EXERCISES

EXERCISE 1, IDIOMS. *In your desk dictionary find the idioms listed under several of the following words. You will find idiomatic phrases printed in boldface type, usually after the synonyms. Bring to class a number of these for class discussion. Try to decide why some are marked* colloq. *and some are without a label.*

eat	go	head	mouth	stand
foot	hand	heart	pick	take
get	have	horse	run	word

EXERCISE 2, MISUSE OF IDIOMS. *Rewrite the following paragraph, correcting the misuses of idiom.*

He was superior than all of us, or so he thought, but his bragging was no substitute of ability. He felt himself independent from the rest of us, though he was usually agreeable with going along with the majority. I was often angry at him, since he differed from me so often.

EXERCISE 3, IDIOMATIC PREPOSITIONS. *Supply the idiomatic prepositions as required in the following sentences.*

1. Since I was so concerned (   ) my business at that time, she was concerned (   ) my health.
2. At that period we differed (   ) almost everything.
3. She especially differed (   ) me about money matters.
4. Finally we separated (   ) one another.
5. Neither of us, however, proved to be capable (   ) living alone.

§ 25. CONCRETENESS

The concrete or specific or homely word is more likely to touch the reader's imagination than its abstract or general or bookish counterpart.

General words name classes or groups; specific words name the individual objects, actions, or qualities that compose the group. The terms are to some extent relative: *furniture* is a class of things; *chair* is more specific than *furniture*, more general than *armchair* or *rocking chair*.

Let us illustrate the effectiveness of specific words by taking another word. *Weapon* is a general noun. When, for example, you write, "Mrs. Hanks assaulted her husband with a deadly weapon," just what control do you have over what goes on in your reader's mind? What picture do your words call up? Did she stab him with a letter opener, club him with a brass book end, slash him with a safety razor blade that she had picked out of her sewing basket, or shoot him with a Derringer? You say that the police found an ornament that she had dropped in the scuffle. It was probably a piece of jewelry—which is more specific than *ornament*—but it would have been more specific and more effective to say "a green jade earring."

The verb *move* is general; *stride, amble, creep, glide, fly, lope* are all more specific ways of moving. The adjective *large* is general; when you try to make it more specific, you discover that different varieties of largeness are associated with different nouns. For instance, *bulky, towering, brawny, fat, spacious, hulking* are applicable to which of these—a building, a man, a room, a tree?

A concrete noun, such as *bridge, wall, needle, cloud, smoke, shoe, clatter,* or *apple,* names something that can be perceived through any of the senses. In other words, it names something you can touch, see, hear, taste, smell, feel. Abstract words name ideas, or qualities, more or less detached from any particular thing bearing those qualities, as *beauty, cleverness, empiricism, truth, devotion, weariness.* Now of course you can seldom give a concrete equivalent of an abstract word, but you can—and should—spell out your concept of the abstraction that you use. To say "Father is both stubborn and easygoing" is not enough if you want to develop him dramatically; bring him out on the stage for us to see, and show him in a typical action.

Homely words are those associated with the objects and activities of everyday living; bookish words are those associated with literary formality.

The following pairs of words and expressions will help to make the distinctions clearer:

GENERAL WORDS
Furniture, apparel, cutlery, kitchen utensil, a crime, an industrial worker, a flower, an animal.

SPECIFIC WORDS
Davenport, overcoat, a carving knife, a frying pan, burglary, a welder, dahlia, mongoose.

ABSTRACT WORDS
The faithfulness of an animal; the harmony of music; a misfortune of battle; extreme intoxication.

CONCRETE WORDS
She served him like a dog; my mother hummed a lullaby; a shell splinter ripped open his right arm; he was lit up like a Christmas tree.

BOOKISH WORDS
Frigidity, inebriated, suspend, incarcerated, the matutinal meal, to delve, to cultivate.

HOMELY WORDS
Cold, drunk, hang, jailed, breakfast, to dig, to plow.

Let us hasten to say at this point that these are by no means scientific classifications applicable to all words in the language. We are merely picking out handfuls of words as samples, and saying in effect: "Look at these. This type of word seems to do something more to your imagination and comprehension than that one." Abstract and general words are not bad words; they are necessary for the expression of abstract qualities and general ideas. Bookish words are natural in a scholarly, formal context. But in the writing of the average student, abstract and general words are used too often where concrete and specific words would do a better job.

The following examples will help to make the idea clearer:

GENERAL AND INEFFECTIVE

They would usually serve us a good breakfast in cheerful surroundings.

CONCRETE AND SPECIFIC

There would be a brisk fire crackling in the hearth, the old smoke-gold of morning and the smell of fog, the crisp cheerful voices of the people and their ruddy competent morning look, and the cheerful smells of breakfast, which was always liberal and good, the best meal that they had: kidneys and ham and eggs and sausages and toast and marmalade and tea.

—THOMAS WOLFE, *Of Time and the River*

GENERAL AND INEFFECTIVE

I took the spores from the puffball home, set up my microscope, and was startled when I saw the spores magnified.

CONCRETE AND SPECIFIC

At my desk, I draw the microscope out of its case, and though it is heavy, it slides out to me, when I grasp it by the middle, with an ease like a greeting. It is a matter of a moment to whisk the fungus spores on a glass slide, a moment more to find them in the lower magnification, and then with a triumphant click to swing the intense myopic gaze of the tinier lens upon them. From a speck as fine as a particle of wandering cigarette smoke, a spore leaps suddenly up at my eyes as a sphere of gold meshed with vitreous green bands that cut up this tiny world, this planetesimal of sealed-up life, into latitude and longitude.

—DONALD CULROSS PEATTIE, *Green Laurels*

GENERAL AND INEFFECTIVE

The inconvenience of taking a bath in one of these old English homes is hard to realize.

CONCRETE AND SPECIFIC

I do not mind taking sectional baths with two pints of water in the country, where it seems unexceptional and goes along with fresh air, old clothes and being sleepy by nine o'clock in the evening. But segmented bathing in this weary, constricted, suburban household has nothing of rural simplicity about it, only skimpiness and inadequacy, and it makes you feel when you finish like a postage stamp that has been licked and then not used.

—MARGARET HALSEY, *With Malice Toward Some*

INEFFECTIVE

He removed his shoes and walked more comfortably in his bare feet.

MORE VIVID

He leaned down and untied the laces, slipped off first one shoe and then the other. And he worked his damp feet comfortably in the hot dry dust until little spurts of it came up between his toes, and until the skin on his feet tightened with dryness.

—JOHN STEINBECK, *The Grapes of Wrath*

GENERAL AND INEFFECTIVE

The entryway was dirty and messy.

CONCRETE AND SPECIFIC

The space inclosed within the skewed and bent gate pickets was a snug harbor for the dust of many a gritty day. There were little grey drifts of it at the foot of each of the five steps that led up to the flagged floor level; secretions of grime covered the barred double doors on beyond the steps, until the original color was only to be guessed at; scraps of dodgers, pieces of newspaper and tattered handbills adhered to every carved projection at the feet of the columns, like dead leaves about tree boles in the woods.

—IRVIN S. COBB, "The Great Auk"

EXERCISES

EXERCISE 1, GENERAL AND SPECIFIC WORDS. *Find several specific words for each of the following general words.*

jewelry	animal	to move	road	to laugh
flower	ship	to speak	grass	to clean
entertainment	hat	to sing	bird	to hit

EXERCISE 2, ABSTRACT AND CONCRETE WORDS. *Construct sentences in which you give concrete examples of each of the following abstract terms.*

| unselfishness | pugnacity | fear |
| efficiency | stubbornness | laziness |

EXERCISE 3, REVISING WITH SPECIFIC AND CONCRETE WORDS. *Rewrite the following sentences, making them more specific and concrete.*

1. On the porch a row of elderly women sat and rocked and watched the new guests come in.
2. An irritated and impatient policeman was trying to give directions to a driver.
3. The sounds at midnight are interesting to hear.
4. A little boy was happily playing in the alley.
5. The man leaned against the wall and fell asleep.

§ 26. CONCISENESS

Avoid using more words than are necessary for the adequate expression of your thought.

The stylistic fault of *wordiness* has been a concern of writers and rhetoricians for many centuries. Wordiness has been called by many names—verbosity, pleonasm, redundancy, prolixity, diffuseness, circumlocution, periphrasis. By whatever name, wordiness simply means the use of more words than you need in a particular situation. To achieve the goal of conciseness, the student must ask himself whether every word he writes is doing its work, carrying its proper load of meaning, and helping its neighbors with their loads.

Do not mistake brevity for conciseness. A sentence is not concise if it lacks the words necessary for adequate expression. Cutting out words in a good essay might also cut out of it those qualities which make it good—strength, variety, maturity, grace, cleverness, even accuracy.

Study the difference in effect produced by the following pairs of sentences. Notice that in each case the first, although longer, is also stronger and richer.

1. The ant and the moth have cells for each of their young, but our little ones lie in festering heaps, in homes that consume them like graves;

and night by night, from the corners of our streets, rises up the cry of
the homeless—"I was a stranger, and ye took me not in."

2. Insects are more careful about their young than are human beings.

1. When we had done all this, there fell upon us the beneficent and deliberate evening; so that as we sat a little while together near the rakes,
we saw the valley more solemn and dim around us and all the trees and
hedgerows quite still, and held by a complete silence.

—HILAIRE BELLOC

2. When we had finished, it was evening; so that we sat a little while
near the rakes and looked out upon the quiet valley.

Now study the following sets of sentences. Do you see what is
meant by conciseness?

1. Whenever anyone called for someone to help him do some certain
thing, Jim was always the first to volunteer and lend his help for the
cause.

2. Whenever anyone called for help, Jim was always the first to volunteer.

1. This spirit of cooperation is essential and necessary for anyone to have
in order to get along with other people, and this is a quality that Jim
had.

2. Jim had the spirit of cooperation which is necessary if one wishes to
get along with people.

1. Jim was one of those people of whom there are few in this world like
him.

2. There are few people like Jim.

1. Lumbering is placed in the upper ten industries in the United States
from the standpoint of importance.

2. Lumbering is one of the ten most important industries in the United
States.

This section will concern itself with several kinds of wordiness
which are to be avoided by the writer who hopes to be concise,
direct, and to the point.

26a. Avoid careless repetition of the same word.

A word carelessly repeated weakens the effectiveness of a sentence. Careless repetition is frequently associated with wordiness,

as may be seen in the following examples. The fault may be corrected by using synonyms, by using pronouns, or by completely rewriting the sentence.

POOR

I have been asked to write on a controversial subject that has been the subject of controversy among historians for years. That subject, as you have probably guessed, is none other than how to account for the rise of Hitler's Germany. The rise of Hitler's Germany has fascinated me for a longer time than I can remember.

BETTER

I shall try to account for the rise of Hitler's Germany, a controversial subject that has fascinated me for some time.

The importance of avoiding awkward repetition must not distract the writer from the possibilities of repetition for emphasis—a tried and true device for securing certain kinds of attention from the reader. It is especially appropriate in persuasion and oratory, as the famous selection from Winston Churchill below suggests, and it is used sparingly by most contemporary writers.

We shall go on to the end, *we shall fight* in France, *we shall fight* on the seas and oceans, *we shall fight* with *growing* confidence and *growing* strength in the air, *we shall defend* our Island, whatever the cost may be, *we shall fight* on the beaches, *we shall fight* on the landing grounds, *we shall fight* in the fields and in the streets, *we shall fight* in the hills; we shall never surrender, and even if, which I do not for a moment believe, this Island or a large part of it were subjugated and starving, then our Empire beyond the seas, armed and guarded by the British Fleet, would carry on the struggle, until, in God's good time, the New World, with all its power and might, steps forth to the rescue and the liberation of the old.

—Winston Churchill, *Blood, Sweat, and Tears*

The effectiveness of a sentence, or of a series of sentences, may be strengthened by repeating the same form of construction.

To differ is grotesque and eccentric. To protest is preposterous. To defy is incendiary and revolutionary.

—George William Curtis

Made drunk with the freedom of ideas, college students should charge destructively against all the institutions of a faulty world and all the conventions of a silly one.

—Bernard DeVoto

The life of Man is a long march through the night,
|| surrounded by invisible foes,
|| tortured by weariness and pain, towards a goal that
|| few can hope to reach, and where
|| none may tarry long.

—Bertrand Russell

To make parallels clearer, such signal words as prepositions, conjunctions, articles, and auxiliaries may be repeated:

When he was at the beach, he longed
|| *for* his humid office in the city,
|| *for* the sweltering crowds on the subways,
|| *for* the hurried noonday snack at the drug store.

They left the world || *as* wicked and
|| *as* ignorant as they found it.

26b. Avoid repetition of words with the same meaning (tautology).

WORDY

The analysis was *thoroughly and wholly complete.*
All the requirements of *frank* and *honest candor* made his speech popular.
The *basic fundamental essentials* of a college education are *simply* and *briefly* these.
He woke up at six *a.m. this morning.*

26c. Avoid the double *that* before a clause (pleonasm).

WORDY

I was very glad that when I came into the house that I found everything in order. [Omit the second *that*.]

26d. Avoid roundabout expressions (circumlocution or periphrasis).

WORDY

The reason why I was so upset was because she seemed so angry with me. [reason—why—because] [*Revise:* I was upset because she seemed so angry with me.]

26e. Avoid wordy use of intensives and other modifiers.

It is wise to question critically all modifiers (adjectives and adverbs), because it is often here that wordiness gets a foothold. The so-called "intensives"—*very, much,* and so on—are especially likely to weaken a sentence.

WORDY
They were absolutely so much astonished to find so very much still to do that they were absolutely speechless. [They were speechless with astonishment to find so much still to be done.]

She was completely and totally pleased by the very fine report that the children gave her. [She was pleased by the children's fine report.]

26f. Avoid repetition of similar sounds.

The awkward repetition of similar sounds in prose may seriously distract your reader from what you are trying to communicate. Consider the following warning on the subject and note the examples:

Bad prose is bad business, even if the badness be nothing worse than discord. Let the ear then have its way as the phrases are conned; rougher rhythms and inharmonious sounds will drag; as we read we resent something wrong, so that we hesitate, and look back to see where was the jar or the limp. *E.g.* "A more ac*commo*dating deno*mi*nation is *commonly* given to it." "*Gratitude* for his *rectitude*"; "an organisational centre of crystallisation"; "necessari*ly* tempora*ry*"; "very near*ly* entire*ly*"; "so that it at once commenced"; "the native rulers were as a rule," etc. . . . "Of all I have kn*own* he could at least hold his *own*," is not only an untimely assonance but imparts the alien rhythm of verse.

—Sir T. Clifford Allbutt, *Notes on the Composition of Scientific Papers*

26g. Avoid officialese.

The language of official life, government and the military, is seldom concise. You will find there many examples of wordiness such as we have been illustrating. Note especially, in such writing, the overuse of passive verbs (see Section 6) and a fondness for abstract nouns (Section 27a). A similar kind of stuffiness infects the report writing of committees—writing created, that is, by more than one author. And extracurricular student writing, strange to say, is not always free from the wordiness of hot air. See your own campus newspaper.

For an example of official style—by no means an extreme one— study this important passage from the Surgeon General's 1964 advisory committee's report on smoking.

> Cigarette smoking is causally related to lung cancer in men; the magnitude of the effect of cigarette smoking far outweighs all other factors. The data for women, though less extensive, point in the same direction.
>
> The risk of developing lung cancer increases with duration of smoking and the number of cigarettes smoked per day, and is diminished by discontinuing smoking.
>
> The risk of developing cancer of the lung for the combined group of pipe smokers, cigar smokers, and pipe and cigar smokers, is greater than for nonsmokers, but much less than for cigarette smokers. The data are insufficient to warrant a conclusion for each group individually.

Here is a possible revision of those three paragraphs into more concise English.

> Cigarette smoking is the major cause of lung cancer in men, and probably in women too.
>
> The longer one smokes, and the more cigarettes one smokes per day, the greater the chance of developing lung cancer. This risk is reduced when one stops smoking.
>
> People who smoke pipes or cigars, or both, also risk cancer, but to a lesser degree than cigarette smokers. We cannot say exactly what the risk is for each of these groups.

26h. Avoid "fine writing."

"Fine writing" is not, as the phrase seems to indicate, good writing. It is flowery, artificial, overblown writing. In an effort to be literary, the writer loads his style with too many adjectives and adverbs, with big words, awkward repetitions of high-sounding phrases, and trite figures of speech. (See also Section 27c.) "Fine writing" is often the result of an over-complicated sentence structure. Its effect is that of a voice that sounds pompous and stuffy, and no sensitive reader will listen to such a voice for very long.

EXERCISES

EXERCISE 1, AWKWARD REPETITIONS. *In the following sentences, underline the awkward repetitions and examples of wordiness. Then rewrite the sentences, making them more concise by cutting or other revision.*

1. The several features of the situation were complex, and altogether the situation was complicated because of the many elementary elements involved.
2. It was perfectly clear that if she had come along with you as your companion that she would have been welcome.
3. I need hardly say to you all at this time and place that the very great economic loss is a serious source of loss to us all.
4. The chief significant reason why the economy failed was on account of an economic imbalance in the balance of trade.
5. I told him about the courses we were taking, French and history and so on and so forth, so he would get a good idea of the curriculum in which we take courses.
6. He had an arbitrary, set, inflexible rule for everything that he did, and for anything on which he had made up his mind it was very difficult to persuade him otherwise.
7. I really mean it, I certainly was relieved to make that discovery, to my real relief.
8. Unless a person is thoroughly and completely prepared, both mentally and psychologically, the chances of success in marriage are dim, doubtful, and obscure.
9. In regard to this matter of your new insurance policy, please be advised that your new policy is being taken up in a matter of approximately a week or thereabouts.
10. Without any doubt it is very true and unarguable that this great nation of ours is very ready to prepare to defend itself to the very last launching pad.

EXERCISE 2, OFFICIALESE. *Here is an example of officialese, not much exaggerated. Rewrite in plain English.*

It is desired by the administration at this particular time that students refrain and desist from the excessive noise and horseplay that has characterized their behavior in halls and corridors during recent occasions that I have observed. The magnitude of the noise involved has reached a degree where, in some cases of particularly recalcitrant offenders, the awarding of the degree in June may be jeopardized. All faculty personnel are enjoined to be alert to dispatch to this office any flagrant discrepancies of this sort that may come to their attention from time to time.

§ 27. VIVIDNESS AND METAPHOR

27a. Try to use words and phrases that give life and freshness to your style.

There are of course dozens of ways to make a style vivid. Some of them were discussed in previous sections under the headings of "concreteness" and "conciseness." In this section we consider some other devices available to the writer who wishes to create fresher, livelier language. Such a writer, first, should be aware of the possibilities for freshness in the various parts of speech—nouns, modifiers, verbs. Second, the writer should be aware of the possibilities in figurative language, or metaphor. Then he must also be aware of the dangers of metaphor, particularly since so much figurative language has been used before and has lost its freshness. Finally, he must recognize the related problem of over-used language generally: the problem of triteness and clichés.

1. *Specific rather than general nouns will help to produce a vivid style.* (Go back to Section 25 to find out what is meant by *specific* and *general.*) When you write, "I heard a bird singing," your words may call up a definite sense image in the mind of your reader—or they may not—but you do not know what that image is. Have you suggested to him a canary or a robin or a song sparrow? If instead of "bird" you say "meadow lark" or "hermit thrush," your reader will at least make an effort to recall or imagine the song of a meadow lark or a hermit thrush. Whenever you use a specific noun, you make it easy for your reader's mind to create a specific image. You do more than suggest images by your words; you direct the picture-making that goes on in your reader's brain.

2. *Try to use strong, picture-making adjectives and adverbs.* (See also 26e.) No part of speech, generally speaking is more

likely to lie down and die than a flat, uninspired adjective or adverb. You say, "That was a good lecture," when you mean that it was witty, or stimulating or instructive, or entertaining. You say "She is a nice girl," when you mean that she is friendly, or sympathetic, or generous, or vivacious, or modest, or conventional. You can find many adjectives that are more accurate and more vivid than *nice, swell, big, easy, hard.* A book of synonyms will help you find them.

It is a good idea to be on guard against all weak, overused adverbs, such as *very, pretty, rather, little.* Often a weak verb-adverb group can be replaced more effectively by a single strong verb. Note the following examples:

He ran quickly. [He fled, sprinted, trotted, rushed, surged, dashed.]
He was breathing rapidly. [He was panting, blowing, wheezing, puffing, gasping.]
He cut through it. [He pierced it, sliced it, tore it, split it, ripped it.]
He threw it down violently. [He hurled it, flung it, heaved it, pitched it.]

3. *Try replacing general or colorless verbs with more specific and descriptive verbs.* Here are some examples.

He moved toward the door. [He crept, sneaked, crawled, strolled, sidled, inched, drifted, flitted toward the door.]
He spoke several words. [He whispered, roared, shouted, hissed, mumbled, muttered several words.]
We put it on the truck. [We tossed, lifted, pitched, threw it on the truck.]
He got on the horse. [He scrambled, leaped, jumped, vaulted on the horse.]

27b. Figurative language can be used to add freshness to your style.

Some college freshmen feel that figurative language is a bit insincere, a little arty perhaps, good enough for poetry but out of place in honest prose. The truth is that all writing, from the deeply serious or reverent to the lightest or gayest, is often metaphorical. Our daily talk is salted with figures of speech. We meet metaphors in our reading and take them as they come, hardly realizing what they are. Churchill speaking before Parliament ["the life of the world may move forward into *broad, sunlit uplands*"], a historian, Oscar Handlin ["mariners *hugged* the margins of the continent"], a nuclear scientist, J. Robert Oppenheimer ["broken the *iron circle* of his frustration"], a scholar and naturalist, Joseph Wood Krutch, describing a tarantula ["Plainly, he is a discontinued model—still running but very difficult, one imagines, to get spare parts for"]—all use figurative language.

Although all figurative language is usually called metaphorical, some elementary distinctions are useful. A metaphor is a figure that likens one thing to another; it says that one thing *is* another, not literally of course, whereas a simile says that one thing is *like* another. "Life's but a walking shadow, a poor player" . . . "all the world's a stage" . . . "a critic is a legless man who teaches running" . . . "a camel is a greyhound designed by a committee"— these are metaphors. But when the likeness is actually expressed by the use of *as* or *like*, the metaphor becomes a simile. "All the world is like a stage" . . . "insubstantial as a dream" . . . "the water lay gray and wrinkled like an elephant's skin"—these are similes.

Figurative language, it is true, can be overdone, especially by a writer reaching out for a gaudy style, like a boy who always either shouts or growls, but rarely is this a fault in college writing.

Figures of speech are best observed in context, where they look at home, as in the following selections. Seen by themselves as specimens they too often remind us of brightly colored butterflies pinned to a board. In the following, observe also the vivid nouns, verbs, and adjectives:

Many of us, if we have happy childhoods, are tempted to believe that life is a pony, beribboned and curried, which has been given to us as a present. With the passing of years we, sooner or later, come to learn that, instead of being a pony, life is a mule which unfortunately has more than four legs. To the best of my knowledge, no one who lives long enough fails to be kicked, usually again and again, by that mule. Why this should surprise us or unnerve us, I as an older person have long since ceased to understand.

—JOHN MASON BROWN, "Prize Day Address," at Groton School for Boys

Then the creeping murderer, the octopus, steals out, slowly, softly, moving like a gray mist, pretending now to be a bit of weed, now a rock, now a lump of decaying meat while its evil goat eyes watch coldly. It oozes and flows toward a feeding crab, and as it comes close its yellow eyes burn and its body turns rosy with the pulsing color of anticipation and rage. Then suddenly it runs lightly on the tips of its arms, as ferociously as a charging cat. It leaps savagely on the crab, there is a puff of black fluid, and the struggling mass is obscured in the sepia cloud while the octopus murders the crab. On the exposed rocks out of water, the barnacles bubble behind their closed doors and the limpets dry out.

—John Steinbeck, *Cannery Row*

In the meanwhile all the shore rang with the trump of bullfrogs, the sturdy spirits of ancient winebibbers and wassailers, still unrepentant, try-ing to sing a catch in their Stygian lake,—if the Walden nymphs will pardon the comparison, for though there are almost no weeds, there are frogs there,—who would fain keep up the hilarious rules of their old festal tables, though their voices have waxed hoarse and solemnly grave, mock-ing at mirth, and the wine has lost its flavor, and become only liquor to distend their paunches, and sweet intoxication never comes to drown the memory of the past, but mere saturation and waterloggedness and disten-tion. The most aldermanic, with his chin upon a heart-leaf, which serves for a napkin to his drooling chaps, under this northern shore quaffs a deep draught of the once scorned water, and passes round the cup with the ejaculation *tr-r-r-oonk, tr-r-r-oonk, tr-r-r-oonk!* and straightway comes over the water from some distant cove the same password repeated, where the next in seniority and girth has gulped down to his mark; and when this observance has made the circuit of the shores, then ejaculates the master of ceremonies, with satisfaction, *tr-r-r-oonk!* and each in his turn repeats the same down to the last distended, leakiest, and flabbiest paunched, that there be no mistake; and then the bowl goes round again and again, until the sun disperses the morning mist, and only the patriarch is not under the pond, but vainly bellowing *troonk* from time to time, and pausing for a reply.

—Henry David Thoreau, *Walden*

27c. Metaphors and other phrases that have become trite should be avoided.

Trite expressions, whether they were once metaphors or not, are also called hackneyed phrases or clichés. At one time they may have been apt or witty and felicitous, but now, because they have been used so often, they are stale and flat. They offend the reader. The following list may help to put you on your guard:

aching void
acid test
after all has been said
all in all
all work and no play
among those present
ardent admirers
arms of Morpheus
as luck would have it
at a loss for words
at one fell swoop
beat a hasty retreat
beggars description
better half
better late than never
blissfully ignorant
blushing bride
bolt from the blue
bountiful repast
breathless silence
briny deep
budding genius
busy as a bee
by leaps and bounds
caught like rats in a trap
checkered career
cheered to the echo
clear as crystal
conspicuous by his absence
course of true love
devouring element
discreet silence
doomed to disappointment
downy couch
drastic action
dull, sickening thud
each and every one
easier said than done
equal to the occasion
fair sex
familiar landmark
favor with a selection
festive occasion
few and far between

filthy lucre
goes without saying
great open spaces
gridiron warriors
grim reaper
holy bonds of matrimony
in all its glory
in the last analysis
irony of fate
justice to the occasion
last but not least
lonely sentinel
long-felt want
mantle of snow
meets the eye
method in his madness
monarch of all he surveys
mother nature
motley crowd
nipped in the bud
none the worse for his experience
none the worse for wear
no sooner said than done
partake of refreshments
pleasing prospect
powers that be
presided at the piano
proud possessor
psychological moment
reigns supreme
rendered a selection
replete with interest
riot of color
ripe old age
sadder but wiser
shadow of the goal posts
silence reigned supreme
single blessedness
specimen of humanity
sumptuous repast
sweat of his brow
sweet girl graduate
table groaned
tired but happy

vale of tears	where ignorance is bliss
venture a suggestion	with bated breath
watery grave	words fail to express
wee small hours	worked like a Trojan
wends his way	wrought havoc

EXERCISES

EXERCISE 1, WRITING FOR VIVIDNESS. *Rewrite the following paragraph. Pay special attention to the verbs, adjectives, and adverbs, and try to make use of metaphors or similes where they can be made appropriate.*

The boy walked home from school very slowly. It was April, and he observed as he went the various signs of the spring season. As he approached his own house, he paused to speak to his neighbor, who was puttering about on his lawn. Finally he turned and walked indoors, for he was hungry.

EXERCISE 2, CLICHÉS AND TRITE PHRASES. *Now rewrite this passage again, this time using as many clichés and trite phrases as you can.*

EFFECTIVE SENTENCES

§ 28. SENTENCE UNITY

The problem of unity in a sentence concerns itself primarily with either "not enough" or "too much."

NOT ENOUGH IN THE SENTENCE

28a. In standard English, the structural unity of the written sentence depends on the presence of a finite verb with its subject.

The completeness or unity of a sentence is based, in one sense, on its structure. As we shall see later, it is also based on its thought or content. The sentence, however, is not a formula or an unchangeable pattern. On the contrary, it is a unit of such variety and flexibility that no rule, only the good sense of the writer, can decide when "not enough" becomes "complete," and when "complete" becomes "too much."

Obviously, a sentence is "not enough" when it is not grammatically complete; that is, when it does not have an expressed or implied subject and verb. For a discussion of sentence fragments see Section 1.

TOO MUCH IN THE SENTENCE

28b. Sentence unity may be destroyed by the inclusion of words, phrases, or clauses that have no direct bearing on the principal thought of the sentence.

A sentence may have "too much" in several ways. First, two unrelated ideas of the same weight and importance may be thrown together to make a compound sentence. The proper cure for this sort of fault is subordination. The methods of subordination are discussed in Section 29. Second, a sentence may appear bulging and baggy from having too many related minor details thrown into it. Finally, a sentence may lack unity because the writer tossed into it some unrelated minor detail that happened to pop into his mind while he was writing.

See also the warning against the grammatically mixed construction, Section 34d.

UNRELATED DETAILS
The library, old and dusty and well lit with bright new fixtures, was a melancholy place to work. ["Melancholy" seems related to "old and dusty" but not clearly to the new lighting.]

UNIFIED
The library, though well lit with new fixtures, was old and dusty and a melancholy place to work.

UNRELATED DETAILS
After the junta took control in Vietnam, freedom of the press, which is guaranteed by a Constitutional amendment in the United States, was suppressed by the new regime. [If the sentence is about Vietnam, the reference to the United States is merely thrown in. If it is part of a contrast between the two governments, it might be acceptable.]

UNIFIED
After the junta took control in Vietnam, freedom of the press was suppressed by the new regime.

UNRELATED DETAILS
The good sense of the chairman, who is a corpulent individual, is respected by all who know him. [His good sense has nothing to do with his shape.]

UNIFIED
The good sense of the chairman is respected by all who know him.

Overloading a sentence with details can obscure its unity and destroy its clearness and order. If the details are important, they should be told in separate sentences where they can be given proper value. If they are unimportant, they may be omitted.

CONFUSED
Military training teaches a person to stand up straight and walk with his head up; this helps in future life because it becomes a habit and so

many people have the bad habit of walking stooped and this leads to poor health and poor appearance.

Military science teaches also common courtesies, not only to your superior officers but to everyone to whom courtesy is due; for instance when you enter offices, or the courtesies you should use when you are using firearms while hunting or shooting in the presence of another person.

If you write sentences like these, your remedy is to go back to the first principles of thought communication: say one thing at a time; say it as simply and clearly as you can; say it so that it cannot be misunderstood.

Let us try to dissect these sentences in order to discover what the writer tried to say.

REVISED

Military training teaches a person to stand erect and to walk with his head up. [That is enough for one sentence.] Good posture [Is that what the writer meant by "this" and "it"?] becomes habitual. It leads directly to better health and better appearance.

Military science also teaches common courtesy, not only to officers superior in rank but also to everyone. [Are there some persons to whom "courtesy is not due"?] For instance, it teaches one how to enter an office, or how to handle firearms with safety to others. [These two examples are so badly chosen that no sentence can make them apt or congruous.]

E X E R C I S E

EXERCISE, ELIMINATING UNNECESSARY DETAILS. *Here is a paragraph of overloaded sentences. Reorganize these sentences, discarding unnecessary details.*

The desert of the Negev in Israel, whose principal port is Haifa, looks from a plane like the surface of an unknown moon seen from a rocket ship around the year 2165. This is the land the Israelis, a very ancient people, hope to irrigate with their new pipeline from the Sea of Galilee, which is a reservoir in the Jordan River, which rises on the slopes of Mount Hermon, a mountain range in Syria. The great pipeline from the Jordan (Jordan means "impetuous") has cost about 150 million dollars for bringing water from the Sea of Galilee to the Negev, which is all broken rock and sand. Perhaps before long it may be another promised land, sending produce to Haifa and Elath, the principal ports of Israel, for shipment to other countries.

§ 29. SUBORDINATION

Make proper use of subordination of sentence elements in your writing.

Turn back to Chapter 3 and read what has been said there about the various uses of subordination. Subordination is a device that may be used to correct two types of sentence faults: (1) putting minor details into main clauses within the sentence and (2) putting minor details into a succession of short, choppy sentences.

The subordinate elements to which a main clause may be reduced are a dependent clause, a prepositional or verbal phrase, and an appositive. Occasionally something that a writer has expressed in a main clause may be reduced to a single word.

29a. Dependent or minor details should be placed in subordinate constructions in the sentence.

Too much coordination is a sign of immaturity, in thinking as well as in writing. A child will say, "We had a party yesterday, and it was my birthday, and it rained, and the rain spoiled my party." A maturer person might say, "Our daughter's birthday party yesterday was spoiled by the rain." A mature person will not assume that all ideas, details, or facts are of the same importance or that they should be expressed on the same level. He knows that some are of primary importance, that others are supporting or explaining details, and he will try to show the relationship of one part of the sentence to another.

The following are suggested revisions of single-level sentences. Of course only the writer can know exactly what he intended to stress.

IMMATURE
The opening to the tunnel was covered by a grating, and this was made of iron, and it was very heavy.

REVISED

The opening to the tunnel was covered by a very heavy iron grating. [*or*]
A massive iron grating covered the opening to the tunnel.

IMMATURE

The aardvark lives in Africa, and it eats ants and termites, and it has
sharp claws to dig them out.

BETTER

The African aardvark lives on ants and termites, which it digs up with its
sharp claws.

29b. Long, straggling sentences may be improved by being broken up into more compact units.

The weakness of a long sentence lies not in its length but in its
shapelessness. A long sentence may be highly effective because
of its easy flow and rhythm. Note how Joseph Conrad builds up a
powerful climax in the following long sentence:

> There are many shades in the danger of adventure and gales, and it is
> only now and then that there appears on the face of facts a sinister vio-
> lence of intention—that indefinable something which forces it upon the
> mind and the heart of a man that this complication of accidents or these
> elemental furies are coming at him with a purpose of malice, with a
> strength beyond control, with an unbridled cruelty that means to tear out
> of him his hope and his fear, the pain of his fatigue and his longing for
> rest: which means to smash, to destroy, to annihilate all he had seen,
> known, loved, enjoyed or hated; all that is priceless and necessary,—the
> sunshine, the memories, the future—which means to sweep the whole
> precious world utterly away from his sight by the simple and appalling
> act of taking his life.
>
> —JOSEPH CONRAD, *Lord Jim*

The cure for the straggling sentence is "subordinate and
divide"—subordinate what seems to be of secondary importance,
and divide if you cannot subordinate.

STRAGGLING

When I was a little girl I did not care for motion pictures, but as I grew
into high-school age I began to go every week and now that I am out of
high school I do not go so often and I am more particular about the
quality of the picture that I see.

REVISED

My taste in motion pictures has developed through three stages—a complete indifference to them in my childhood, a movie-a-week stage in my high-school days, and my present discriminating enjoyment of a few of the best.

STRAGGLING

In my sophomore year the teacher thought that we needed more drill in creative writing, which was the same course we had had the previous year, but in my junior year we did not have any English course but instead spent two terms studying literature.

REVISED

My high-school training in English consisted of a two-year course in creative writing, the second year a repetition of the first, and a year's study of literature.

Coordination and subordination are devices by which a writer may give different degrees of emphasis to different parts of his sentence. No one but the writer can know what his intentions were when he wrote a certain sentence. All we can do is to say, "Is this really what you meant to say? Try combining your main clauses. Try subordinating one of them. There will be a difference in the emphasis that you get, but your revised sentence may be closer to what you meant to say."

29c. Avoid upside-down subordination.

The English language has evolved certain sentence patterns that often go contrary to the norms. For instance, in a sentence like this: "It is assumed that what a man displays on the walls of his living room is more important to him than what he throws into a corner," the important idea is obviously in a subordinate clause. Yet we accept the pattern. It is good English. There is wide objection, however, to putting the main idea into a *when*-clause, as in: "One evening I was reading in the library when I saw a student tear out a sheet from a valuable reference book." That sort of thing is usually called "upside-down subordination." It makes many educated people squirm. They say you should have written, "One evening, as I was reading in the library, I saw a student tear out a sheet from a valuable reference book."

29d. Avoid the overlapping or tandem subordination.

Overlapping subordination occurs when there is a succession of subordinate clauses, each depending on the one preceding it.

POOR
I had heard the warning so often that I was so used to hearing it that I failed to realize that it was important. [Three that-clauses in succession]

BETTER
Repeated warnings had dulled my appreciation of their importance. [Or] The warnings had been repeated so often that I failed to realize their importance.

29e. Avoid a series of short, choppy sentences if the content can be expressed more precisely by using subordination.

Again, the reader cannot look into the writer's mind to see what his intentions were when he wrote a sentence. Short sentences *can* be effective. Turn to page 73 and note what Ernest Hemingway could do with them. But see also Section 29a.

POOR
The performance was over. I arose to go out. I was so nervous that I had to sit down on a chair. Soon I grew calm again.

BETTER
After the performance I arose to go out, but I was so nervous that I had to sit on a chair until I grew calmer.

POOR
Back of the grandstand are the stables. The stables are long, rambling, one-story barns. Each barn is divided into box stalls. Each stall is large enough to accommodate one horse.

BETTER
The stables, situated behind the grandstand, are long, rambling, one-story barns, each barn divided into stalls large enough to accommodate one horse apiece.

EXERCISES

EXERCISE 1, USING SUBORDINATE CLAUSES. *In each of the following sentences change one of the main clauses to a subordinate clause.*

1. It was still early afternoon, but we stopped to look for a motel. [Use an adverb clause.]
2. We were nearing Franconia, and we had driven there to view the fall color. [Use adjective clause.]
3. The wooded hills surrounded us and they were gay with color. [Use an adjective clause.]
4. We were driving south from Franconia and we saw the Old Man of the Mountain. [Use an adverb clause.]
5. We looked toward the west, and we saw, far off, a rock formation resembling a man's profile. [Use an adverb clause.]
6. Our guidebook explained it to us; it was the inspiration for one of Hawthorne's famous stories. [Use a noun clause.]
7. We tried to take a picture of the Old Man and we found that it made a tiny speck on the view finder. [Use an adverb clause.]
8. You can use a 300-millimeter lens and you will get a fairly large picture. [Use an adverb clause.]
9. We parked our car near a small park, walked down a path, took a few pictures, and then we drove away to look for a motel. [Use an adverb clause with *after*.]
10. It had been raining in the mountains all week and the traffic was not heavy. [Use a causal adverb clause.]

EXERCISE 2, SUBORDINATION WITH PHRASES. *Subordinate one of the clauses in each of the following sentences by reducing it to a prepositional or verbal phrase.*

1. As I was a native of Quebec, I spoke Canadian French fluently.
2. Some Canadians who come here from British Columbia do not realize how French this province is.
3. The visitor goes into a shop or a hotel and he finds that a knowledge of French is really useful.
4. Our people have lived amid a French culture, and the traditions of their ancestors are dear to them.
5. There are two French universities in Canada and all the instruction is in the French tongue.

EXERCISE 3, SUBORDINATION WITH APPOSITIVES. *Use an appositive to subordinate one of the clauses in each of the following sentences.*

1. A youngish man in an unpressed suit trotted into the classroom; it was Mr. Brooks, and he was our new instructor.

2. Hastily dropping his papers on the desk, he searched for a missing object; it was the class-sheet from which he was to call the roll.

3. He was a young candidate for a doctorate and he unconsciously taught us freshmen the latest thing he had learned in his graduate course.

4. His graduate school had impressed three virtues upon his mind; they were erudition, thoroughness, and indifference to personal appearance.

5. His research project had impressed the scientific world; it was a classification of the mating calls of toads.

§ 30. REFERENCE OF PRONOUNS

30a. The antecedent of a pronoun in a sentence should be immediately clear to the reader.

As a rule, pronouns should have definite antecedents and should be placed as near their antecedents as possible. The hedging in this last sentence, represented by the phrase "as a rule," refers to two or three special situations. First, there are a number of idiomatic phrases in which a pronoun has no visible antecedent, such as *it rained last night; it's the climate; it is time to go home*. There is no lack of clearness in these sentences. Second, the pronoun *you*, in the sense of *one*, or a *person*, has wide currency in informal written and spoken English, and occasionally in good formal writing. Third, the pronouns *which, this, that* may refer to an idea or fact expressed by a whole clause or a sentence, or by a part of a clause, if the reference is unmistakably clear.

In good writing, the meaning of a sentence should be clear to an intelligent reader on the first reading. If the reader has to hesitate, if he has to search for the substantive to which the pronoun refers, or if he has to puzzle over which of two possible antecedents it does refer to, the sentence is not as good as it should be. And we may add here that even if you can find a bucketful of muddled sentences in the writing of great scientists, great educators, or great public servants, those sentences still are muddled and not as good as they could have been.

INDEFINITE

She saw a play at the elegant new Plymouth Theatre, but later she was not able to remember it very well. [What could she not remember, the play or the theatre?]

CLEAR

At the elegant new Plymouth Theatre she saw a play, which later she was not able to remember very well.

OR

She saw a play at the elegant new Plymouth Theatre, but later she was not able to remember the building very well.

INDEFINITE

Since my grandfather was a doctor, it is not surprising that I have chosen *that* for a career. [The antecedent of *that* is only vaguely implied.]

CLEAR

Since my grandfather was a doctor, it is not surprising that I have chosen medicine for my career.

It is usually awkward to have a pronoun refer to an antecedent in a subordinate position. The reader will instinctively associate a pronoun with the most prominent substantive in the clause he has just read. The result is confusion—possibly a momentary confusion but still an undesirable one.

CONFUSING

Men have lounged and crouched around their fires; they have been the companions of their dreams and meditations. [The reader will hesitate when he comes to "they have," because he will assume that the subject of the sentence is still "men."]

CLEAR

Men have lounged and crouched around their fires, which have been the companions of their dreams and meditations.

OR

Men have lounged and crouched around their fires—the companions of their dreams and meditations.

30b. The reference of a pronoun should not be ambiguous.

AMBIGUOUS

The title of the book was so dramatic that *it* was a great help in remembering *it*. [Does the first *it* refer to the title, or to the drama of the title? Does the second *it* refer to the book, or to the title of the book?]

CLEAR
I remembered that book easily because of its dramatic title.

AMBIGUOUS
The players and umpires know one another well and sometimes they call them by their first names.

CLEAR
Players who know umpires well sometimes call them by their first names.

AMBIGUOUS
Mr. Beamis told his brother that he did not yet know the situation thoroughly.

CLEAR
As Mr. Beamis admitted to his brother, he did not yet know the situation thoroughly.

OR
Mr. Beamis charged his brother with not knowing the situation thoroughly.

It is usually unnecessary to resort to an explanatory antecedent in parentheses after a pronoun.

AWKWARD
Mr. Beamis told his brother that he (Mr. Beamis) did not yet know the situation thoroughly.

30c. In formal and serious writing, the indefinite reference is less common than in informal writing and in speech.

We are here referring to two particular situations: (1) the use of the indefinite *you* to mean *one, a person* and the indefinite *they* to mean *people,* and (2) the use of *this, that,* and *which* to refer to a clause, sentence, or a general idea.

1. The indefinite *you* and *they* are common in speech and in many forms of informal writing; they are less appropriate in formal writing. The student should guard against making their use a habit, especially in papers of explanation.

FORMAL
First the seed is scattered evenly over the ground; then the soil is raked lightly and firmed with a roller. [Note the passive voice here.]

COLLOQUIAL
First you scatter the seed; then you rake it in and firm the soil with a roller.

FORMAL
When a soldier salutes, he must stand up straight and bring his right hand up smartly to the visor of his cap.

COLLOQUIAL
When saluting, you must stand up straight and bring your right hand up smartly to the visor of your cap.

FORMAL
In the army, a soldier does not ask; he obeys.

COLLOQUIAL
In the army, you do not ask; you do what you are told.

2. A pronoun may have a clause or a sentence for its antecedent; it may even refer to a thought expressed by a part of the preceding sentence. As long as the reference is unmistakable, the sentence is clear. But the careless writer may fall into the habit of stringing together a series of *this-*, *that-*, and *which*-clauses without troubling himself about either clearness or exactness. See also Section 28 on the overloading of sentences. When the writer suspects the clearness or definiteness of an antecedent, he can sometimes summarize the idea of the clause referred to by an expression such as *this fact, this condition, a fact which,* and so forth. If the result is still unsatisfactory, he should rewrite the sentence.

Notice that the references are clear in the following sentences.

CLEAR
I have finished my work at last. That should satisfy the boss.
He recommended that I write to the secretary, which I did without delay.
If you have decided to speak out on this issue, it should be done quickly.

Now notice the vague references in the following sentences.

VAGUE
The antismoking campaign in England, which had such little effect, has cost a good deal of money and energy, and this leads to pessimism about our own campaign.

CLEAR

The costly and energetic antismoking campaign in England has had little effect, a fact that leads to pessimism about our own campaign.

VAGUE

The fish are kept alive and fresh in glass tanks, and it also attracts people, which helps the business considerably. [What do *it* and *which* refer to?]

CLEAR

The fish are kept alive and fresh in glass tanks. The display of live fish helps business by attracting people to the place.

30d. The careless use of *same, such, above,* and *said* as reference words often produces an awkward sentence.

These words are used as reference words in legal or technical writing; in ordinary writing they should be avoided, not because they are incorrect but because they usually lead to awkwardness of expression. Use one of the common pronouns (it, them, this) or the name of the thing to which you refer.

POOR

I stood there holding the monkey wrench and oil can in my hands. The foreman ordered me to return the same to the engine room.

BETTER

I stood there holding the monkey wrench and oil can in my hands. The foreman ordered me to return the tools to the engine room.

POOR

The significance of said decision is not yet fully comprehended.

BETTER

The significance of the decision referred to is not yet fully comprehended.

POOR

Please return same to me by bearer.

BETTER

Please return it [or name the object] to me by the bearer of this note.

POOR

The above is a complete refutation of their arguments.

BETTER

These facts completely refute their arguments.

30e. A pronoun should agree with its antecedent in number, gender, and person.

For a discussion of the agreement of pronouns, see Section 4j.

POOR IN FORMAL ENGLISH
Every student is required to bring their books with them.

BETTER
Every student is required to bring his books with him.

POOR
A team that loses most of its games may owe its failure to the fact that they do not have a good coach. [You must be consistent. If you begin by considering *team* as singular, you must continue to refer to it as one unit.]

BETTER
A team that loses most of its games may owe its failure to its lack of a good coach. [Or, more simply, "may owe its failure to poor coaching."]

30f. It is usually considered awkward to begin an essay with a reference to the title.

It is better to repeat the words of your title, in your first sentence, than it is to refer to your title with a pronoun. For example, if your title is "Coming About in a Small Boat," do not begin your paper, "This was very difficult for me to learn." Say instead, "The operation of coming about in a small boat was very difficult for me to learn."

E X E R C I S E

EXERCISE, FAULTY REFERENCE. *In each of the following sentences underline the pronoun or pronouns with faulty reference. Rewrite each sentence so as to correct the error.*

1. The baggage was loaded onto a small handcart which was the only way to get it through the crowded station.
2. I worked for the college physics department last year, washing equipment for them and cleaning their laboratories.
3. He told me all about it, and very well too. It was something I would like to have done myself.
4. The history of this community goes back to the seventeenth century which makes a visit well worth while.

5. The obligations of an army sergeant are that of any leader in a small group.
6. While a person would suppose that she wanted nothing else in life, you could be very wrong about this.
7. The wealth of the country is controlled by a few who live in the city, which is usual in such societies.
8. Every player must learn his signals which will make an efficient and coordinated team.
9. He laughed at what I had said. This was amazing.
10. Everybody knows the reason why the economy is in such poor shape. It is a source of dismay to us all.

§ 31. PROPER ARRANGEMENT

The parts of a sentence should be so arranged that the meaning of the sentence is clear at the first reading.

Since English is not a highly inflected language, the meaning of an English sentence depends largely on the arrangement of the words in it. The reader naturally assumes that the parts of a sentence that are placed next to each other are logically related to each other. You must therefore be careful to arrange words in a sentence in such a way that its meaning will be clear on the first reading. The rule that will guide you may be stated in two parts: (1) place all modifiers, whether words, phrases, or clauses, as close as possible to the words they modify; (2) avoid placing these elements near other words they might be taken to modify.

31a. In formal writing, place adverbs logically.

Let us use *only* as an illustration of what happens when idiom contradicts logic. Logically, an adverb should be placed near the word it modifies; idiomatically, it is often placed elsewhere. For instance, would you say, "We have room for only two more," or, "We only have room for two more"? The person with a logical mind says that "only" modifies "two"; the person who prefers the second form answers that idiom does not pay much attention to logic. Both forms are used. The second is used generally in speech, in a great deal of informal writing, and often in formal writing.

The first is used by writers and speakers who are disturbed by the logic of the other form. No statistical study of the incidence of each form in formal writing has been made.

The same explanation applies to *not*. Compare "Not everyone can be first" and "Everyone cannot be first." Logic sanctions the first form; idiom sanctions the second form—at least in speech and informal writing.

Only slightly less controversial is the placing of several other adverbs, such as *hardly, just, almost, nearly, merely, scarcely.*

COMMON IN SPEECH
He *only* worked half a day.
Everyone is *not* honest.
The child *hardly* ate any food.
He *just* took one apple.
He *almost* weeded the whole garden.

MORE LOGICAL AND PREFERRED BY MANY
He worked *only* half a day.
Not everyone is honest.
The child ate *hardly* any food.
He took *just* one apple.
He weeded *almost* the whole garden.

31b. Avoid ambiguous placement of phrases.

There is no exact position in a sentence that phrases must always occupy; the best rule to follow is to keep them away from words they must *not* be understood to modify. The result of such misplacement is often ludicrous.

MISPLACED
He began to lose his desire to reach the summit *after a time.*

BETTER
After a time he began to lose his desire to reach the summit.

MISPLACED
I was dressed and ready to start climbing *within an hour.* [Does the phrase refer to *being dressed* or to *starting to climb?*]

BETTER

Within an hour I was dressed and ready to start climbing. [*Or*] I was dressed *within an hour* and ready to start climbing.

31c. Avoid ambiguous placement of clauses.

Clauses, like phrases, may be placed wherever they seem to fit in a sentence—except near words they can be mistaken to modify.

AMBIGUOUS OR LUDICROUS

I hid the ring in my pocket *that I intended to give to her.*

BETTER

The ring *that I intended to give to her* I hid in my pocket.

31d. Avoid squinting modifiers.

Modifiers so placed in a sentence that they may be understood with either the preceding or the following words are called squinting modifiers. As a rule, it is better not to try to cure the fault by means of punctuation.

SQUINTING

I firmly decided *the next day* to start studying.

CLEAR

I firmly decided to start studying *the next day.*

SQUINTING

After we had stopped at a service station *with the help of a lady attendant* we found our position on the map.

CLEAR

After we had stopped at a service station, a lady attendant helped us to locate our position on the map.

SQUINTING

The girl who had sat down *quickly* opened her textbook.

CLEAR

The girl who had sat down opened her textbook *quickly.*

31e. Use the split infinitive only to avoid awkwardness.

Placing an adverbial modifier between the sign *to* and the verb of an infinitive results in what is traditionally known as a "split infinitive." The split infinitive is no longer considered one of the seven deadly sins of college composition—if it ever was. It is not true that the parts of an infinitive are inseparable. But since a split infinitive still causes many persons discomfort, if not actual suffering, it is better for the student not to split his infinitives too rashly or promiscuously. A good rule to follow is this: place the adverbial modifier between *to* and the verb of an infinitive only when such an arrangement is necessary to avoid an awkward phrase. For a long list of split infinitives one may consult George O. Curme's *Syntax*, pages 460–467. Here are a few from that list: "to actually mention the name," "to even wish" "to seriously cripple," "to further confirm," "to utterly forget," "to further complicate," "to first consider."

31f. Avoid the awkward separation of any words that normally belong near each other.

Words that usually belong near each other are subject and verb, verb and object, the parts of a verb phrase, nouns and adjective modifiers, and nouns and appositives.

AWKWARD
Justice Holmes, in a brilliantly written interpretation of the Fourteenth Amendment, dissented. [Subject and verb split by long phrase]

BETTER
Justice Holmes dissented in a brilliantly written interpretation of the Fourteenth Amendment.

AWKWARD
Finally, we caught, after sitting in our rowboat for hour hours, a small salmon. [Verb and object split]

BETTER
Finally, after sitting in our rowboat for four hours, we caught a small salmon.

AWKWARD
After it got dark, the boys bedded down beside a stream, wet, tired, and discouraged.

BETTER
After it got dark, the wet, tired, and discouraged boys bedded down beside a stream.

E X E R C I S E S

EXERCISE 1, ELIMINATING SPLIT INFINITIVES. *Improve each of the following sentences by eliminating an awkward split infinitive.*

1. I hope to some day in the near future visit Paris again.
2. You should now begin to methodically and carefully budget your time for study.
3. If you care to remain in college, you must plan to quickly change your habits.
4. Your first concern should be to not carelessly waste your time.
5. If you really care to materially improve your grades, you should promise to immediately give up your trips to the city.

EXERCISE 2, CORRECTING MISPLACED ELEMENTS. *Point out the misplaced element in each of the following sentences. Then show how the sentence can be improved. Do not use punctuation as a means of correcting an error in arrangement.*

1. We decided at nine o'clock to call him at his home.
2. Taking too many vitamin pills frequently causes bad effects.
3. Her dropped parcels were collected before any had been stepped on by the bus driver.
4. The fullback returned to the team after two days' absence on Friday.
5. Father, not wishing to prolong the argument far into the night, agreed.
6. To be misunderstood often is the fate of an original poet.
7. The departing train brought thoughts of distant friends to the poor girl rumbling over the high bridge.
8. Our teacher has many theories about things that are different.
9. The sheriff was stabbed while sleeping by an unknown person.
10. He needs someone to show him how to put his affairs in order badly.

§ 32. DANGLING OR MISRELATED MODIFIERS

32a. Awkward dangling modifiers should be avoided.

At present there is considerable difference of opinion among educated people over the use of what is traditionally known as the "dangling modifier." Some say that it should be called the "misrelated modifier," for instead of dangling it actually attaches itself too easily to the wrong word. When it does, especially when it results in confusion or in unintentional humor, it is bad. When it calls attention to itself and away from the intended meaning of the sentence, it is bad. One might add that it can be bad because so many educated persons have been taught to regard it as a slovenly way of writing.

Here are some examples of dangling participles, the most common error in this category. Notice that the phrasing often results in unintentionally ludicrous meanings.

Walking along the quiet street, the houses looked old and comfortable.
While waiting for the coffee to warm, the cereal boiled away.
Strewn on the floor in clumsy piles, he glanced idly through the remains of his books.
I had a summer job that year, thereby enabling me to return to school. [This is more awkward than plain wrong. Who or what enabled me to return to school?]

In addition to participles, infinitives are sometimes left dangling. The problem here is that there is no visible subject of the infinitive in the sentence.

To see this view properly, the sun must be shining. [Does the sun see the view?]
To succeed as a businessman, the basic facts of economics are apparently not always necessary.

In each of these sentences, it does not matter whether the phrase dangles because it is not attached where it should be or is misrelated because it attaches itself where it should not be. Each sentence is awkward or misleading, to say the least.

A dangler may be corrected in three ways: (1) by changing the phrase to a clause, (2) by providing a noun or pronoun to which the dangler can properly attach itself, or (3) by reordering the sentence.

EXAMPLES
As I walked along the quiet street, the houses looked old and comfortable.

While I waited for the coffee to warm, the cereal boiled away.

He glanced idly through the remains of his books, which were strewn on the floor in clumsy piles.

The money I made on a summer job that year enabled me to return to school.

To appreciate this view properly, one should see it when the sun is shining.

In order to succeed as a businessman, it is apparently not always necessary to know the basic facts of economics.

Note that the absolute phrase does not dangle. In the absolute phrase the word that the participle attaches itself to is in the phrase itself.

EXAMPLES

The day's work being over, we returned to town.

The guests having arrived, Mother went to the door.

Three more girls, their wet hair plastered down over their eyes, stumbled into the classroom.

It may be helpful to think of the participle as a kind of preposition in such sentences as these:

Considering the size of the house, it seemed remarkably cheap.

Judging by his voting record, he is a responsible congressman.

A slight shift in phraseology, however, produces a dangler, even though the meaning is essentially unchanged:

Viewing his voting record, he is a responsible congressman.

Certain idiomatic phrases, especially those that express a general action and those that serve as directive and transitional links, are always acceptable in either formal or informal situations. These are phrases like *generally speaking, looking at it from another point of view, taking everything into consideration, providing that, failing,* and others that are similar.

EXAMPLES

Failing agreement, the meeting was adjourned.

Generally speaking, the worse a pun is, the better it is.

32b. A sentence with any sort of expression, like a phrase or an appositive, that is not easily understood with the rest of the sentence is awkward and usually misleading.

ILLOGICAL
A gentleman farmer, his wardrobe ranges from faultlessly tailored suits to four-buckle rubber boots. [The expression *a gentleman farmer* seems to be in apposition with *wardrobe*.]

REVISED
As he is a gentleman farmer, his wardrobe ranges from faultlessly tailored suits to four-buckle rubber boots.

ILLOGICAL
After five years in a city school, a country school presents many problems in adjustment. [One naturally associates the opening phrase with a *country school.*]

REVISED
A person who has spent five years in a city school encounters many problems in adjustment when he goes to a country school.

The dangling or misrelated modifier, it can be seen from the examples offered, is a stylistic blunder. If it causes confusion, even momentary confusion, or if it is associated with an unasked for ludicrous image, it is undesirable. For a discussion of danglers used by many professional writers, see Pooley's *Teaching English Usage*, pages 107–113.

E X E R C I S E

EXERCISE, CORRECTING DANGLERS. *Some of the following sentences are correct, while some contain objectionable danglers. Pick out the faulty sentences and correct them.*

1. Buying her ticket at the box office, she walked into the opera house.
2. While waiting to be seated, the usher approached her.
3. He delayed taking her ticket, thus causing a small traffic jam.
4. Seated at last, she glanced through her program.
5. The opera, based vaguely on Shakespeare, was the famous *Falstaff.*

6. One of Italy's most beloved composers, the music was by Verdi.
7. The curtain having gone up at last, she sat back in her seat feeling thoroughly relaxed.
8. While sitting there quietly, the stage exploded with excitement.
9. To see an opera at its best, the scenery too must be appreciated.
10. Rising at the intermission, she strolled into the outer lobby.
11. She heard a familiar voice, thereby meeting an old friend.
12. Being an old opera lover, they got along famously.
13. When young, the opera had seemed too complicated.
14. Now, however, having matured, she enjoyed almost all performances.
15. Returning home in a taxi, the music of Verdi still seemed to sing in her ears.

§ 33. EMPHASIS IN THE SENTENCE

The relative importance of ideas in a sentence may be shown by various devices of structure. The principle used is known as *emphasis.*

Emphasis is a word that may be understood in more than one sense. A speaker may emphasize his words by shouting or screaming them; a writer may emphasize words by indicating that they be printed in italics or capitals. Some writers and speakers have used these methods. But that is not the sense in which we use the word here. By *emphasis* we mean using rhetorical devices that show the relative importance or prominence of ideas and details in a sentence or paragraph. Some of these devices we have discussed elsewhere in connection with other qualities of good writing— clarity, directness, order, coherence, conciseness, directness. Two or three others will be pointed out here and in the following sections.

It may be well to restate here the various devices by which the relative importance of ideas can be shown:

1. By placing the important idea by itself in a short sentence.
2. By placing the idea in a main clause of a complex sentence.

3. By changing the usual order of a sentence. [Sympathy I did not want!]
4. By using parallel structure. [See Section 35.]
5. By using the order of climax.
6. By repeating key words. [See Section 26a.]
7. By using the active instead of the passive voice.
8. By giving an important idea fuller treatment.
9. By placing important words in prominent positions.
10. By using periodic structure.

33a. Placing important words in the important positions in the sentence will help to show the relative importance of ideas.

The most conspicuous positions in a sentence of some length are the beginning and the end. These are the positions that should be used for ideas that deserve attention and emphasis. The less important details, the modifiers, the qualifying comments should be tucked away inside the sentence.

WEAK
The student who cheats in an examination is cheating only himself in the final analysis.

BETTER
The student who cheats in an examination is, in the final analysis, cheating only himself.

WEAK
Public speaking should be taught in freshman English, I think.

BETTER
Public speaking, I think, should be taught in freshman English.

No writer can consistently rearrange his sentences so as to begin and end them with important ideas. Many sentences are so short that the reader's mind comprehends them as units. In many others the word order is determined by the nature of the English language. A writer may occasionally construct a sentence such as this—as Stephen Leacock once did—"Him they elected president," but in sentences such as the following no problems of emphasis can arise: "He is a good man." "Her son was killed in France." "The day's work is done." "The President saluted the flag."

33b. Occasionally one may express a thought more effectively by changing a sentence from the loose to the periodic form.

A periodic sentence is one in which the main idea is held until the end; a loose sentence is one in which the main idea is followed by details and modifiers. The effect of a periodic sentence is one of suspense—that is, the reader is asked to wait for the main idea until after he has comprehended the deails upon which the main idea is based or by which it is limited or changed. Not all sentences in English are periodic; a large majority of them, in fact, are loose. It is precisely for this reason that an occasional periodic sentence is emphatic.

LOOSE

In recent years many factories were established in the city, especially plants engaged in the manufacture of brass products.

PERIODIC

In recent years many factories, especially plants engaged in the manufacture of brass products, were established in the city.

LOOSE

Stop talking if you have nothing more to say.

PERIODIC

If you have nothing more to say, stop talking.

LOOSE

It is of course impractical to legislate for those who will behave themselves while completely ignoring those who will not.

PERIODIC

To legislate for those who will behave themselves while completely ignoring those who will not is, of course, impractical.

The periodic effect, one of suspense, of waiting, is not limited to sentences in which the dependent clauses all come before the main clause. Note the following two sentences:

Metaphors are so vital a part of our speech, so common and used so unconsciously, that they become, as William Empson has indicated, the normal mode of development of a language. And it is the incalculable reach of the image—the establishment of a kinship between unrelated objects, the combination of exactness and ambiguity—which is its charm and power.

—Louis Untermeyer, "Play in Poetry"

Then note the way a writer creates suspense by using a summarizing main clause with *all* or *such*:

To transfer admiration from the thing possessed to its possessor; to conceive that the mere possession of material wealth makes of its possessor a proper object of worship; to feel abject before another who is wealthier —such emotions do not so much as enter the American mind.

—Hilaire Belloc

33c. Use the active instead of the passive voice where the active is more direct and natural.

Please note that the use of the passive voice is not in itself a grammatical or stylistic fault; it is the *overuse* of it that is a fault. The passive voice has several proper and necessary uses: (1) when the object or receiver of the action of the verb is more important than the doer; (2) when the doer of the action is not known; (3) when the writer wishes to place the emphasis on the receiver instead of on the doer.

To the satisfaction of everyone, Grabowski was chosen best player of the tournament.
Several priceless old manuscripts were destroyed.
The wounded prisoner was dragged into the trench.

Then note the difference in the following sentences when the active voice replaces the passive:

PASSIVE
A good time was had by all.
Then a driver's test was taken by me.
A period of weightlessness is endured by the astronaut.

ACTIVE
Everyone had a good time.
Then I took a driver's test.
The astronaut endures a period of weightlessness.

EXERCISES

EXERCISE 1, EMPHASIS. *Using the principle of emphasis by position, improve the following sentences.*

1. A fool can ask more questions than a wise man can answer, according to the Italian proverb.
2. Long sentences in a short theme are like large rooms in a small house, the professor explained.
3. Generally speaking it is well not to speak generally, as someone has said.
4. Generally speaking, one good teacher is worth a dozen good books.
5. When in danger or in doubt, run in circles, scream and shout, the sergeant advised.

EXERCISE 2, LOOSE AND PERIODIC SENTENCES. *Change the following loose sentences to periodic sentences.*

1. Stress has a harmful effect on our ability to learn, it was discovered by these experiments.
2. For this experiment two controlled groups were selected who had the same ability to memorize.
3. One group was told that its scores were poor after they had completed about half the test.
4. Their performance at once deteriorated when the testing was resumed.
5. But their ability improved considerably after they had been praised for their improved performance.

EXERCISE 3, ACTIVE OR PASSIVE VERBS. *Improve the following sentences by changing the verb from the passive to the active.*

1. The skidding car was brought safely to a stop by the alert driver.
2. The policeman's warning was accepted by her with humility.
3. I thought that she would be nervous and tearful, but a very different reaction was observed by me.
4. As she informed me, a set of new tires had been bought by her husband a few days ago.
5. But the need for new tires, she said, was vetoed by her.
6. Instead, the new tires were returned to the dealer and a new dress was purchased with the money by her.
7. "Do you think now that a new dress is worth your life?" was asked by the officer.

8. The workings of a woman's mind cannot be understood by a simple man.
9. After a few minutes the trip to our destination was resumed by us.
10. Glancing up at the rear-view mirror, it was observed that the woman's car was now following us.

§ 34. SHIFT IN POINT OF VIEW

Any unnecessary and illogical shift in point of view should be avoided.

In Section 43, we consider problems of consistency in point of view that involve fairly large matters of style. There we take up the *position* in time and space chosen by the writer, his *tone* toward his reader (including his consistent use of formal or colloquial language), and his *attitude* toward his subject. Here we consider some smaller, largely grammatical dangers—but they are just as important as the larger questions in the completion of a finished essay.

Three common grammatical shifts in point of view are (1) from active to passive voice, (2) from past to present tense, and (3) from *one* to *you* and similar shifts of person. These and other shifts are described below. Writing is both clearer and more pleasing if the writer maintains his point of view, unless, of course, he has some logical reason for changing to another.

34a. Unnecessary shifts from active to passive voice are undesirable.

SHIFT

You wrap the bundle carefully in paper; it is then tied securely.

We were acquainted with his brother, and his eighty-year-old father was also well known to us.

BETTER

You wrap the bundle carefully in paper and tie it securely.

We knew both his brother and his eighty-year-old father.

[415]

34b. Needless shifts in tense—from past to present or from present to past—are usually objectionable.

See also Section 6.

SHIFT

I *go* right on into the room and then *looked* around me to see what he *would be doing* with all that furniture. [Such shifts in tense must be watched for especially in narrative accounts.]

BETTER

I *went* right on into the room and then *looked* around me to see what he *might be doing* with all that furniture. [Or *might have done* with all that furniture]

SHIFT

After *planning* the trip I *had thought* I *deserved* a little credit for its success.

BETTER

After *having planned* the trip, I *thought* I *deserved* a little credit for its success. [All verbs in past tense]

34c. Needless shifts in number or person should be avoided.

SHIFT

If one really wishes to sample fine cooking, try that restaurant on the corner.

BETTER (INFORMAL STYLE)

If you really want to try some good eating, try that restaurant on the corner.

CORRECT IN A FORMAL CONTEXT

If one really wishes to sample superior cooking, he should try the restaurant on the corner.

See also Section 30e for a discussion of number in pronouns.

34d. A writer should guard against mixing two distinctly separate constructions in a sentence.

A "mixed construction" is usually the result of hasty and careless writing. The writer begins one construction, and immediately, without troubling himself to look back on what he has written, continues with another construction.

MIXED

In our basement we found a small wood stove, which upon removing the front, made it resemble a fireplace. [*Which* refers to *stove*. The stove cannot remove its own front, nor can the stove make itself resemble anything.]

CLEAR

In our basement we found a small wood stove, which we made into a fireplace by removing its front.

In our basement we found a small wood stove. By removing its front, we made it resemble a fireplace.

MIXED

She did not say a word, but took me to the back yard in what seemed to me a bit hurriedly. [The writer has forgotten his original intention. He could say either *took me in what seemed a hurried manner* or *took me a bit hurriedly*.]

Occasionally a writer will run an independent clause into a sentence in such a way that it appears to stand as the subject of a verb.

MIXED

We were tired of traveling is the main reason we came here.

I was all alone was what truly frightened me.

CLEAR

We came here mainly because we were tired of traveling.

What truly frightened me was that I was all alone.

34e. Mixed figures of speech are inappropriate in serious writing.

In the teaching of writing, warnings against scrambled metaphors may have been given an undeserved and an unfortunate prominence. A mixed metaphor is often a sign of mental vitality. It is surely a lesser literary crime than page after page of dull and uninspired prose. If you scramble two incongruous images, you probably need little more than a hint to show you that your metaphors are inappropriate. It is manifestly absurd to speak of "watering the spark of originality," or "blazing a trail over the sea of knowledge," or of "being blinded by a thirst for revenge." Even Shakespeare spoke of taking up arms against a sea of troubles. If your instructor points out a mixed figure of speech in your writing, laugh over it. He will laugh with you and then "encourage the spark of imagination which the mixed metaphor foreshadows, water it with drops of kindness and fertilize it with praise, so that the springs of originality may blossom forth like a tree and shed their light over many arid pages of prose writing!"

The following samples illustrate what is meant by "mixed imagery."

Many high-school athletes think they can ride on their high-school laurels right into a position on the college team. [How can one ride on a laurel?]

The future of jazz was at its lowest ebb. [Even were the future not transported to the past, a rare feat in itself, how could a future ebb?]

Instead of narrowly pursuing the mechanics of grammar, the clever teacher will often digress into anecdotes which will make the class fairly rock with laughter. [Can "mechanics" be pursued, either narrowly or broadly?]

A college education enables the graduate to meet the snares and pitfalls of life with a broader point of view.

E X E R C I S E S

Exercise 1, Illogical Shifts. *In each of the following sentences specify the type or types of illogical shift that you find—in tense, voice, number, or person. Then make the necessary corrections.*

1. The submarine *Thresher* goes down in April of 1963, and many scientists participated in the investigation that followed.
2. They conducted research from several ships; also a survey of the ocean bottom was made.
3. One would suppose the task would have been easy, since all you have to do is find the hull on the ocean floor.
4. The scientific group had its hands full, however, for they could discover no trace of the missing craft.
5. The Navy called off its search in September; they had done all they could.
6. New efforts have been undertaken by private scientific organizations and universities have continued research into the mishap.
7. Until late 1964, no one knows just where the ship is lying

—you would have been amazed to learn how the discovery was finally made.

8. A bathysphere is ordered; it has been at work for some time on the scene.
9. No doubt many scientists on the project would prefer to return to shore as a laboratory researcher.
10. In the process, however, the ocean floor in the area has been fully investigated, which had been useful for future oceanographers.

Exercise 2, Mixed Constructions. *Here are ten badly muddled sentences. Rewrite them. Do not be afraid to break them up if they can be improved in that manner.*

1. You could view that painting as a complex pattern of colors or as an amateur who knows very little about art.
2. They had a magnificent wedding which I regret to say they never asked me to come.
3. The table was made of inlaid wood and a source of admiration to all who saw it.
4. Everybody considered her a beauty that she was an ornament to the community.
5. The dean said he believed in a straightforward, middle-of-the-road, thoroughly well-rounded plan of education which everyone ought to have the opportunity.
6. Industriousness has always been a bad point with me due to my time has always been so preoccupied with fun.
7. He looked bravely into the eye of the future with a brisk and unfaltering step.
8. The reason things are at such a low ebb is due to the inevitable swing of the economic pendulum.
9. Sometimes you see a student reading comfortably in the library and looks as if he has fallen asleep as indeed he has.
10. Anyone who writes sentences like these that thinks he can write English ought to know better.

§ 35. PARALLEL STRUCTURE

35a. Parallel structure expresses similar ideas in the same grammatical and rhetorical patterns.

Parallel structure is primarily a rhetorical device, which writers use to give their sentences force, clearness, grace, and rhythm. In its more elementary uses it can give sentences greater clarity and smoothness. For a more complete discussion of rhetorical uses of parallelism and balance, turn to Chapter 3, pages 78–81. Here are two examples from the works of writers to whom style is important:

Then she would fill the page
|| with recommendations and suggestions,
|| with criticisms of the minutest details of organisation,
|| with elaborate calculations of contingencies,
|| with exhaustive analyses and statistical statements piled up in
     breathless eagerness one on the top of the other.
And then her pen, in the virulence of its volubility, would rush on
|| to the discussion of individuals,
|| to the denunciation of an incompetent surgeon or
    the ridicule of a self-sufficient nurse.

—LYTTON STRACHEY, *Eminent Victorians*

The city [New York] at last perfectly illustrates both
|| the universal dilemma and
|| the general solution,
this riddle in steel and stone is at once
|| the perfect target and
|| the perfect demonstration || of nonviolence,
                           || of racial brotherhood,
this lofty target || scraping the skies and
                || meeting the destroying planes halfway,
|| home of || all people and
               || all nations,
|| capital of everything,
housing the deliberations by which || the planes are to be stayed and
                                         || their errand forestalled.

—E. B. WHITE, *Here Is New York*

In its simpler and more elementary form, parallel structure is a balancing of noun with noun, an infinitive with another infinitive, a phrase with another phrase, and a clause with another clause. Used at this level, the device will cure many a deformed or arthritic sentence:

AWKWARD

Sororities teach a girl to be a lady and courteous. [Noun paralleled with adjective]

PARALLEL IN FORM

Sororities teach a girl to be || *ladylike* and
courteous.
[Adjective || adjective]

AWKWARD

Our English teacher asked us to close our books, to take pen and paper, and that we were to write a short theme. [Two infinitives and a clause]

PARALLEL IN FORM

Our English teacher asked us || *to close our books,*
to take pen and paper, and
to write a short theme.
[Infinitive || infinitive || infinitive]

AWKWARD

Few of the leaders anticipated the bitterness of the strike or how long it would last. [A noun and a clause]

PARALLEL IN FORM

Few of the leaders anticipated || *the bitterness* or
the duration of the strike.
[Noun || noun]

35b. Avoid the *and who* and the *and which* constructions.

The "and who" or "and which" fault, as it is called, consists of using *and who* or *and which* in a sentence that does not have a preceding *who* or *which* clause.

FAULTY

He is a man of wide experience *and who* is also very popular with the farmers.

PARALLEL

He is a man of || wide experience and
great popularity among the farmers.

FAULTY

I am interested in electronics, because it is a new field *and which* offers interesting opportunities to one who knows science.

PARALLEL

I am interested in electronics, || which is a new field and
which offers interesting
opportunities . . .

35c. The false parallel should be avoided.

Straining for parallelism where it is not natural is a fault that occurs rarely in college writing. The false parallel, however, is not the result of too much care for form; it is purely accidental.

ILLOGICAL
I finally realized that my daydreaming was not making me beautiful, slender, or friends. [The three words seem to depend on *making me*, but two of them are adjectives and one is a noun. They are not logically parallel.]

REVISED
I finally realized that my daydreaming was not making me beautiful and slender or bringing me friends.

Parallel forms may be used with the correlative conjunctions *both—and, either—or, neither—nor, not only—but also*. Care should be taken in placing these correlatives so that the intended meaning of the sentence is not obscured.

EXERCISES

EXERCISE 1, PARALLEL FORM. *In the following sentences underline the parts that should be expressed in parallel form. Then revise each sentence.*

1. Professor Macy is a middle-aged man, short, stocky, blue eyes, and partly bald.
2. His lectures are witty, interesting and he outlines them carefully.
3. He told us that we should read our text and to write a short review of it.
4. The book is interesting and I can learn from it.
5. Mr. Macy said he would give us a quiz on the first chapter and for us to review it carefully.

EXERCISE 2, FALSE PARALLELS. *In the following sentences correct the faulty use of correlatives.*

1. My summer's work proved not only interesting but I also learned much from it.

2. I wondered whether I should continue with it or should I return to college.
3. My boss was not only pleasant but he was also generous.
4. A college education was both necessary and I could afford it.
5. Not only was I getting older fast, but I also planned to be married soon.

§ 36. COMPARISONS

36a. In standard formal English, comparisons should be logical and complete.

Written English, especially formal written English, requires a logic and a precision in expressing comparisons that is often lacking in loose, informal speech. In informal speech certain elliptical or illogical comparisons have become idicmatic. Some of these shortened comparisons, or illogical comparisons, are becoming more and more common in writing, both formal and informal; as in other cases of divided usage, the choice made by the student should be based on an understanding of the facts of usage.

1. In informal writing do not omit than *or* as *in a double comparison.*

USUALLY INAPPROPRIATE IN FORMAL USAGE
The bus is about as fast if not faster than the train.
Football coaches earn as much if not more than college presidents.
California is now as populous, if not more populous than New York.

LOGICAL BUT AWKWARD
The bus is about as fast as, if not faster than the train.
Football coaches earn as much as, if not more than college presidents.
California is now as populous as, if not more populous than New York.

The last three examples illustrate what is often called the "suspended construction." Some writers use it; others object to it on the score of awkwardness. It can be easily avoided.

LOGICAL AND SMOOTH
The bus is about as fast as the train, if not faster.
Football coaches earn as much as college presidents, if not more.
California is now as populous as New York, if not more so.

2. *Avoid ambiguity in making comparisons.*

AMBIGUOUS
I saw more of him than Jones. ["more than Jones did" or "more than I saw of Jones"?]

CLEAR
I saw more of him than I saw of Jones. [Or *more of him than Jones did*]

AMBIGUOUS
Our country helped France more than England.

CLEAR
Our country helped France more than England did. [Or *more than our country helped England*]

3. *Do not omit* other *after* than *or* as *in comparing two members of the same group or class.*

MISLEADING
Miss Jenkins is more literate than any girl in the class. [If Miss Jenkins is not a member of the class, the sentence is clear. If she *is* in the class, she cannot be more literate than herself.]

CLEAR
Miss Jenkins is more literate than any other girl in the class.
Miss Jenkins is the most literate girl in the class.

4. *Finish your comparisons so that you will not seem to be comparing something that you do not intend to compare.*

MISLEADING
The salary of an English teacher is lower than a lawyer. [Are you comparing salaries, or are you comparing salary and lawyer?]

CLEAR
The salary of an English teacher is lower than that of a lawyer. [In your desire to escape awkwardness you should not say, "An English teacher earns less than a lawyer." If you want to be accurate in fact as well as

logical in expression, you could say, "An English teacher earns more than does a lawyer, but he gets less."]

MISLEADING
The duties and responsibilities of a traffic officer are more complex than a game warden.

CLEAR
The duties and responsibilities of a traffic officer are more complex than those of a game warden. [Name the second term of the comparison.]

36b. In standard English, comparisons are completed except when the missing term of the comparison can be easily supplied by the reader.

NOT CLEAR
It is easier to remain silent when attacks are made upon the things one loves. [Easier than what?]

CLEAR
It is easier to remain silent when attacks are made upon the things one loves than to risk criticism by defending them.

NOT CLEAR
Students who live in a dormitory do better work. [Better than students who live where?]

CLEAR
Students who live in a dormitory do better work than those who room in private homes (*or* who live in fraternity houses).

There are, however, many idiomatic expressions in which an unfinished comparison is easily understood, such as "It is always better to tell the truth"; "her explanation is simpler"; "we thought it wiser to agree." No misunderstanding is possible in statements like these. The uncompleted superlative is also used, especially in speech, and its sense is not that of a comparison but of an intensive, as in: "She is the most unselfish woman," "he is a most peculiar man."

We must also add here that although in general a comparative refers to two and a superlative refers to three or more, idiomatically the superlative is often used with two persons or objects. This use of the superlative is undoubtedly more common in speech than in informal writing.

EXERCISE

EXERCISE, COMPARISONS. *Revise the comparisons in the following sentences. Use the forms appropriate in standard written English.*

1. The snails of South America known as apple snails are as interesting if not more interesting than the allied *Pila* of the Old World.
2. Their shells are like apples, greener and rounder than other snails.
3. They are one of, if not the most amphibious kind of snail known to science.
4. Equipped with both gills and lungs, they are better swimmers than any snails.
5. When one compares the two types, the apple snail is clearly the best adapted to its environment.
6. The English periwinkle is as common if not more common than most other snails.
7. The lungs of the periwinkle are more developed than most other such sea animals.
8. Here the development of the lungs has reached a point higher than any place on earth.
9. Some snails can live as long if not longer than six months out of water.
10. Snails are the most fascinating animals; they are so attractive and varied in appearance.

§ 37. WORDS LEFT OUT

Words necessary for clearness should not be left out.

Two kinds of omissions need to be considered here. One is the result of carelessness. The cure for that type is more careful proofreading. The second kind results from the carrying over of speech habits into writing. We often speak in a more clipped or telegraphic manner than is permissible in writing, especially in serious and dignified writing on serious subjects.

The following are some of the omissions that need to be guarded against.

37a. Avoid the misleading omission of "that."

MISLEADING

I soon observed nearly all the women, especially the young and pretty ones, were carrying strange little baskets. [Did he "observe the women, especially the young and pretty ones," or did he observe *that* the women were carrying baskets?]

He told me his story in its original version had been rejected by thirteen publishers. [Supply *that*. "He told me *that* his story . . ." The confusion is undesirable even if it is momentary.]

37b. Avoid the omission of a part of a verb or of a verb phrase.

MISLEADING

The patient was given an anesthetic and the instruments made ready. [It is better to say *were made ready*, because *patient* is singular, and the verb *was*, which follows it, cannot be understood with *instruments made ready*. We need a plural verb.]

His ideas were progressive and adopted without debate. [Repeat *were*. The two verbs are not parallel. The first *were* is used as a main verb—*ideas were*—but the second *were* is an auxiliary verb—*were adopted*. *Progressive* is not part of the verb phrase.]

37c. Avoid omissions that result in the use of a noun or a verb in a double capacity.

AWKWARD

He never has and never will deceive a customer. [Say *never has deceived*. Although this sort of construction is common in speech, many people object to it in written English.]

This boy is one of the best, if not the best fullback I have ever watched. [Say: *one of the best fullbacks*.]

37d. Avoid the omission of necessary prepositions in idiomatic expressions.

INCOMPLETE

Spring term the course will be repeated for all new students. [Say *During the spring term. . . .*]

We must show our faith and devotion to our country. [Say *faith in*. *Faith to* is not idiomatic.]

Customers have neither respect nor faith in a merchant who cheats. [Say *respect for*. *Respect in* is not idiomatic.]

For a more complex sentence in which idiomatic prepositions are used with precise care, examine this sentence from Galsworthy's "Some Platitudes Concerning Drama":

This third method requires a certain detachment; it requires a sympathy with, a love of, and a curiosity as to, things for their own sake; it requires a far view, together with patient industry, for no immediately practical results.

37e. Avoid the omission of function words that indicate balanced and parallel constructions.

WEAK

He said that Communism had never had many adherents in the United States and there were fewer party members today than at any time since the Russian revolution.

STRENGTHENED

He said *that* Communism had never had many adherents in the United States and *that* there were fewer party members today than at any time since the Russian revolution.

WEAK

We thanked her for her kindness, which we had not always reciprocated, the stimulation we found in her classroom, and the long hours she had spent helping us with extracurricular activities.

STRENGTHENED

We thanked her *for* her kindness, which we had not always reciprocated, *for* the stimulation we found in her classroom, and *for* the long hours she had spent helping us with extracurricular activities.

EXERCISE

EXERCISE, MISSING WORDS. *Supply the missing words in the following sentences. Rearrange the wording wherever it is necessary.*

1. This student, I feel sure, never has and never will write a passing theme.
2. We visited one of the oldest, if not the oldest church in Vermont.
3. We noticed many churches were almost surrounded by graveyards.

4. He needed better evidence to prove his demands were justified.
5. Sundays more men studied their lessons than women.

§ 38. VARIETY

Variety in the length and the structure of sentences usually makes writing more effective.

A writer may avoid monotony of sentence structure by avoiding the following:

1. Beginning a series of sentences with the same word or the same subject.
2. Beginning a series of sentences with participial phrases.
3. Using the same sentence pattern in a group of sentences.
4. Beginning each of a series of sentences with the same kind of subordinate clause.

Here are some elementary examples of monotony. Notice the consistent shortness of the sentences, the immature vocabulary, and the dreary repetition of sentence structure.

SHORT SENTENCES, ALL BEGINNING WITH THE SUBJECT
Mrs. Helmer is a fine woman. She has always been most kind to me. I have appreciated her efforts in my behalf. She helped me find a summer job. I met a number of interesting people through her. She has always been a good friend of mine.

SHORT SENTENCES BEGINNING WITH A PARTICIPIAL
PHRASE
Waking up in the morning, I dressed quickly. Hurrying into the kitchen, I saw my mother at the stove. Pouring me a cup of coffee, she advised me not to delay. Gulping my coffee quickly, I began to collect my thoughts for the day ahead.

Few college students should be guilty of such monotonous writing as that. Some common techniques for introducing variety include the following:

[429]

1. Mixing simple sentences with complex or compound sentences.
2. Putting a short sentence in the midst of several long ones.
3. Occasionally beginning a sentence with modifiers instead of with the subject.
4. Occasionally beginning with a conjunction instead of with the subject.

In the selection that follows, observe how richness and variety are achieved by weaving various details, in phrases, clauses, appositives, into the sentence themselves.

Very different was dapper Mr. Groce, our teacher of English composition and literature, a little plump man, with a keen, dry, cheerful, yet irritable disposition, a sparkling bird-like eye, and a little black mustache and diminutive chin-beard. I suspect that he was too intelligent to put up patiently with all the conventions. Had he not been a public-school teacher, dependent on the democratic hypocrisies of a government committee, he might have said unconventional things. This inner rebellion kept him from being sentimental, moralistic, or religious in respect to poetry; yet he *understood* perfectly the penumbra of emotion that good and bad poetry alike may drag after them in an untrained mind. He knew how to rescue the structural and rational beauties of a poem from the bog of private feeling. To me this was a timely lesson, for it was precisely sadness and religiosity and grandiloquence that first attached me in poetry; and perhaps I owe to Mr. Groce the beginnings of a capacity to distinguish the musical and expressive charm of poetry from its moral appeal. At any rate, at sixteen, I composed my first longish poem, in Spenser's measure, after *Childe Harold* and *Adonais*, full of pessimistic, languid, Byronic sentiments, describing the various kinds of superiority that Night has over Day. It got the prize.

—George Santayana, *Persons and Places*

§ 39. AWKWARDNESS AND OBSCURITY

Sentences that are confused, awkward, illogical, or obscure should be rewritten.

An awkward and confused sentence may occasionally be a sign of slovenly thinking, but it is probably more often a result of haste and carelessness in writing and revision. A confused sentence may have several faults:

1. The central thought may be lost in a tangle of modifiers.
2. The thoughts may not be arranged properly.
3. The words used may be inexact, ambiguous, or inappropriate.
4. Several constructions may be telescoped into one.

See also Section 34.

CONFUSED

My belief is that if more emphasis was stressed in college on extempore speaking, the graduating student would be better prepared to face people of social prominence and college professors.

REVISED

I believe that colleges should stress courses in extempore speaking in order to give their graduates more confidence and social ease.

CONFUSED

The word *laureate* comes from the Greeks when they used laurels to crown certain people.

REVISED

The word *laureate* comes from the language of the ancient Greeks, who used a laurel crown as a mark of special honor.

EXERCISE

EXERCISE, AWKWARD AND OBSCURE SENTENCES. *Revise the following sentences.*

1. Some allergic people live in pollen-proof rooms created by air-conditioning, not including air-cooling, to escape paroxysms of sneezing caused by chilling.
2. The hay fever patient should be wary of squirting insecticides about the yard or house, for squirting pyrethrum, the ground-up flower of the chrysanthemum, which is a member of the composite family, also is contained in these.
3. A student spends two or three terms in college to become accustomed with the rules needed for comprehensive learning.

4. Proper use of the English language is very essential in any type of work, whether a business man or a profession.

5. Many people have sacrificed wonderful professions because of simple misconceptions of their judgment.

6. There are some girls who really cannot afford to live in a sorority house but who would rather have it known that she belongs to a sorority and do without other things like food and clothes.

7. Having never attended college before gives me the opportunity to develop to the fullest extent my study habits and idle time.

8. Still half asleep and unconscious of what I was doing, I applied the makeup on the left-hand side of the table, which happened to be the kind used for evening wear.

9. Privacy hindered my studying while in high school because living in a house where there are many children it is very hard to secure privacy.

10. The subject of classifying what I think is an ideal roommate should be written to an unlimited length if one was to take every point in doing so.

THE PARAGRAPH

§ 40. ADEQUATE PARAGRAPH DEVELOPMENT

40a. Effective presentation of ideas requires paragraphs of suitable length.

Rarely do college freshmen write paragraphs that are too long; their chief difficulty is finding enough to say so that their paragraphs will not resemble a series of stunted sentences.

If a writer has three or four paragraphs on every page of his theme paper, his paragraphs are probably too short. If he splits up a five-hundred-word essay into ten or twelve paragraphs, his paragraphs are certainly too short. The paragraphs of a newspaper story are short, it is true; so are the paragraphs of a business letter. But we are not speaking of those special types of writing when we say "expository" writing. In expository writing it is customary to develop ideas more fully, or to group ideas into larger units than in news stories or in letters. In expository writing, a series of very short paragraphs is an indication of malnutrition; the paragraphs need to be fed details to make them effective.

If your instructor refers you to this section, rewrite your paper. Start with a plan, or an outline, which calls for a limited number of facts or ideas. Your trouble may be too ambitious a subject. Cut it down to fit your space. Then write a thesis sentence stating your central idea. Write a topic sentence for each paragraph. With these as your guide, proceed to make your paper interesting by means of details, concrete examples, illustrations, comparisons, specific instances, reasons—all those things which transform a skeleton into writing that is alive.

The following examples illustrate some of the weaknesses in

paragraph development that are common in student writing. See also Chapter 4, especially the section "Problems of Internal Organization."

UNDEVELOPED PARAGRAPH

Advertisements in magazines and on television these days are a lot better than they are given credit for. Some of them are quite funny. I think advertising is more interesting than a lot of other things going on nowadays. [This is vague, repetitious, undeveloped. Note especially some of the undefined words and phrases: *a lot better* (how is it better?), *more interesting* (in what way?), *a lot of other things* (what sort of things?).]

REWRITTEN PARAGRAPH

The growth of wit in the writing of advertisements is a pleasant phenomenon of recent years. In magazines and on television many writers of ads have been exploiting a sense of the absurd, almost as if they were making fun of themselves. The famous series advertising a New York bank, featuring a huge egg held in a gold chain, is a case in point. With a comic kind of approach, the bank offered "a better way to take care of your nest egg." Then there is the gasoline which, the adwriter promised, would move your car not only forward—but back! Altogether this kind of fun-making is a healthy development in a profession that often appears to take salesmanship all too solemnly.

UNDEVELOPED PARAGRAPH

I like to travel all right, but it is the people you meet rather than the things you see that I appreciate. When I visit a new place I am really happy to find some new faces and names that I can make friends with. [This paragraph has reduced informality to not much more than chattering. Again it is vague and unconvincing. Note how, in the revision, the writer has exploited the unintended rhyme—new places, new faces—to enliven his first sentence. Then he proceeds with some relatively concrete, memorable examples.]

REWRITTEN PARAGRAPH

When I go traveling, it is new faces, not new places, that I go to see. The Grand Canyon is certainly an awesome sight, but what I remember most vividly from my visit there is the figure of a priest I met in a hotel lobby. Lean, ascetic, with flashing black eyes, he spoke to me of his order and its commitment to teaching. And at Yellowstone Park, where I was duly impressed by Old Faithful, an elderly woman with bright silver hair and the manner of an actress took one look and sniffed. "Another dull show in the provinces," she concluded scornfully. Traveling is all very well but I suspect our own human depths may be more mysterious and fascinating than any canyon. Thoreau put it better, at a time when maps still contained large, unexplored blank spaces. "What does Africa, what does the West stand for?" he asked. "Is not our own interior white on the chart?"

Some scrappy paragraphs are the result of the student's failure to think in larger units. The writer fails to determine his central idea, and he fails to recognize his miniature paragraphs as merely parts of his topic idea.

SCRAPPY PARAGRAPHS

Father and Mother marveled at the way my sister Lois and I got along; they still do in fact. They are proud of the family unity we show.

When Lois married, I was as thrilled and happy as she, I am sure. I think I knew better than anyone else what a wonderful wife she would be. Her marriage is an example to me.

Although my sister never attended college, she has encouraged me greatly. I am working to live up to the high standards she set for me, and I am constantly hoping that some day I can in some way repay her.

[Try combining under a topic sentence like this: *My sister Lois has been a companion and an example to me.*]

The buzzard usually glides over wooded areas in search of food because a domestic animal is more likely to meet a mishap in the forest than out in a plain pasture. Also one will find buzzards around the sloughs in the summer because the water is drying up and the buzzard will feed on the dead fish.

The buzzard lives in a nest on top of high cliffs and in tree tops.

It is against the law to shoot buzzards because they scavenge the animals that have died in the woods through accident.

[Try combining these three paragraphs under a topic sentence that makes a statement about the feeding and nesting habits of buzzards.]

I suppose any mother is happy and proud when her daughters surprise her by cooking a meal. I know that my mother always is. This is one way in which we like to make her happy.

Mother always remembers kindness, whether it be in thoughts or actions, and always forgets the unkindness of others. She appreciates having us cook for her.

[Try constructing a topic sentence about Mother's appreciation of a kind act.]

40b. Concrete details help to make a paragraph interesting and effective.

The tendency of beginners is to write in generalizations and abstractions: "The closing hour at the cafe is always a scene of great confusion." What actually is going on? Why not make us see—hear and smell, too—the various details of that confusion? Just what did you see that justified your conclusion that the closing hour at the cafe is a scene of confusion? In criticism, the statement "I like this poem" is of course practically meaningless. Why do you like it? Because it irritates you? or because it soothes you? In presentation of character—"My father is an honest man." How is he honest? What does he do that shows honesty? Drag him out on the stage and let us watch him being honest. In discussions of college problems—"College men are more conventional and conservative than college women." Give us examples, many of them. Let us see these college men and women in situations that require choice; let us see how they behave and what they think in relation to political questions, to books, to art, to social morality. Give the reader action and proof. Give him the evidence that you have observed.

Here are some examples to show how details can be used.

BEFORE

Holding a little boy by the hand, a fat old woman waddled slowly up the staircase.

AFTER

Her carpet slippers flapping against the stone steps, the huge woman made her way laboriously up the staircase. Her dark shapelessness almost hid the little boy beside her, whose thin white arm stretched taut as she pulled him along. His wispy red curls bobbed as he pumped himself up, one step, then another step. Panting almost in unison, they sang together as they climbed: "London Bridge is falling down ... falling down ... falling ... down."

BEFORE

The closing hour at the cafe where I work is always a scene of great confusion. The juke-box is playing, the customers are shouting their orders, everyone is impatient and in a hurry.

AFTER

The air is blue and suffocating with smoke. Everyone screeches orders at once, and someone wants me to turn up the juke-box because the crowd cannot hear the music. One freshman, who must have been on the campus for several weeks, wants to know where the Pi Phi house is; another, who is obviously exaggerating, says that he has waited ten minutes for his hamburger. Some helpful soul says, "Just give me anything; I don't care what," or "What have you got that's good?" Someone wonders what kinds of shakes we have, and after I have named all fourteen flavors, says, "I'll take vanilla." At 9:30 we are out of glasses, silverware, and ice cream, and someone has spilled a cup of coffee on the floor. Then the carbonator freezes, and while I am concentrating on defrosting it, a mathematical genius shoves a handful of coins at me and drones, "I want five cents out of this, fifteen out of this, forty out of this, with two nickels change, a hamburger out of this, three shakes from this, and change this bill to three ones, two fifty-cent pieces, two quarters, four dimes, a nickel, and five pennies—have you got that?" A girl who has been lounging in a booth all evening elbows her way to the counter and shouts, "I have to be in by ten. Will you get me six hamburgers to go right away? One with lettuce and no mayonnaise, one with mayonnaise and no lettuce, one with both and mustard, one with nothing but meat, and onions in the other two. I don't know what else they want besides onions. Hurry, please!" Some shrewd thinker will corner me, demanding to know if we don't have some cigarettes hidden under the counter. And then—as suddenly as it came, the mob has vanished, leaving stacks of dirty dishes, whatever silverware could not be used at home, and a quaint little professor to tell us fish stories until long after order has been restored.

§ 41. UNITY IN THE PARAGRAPH

41a. Effective paragraphs of exposition observe the principle of unity.

A paragraph of exposition is a unit of structure. It deals with one idea, or with one phase of a larger idea. Its unity may be destroyed by:

1. Digressions from the main thought or topic idea, usually expressed by the topic sentence.
2. The addition of irrelevant details.

3. Afterthoughts that should have been disposed of earlier in the composition.

If your instructor refers you to this section, you may do one of two things. If the detail that destroys the unity of the paragraph is a minor digression, you may cross it out. Turn to Section 7 to learn how deletions should be indicated in manuscript. If your paragraph is a muddle of two or more major ideas, you may select the idea that you wish to develop and rewrite the entire paragraph. See Section 40 and Chapter 4 for help in building up and presenting an idea in paragraph form.

The following are paragraphs that violate unity. Study them and the criticisms that show the error and the method of revision:

PARAGRAPH 1

Well-built and comfortable houses can be built for a small amount of money. [Topic sentence] Any family with small means may build a well-equipped home a short distance from the city limits for less than they could live on in a run-down apartment. Materials for building are also important. Houses are more and more being built with steel frames. The windows are usually steel sashes. The outside may be almost any type —brick, stone, wood, or stucco.

CRITICISM

This paragraph breaks in half after the second sentence, since the writer seems to have forgotten his original idea, that families of small means can build inexpensive houses. The material here should be developed more fully in two paragraphs.

PARAGRAPH 2

Little is known about McGuffey's early theories of education because he failed to write down his sermons and lectures. It is known, however, that he felt the need of a systematic education and textbooks. He liked to do his teaching outdoors. He would seat his children on logs. He had a log for each subject. The best students would sit at the head of a log and the poorest at the foot. He would often question his students until they could see the truth or falsity of their reasoning. By these methods he encouraged the competitive spirit among his students, and taught them to think logically and speak clearly. He established the tastes of four fifths of the nation's school children in regard to literature, morality, social development, and—next to the Bible—their religion.

CRITICISM

This paragraph has an understood topic sentence. The paragraph deals with what little we know about McGuffey's early theories of education, which we infer from what he did. Hence the last sentence violates unity, for although it is about McGuffey's teaching, it is not about his early theories or methods. If the facts in the last sentence are important or pertinent, they should be put into a paragraph dealing with his lifetime influence upon American youth.

41b. The topic sentence is a useful device for security unity in a paragraph of exposition.

When your instructor refers you to this section, you should underline the topic sentence of your paragraph or write a topic sentence if it is implied in your paragraph. It is quite probable that your instructor is trying to make you see that your paragraph lacks unity, or a close-knit structure, faults that your attention to a topic sentence would help to correct.

Not all expository paragraphs, of course, begin with a topic sentence. In some paragraphs the summary is left to be made by the reader; the paragraph details do aim at one central idea, but they are not conveniently tied together by a topic sentence. In some paragraphs, however, it seems as if all that held the ideas together was a mutual friendship, or a common interest in the same subject. Such paragraphs are hard to write successfully. The fact remains that the most common, the most typical, and to the student the most useful paragraph of exposition has a topic sentence, usually expressed somewhere near the beginning, either after the transitional phrases or combined with them.

What has been said here and in Chapter 4 about the topic sentence applies primarily to fully developed paragraphs of exposition, not to special paragraphs such as transitions or summaries, nor to paragraphs of narration or description.

Here are some examples of different methods of using a topic sentence. They merit careful study. The first example shows topic sentences beginning two consecutive paragraphs:

The wings of both male and female monarchs [butterflies] have another characteristic which has interested naturalists for generations. [Topic sentence] This is their striking, contrasting pattern which makes them easily seen. These brilliant wings are more than adornments. They are warnings to insect-eating birds to keep away. The exact opposite of protective coloring, their purpose seems to be to attract attention, to let the birds know they are the wings of a monarch. For these insects have an evil-tasting blood which nauseates the bird that tries to eat them. By warning inexperienced birds away, the wings of the insect protect it from attack. Otherwise, in learning that the monarch is not good to eat, birds would kill or injure numbers of the insects. Its "aggressive coloration" is an advertisement; and, for the monarch, it pays to advertise.

A notable and oft-cited instance of "mimicry" among insects which already has been mentioned is connected with the flaunting wings of the monarch. [Topic sentence] A butterfly of a different family, the viceroy, an insect with entirely different history and habits, rides about on wings that have almost exactly the same pattern as those of the monarch. Its eggs, its caterpillar, its chrysalis are different. Its body contains no nauseating fluids. Yet, because it looks like a monarch, it, too, is immune from the attacks of birds. As the New England entomologist Clarence Weed once put it: The viceroy is a sheep in wolf's clothing. The advertising of the monarch aids it, too. It thrives through mistaken identity.

—EDWIN WAY TEALE, *The Strange Lives of Familiar Insects*

Here is an example of a paragraph of exposition that uses narration as its method of explaining something. Notice that the topic sentence at the end clearly indicates that the purpose of the paragraph is not to tell a story but to explain how something was done.

One day in June at Wolf Camp in the Gobi Desert, Walter Granger and I were prospecting for fossils on the gray white sediments below the tents. A tiny piece of bone caught my eye. It was not more than an inch long, but I knelt down and with a whisk broom began to brush away the loose gravel. More and more of the bone was exposed, and it kept getting bigger as I went deeper. It was solid, too, and that meant that it belonged to a large piece. I called Walter. Under his expert hands a flat stone was exposed right over the bone, and he moved the block with the greatest care. It was like lifting a trap door, for under it lay a mastodon's molar tooth firmly set in bone. Granger followed it down while I looked on seething with excitement. The enormous spoon-shaped lower jaw of a rare shovel-tusked mastodon slowly took shape under his brush. Near its lower end a second tip of bone just showed in the sediment. As that was exposed, still another came to view. This went on bit by bit until we had excavated the skull, jaws, and parts of the skeletons of a big mother shovel-tusker and her baby. For two million years they had been lying there covered with unknown tons of sediment which had gradually worn away by the action of weather until that first telltale point of bone which I had seen had been exposed. That is the way fossils are found. [Topic sentence]

—Roy Chapman Andrews, *This Amazing Planet*

Quite often the topic sentence takes the form of a question. The paragraph then is the answer to that question. In the preceding paragraph, the author could very easily have written: "How are fossils found?" or "Are fossils found by plan or by accident?" The paragraph would have followed the question. Occasionally the question is a question merely in form, as in the following example. Here the author could have opened with: "Buying or fantasy-buying is an important part of everyone's emotional life," and the paragraph would have lost some of its charm.

Reader, isn't buying or fantasy-buying an important part of your and my emotional life? (If you reply, *No,* I'll think of you with bitter envy as more than merely human; as deeply un-American.) It is a standard joke that when a woman is bored or sad she buys something, to cheer herself up; but in this respect we are all women together, and can hear com-complacently the reminder of how feminine this consumer-world of ours has become. One imagines as a characteristic dialogue of our time an interview in which someone is asking of a vague gracious figure, a kind of Mrs. America: "But while you waited for the intercontinental ballistic missiles what did you *do?*" She answers: "I bought things."

—Randall Jarrell, *A Sad Heart at the Supermarket*

Finally we have here a paragraph in which the topic idea is loosely expressed in the first two sentences, the first one being partly a quick summary of what has been said before.

The way in which man has tamed and developed his emotions is, of course, the story of civilization, told in art, music, and literature, in the rise and fall of nations, in the tragedies and comedies of human existence, in the development of religions and loyalties. But to achieve its purpose, this story cannot be told with scientific objectivity. The emotions of the student must be involved; his own imagination must be set on fire and his brute emotions converted into a scale of values. He must not merely know about Hamlet; he must for at least a brief instant *be* Hamlet, through a flash of what Bergson calls intuiton. The Parthenon or Chartres must for a moment be his and no one else's—no one has ever seen them so clearly before. He must defy the jury with Socrates, and he must feel for himself the sorrows of Werther. Tears must spring to his eyes as he hears the Saint Matthew chorale, and he must suddenly see the country-side through the eyes of Constable. Then his own subjectivity will acquire the objectivity of beauty and goodness, and the world itself will take on meaning and significance for him.

—Mason W. Gross, President of Rutgers University

§ 42. COHERENCE IN PARAGRAPHS

42a. A skillful arrangement of details helps to produce an effective paragraph.

If your problem of coherence is with an *opening* paragraph, recall the section in Chapter 4, "Kinds of Introductory Paragraphs," in which the three familiar ways of beginning are analyzed. To review briefly, you might begin an essay in any one of the following ways:

1. You might state in your first paragraph a thesis that you are about to defend. Often this statement may include a reference to general opinion on the subject and how your treatment will differ.

2. You might begin with an anecdote that will become an example or piece of evidence to support your argument.

3. You might concentrate on a single key term, using your opening paragraph to define it carefully.

If your problem is with a paragraph in the body of your paper, one of the following suggestions may help:

1. Try presenting your material from "the general to the particular." Most paragraphs of exposition follow this order. The writer states his general idea first in a topic sentence, and then he presents the reasons, details, examples, illustrations, and so on, that make his general statement understandable and convincing.

2. Try the "order of enumeration." In your topic sentence state that your idea may be seen from two points of view, that it has three important aspects, that you are going to use four illus-

trations, that you have two excellent reasons for believing it, and so on. You can see various uses for this method. You should also see that this order may help you to write a clear, compact, and well-organized paragraph.

The following topic sentences from the works of professional writers demonstrate how this method is used:

All social organization is of two forms.

There were also three less desirable results of the Peace Conference.

There are two uses of knowledge.

Among the leading purposes of law today we may list three.

Remember, however, that this sort of beginning gives a formal tone to your writing. Use the device occasionally, when the material of your paragraph is adapted to classification and enumeration.

3. Try the "time order." If details can be arranged in the order of happening, there is no particular advantage to be gained by trying any other arrangement. The order of time (often called the "chronological" order), or happening, produces a clear and orderly paragraph. It is inherently simple, perhaps elementary— but it has the unquestioned virtue of being almost foolproof. It may be used with material that at first glance does not arrange itself in the order of time. For instance, "How to Train a Horse" can become "How I Trained My Horse"; "Academic Freedom" can become "The Historical Development of the Concept of Academic Freedom"; "The Right to Work" can become "How the Notion Grew Up That a Job Is Property."

4. Try using the "inductive order." It may be that your paragraph idea should not be stated bluntly in the first sentence. The reader may not be ready for it. Prepare him for it by using your details, your examples and instances, to guide his thoughts, so that when you are ready to use your summarizing topic sentence he will also be ready to accept it.

If your problem of coherence is with your concluding paragraph, especially with its relation to your beginning, review the section on "Beginnings and Endings" in Chapter 5. In that section, eight possible beginning-and-ending combinations are listed, with examples.

42b. Paragraphs are made more effective by the skillful use of connectives and transitions.

In Chapter 4 ("Problems of Internal Organization"), we list four main ways of linking ideas—by using conjunctions and transitional words and phrases, by using pronouns, by repeating key words, and by expressing related ideas in parallel structure.

1. Transitional Expressions. The following is a brief list of transitional words and phrases. You must not think that this list is complete; neither should you assume that the natural, spontaneous phrases of transition that occur to you as you write are either incorrect or unliterary.

on the other hand	conversely	finally
in the second place	of course	after all
on the contrary	in conclusion	I mean
at the same time	to sum up	indeed
in particular	moreover	next
in spite of this	in addition	similarly
in like manner	for example	again
and so again	for instance	I repeat
as I have said	furthermore	and truly
in contrast to this	accordingly	meanwhile

EXAMPLES OF TRANSITIONS

In like manner, all kinds of deficient and impolitic usages are referred to the national love of trade; though, *oddly enough,* it would be a weighty charge against a foreigner that he regarded the Americans as a trading people.

—CHARLES DICKENS

I am not blaming or excusing anyone here. . . . I find, *for instance,* that prejudice, essentially, is worse on the prejudiced than on their targets.

—LOUIS ADAMIC

There were then very few regular troops in the kingdom. A town, *therefore,* which could send forth, at an hour's notice, twenty thousand men . . .

—THOMAS BABINGTON MACAULAY

Their [the immigrants'] children, *however*, follow the general increase which is found in the American population. *Furthermore*, the form of the body of immigrants' children undergoes certain changes. . . .

—FRANZ BOAS

2. Pronouns Referring to Antecedents in the Preceding Sentences.

The technique of using pronouns for transition is a standard practice, but often runs the risks of vagueness of reference.

EXAMPLES

In the summer, Father had his usual two or three weeks of vacation. *These* were spent usually at our cabin in the mountains.

I know a writer of newspaper editorials. *Himself* a liberal, *he* has to grind out a thousand words daily which reflect the ultra conservative policy of the paper for which *he* works. *He* keeps a record like a batting chart. . . .

—STUART CHASE

3. Key Words Repeated.

In the two following passages, the words *civilization* and *understanding* are repeated to hold the arguments together.

EXAMPLES

Nothing in the way of civilization is inborn, as are the forms and workings of our bodies. Everything that goes to make up civilization must be acquired anew in infancy and childhood, by each and all of us.

—JAMES HARVEY ROBINSON

In some of my early writings I spoke of the twofold problem of understanding—there was the problem of understanding the world around us, and there was the problem of understanding the process of understanding, that is, the problem of understanding the nature of the intellectual tools with which we attempt to understand the world around us.

—P. W. BRIDGMAN

4. Parallel Structure.

In the example, the repeated subject-verb phrasing relates each clause to all the others.

EXAMPLE

While I talk and the flies buzz, a sea gull catches a fish at the mouth of the Amazon, a tree falls in the Adirondack wilderness, a man sneezes in Germany, a horse dies in Tartary, and twins are born in France.

—WILLIAM JAMES

§ 43. POINT OF VIEW

Maintain a consistent point of view.

In Section 34 we discussed some dangers, largely grammatical, involving shifts in point of view. We pointed out, for example, what happens when there is an abrupt change in the voice or tense of the verb. Here we consider some larger questions of consistency. It is important, however, to make plain that all our ways of putting words together, including the most lowly routines of grammar, contribute to creating a point of view. In fact, to maintain a consistent point of view is to be sensitive to all the principles our handbook has outlined. Sentence structure, vocabulary, even mechanics and spelling—all these have a direct bearing on your central problem as a writer: that of producing a consistent, controlled prose style.

43a. Maintain a consistent point of view in time and space.

One way to understand the phrase "point of view" is to think of it quite literally as a *point* from which one *views* one's subject.

Having chosen a particular "point" from which the material is to be "viewed," the writer owes it to his reader to maintain his position, and not to skip around unless he does so for a very good reason. This injunction applies to points in *time* as well as in *space*. At its simplest, it means that a paragraph in the present tense should be followed by a paragraph in the past tense only if the break in point of view is deliberate and desirable. Similarly, if a scene is to be described from the vantage point of one particular spot, or through the eyes of one particular person, then an abrupt removal to another spot or another person, simply to suit the author's whim or convenience, is sure to disturb a careful reader.

Here are some passages from a brief anecdote, written by a college student, that will help us to define some of these difficulties.

The small gray Chevrolet pulled up to the side of the road and halted as the hitchhiker dropped his solicitous thumb and moved to the car. He looked inquiringly at the driver, his companion, and the back seat, and opened the door.

"Going to Baker?"

The driver, decked out in blue denims and with a short peaked cap covering a head of silver hair brushed down on the sides, gave a nod and replied, "Sure am. Hop in back."

The stranger got in and found the back seat already taken by a large German police dog, stretched out full length on the seat. His surprised grunt came just as the farmer's companion, apparently his wife, turned around and rasped, "Don't worry about him, son, he's pretty friendly. Get down, Boss."

The object of her order gave a perturbed gesture with his front paws and jumped to the floor as the new rider took over the back seat. He glanced at the backs of his two benefactors.

The *point* from which we are asked to *view* this scene is, of course, the physical position occupied by the hitchhiker. Notice how we follow him about, and when he is in the car, we too see the car from the back seat where he is situated. This is logical and proper enough. The woman in the front seat is "apparently" the farmer's wife; we know no more about her than the hitch-hiker does. But note too that we are not so placed as to know what's going on in the hitchhiker's mind. The speaker refers to him as "the stranger" and "the new rider." We are observing the situation from outside any one person's consciousness, and this too is part of our point of view. The writer has placed us in a certain position of distance from "the stranger," and he must be careful to maintain that distance unless he has a good reason for changing it.

The story goes on:

The dog was resting, head on his paws, with his eyes fixed on the new rider. He was a massive beast, and the result of good care showed in a well-filled body that rested firm under a sleek gray coat. The stranger passed his eyes from the dog's rump along the line of his back to his head, and noticing the canine gaze still upon him, glanced briefly at the long angular jaws.

The gaze prompts a sudden thought, and half to himself he comments, "That dog must have been raised in the Arctic."

Here a change in point of view has taken place—a change that is probably too abrupt, though it is not absolutely drastic. We have moved closer to the "stranger": first we are aware that he notices "the canine gaze"; then, with a curious and awkward change of tense, we are told that a "sudden thought" is prompted inside him. A few sentences later, however, as the author describes a conversation taking place in the car, we find this sentence:

"Just what breed of dog is this?" came from the back seat.

Can you see what has happened? We have suddenly been catapulted, in our point of view, from the back seat to the front seat, right over the upholstery! The scene that we saw from one point in space, we now see—for no good reason—from quite another point. And a few sentences later, the writer slips even further from his original place next to the hitchhiker as he tells us:

The woman was intent on continuing the discussion, but then the idea of some new plan faded from her mind and she turned full around to face the front and the road unwinding ahead of them.

As you can easily see, we have now come almost full circle, for when we know what is going on inside the woman's mind, we have been shunted about inside that automobile in a pretty thoroughgoing fashion. (Only the farmer has remained inscrutable!) In the hands of a skilled professional writer, such shifts might be meaningful and desirable, but for most beginning writers a shift in point of view is perilous. Though the problem is most obviously demanding in fiction, as in this example, it is crucial in all writing and must be watched carefully.

43b. Maintain a consistent *tone* toward your reader.

You will recall from our discussion in Chapter 1 that when a writer selects language to express what he has to say, he inevitably creates as he does so a particular speaking "voice," a kind of personality through which he projects his meaning. (We are not now speaking of voice in the grammatical sense, of course, as in active or passive voice.) This dramatic identity, this mouthpiece must suggest by its language a certain relation with the reader—informal or formal, intimate, friendly, even hostile. It is this relation with the reader that we call *tone,* and it is an indispensable part of a point of view.

By leafing through the columns of any daily newspaper, you can discover any number of different voices that make their appeals to you with many different tones. Some of them, as in the more formal news articles or editorials, may hold you at arm's length, or they may chide you as from a pulpit.

It has been announced that a government delegation will depart from Hong Kong tomorrow for technical discussions on a new Communist proposal to increase the amount of water which the British Colony receives from the mainland.

The nominee for the Vice Presidency on both the Republican and the Democratic tickets should be selected solely because he is the best-qualified person available to step into the Presidency, if fate should call him there. Considerations of religion or sex or race or family or place of residence should not enter into this choice. Ability to carry on the duties of the Presidency of the United States with distinction is the proper, and the only proper, criterion.

Note the relatively long sentences, the elaborate structures, and the passive verbs in these passages—all devices for promoting a formal tone. On the other hand, in other columns of the daily paper, you can be addressed in an excessively friendly way by other voices as they assume an intimacy with you that may be quite surprising. This is most obvious in the advertisements, of course: an ad for soap may cry out at you, in black print, "Dry skin? Not me, darling!" Or a shipping line may assume it knows just what you want:

Why just get there when you can *cruise* there? Our ships offer you far more than just transportation. They slow down your pace and help you relax and revel in lazy, sunny days at sea.

Sometimes, in other passages, the voice that addresses you may be so extremely detached and formal as hardly to exist at all, except as something dry, crisp, and impersonal:

Pursuant to the provisions of the amended Certificate of Incorporation, notice is hereby given that the Board of Directors will dispose of said property on Wednesday, 16 May, at ten o'clock in the forenoon.

These examples will suggest the enormous range of possibilities in manipulating tone. The problem of consistency, of course, is simply not to change personalities as you move from paragraph to paragraph.

43c. Maintain a consistent *attitude* toward your subject matter.

A familiar use of the phrase "point of view" occurs in a question like "What is his point of view on that?"—meaning, What is his attitude, his value judgment, his opinion? This aspect of the problem is also part of the character or voice you are creating with your language. Consistency in attitude is simply a matter of taking a stand and sticking to it, without wavering or contradictory statements. If you have expressed appreciation for the United States foreign policy in your first paragraph, do not deride it in your fourth unless the intervening sentences demonstrate and defend the change in attitude. The part of speech to watch with particular care in expressing attitude is, of course, the adjective. A great many adjectives state by definition a speaker's approval of the modified noun; examples are *attractive, beautiful, industrious, virtuous, warm-hearted*. Such adjectives are called *honorific*; they almost always commit their users to a favorable view of the subject. On the other hand, many adjectives act by definition in just the opposite way: *unattractive, ugly, lazy, evil, cold-hearted*. Such adjectives are called *pejorative*, and they are very difficult to use without suggesting disapproval. Between these extremes, there are infinite subtle variations of approval and disapproval to be controlled by the skilled writer.

EXERCISES

Exercise 1, Point of View. *Look through the pages of a large national magazine that offers a varied table of contents. Find the opening paragraphs of a piece of fiction, and define carefully the time and place of the narrator's point of view. Show what shifts in position there may be, and try to decide why such shifts are there.*

EXERCISE 2, TONE. *In the same magazine find half a dozen paragraphs from various pages to show different speaking voices in action with markedly different tones. Show what kind of person the reader is expected to be, as he responds to the language in each case.*

EXERCISE 3, INTIMATE TONE. *Select an advertisement from the magazine that employs a particularly intimate tone. Point out the grammatical and rhetorical devices by which this tone was created. What happens to the advertisement if you try rewriting it in formal style?*

EXERCISE 4, DISTANT TONE. *Find a voice in the magazine that is particularly distant or detached from the reader. Rewrite the passage to bring the speaker closer to the reader.*

EXERCISE 5, WORDS THAT EXPRESS ATTITUDES. *In all the passages you have chosen, show what words have been used to express attitudes toward what is being talked about. Rewrite two or three of the passages, reversing or drastically changing the attitude by replacing the modifiers and other language as necessary.*

GLOSSARY

§ 44. A GLOSSARY OF USAGE

This section is to be consulted for information about current usage.

An introduction to the problems confronted in this glossary can be found in the paragraphs on "Levels of Usage" and "Functional Varieties of English" in Chapter 1. As you recall from that chapter, and as we have repeatedly made plain throughout this book, correctness and incorrectness in English usage are relative terms. We usually prefer to speak of the appropriateness of an expression in a given context, rather than of its correctness. An expression is appropriate in a certain situation, on a certain occasion, in a certain locality, among certain people; it may be inappropriate in another situation, on another occasion, in another locality, among other people.

But saying this much hardly solves the student's difficulties in deciding what is or is not appropriate in various situations. The student has a right to expect some firm assistance on such questions from his English handbook, in spite of the relativity in usage that we all recognize. His problem arises particularly in a number of cases where the current status of an expression is debatable, and the list that follows is intended to help the student respond intelligently to some of these cases, as well as to those many other cases of confusing or troublesome usage where no argument exists.

In considering this matter of status, important in perhaps half the items in our glossary, we will speak of three classifications of language, conscious as we do so of the artificial nature of such constructions. First, there are all those words and expressions that are part of Standard Literary English, and as a matter of fact these account for most of the words in the language. Very many words in Standard English are appropriate on any occasion, formal or informal, anywhere. Second, we label certain expressions Colloquial or Informal, which simply means that these expressions are perfectly natural in most conversations, and perhaps in some informal writing, but are usually not appropriate in formal expository writing. An example is the expression *I guess*: "I guess his analysis was correct." Most student problems with usage arise from a failure to recognize and avoid the Colloquial-Informal in the writing of serious essays. (The fact remains, of course, that many fine writers of serious prose are able to modify their formality of style by the deliberate, occasional use of informal language. Their skill depends, naturally, on a high sensitivity to the current status of words, so that just the right mixture can be concocted.) Finally, there is a small body of language that simply has to be called Illiterate. For example, to use the phrase *could of* for *could have* ("I could of come if I'd wanted to") is conceivable in writing only if you are quoting someone who uses language of that sort.

As we have said, there are some expressions whose current status is a matter of argument, and their number is probably increasing in our fast-changing society. For example, no one can tell just when it will become appropriate to use *like* as a conjunction in formal prose—if it ever will. Similar fluid and unpredictable conditions in words have reached a point where, as noted earlier, the editors of *Webster's Third New International Dictionary* (1961) have simply omitted such labels as *Colloq.* in many of their dubious entries. This does not of course mean that these editors believe the status of all language is the same, but simply that the status of current English words has become so complicated and various that strict labels would be misleading.

The student can learn much that is both useful and entertaining by following some of these controversies, or by examining the recent history of some fast-changing expressions. The books listed below, arranged in chronological order, will help him pursue a study of any doubtful expressions he chooses. (Our own glossary contains only a small fraction of the words included in a full dictionary of usage.) The first two books listed, by British authorities, are relatively conservative, ready to call words illiterate that we might classify as merely colloquial. The later, American books are likely to be more permissive in basing their findings on the way masses of people actually do use the language. It is important to recognize, however, that popular usage, in conversation or in informal writing, is *not* the same as usage in formal expository prose. For our purposes in this handbook, the differences matter. Though colloquial expressions may often be included in serious formal writing, they are usually effective only when the writer is clearly aware of the shifts in tone that he is introducing. The books below, and our glossary of usage, should help the beginning writer become aware of his available choices, so that he can be genuinely discriminating in his acts of composition.

H. W. Fowler, A *Dictionary of Modern English Usage*. New York: Oxford, 1926.

Eric Partridge, *The Concise Usage and Abusage*. London: Hamish Hamilton, 1954. (Abridged edition of an earlier work)

Margaret Nicholson, A *Dictionary of American-English Usage*. New York: Oxford, 1957. (Based on Fowler)

Bergen Evans and Cornelia Evans, A *Dictionary of Contemporary American Usage*. New York: Random House, 1957.

Margaret M. Bryant, *Current American Usage*. New York: Funk and Wagnalls, 1962.

a, an. Use *a* before a word beginning with any consonant sound except silent *h*. EXAMPLES: *a book, a tree, a European, a union, a house.* Use *an* before a word beginning with a vowel sound. EXAMPLES: *an American, an onion, an hour, an honorable man.*

accelerate, exhilarate. Sometimes confused because of resemblance in sound. To *accelerate* is to quicken or speed up. To *exhilarate* is to arouse joy, to give pleasure. EXAMPLE: *An exhilarating experience can accelerate the heartbeat.*

accept, except. Often confused because of resemblance in sound. *Accept* means to receive, to agree to; *except* means to exclude or make an exception. EXAMPLES: *He accepted the invitation. She was excepted from the list of guests.*

ad. This clipped form and others like it (such as *math, exam, auto*) are appropriate in informal speech, but in formal writing the words usually appear in full.

adapt, adept, adopt. To *adapt* is to change something for a purpose. *Adept* (adjective or noun) means skillful, or one skilled. To *adopt* is to take possession of. EXAMPLES: *He adapted the motor to another current. He was adept at fixing electric appliances. She was an adopted child.*

affect, effect. A familiar confusion. To *affect* is to influence. To *effect* means to bring about. *Effect* as a noun means result, what has been brought about. EXAMPLES: *The strike will affect the industry. The effect of the strike will be severe. The labor board will try to effect a settlement.*

aggravate. *Aggravate* means to intensify, to increase. Colloquially it means to irritate, to annoy. COLLOQUIAL: *The speaker's mannerisms aggravated everyone.* FORMAL: *The speaker's mannerisms annoyed everyone.*

agree to, agree with. You *agree that* something is true. You *agree to* a proposal. You *agree with* a person. One thing *agrees with* (corresponds with) another.

ain't. Never used in standard written English.

all right. See *alright.*

all the farther, all the faster. Frequently used in conversational English. In formal or literary English, *as far as, as fast as* are more commonly used.

allude, refer. *Allude* means to refer to a person or thing indirectly or by suggestion. EXAMPLE: *When the teacher spoke of "budding Swifts," every student wondered to whom he was alluding.* To *refer* to something means to mention it specifically. EXAMPLE: *I shall now take time to refer to the question of smoking on the campus.*

allusion, illusion. An *allusion* is an indirect reference. (See *allude.*) An *illusion* is a deceptive appearance or false notion. The two words have nothing in common except a resemblance in sound.

already, all ready. *Already*, an adverb, means by this time, before this time. *All ready*, two words, means entirely ready or that everyone is ready. EXAMPLES: *The war had already started. The men were all ready to go.*

alright. The correct spelling is *all right. Alright* is a colloquial expression.

altogether, all together. *Altogether* (one word) is an adverb meaning entirely, completely, on the whole. *All together* means in a group. EXAMPLES: *He was altogether too generous. They were all together again at last.*

among, between. *Among* is used with three or more things or persons, as: They divided the property among six relatives; talk this over among yourselves. *Between* usually refers to two things or persons, as: Let nothing stand between you and me; much must be done between sunrise and breakfast. *Between* can sometimes refer to more than two things in such expressions as "between the leaves of a book."

amount, number. *Amount* refers to quantity; *number* refers to things that can be counted. EXAMPLES: *the number of pages, the amount of steel.*

A.M., P.M., a.m., p.m. Should not be used for *in the morning, in the afternoon.* Correct only with the name of the hour.

and etc. *Etc.,* for *et cetera,* means "and so forth." *And etc.* is obviously redundant. In any case it is better for most purposes not to use the abbreviation.

any place, anyplace. These are colloquial forms for *anywhere,* like *no place* for *nowhere, every place* for *everywhere,* and *some place* for *somewhere.*

anyways, anywheres. Colloquial forms of *anyway* and *anywhere,* to be avoided in formal prose.

a piece, apiece. A *piece* is a noun; *apiece* is an adverb. EXAMPLE: *All those present are to have a piece of pie apiece.*

apt, likely, liable. *Apt* suggests a habitual or inherent tendency. *Likely* suggests a probability. *Liable* suggests a chance, a risk of some sort, or a danger. But in American speech all three are often used to mean a probability and nothing more. EXAMPLES: *She is apt to be irritable because she is not well. A cheerful boy is likely to succeed. You are liable to break your neck if you climb that rock.*

as. (1) Highly colloquial when used in place of *that* or *whether.* EXAMPLE: *I cannot say as I care much for that.* (2) *As* in the sense of *because* is frowned upon by some writers, but is widely current in speech and writing nevertheless, especially in clauses at the beginnings of sentences. EXAMPLE: *As I was free that day, I went along with him.*

as—as, so—as. In negative statements some careful writers prefer *so—as* to *as—as.* At present, *as—as* seems to be established in both speech and writing for both positive and negative statements. For negative statements in a very formal style, *so—as* is probably preferable. EXAMPLES: *Your promise is as good as your bond.* FORMAL: *A vast army is not so important as a well-equipped air force.* INFORMAL: *A vast army is not as important as a well-equipped air force.*

at. Redundant, both in speech and writing, in such sentences as: Where are we at now? Where does he live at?

avocation, vocation. A *vocation* is one's principal life work. An *avocation* is not. EXAMPLE: *His vocation was medicine; his avocation was collecting stamps.*

awful, awfully. Colloquially these words, and others like *frightful, terribly, shocking, disgusting,* are used as mild intensives. Often they mean little more than *very*. In formal writing, *awful* and *awfully* should be saved for their precise meaning, to describe something truly awe inspiring. EXAMPLE: *He accepted the awful responsibility of carrying on the war.*

balance. When used for the *remainder, the rest,* it is usually considered colloquial. COLLOQUIAL USES: *The balance of the crew will be released. We listened to records the balance of the evening.* FORMAL: *The rest of the crew will be released.*

bank on. In the sense of *rely upon* it is a colloquial idiom.

because. Often used in informal speech, and sometimes in literary English, as a substitute for *that* in constructions like "the reason was because . . ." *That* is still preferable in formal written prose.

being as, being that. Dialectal for *since, because.* EXAMPLE: *Since* (not *being as*) *it is long past midnight, we should abandon the search.*

beside, besides. According to present usage, *beside* is used as a preposition meaning at the side of, as in: Please sit down beside me. *Besides* is ordinarily used as an adverb, meaning in addition to, as in: There were no casualties besides the one reported earlier.

between. See *among.*

bunch. Colloquial when used to mean several, a group. EXAMPLES: *We saw a group* (not *a bunch*) *of men near the gate. Several* (not *a bunch*) *of them belonged to another union.*

but what, but that. Formerly considered colloquial. *But that* now appears to be standard literary English in sentences like: I don't doubt but that he is disappointed. *But what* should not be used to refer to persons. Most careful writers still prefer a simple *that* to both these expressions. EXAMPLE: *There is no doubt that* (not *but what* or *but that*) *the president wishes to avoid war.*

can, may. In formal usage, *may* implies permission or possibility, *can* implies ability. In informal usage, *can* is very often used in the meaning of *may.* INFORMAL: *Mother, can I go now? Can't we stay up until midnight? No, you can't.* FORMAL: *Sir, may I go now? The delegate can speak three languages.*

can't hardly. A double negative, objectionable in conversation, unthinkable in formal writing.

cannot help but, can't help but. These forms are widely used in speech and by some writers in formal prose.

cause and reason. *Cause* is what produces an effect; *reason* is what man produces to account for the effect, or to justify it. EXAMPLES: *His reasons for going were excellent. The cause of his departure remained a mystery.*

cause of. To say that the *cause of* something was *on account of* is a muddled construction. EXAMPLES: *The cause of my late theme was my having* (not *on account of I had*) *too much work to do. The cause of my late theme was the fact that I had too much work to do.* Both of these sentences, however, are awkward. It may be better to avoid the *cause-of* construction entirely and simply say, "My theme is late because I had too much to do."

censor, censure. A *censor* (who is censorious) is one who supervises public morals, expurgates literature, and so on. Censure is adverse judgment, condemnation.

climactic, climatic. *Climactic* has to do with climax, as: The play had reached a climactic moment. *Climatic* has to do with climate, as: Climatic conditions in Bermuda are ideal.

compare to, compare with, contrast. *Compare to* means to represent as similar. *Compare with* means to examine the differences and similarities of two things. To *contrast* two things is to examine the differences between them. EXAMPLES: *One may compare some men to wolves. One may compare the novels of Dreiser with those of Zola. The novels of Dreiser can be contrasted to those of James.*

contact. Widely used in the sense of *communicate with, meet, interview,* but it should be used sparingly, if at all, in preference to the more formal expressions.

contractions. Less appropriate in formal writing, where they are occasionally found, than in speech and informal writing, where they are entirely at home. EXAMPLES: I'd like to go, but I'm tired. Can't he explain *it to you, or doesn't he care?*

could of. Illiterate for *could have.*

couple. Colloquial for *two, a few, several.* COLLOQUIAL: *A couple of men left the theater.* FORMAL: *Two* (or *several*) *men left the theater.* Standard for a man and woman married, betrothed, or otherwise appearing as partners.

cunning. A colloquialism to describe attractive children and small animals. Not to be used in formal writing.

cute. See *cunning.*

data, strata, phenomena. These are the plurals of *datum, stratum,* and *phenomenon.* At present these words seem to be in a transitional stage, inasmuch as some good writers and speakers use them as singular forms while others believe strongly that only the correct Latin forms should be used. There is no doubt, however, that a mixture of forms is undesirable, as: Although the data collected at the laboratory are vouched for by several scientists, much of it has to be restudied.

date. Inappropriately colloquial when referring to an appointment with the dean, but perfectly acceptable when referring to Saturday night at the movies.

deal. Used figuratively in phrases like square deal, new deal. Informal in the sense of a commercial transaction or political bargain. COLLO-QUIAL: *Good deal!* But with the indefinite article it is literary English, as: a good deal of trouble.

device, devise. A *device* is an instrument for performing some action. To *devise* something is to invent it, to contrive or plan it.

differ from, differ with. One thing *differs from* another. One person *differs with* another when he disputes or quarrels with him. One may also *differ from* a person when he disagrees with him.

different from, different than. Both forms have been used by good writers. At present, *different from* seems to be preferred when a single word follows it, as in: His suggestion is different from mine. When a clause follows, many speakers and writers use *than* to avoid a round-about construction, as in: This group of engineers will use a very different method of extracting the ore than the old Quebec miners used.

dissimulate, simulate. To *simulate* is to pretend; to *dissimulate* is to hide by pretense. EXAMPLES: *He simulated drunkenness by weaving around the floor. He dissimulated his drunkenness by an effort to speak rationally.*

double negative. An expression in which two or more negatives are used to make the negative more emphatic is of course illiterate. EXAMPLES: *Nobody never tells me nothing. We ain't seen nobody.* Another type of concealed double negative appears in a very small number of expressions like *can't hardly, didn't hardly, wouldn't scarcely.* These expressions are not appropriate in writing, though they are widely heard in speech. A third type of deliberate double negative is entirely correct, and common in formal writing. EXAMPLES: *The brief rest was not unwelcome. These people were not uneducated.* Notice that these expressions are more cautious and moderate than the corollary affirmative statements: *The brief rest was welcome. These people were educated.*

dove. The most generally used form is *dived,* though *dove* has been widely used in speech and occasionally in writing.

due to, owing to. *Due to* was originally an adjective, and no one questions its use in sentences like these: His lameness was due to an accident. The spring floods, due to prolonged rains, did much damage to the stockyards. The adverbial use of *due to* is also common, as: Due to an accident, we arrived late. If a more formal tone is desired, the expresion *owing to* may be substituted for *due to. Due to the fact that* is a common, and deplorable, substitute for a simple *because.*

each other, one another. The first refers to two people only, at least in formal discourse. The second refers to more than two. EXAMPLES: *The* *two senators started hitting each other. The whole senate started hitting one another.*

end up. Unacceptable colloquialism for *end* or *conclude.*

enthuse. U.S. colloquial for "to be enthusiastic" or "to show enthusiasm." Many people dislike it thoroughly. FORMAL: *She never showed any enthusiasm* (not *enthused*) *about grand opera.*

equally as good. This may be wordy, but many educated people use the expression. It means "equally good," or "just as good." EXAMPLES: *My composition was just as good* (not *equally as good*) *as his.*

etc. See *and etc. Etc.* is to be avoided at the end of a series when the reader cannot grasp the reference. EXAMPLE: *All his friends—John, Al, Len, etc.—were invited.*

everyone, every one. EXAMPLES: *Everyone has arrived by now. Every one of those dishes must be washed thoroughly.*

exam. See *ad.*

except. See *accept.*

exhilarate. See *accelerate.*

expect. Colloquial in the sense of "suppose."

farther, further. The fine distinction between these two words, and between the superlative forms, *farthest, furthest,* is that both can be used to speak of distance, but that *further* and *furthest* have an additional meaning of "additional." STANDARD USAGE: *They could go no farther. The Johansen party penetrated furthest into the jungle. The senator promised further revelations soon.*

faze. American slang or colloquial for *disconcert, worry, disturb, bother, daunt.* It has no connection with *phase.* COLLOQUIAL: *He wasn't fazed by the amount of work he had to do.*

feel. A spineless substitute for *think* or *believe,* in such examples as "I feel that the United Nations is doing more harm than good." Don't feel it—just say it.

fellow. Colloquial for *a person, a boy, a man, a beau, a sweetheart.* It is a very useful word in college, for it dodges the embarrassing necessity of distinguishing between a man and a boy.

fewer, less. Use *fewer* when referring to numbers. Use *less* when referring to quantity or degree. (See also *amount, number.*) EXAMPLES: *There will be fewer* (not *less*) *men on the campus next year. Most women are earning less than they did last year.*

finalize. Many are irritated by this and other recent coinages from business and officialese. Use cautiously if at all. Also see *contact.*

fine. See *nice.* A vague word of approval, entirely proper in conversation, but in exact writing a more exact word should be used.

fix. Colloquial in the sense of *a predicament,* as: The headmaster was in a predicament (not *fix*). Also colloquial in the sense of to *arrange* or *prepare.* COLLOQUIAL: *Give me a few minutes more to fix my hair.*

folks. Colloquial for relatives, family.

fun. Not to be used as an adjective: a fun thing to do. This is a transitory colloquialism.

funny. Colloquial for *strange, queer, odd.*

get. *Get* has a large number of uses, both formal and informal. In formal or literary contexts, it means obtain, receive, procure, acquire. In informal and conversational usage, it has a large number of meanings, figurative, idiomatic, and otherwise. In speech, *have got* in the sense of *have* is very common. The form *have got* in the sense of *must* or *have to* is felt to be more emphatic. *Got* and *gotten* are both past participles found in speech and in writing.

guess. The expression *I guess* is too colloquial for most formal prose. Write *I suppose,* or *I presume.*

had better, had best, had rather. Correct idiomatic forms, as are *would rather, would best, would better.*

had ought, hadn't ought. Colloquial. It is easy to substitute *ought, should, should have, shouldn't have,* all forms appropriate in both speech and writing.

hanged, hung. People are *hanged*; objects are *hung.* EXAMPLES: *The murderer was hanged. The clothes were hung on the line.*

hardly, scarcely. See *double negatives.*

have got. See *get.*

healthy, healthful. Strictly, *healthy* means being in a state of health; *healthful* means serving to promote health. People are healthy, but good food is healthful.

if, whether. Both *if* and *whether* are used to introduce a noun clause in indirect questions after verbs like *doubt, ask, wonder. Whether* is more likely to be used if an alternative introduced by *or* is stated. There is still some feeling among teachers and writers that *whether* is more formal, but both words are used and have been used for many years to introduce noun clauses. EXAMPLES: *I doubt if they can come. He wondered whether or not he should warn the settlers. Ask him if he has any food left.*

in, into. In theory, the distinction between these words is that *in* denotes location inside something, whereas *into* denotes motion from outside to inside something. In practice, however, *in* is also used in the sense of *into.* EXAMPLES: *Throw that in the waste basket. Please jump in the lake.*

in back of, back of. Both forms, still considered by many to belong to informal speech, have been used in writing for some time. The more formal word is *behind.*

in regards to. The correct idiom is *in regard to.*

is when, is where. These expressions when used in definitions appear awkward and juvenile.

its, it's. *Its* is the possessive form of *it*. *It's* is the contraction of *it is*. The two forms should not be confused.

kind, sort. In colloquial usage, these words are often felt to be plural in constructions like this: "These kind of dogs are usually hard to train." In more formal situations, both in speech and in writing, most people prefer the singular, as: "I do not like this sort of entertainment. That kind of man is not to be trusted."

kind of, sort of. Colloquial when used to modify a verb or an adjective. Use *somewhat, somehow, a little, in some degree, rather, for some reason* in formal contexts.

lay, lie. The principal parts of *lay* are as follows: Now I *lay* it down; I *laid* it down; I have *laid* it down. The principal parts of *lie* are these: I *lie* down; I *lay* down yesterday morning; the dog *had lain* in the shade all day. The participles of *lie* and *lay* are *lying* and *laying*. STANDARD: *He had laid* (not *lain*) *his bundle on the table. It had lain* (not *laid*) *there all morning. The dog was lying* (not *laying*) *in the road.*

lead, led. The past tense of *lead* (pronounced *leed*) *is led* (pronounced like the metal *lead*.)

leave, let. It is just as correct to say *leave him alone* as *let him alone*. But *leave* cannot be used for *allow* in such a sentence as "I begged my mother to leave me do it."

less. Often used in place of *fewer* with collective nouns: less clothes, less people. But say *fewer hats, fewer persons.*

liable, likely. See *apt*.

lie. See *lay*.

like, as, as if. In written English, *as* and *as if* introduce clauses; *like* generally governs a noun or pronoun. In speech the substitution of *like* for *as* is widespread. It is probable that the use of *like* as a conjunction will eventually gain acceptance in formal writing. It has not done so yet. INFORMAL: *I wish you would do it like I said you should.* FORMAL: *The war, just as he had predicted, lasted more than five years. Few men could sway an audience as he did.*

line. Often vague and redundant, as: Have you anything interesting in the line of fiction? He wrote epics and other works along that line. BETTER: *Have you any interesting novels? He wrote epics and other narrative poems.*

locate. In the sense of *settle*, it is appropriate only in informal use.

lots, lots of. Widely used colloquially for *many, much, a large number, a large amount, a great deal*. COLLOQUIAL: *He has a lot to learn. There are lots of exceptions to this rule.*

mad. Colloquially *mad* is used in the sense of *angry*. In formal usage it means "insane."

majority. Inaccurate when used with measures of quantity, time, distance. The appropriate word is *most*. EXAMPLE: *Most of the day* (not *the majority of the day*) *we stood in line and waited.*

might of. Illiterate for *might have.*

mighty. Colloquial for *very*. Unacceptable in most writing.

most, almost. Most, in formal written English, is the superlative form of *much* or *many*. EXAMPLES: *Much food, more food, most food; many men, more men, most men. Almost* is an adverb meaning "nearly." In colloquial use *most* is often substituted for *almost*. FORMAL: *almost* (not *most*) *all of our friends have returned from college.* In conversational usage, *most* is frequently used to qualify *all, everyone, everybody, anyone, anybody, always.*

much, many. *Much* should not be used in place of *many* with most plural nouns. EXAMPLES: *There was too much food. There were too many courses.*

neat. When used as a general honorific (*That's neat!*), it is another overused and transitory colloquialism, like *the greatest*, or *fun* (adjective). To be avoided in writing.

neither, nor; either, or. *Neither* should be followed by *nor* and *either* by *or*. Both *neither* and *either* may be used with more than two alternatives, as: Either past, present, or future. . . .

nice. Strictly used, *nice* means discriminating. When used as a vague word of mild approval, it is to be avoided in serious writing.

no good, no-good. Colloquial when used for *worthless, useless, of no value.*

no one. Not *noone.*

nowhere near, nowheres near. The first is common in both speech and writing; the second is common in colloquial speech. In formal writing it is better to use *not nearly*. EXAMPLE: *That was not nearly* (not *nowhere near*) *as much as he had expected.*

O, oh. *O* is used with another word, a substantive, usually in direct address, often in poetry. It is always capitalized and is not followed by any mark of punctuation. *Oh* is an exclamation, not capitalized except when it begins a sentence, and is followed by either a comma or an exclamation point.

off of. The *of* is unnecessary. EXAMPLE: *He took the book off* (not *off of*) *the shelf.*

one another. See *each other.*

oral, verbal. *Oral* refers to spoken language; *verbal* refers to all words, spoken or written.

out loud. Somewhat less formal than *aloud, loudly, audibly.*

outside of. Colloquial for *except, besides*. EXAMPLE: *There was no witness to the robbery except* (not *outside of*) *the mailman.*

over with. Colloquial in the sense of *finished, ended.*

party. Except in legal and telephone usage, *party* is colloquial and semi-humorous when it means a person.

per cent. Used after numbers. The sign % is not used except after figures in tabulations or in technical writing. *Per cent* is not an exact synonym for *percentage.*

personal, personally. Students are understandably disposed to hedge their bets, with expressions like *in my personal opinion, personally I believe, my view is,* and so on. In essays on literary interpretation, expressions such as *I get the feeling that* . . . are common. In many cases such qualification weakens the force of what is being said. If you are wrong in what you say, then you are wrong, whether you say it's your personal opinion or not.

plenty. Colloquial when used as an adverb in such expressions as *plenty good, plenty good enough, plenty rich,* and so on, or as an adjective before a noun. COLLOQUIAL: *He was plenty rich. The room is plenty large. There is plenty wood for another fire.* FORMAL: *He was very rich. The room is large enough. There is plenty of wood for another fire. Ten dollars is plenty.*

P.M. See *A.M., a.m.*

poorly. Colloquial for *in poor health, not well, unwell.*

practicable, practical. *Practicable* means "something possible, feasible, usable." *Practical* means "useful, not theoretical, experienced." *Practical* may apply to persons, things, ideas; *practicable* may not apply to persons.

proposition, proposal. *Proposal* implies a direct and explicit act of proposing; *proposition* implies a statement or principle for discussion. The loose use of *proposition* to mean "idea, thing, a task, a business enterprise, a problem," is disliked by many people. EXAMPLES: *It is a poor practice* (not *proposition*) *to study until three in the morning. Moving the settlers out of the district was an impractical plan* (not *proposition*).

quiet, quite. Two words carelessly confused. *Quiet* has to do with stillness or calmness. In formal standard usage, *quite* means "entirely, completely." *You are quite right.* In informal usage it may also be used to mean "very, to a considerable degree." *The dog seems quite friendly.*

quite a few, quite a bit. Overused in student writing.

raise, rise. Two verbs often confused. The principal parts of *raise:* I raise my hand, he raised the window, they have raised the flag. The principal parts of *rise:* I rise in the morning, they rose before I did, they had risen at sunset.

real. *Real* as an adverb, in the sense of *very* (it was a real exciting game) is colloquial. Its formal equivalent is *really.* Both, however, are vague and weak intensifiers, of little use in promoting meaning. See *awful, so, such.*

reason is because. See *because.*

refer. See *allude.*

same, such. Appropriate in legal documents. In ordinary speech and writing it is better to use *it, this, that.* EXAMPLE: *When you have repaired the watch, please ship it* (not *same*) *to me.*

see where. For *see that,* as: I see where the team lost another game. Permissible only in colloquial speech.

sensual, sensuous. *Sensual* usually means lewd or unchaste; *sensuous* means pertaining to the senses. A *sensuous* man is one who puts value in experiences of the senses, but he need not be *sensual* as he does so.

set, sit. Two verbs often confused. Learn the principal parts: I *set* it down; I *have set* it down; now he *sits* down; I *sat* down; they *have sat* down. But of course one may speak of *a setting hen,* and *the sun sets,* not *sits.* You may set the cup on the shelf and then sit down. I sat on the stool after I had set the cup down.

shape. Colloquial for *condition.* COLLOQUIAL: *The athlete was in excellent shape.* FORMAL: *The equipment was in very good condition* (not *shape*).

simulate. See *dissimulate.*

so. As a conjunction between main clauses, *so* is much overused in student writing. Usually the primary fault is too little subordination instead of too much use of *so.* EXAMPLES: *The bridge was blown up during the night, and so the attack was delayed. The attack was delayed because the bridge had been blown up during the night. The Russians were not ready, so they waited until August to declare war on Japan. Since the Russians were not ready, they waited until August to declare war on Japan.*

In clauses of purpose, the standard subordinating conjunction is *so that,* as in: They flew low so that they could observe the results of the bombing. But *so* is also used, especially in spoken English.

So as a "feminine intensive" can be easily overworked in speech— and it often is. It has a long literary tradition, however. EXAMPLES: *She is so kind and so charming. The work is so hard.*

sort of. See *kind of.*

strata. See *data.*

such. As an intensive, it is used like *awful* or *so.* Also see *real.* Such introducing a clause of result is followed by *that.* EXAMPLE: *There was such an explosion that it could be felt for miles.* When introducing a relative clause, *such* is followed by *as.* EXAMPLE: *Such improvements as are necessary will be made immediately.*

sure. Colloquial for *certainly, surely, indeed.*

swell. Another hardy colloquialism, in the sense of *excellent, very good, admirable, enjoyable.* Avoid in writing.

that there, this here. Illiterate forms.

their, they're. *Their* is a possessive pronoun. *They're* means *they are.* EXAMPLE: *They're happy because their team won.*

thorough, through. An elementary spelling problem.

to, too, two. Another elementary spelling problem. EXAMPLE: *He too should make two trips to the dictionary to learn how to spell. It's not too hard.*

verbal. See *oral.*

very, very much. Many educated persons object to *very* instead of *very much* or *very greatly* as a modifier of a verb or a participle in a verb phrase. Other persons point out examples of its use in the works of reputable writers. See the note under *very* in *Webster's New International.* EXAMPLES: *They were very pleased. They were very much pleased. They seemed very disturbed. They seemed very greatly disturbed.*

vocation. See *avocation.*

wait on. Regional for *wait for, stay for.* Standard in the sense of *attend, perform services for,* as: It was the other girl who waited on me.

want in, want out, want off, etc. Dialectal forms of *want to come in, want to go out, want to get off,* etc.

way, ways. *Way* is colloquial for *condition. Ways* is dialectal for *distance, way.* FORMAL: *When we saw him, he was in bad health* (not *in a bad way.*) *We walked a long distance* (not *ways*) *before we rested.*

where at. The *at* is unnecessary. EXAMPLE: *Where is he now?* (not *Where is he at now?*)

which and that, who and that. *Which* refers to things; *who* refers to people. *That* can refer to either things or people, usually in restrictive clauses. EXAMPLES: *The pictures, which were gaudy and overdecorated, made me wince. The pictures that I bought yesterday were genuine; the others were fake. Who* can also be used in a restrictive clause, as: I want to see all the people who care to see me. With *that,* the same clause is still restrictive: I want to see all the people that care to see me.

while. Frequently overused as a conjunction. Usually *but, and,* or *whereas* would be more precise. It is standard in the sense of *at the same time as* or *although.* It is colloquial in the sense of *whereas.*

-wise. This suffix has been so absurdly overused that it has become largely a joke. He is a competent administrator economy-wise, but politics-wise he is a failure. Avoid. Educated people have taken to using the term almost entirely facetiously. That's the way it goes, cookie-crumblewise.

you all. In Southern speech, *you all* is the plural form of *you.*

INDEX TO QUOTED
PASSAGES

INDEX

Chronological order of presenting material, 133
Cite, sight, site, defined, 347
Clauses:
adjective, defined, 60
adjective:
nonrestrictive, 60, 302
punctuation with, 60
restrictive, 60, 302
adjective, uses of, 60
adverb:
defined, 61
uses of, 61–62
coordinate:
diagrams of, 57
excessive coordination, 67–77
punctuation of, 296
dependent:
diagrams of, 59–62
main thought in, 58
for variety in sentence structure, 66–68
misused as sentences, 219–220
noun, uses as subject, object, subjective complement, object of verbal, appositive, 59–60
overlapping dependence, 394
principal, *see* Coordinate
subordinate, *see* Dependent
substantive clause, *see* Noun
Clauses, parenthetical, punctuation of, 303
Clearness, commas used for, 280, 299
Clearness and order in sentences:
awkwardness and obscurity, 431
correlatives, 422
dangling modifiers, 406–409
destroyed by overloading, 388–389
misplaced modifiers, 396–401
mixed constructions, 416
mixed imagery, 417
parallel structure, 419–422
proper arrangement, 402–405
reference of pronouns, 396–401
shift in point of view, 415–418
squinting reference, 404
subordination, 391–394

Clichés, 368
see also Trite phrases
Climactic, climatic, differentiated, 458
Coarse, course, defined, 347
Coherence in paragraphs:
by arrangement of details, 442–443
outlining for coherence, 85–86
relating parts, 84–102
transitional devices listed, 101, 444–445
conjunctions, 101, 444
parallel structure, 101, 445
pronouns, 101, 445
repetition of key words, 101, 445
Coherence in sentences, improved by:
parallel structure, 419–422
proper arrangement, 402–405
proper reference, 397–401
transitions, 444
use of connectives, 444–445
Coherence in theme, *see* Order of presentation
Collective noun, verb with, 234
Collier's Encyclopedia, listed, 156
Colloquial diction, 25–34, 366, 453–454
defined, 366
levels of usage, informal, 25–33
varieties in speech, 33–34, 453–454
Colon, uses of:
after salutation in letters, 206
before enumeration, formal list, quotation, explanation, 325
between two clauses, 327
capitalization with, 326
Comma fault, comma splice:
corrected by:
coordinate conjunction, 224
subordination, 224–225
using period, 225
using semicolon, 224–225
legitimate comma junctions, 225–226
Commas, unnecessary, 332–335
after coordinating conjunction, 33
between subject and verb, verb and object, preposition and object, adjective and noun, 332